Development, Ethnicity and Human Rights in South Asia

Development, Ethnicity and Human Rights in South Asia

ROSS MALLICK

Sage Publications
New Delhi/Thousand Oaks/London

First published in 1998 by

Sage Publications India Pvt Ltd
M–32, Greater Kailash Part–I
New Delhi–110 048

Sage Publications Inc Sage Publications Ltd
2455 Teller Road 6 Bonhill Street
Thousand Oaks, California 91320 London EC2A 4PU

Published by Tejeshwar Singh for Sage Publications India Pvt Ltd, laser-typeset by Line Arts, Pondicherry and printed at Chaman Enterprises, Delhi.

Library of Congress Cataloging-in-Publication Data

Mallick, Ross.
    Development, ethnicity and human rights in South Asia / Ross Mallick.
        p. cm.
    Includes bibliographical references and index.
    1. South Asia—Economic conditions—Regional disparities. 2. Ethni-city—South Asia. 3. South Asia—Ethnic relations—Economic aspects. 4. Economic development—Social aspects. 5. Human Rights—South Asia. I. Title.
    HC430.6.M35   305.8′00954—dc21   1998   97–45134

ISBN: 0–7619–9227–8 (US-hbk)   81–7036–681–X (India-hbk)
          0–7619–9228–6 (US-pbk)   81–7036–682–8 (India-pbk)

Sage Production Team: Shyama Warner, N.K. Negi and Santosh Rawat

Contents

List of Tables

Preface

South Asia is facing seemingly intractable problems of uneven development, ethnic conflict and human rights violations. The pressures on the South Asian states from their peoples have led to frequent resort to coercion. Human rights are routinely violated, even in institutionalized democracies such as India. Maintaining a semblance of democracy while preserving the integrity of the country is proving an increasingly difficult goal to achieve. This is a task every state undertakes, but in South Asia the pressures from diverse and impoverished peoples present problems of a scale and diversity few other regions have to face.

The difficulties in achieving equitable development during ethnic conflict and repression cannot be exhaustively addressed in a single book. Rather, some of the issues are selected for in-depth analysis, thereby contributing more original material to the topic than is commonly found in syntheses of the secondary literature that attempt to cover the whole region. The selection emphasizes the problems of minority rights in societies with inegalitarian cultural values and highly skewed property distribution. How these issues will be resolved, or at least ameliorated, will determine the future of the region and have an influence on the world's future. As a fifth of humanity is South Asian, and half of the world's poor live in the region, events there will have a profound effect on how problems of development and ethnic conflict are dealt with. Already India alone is the world's fifth largest contributor to global warming. Unless sustainable development can be achieved in the region, there will be a downward spiral of resource depletion and population growth that will leave large numbers without even the minimal income they now have. To maintain democracy in such circumstances could be virtually impossible. If it is maintained it will be through increasing state repression, something that is becoming evident in India, the subcontinent's only institutionalized democracy. If this tendency towards increased repression continues, India could become like Sri Lanka, a country with the institutions of democracy but without the degree of freedom to genuinely warrant the description. Nominal democracy is still the rule in Pakistan and Bangladesh where military regimes, though not long removed from political office, still continue to determine who will stay in power.

Though the region has achieved growth in real terms, its relative position in the world has been steadily declining. In 1955 India was the 10th biggest industrial power, but despite growth its relative position slipped to 20th place two decades later. India's manufactured exports as late as in 1965 were eight times that of Korea, but by 1986 Korea's exports were 4.5 times the value of India's. By 2025 India's population may exceed China's predicted population. With 1.5 billion people, the prospects are that even the real gains in average per capita income may no longer be environmentally and economically sustainable and, without this, democracy may not be sustainable either. It has been argued that one of the reasons that democracy has survived in India is that its people place only limited demands on the government and have low expectations of what it will do for them. This provides opportunities for incremental changes and the accommodations that enable competing groups to coexist in a democracy. Another reason may be the lack of a dominant ethnic group in control of the government, which enables minorities to form coalitions and obtain state benefits. This has been consistently lacking in Pakistan where West Pakistanis dominated East Pakistan, and after the creation of Bangladesh this dominance continued, with Punjabis repressing the minorities within the truncated western wing.

How dominant groups deal with their minorities will determine the survival of genuine democracy, and this central theme of the book asks the hard questions about the capability of states controlled by dominant groups to make the necessary concessions to minority human rights. It is commonly understood that democracy cannot survive and development cannot be maintained without a coercive state. The degree of repression varies enormously among democracies and over different periods of development. The democracies in South Asia are probably more repressive than most, but few others face the magnitude of poverty and ethnic diversity that now confronts their governments. Nevertheless, human rights are now recognized to supersede the rights of states, and hence the minorities in South Asia must be included in any evaluation of their societies and governments.

In making this evaluation, the analysis in this book ranges from previously privileged minorities such as the Sri Lankan Tamils who have the capacity to sustain a civil war against the Sri Lankan government, to those minorities such as the Untouchables who lack the resources to maintain even a unified and effective political movement. The disparities among minorities illustrate the difficulty in making generalizations about development and human rights for ethnic groups. The most repressed, such as the Untouchables, are too poor and isolated to represent their own interests effectively, while others, such as the Sikhs and Tamils, have international networks to sustain and fund major insurgencies that stretch the capacities of central governments to control their own territory. The minorities with the most legitimate grievances, such as the Untouchables who are the world's last segregated population and comprise 2.6 per cent of humanity, receive little publicity and have no effective lobby. The much smaller population of Sikhs on the other hand were a relatively privileged group in India, whose influence and prosperity have been at least temporarily eroded in a long and fruitless attempt to create an ethnically exclusive theocracy. Determining the relative legitimacy of minority grievances is fraught with bias, and world reaction has little to do with the relative merits of the case of a minority. In examining some of the largely forgotten issues of human rights in South Asia, such as those of Untouchables and tribals, it is hoped that a new and more realistic understanding of the region's problems will be reached.

CHAPTER 1

Culture and Development

Half of the world's poor are South Asian, yet overseas development assistance for the subcontinent is less in per capita terms than for many other Third World regions. Foreign aid programmes have not regarded poverty eradication and human rights as their top priority, all the rhetoric to the contrary notwithstanding. Even if it were otherwise, it is doubtful that much of the aid would ever reach the 'poorest of the poor'. There are fundamental reasons that this state of affairs has continued. The poor of South Asia are caught in a double bind in which the developed nations pursue political self-interests, which leaves little room for the absolute poor, while South Asian elites are similarly unconcerned, as evidenced by the low priority given to poverty alleviation in their budgets.[1]

There is no necessary correlation between development and human rights. Some of the most oppressive regimes have maintained impressive growth rates, while economically stagnant countries have retained an effective social assistance net. Yet the consensus is that a combination of both is a desirable policy objective, even if not always implementable. In South Asia there has been a modest measure (by Third World standards) of economic development, but human rights have been more observed in the breach. India, which has prided itself on the maintenance of democratic institutions, is at best a flawed democracy, tolerating gross violations of human rights alongside its democratic institutionalization. The neighbouring states have yet to achieve any institutionalization of democracy, and their human rights record is even more dismal.

These failures are well known, but the causes are controversial. There has been a tendency to obscure the reasons rather than analyze them. No government wants to reveal its shortcomings in human rights, and nations are uncomfortable discussing cultural inadequacies. Yet culture is at the root of human rights abuses in South Asia, as it is of development problems. There are too many cultures to decipher them all adequately, yet there are common cultural traits that can be traced in the way development is implemented and human rights violated. In focusing first on the problems and failures of regional cooperation at the macro level, the ethnic roots of regional conflict will be indicated. A discussion of the inadequacy of the regional reconciliation approach is followed by an analysis of state-level development by a Communist regime which also ends in failure. The use by the Sri Lankan government of foreign development assistance to marginalize the Tamil minority leads to the section on ethnicity. The failures of regional and state-level development raise the problems of ethnic movements and of how the issues of human rights of the world's last segregated population, the South Asian Untouchables, are to be resolved. This is dealt with in terms of the British and post-colonial ethnic policy and its treatment in scholarly literature. The cultural roots of these problems are illustrated by detailed examination of selected issues of development and human rights in South Asia. The concluding chapters look at prospects for implementing development with human rights in the 'new world order' and in forthcoming Dalit (Untouchable)-influenced governments.

The cultural roots are to be found in the dominant elite of South Asia who have determined the policy agenda and controlled state power. How elites perceive equality, and comparative studies of their values have revealed national cultural differences which are reflected in the priority given to welfare state policies. Myron Weiner has argued that Indian cultural values underlie the continuous lag in Indian state policies in implementing primary education and abolishing child labour, in comparison with the policies of industrialized nations at similar stages of economic development. Sidney Verba's comparison of Japan, Sweden and the United States indicates that the United States lacks the cultural elite egalitarian values of these other nations. Though Verba does not make a comparison with it, South Asia is like the United States in its relative neglect of welfare-type state intervention. America lags behind other industrialized states in much the same way as South Asia neglects its poor. The cultural values of the dominant elites in both places stem from very diverse historical roots and cultures, but the resultant neglect of the poor in terms of state welfare implementation is common to both. That the United States is the only industrialized nation not to have universal health care is indicative of how out of step it is with the rest of the industrialized world. The continued rural segregation of Untouchables makes India unique among developing nations. These two very different realities have nothing in common except cultural and political values that neglect the generally perceived 'universal human entitlements'. While in the United States this in part reflects a frontier individualism and entrepreneurship which resists state intervention for redistribution of wealth, in India the roots lie in the traditional caste hierarchy.[2] These differing organizing principles, of individual rights in the United States and group/caste obligations and duties in India, have opposite philosophical roots but, when mediated by state policies, produce surprisingly similar results in their neglect of the poor. While traditional America stresses individual rights, India stresses duties.

There is no concept of rights in traditional India comparable to the western meaning of the term. Though Third World nations have adopted such things as the UN 'Universal Declaration of Human Rights', these are western traditions which Third World elites have adopted formally but do not necessarily practise. Human rights groups attempt to claim that these rights are universal, thereby glossing over their western origins, but this is disingenuous since their eurocentric roots have been revealed by those who have studied the issue.[3] This does not negate the superiority of these rights over other concepts, but to admit their European origins would be tantamount to imposing cultural values on other peoples, and thereby indicating that some values and cultures are superior to others. However, the superiority of these western values over indigenous ones has received wide recognition among westernized Third World elites, including those in South Asia. Few in India would make a traditional defence of the caste system, even though it is almost universally practised at some level. In a fundamental sense therefore, traditional hierarchical values have been modified by modernity. Whether this strengthens the traditional core concepts, or enables the creation of new secular values is difficult to determine. Although the empirical evidence for exceptional exploitation and the neglect of the lower classes is largely accepted, that there are cultural reasons behind this state neglect of the poor, as Weiner argues, is difficult for anyone to prove conclusively. His isolating of the cultural variable from other explanations, through comparison with nations at similar levels of development, is as conclusive as can be expected on issues of culture, which are difficult to analyze and quantify. Comparative attitudinal surveys such as Verba's of elites in industrialized nations would be difficult in the Indian context, given the deceptions and public adherence to egalitarian values commonly expressed by politically astute elites. One therefore falls back on impressionistic observations of the South Asian elites, and their empirically verifiable neglect of the lower classes in budget allocations and their ineffectual implementation.[4]

The cultural roots of human rights violations make change in South Asia difficult. A genuine modification of culture would presumably take generations, if it occurs at all. The failure of British rule to change values fundamentally has continued in post-colonial society. Foreign pressure on the state may be difficult to sustain; in any case state power as an instrument of cultural change is both a complex and a delicate issue. Still the cultural gap between the industrial and underdeveloped countries is obvious.

> Throughout the non-Western world, societies have judged themselves by Western standards and have found themselves wanting. Maybe the time has come to stop trying to change these societies and to change the model, to develop models of a modern Islamic, Confucian, or Hindu society that would be more relevant to countries where those cultures prevail.[5]

This is the purpose behind UNESCO's 'World Decade for Cultural Development'.[6] The substitution of westernization by modernization however is problematic. Though Huntington argues that 'the partnership between modernization and westernization has been broken', no society has successfully modernized without westernization even if the cultural roots, as in the case of East Asia, were elsewhere. Modernization without westernization, if at all possible, could mean continued oppression of minorities such as women, lower castes and tribal peoples. It is the western values which have served to uplift their status. Islamic societies which have attempted modernization without westernization have done so imperfectly, and left most of their population with few civil liberties. Westernization has universal human rights as its inherent goal, which poses a problem for attempts at Islamic or Hindu modernization. This is hardly surprising since human rights is an inherently western concept that finds limited resonance in many Third World cultures. Even adherence to it in the western cultures from which it originated is unevenly implemented, as critics of the North frequently point out.

There has been a long history, dating from the early 19th century, of Hindu reformers attempting to incorporate humanist values into their religion, but these are western concepts being adopted rather than indigenous traditions being asserted. The resultant hybrid reform movements never caught on with most of the population. Nevertheless, among the elite their influence was profound enough for them to adapt to scientific and humanist thought, even if it was not always put into practice. Westernization frequently is manifested in the superficial aspects of entertainment and dress, but work culture remains unaffected. The secular never really caught on, nationalist rhetoric notwithstanding.

This unevenness of modernization makes human rights adherence difficult to implement. The United Nations' declarations attempt to universalize eurocentric concepts which contradict the values of many cultures which reject minority rights. Changing the way governments operate goes against their self-interest and when indigenous cultural values do not require any change of norms, foreign incentives are usually inadequate. A nation of India's traditions, size and autarchy is particularly impervious to foreign influence since there are few indigenous values to which an appeal can be made, and few in the elite who are really committed to implementing human rights legislation.

A state policy or external intervention to change these conditions would have to confront the lack of an organizational basis for these values. As Hinduism is not institutionalized in a hierarchical religious organization, a change of institutional personnel will not alter the culture or religious beliefs. In fact the values are so all-pervasive in the subcontinent that even religions such as Islam, Sikhism and Buddhism which profess not to believe in caste have come to have caste-like divisions in their communities.

Caste influence is so pervasive that an attack on caste would have to involve all the major religions of the subcontinent.

If cultural reform for human rights is problematic, the implementation of human rights along with development is even more so. It is far from clear whether human rights facilitates or hinders economic development, particularly in the 'take-off' phase of industrialization.[7] Development is a traumatic and sometimes an all-consuming process. Industries and livelihoods are lost and alternative sources of income may be slow in coming or not come at all. The motivation of those adversely affected to destabilize the system is high and the temptation of states to resort to repression in defence of their elite interests is strong.[8]

A certain measure of stability of the state is important for growth and investment. Finding the correct balance between rights and development is far from easy. While most would argue for the need to eradicate torture and implement multiparty elections with universal franchise, demanding entitlements is a totally different and a more difficult issue. They often involve investment of scarce resources that might be better placed in longer term growth projects, or in those which can give return on investment quickly. Too high an investment in basic needs for the poor may provide few tangible returns and reduce work incentives. In the Third World, only the most basic needs can possibly be met, and state corruption could prevent some of the benefits from reaching the intended beneficiaries anyway. Those who already have access to power and resources are likely to get more, as they are already integrated into the system. They can resist cutbacks and have them apply to those most vulnerable. At the same time, resort to repression is an admission of failure by the state, which in the long term can have more serious consequences as the repression becomes more widespread and indiscriminate.

The management of dissent has been something in which only India can claim any finesse. Even here, however, the problems of Kashmir, Punjab and Assam, and the commonplace use of torture and police firings on demonstrators reveal the high degree of repression that accompanies democratic institutionalization. To what extent was this repression necessary and inevitable if democracy was to be maintained? Would foreign pressure for human rights merely serve to unravel the system and produce anarchy instead? All nations that have become developed have been guilty of human rights violations and it is doubtful if a case can be made that this hindered industrialization. The justification of repression to achieve development is also dubious. Human rights implementation can be justified on moral grounds without having to prove its efficacy on development grounds. Thus, while there is no necessary correlation between development and human rights, both can be promoted for the benefits they provide in their own terms.

REFERENCES

1. United Nations Development Programme, *Human Development Report* (New York: Oxford University Press, various years). World Bank, *World Development Report* (New York: Oxford University Press, various years).
2. Sidney Verba, *Elites and the Idea of Equality* (Cambridge: Harvard University Press, 1987), p. 41; Myron Weiner, *The Child and the State in India* (Princeton: Princeton University Press, 1991).
3. Emanuel de Kadt, 'Some Basic Questions on Human Rights and Development', *World Development*, Vol. 8, No. 2, February 1980, p. 98.
4. United Nations Development Programme, *Human Development Report* (New York: Oxford University Press, various years).
5. Samuel P. Huntington, 'The Goals of Development', in Myron Weiner and Samuel P. Huntington (eds), *Understanding Political Development* (Boston: Little, Brown & Company), p. 25.
6. Canadian Commission for UNESCO, *Final Report*, International Workshop on the Cultural Dimension of Development, Ottawa, 14–15 March 1991, January 1992.
7. Jack Donnelly, 'Human Rights and Development', *World Politics*, Vol. 36, No. 4, January 1984, pp. 256–57.
8. Saul Newman, 'Does Modernization Breed Ethnic Political Conflict?', *World Politics*, Vol. 43, No. 3, April 1991, p. 452.

CHAPTER 2

Regional Cooperation

Regional integration has been a major field for conflict resolution studies. The premise is that in the absence of powerful international institutions, intermediate-level regional organizations provide more immediate prospects for effective interstate cooperation. The track record of regional organizations in the reduction of tensions has been mixed. These organizations have endeavoured to increase security through military confidence-building measures and by cultural and economic integration programmes. Yet in the Third World most conflict issues remain outside the mandate of regional institutions.

Though the study of regionalism was spurred by the work of the European Economic Community (EEC), its application to the Third World proved disappointing to its proponents. Regionalism as a useful tool for conflict management had apparently passed its prime, with a number of the academic advocates switching to other fields. However, the ending of the cold war has seen a resurgence of interest in regional conflict management. With the absence of East–West competition to motivate Third World conflict, new possibilities for conflict resolution through foreign intervention seem possible. Though domestic sources of tension continue, the lack of foreign sponsors could de-escalate the process. The study of regionalism as a source of development and conflict resolution thus has a second chance to prove itself in newly favourable international circumstances.

Scholarly interest in regionalism has been reflected in South Asia, where an on-going stream of books and articles on the subject dwarfs the earlier literature on regionalism. The uniqueness of the South Asian experience does not make for the general application of international regional experience and literature to the region. The domestic ethnic basis of South Asian conflict means that the international relations theory has limited application. Fields such as religion, history, economics and comparative politics should also be included in the study of South Asian regionalism.

Regional organizations such as the EEC and the Association of South East Asian Nations (ASEAN) had an implicit function in containing the spread of communism and this common goal provided a context for achieving mutual benefits.[1] They excluded their primary antagonists in favour of uniting with old and newly found allies. These regional organizations were therefore exclusivist in keeping out enemies through the erection of trading and military barriers to rivals outside these alliances. As these rivals also formed their own regional organizations, such as the Council for Mutual Economic Aid (COMECON), the world became divided into mutually exclusive groups which served to reduce tensions among allies but did nothing to reduce tensions among antagonistic regional blocs. The East–West and North–South divides remained and may even have been accentuated by regional integration schemes which excluded outside nations.

In this way, virtually the whole world came to be included in assorted regional alliances which formed in antagonism to each other. The one area that remained without a regional alliance was South Asia. This was because its primary antagonists were not external to the region but were within it. A South Asian regional bloc could only be formed if the two protagonists, India and Pakistan, agreed to cooperate. As there had been three wars between these countries, this proved an insurmountable obstacle until 1985 when the South Asian Association for Regional Cooperation (SAARC) was formed. The creation of a regional bloc among antagonists was unique and went against the traditional pattern of regional alliance formation. For this reason there was considerable scepticism about the prospects of SAARC at its formation. From the outset there were assertions that its failure was inevitable due to the lack of a common security perception.[2] Its subsequent track record, while modest, was nevertheless impressive, given the on-going tensions in South Asia and the achievements of other Third World alliances. 'Despite ASEAN being claimed as a relatively successful organization regional cooperation has not done much better in Southeast Asia than in South Asia, and in some respects has lagged much behind.'[3]

That enemies rather than allies were brought together in SAARC makes similarities with other regional alliances minimal. Nevertheless, the literature on regional integration does provide concepts within which South Asian cooperation can be analyzed. The contrasts with other regions invite comparative analysis, and reveal something about the requirements for successful integration and conflict resolution. However, the 'lack of progress towards development of any coherent theoretical or even descriptive framework' of regional integration means that no comprehensive political theory exists that can adequately explain the South Asian integration phenomenon.[4] If regional organization in South Asia can be an effective forum for the reduction of tensions, this experience could provide an example for the incorporation of enemies within regional organizations in other conflict zones.

The use of such organizations raises a number of analytical problems. The most difficult perhaps is crediting any reduction in tensions to the organizations and not to other factors extraneous to the activist conflict-resolution process. The attribution of conflict resolution to particular institutions can be a problematic task, but, given sufficient data, not necessarily an impossible one. The existence of an institution at a crisis point can mediate a settlement, or at least prevent a misunderstanding from leading to a war neither side wants. However, even in the absence of such institutions other channels may be available to fill this void, such as foreign mediation or bilateral diplomatic contacts. The role most difficult to attribute to regional organizations among the normal interstate communications is that of moulding public opinion. Though the programmes of regional organizations can be evaluated, the ripple effects of these cooperative endeavours are more difficult to detect the further they are from the institutional intervention. Whatever effect they have can be swept away by domestic or foreign circumstances over which the regional organization has no control. The waste of effort this represents in human endeavour and funding makes it imperative that optimal interventions by regional organizations be undertaken in those areas where they will have the greatest impact.

The results of cooperation are both short- and long-term. A short-term intervention that can prevent hostilities could be the establishment of annual summit meetings of prime ministers, as SAARC has done in South Asia.[5] This can facilitate communication and ease tensions between individual leaders who ultimately must take the decision to go to war. More problematic, but not necessarily less important in the long term, is the moulding of public opinion by regional organizations in favour of reconciliation with traditional enemies. The creation of multilateral organizations to achieve this falls within the neo-functionalist view that joint endeavour creates understanding and mutual interests which may not have been realized or have existed before.[6]

This approach raises the question of whether there really are grounds for common understandings. Is cooperation a zero-sum game in which there are winners and losers but no positive outcomes for the region as a whole? If there are winners and losers, who will be the likely beneficiaries? If these can be predicted in advance the probable losers will not participate voluntarily unless they receive compensatory benefits from the winners or outside parties. These benefits would have to be sufficient to coax their participation yet not so onerous as to discourage the likely winners from paying the price. A balance of costs and benefits of alliances is difficult to negotiate even between allies, such as the United States and Canada, let alone traditional enemies.

The source of conflict in South Asia has been politicized ethnicity, yet this basis of conflict is very difficult for the state or a regional organization to resolve. The South Asian states have frequently resorted to repression, which has further antagonized public opinion in neighbouring states. However, these states have been implementing both tacit and formal confidence-building measures. On the military side an implicit understanding has existed between India and Pakistan through most of the post-independence period. Though security regimes are considered in the literature to be more difficult to implement than economic cooperation agreements, in South Asia most economies are autarchic in relation to each other.[7] Despite participation in international regimes such as the General Agreement on Tariffs and Trade (GATT), regional economic integration among antagonists is generally minimal. SAARC's creation of an economic regime would be an important advance in building vested interests in cooperation. Thus, while regimes dealing with military or economic affairs would not tackle the root cause of South Asian conflict, these sectors are more amenable to state and regional conflict resolution than the religious values which are beyond state control.

Regional integration and conflict resolution have traditionally followed two paths, those of military de-escalation and cultural and economic exchanges. It is economic integration which has achieved the greatest quantitative sophistication and empirical analysis, enabling the verification of certain conceptions about regional economic integration. The cultural aspect, however, is the most difficult to conceptualize in terms of conflict resolution. Military security through confidence-building measures is the most clearly conceived. Though only in its preliminary stages in South Asia, this offers short-term prospects for conflict management which can be enforced and verified. The prospects for the reduction of South Asian tensions will be examined using concepts in these three subfields, as there is no suitable overall theory that can adequately cover all areas of integration. Which programmes prove the most important in reducing tensions in South Asia have yet to be determined; however, likely areas for productive regional cooperation need to be analyzed in advance of implementation.

Geopolitical Regionalism

The seven members of SAARC range from India, with a population of 898 million people in 1993[8] to the Maldives, with 200,000 in 1992.[9] The most fundamental political difference however remains the rivalry between India and Pakistan. 'The organising principle of Pakistan threatens India with secessionism, while that of India threatens Pakistan with either dismemberment or absorption.'[10] Only Pakistan can have any capability to resist India militarily, yet most members have been able to prevent Indian economic and political interests from determining foreign and domestic policies. 'India has been unable to translate this preeminence into predominance' due to the resistance of smaller states.[11] However, the smaller states combined still cannot match India in economic and military terms. Yet, in a post-cold war world where western powers are unwilling to underwrite an anti-India policy, there is no alternative external power willing to undertake an active policy of containing India. Rather, the American perception has evolved into seeing India as a democratic force in a region of unstable military-influenced regimes. The foreign powers therefore have an interest in maintaining a regional organization that can assist in creating a non-conflictual situation.[12]

Given the autarchy of the Indian economy and its relatively independent foreign policy, external influence on the region is more limited than in some other areas of the world. India's ability to prevent foreign funding of SAARC is indicative of a capacity to forestall its use as an instrument of big power control. This however makes foreign participation in SAARC more problematic.

The differing political and economic interests of the SAARC members make for two contending approaches to regionalism. One implicitly functionalist view, which India advocates, sees SAARC as a vehicle for regional peace and security through advancing socio-economic development and cultural harmony in the region. Pakistan and Sri Lanka show greater interest in arms control measures as do other smaller states. These differences reflect national perceptions of regional interests. India, with the most developed economic capabilities (though not the highest per capita income), sees economic integration as advantageous, while on the cultural front its democratic traditions are subversive for military-influenced governments which would prefer to curb Indian military growth.[13] These differences of emphasis, however, have not prevented cooperation in SAARC and offer prospects for mutually beneficial agreements founded on perceived interests.

Economic Integration

The concept of economic integration as a means of security building found its theoretical basis in the functionalist and neo-functionalist schools of political thought and its practical application primarily in the development of the EEC. The work on regional integration by Haas that came out of the European experience was subsequently found by him and others not to apply in the same way to the Third World.[14] The application of the theory of integration to the developing world by Nye, Axline, and numerous regional specialists has indicated the specific opportunity costs that can be expected from Third World integration.[15] The consensus is that the forces favouring integration are not the same as those in the developed capitalist countries. The role of political parties, business classes and consumer groups is less pronounced in the Third World, leaving the responsibility for integrative functions to the various elites controlling state power. The lack of integrative lobby groups is compounded by the unequal size of Third World nations and consequent inequality of potential integrative benefits. According to the economic theory of integration, market forces will result in the largest benefits going to the most developed nations and regions, which can best exploit existing economies of scale.[16] The manufacturers from the smallest nations will lose out as development increases national disparities.[17] While in theory consumers would benefit from cheaper manufactured products, these products would be more expensive than previously imported consumer goods which were of higher quality but are now priced out of the market through protective tariffs imposed by the new regional trading bloc. The smaller nations thus lose industry they already possess and must pay more for poorer quality manufactured capital and consumer goods.[18] They become more dependent on primary raw material exports which entail increasingly unfavourable terms of trade. It is this uneven distribution of benefits that contributed to the demise of the East African Community, making regional alliances between large and small Third World economies difficult to achieve.[19]

Asymmetry, then, is the fundamental problem in achieving economic integration in South Asia. India has not only a much larger market, but a more diversified economic base which could enable it to outperform industries in neighbouring states. This disadvantage to India's neighbours could only be overcome if India were to forgo the benefits of regional integration by negotiated protection for the economies of its neighbours. In effect, India would have to subsidize regional integration for less developed states, at a cost to its own economy. This cost could be compensated in political terms through the resultant increase in regional influence, and permit defence cutbacks through regional reconciliation. This is a price India has shown little inclination to pay, given its own limited resources and the uncertainty of any tangible benefits that would accrue from the unstable governments in neighbouring states.

Trade-offs between political benefits and development costs are negotiable, but the multifarious nature of the interstate relationships makes an across-the-board agreement for integration unlikely. Progress will have to be made initially on a sectoral basis in which the costs and benefits are readily calculable and can be negotiated to mutual advantage. These negotiations could attempt to find areas of complementarity among the economies of South Asia. Unfortunately the economies are basically competitive rather than complementary as the products tend to be similar in the primary and consumer goods industries.[20] Only in the more advanced manufacturing and capital goods sector would there be scope for a non-competitive trade, but this would overwhelmingly benefit India, which alone has a significant consumer and capital goods manufacturing industry. However, the products from these sectors, despite some lower transportation costs, are not necessarily cheaper than or comparable in quality to foreign goods and therefore there is limited benefit for smaller states to import from India. This could be changed through the creation of a currency zone which allows trade without having to use hard currencies, thereby improving the foreign exchange position of smaller states.[21] A soft currency trading zone would be of limited value to India, however, as there are few products India would require from neighbouring states. The rupee–rouble trade arrangement resulted in India exporting more to the Soviet Union than it imported. This imbalance was partly compensated for by Soviet arms sales, but this is a pattern which neighbouring states would be unable to follow. The use of hard currency would therefore be in India's interest. However, there are areas of mutual advantage; for example, Nepal's hydroelectric potential can be developed for the Indian power sector in return for Indian products. The development of trade complementarities requires careful study to ensure optimal location of industries, avoiding politically expedient locations which could produce money-losing enterprises. This will require a strong regional regime capable of ensuring cost-efficient development implementation with primacy of optimum economic benefits over partisan political decision-making.[22]

Regional economic integration is the most substantive contribution SAARC can make to structural change in favour of conflict resolution. The creation of national complementarities through

SAARC-negotiated development planning would create new consumer and producer interests in expanded regionalism. Given the economic disparities in the region, free trade, which would exacerbate these differences, will be resisted by smaller states. These obstacles can only be overcome by regional planning for mutual benefits, which SAARC is best equipped to facilitate.

Cultural Integration

Culture, or more specifically politicized religion, caused the break-up of South Asia from one administration under the British Empire, into conflicting national quasi-theocracies. As culture and religion have formed the basis for South Asian conflict, any reconciliation must incorporate this dimension. However, the concept of politicized religion is difficult to deal with. The conflicts range from dominant ethnic groups which fear marginalization to prosperous religious groups which have only recently come to feel deprived. Marxist theorists have tended to see the politicization of religion as elite class interests manipulating a false popular consciousness, yet this religiosity has survived under all Communist regimes, and in South Asia has a debatable correlation with class interests. The non-Marxists by contrast see 'religious ethno-communities' as basic to the conflictual groups.[23] Their theoretical argument is that the politicized primordial identities react to the rapid changes brought about by modernity. However, this reaction to change need not be violent or regressive in all instances. Some cultures adapt to change better than others, creating new disparities and disintegration among social groups.[24]

Changing negative religious stereotypes existing in popular culture is extremely difficult, as the Soviet experience illustrates. For predominantly rural countries the influence of the state is minimal at the village level, given the low levels of education and poor communications. The failure of the state to alter public opinion means that regional organizations with even more limited resources and access will face considerably greater difficulties.

If religious differences caused the break-up of India in the independence phase, ethnicity has been the biggest threat to national integrity in the post-colonial period. Pakistan, India and Sri Lanka all face ethnically based secessionist or autonomist movements, which have been only partly repressed or co-opted by national governments. The real or self-perceived relative deprivation of ethnic groups has resulted in autonomist movements that have been supported by neighbouring states, thus creating a downward spiral of mutually fostered ethnic violence and national disintegration.[25]

The concept of politicized culture as manifested in religious and linguistic political movements has been the basis of both interstate and domestic conflict in South Asia. The literature is divided between the 'primordial' view that these identities are intrinsic to humanity, and the 'instrumentalist' view that they are values manipulated by interested parties pursuing a political agenda.[26] The degree to which these conflictual values are inherent in the cultures, or solvable through political and economic compromises, has not been resolved in the literature.

Though religious and cultural conflicts may have an economic basis in deprivation, evidence suggests that these movements acquire dynamics of their own which cannot be readily resolved through economic concessions. The ways in which regional organizations can deal with domestic political crises are limited, but they can help prevent member governments from aggravating the domestic crises of neighbouring states. The cultural programmes SAARC has begun to undertake provide a basis for the development of cross-cultural understanding.

The trend in South Asia has been towards religious fundamentalism rather than tolerance. This is arguably part of a global movement towards the assertion of religious identity.[27] Whether this reflects the shortcomings of other belief systems or more effective political manipulation is debatable. Whatever the causes, the development of religious tolerance will prove the most difficult for SAARC to implement as it is not amenable to negotiation between governments, and the communal religious leadership in South Asia has shown no interest in fostering understanding. Unlike nationalist movements which have a territorial limit, albeit a frequently disputed one, religious movements have a greater 'potential for conflict in that all are based upon a conviction of the possession of truth, which leads to an unwillingness to compromise'.[28] While Islam has no limits in its conversion mission, Hinduism with its caste system of non-conversion is inherently vulnerable to conversion of its lower castes. However, Islamic Pakistan as a subordinate regional power could not threaten a takeover of the subcontinent. Indian secular democracy by contrast enabled the continuity of minority religious practices with the cooperation of minority religious leaders. The assertion of Hindu revivalism now threatens the continuation of this equilibrium. The dominant tendency is to create obstacles to reconciliation, thereby contributing to the current communalism.[29] While direct negotiations with communal religious leaders are problematic, access to the lay public is difficult on account of their isolation and low levels of literacy.

Without such political intervention any attempts at regional institution building could flounder in the wake of communal violence, over which state and private institutions do not have much control. The difficulty is that elites tend to have limited ability to influence public opinion, but have a fair amount of discretion in government policy. While this gap can work to the advantage of regional institution building, which can be fostered by leaders without recourse to public opinion, that public opinion once mobilized against reconciliation becomes difficult to control.[30]

Even the most effective regional institution will fail if public opinion becomes hostile to minority beliefs. Though institutions can help the process of reconciliation, the only permanent solution lies in altering public attitudes from hostility to tolerance of differences of belief. Secular cultural education must therefore be the ultimate objective of SAARC. It has been argued that for regional integration to be effective a common cultural outlook has to be achieved, and this 'civilizational area' exists in South Asia.[31] Though the cultures have much in common, particularly at the elite level where western English education facilitates communication, it is seemingly trivial religious or ethnic differences which have proved the basis for conflict in South Asia. Proximity of habitation and culture have not proved sufficient to produce any discernible impact on conflict levels. Given the grassroots nature of communal violence, regional organizations and national governments have limited influence over this phenomenon and have proved virtually irrelevant in influencing it. Concepts and policies of integration fail when confronted with the popular communal culture, which is generally controlled only through state repression. The repression of minority groups in each others' states only serves to fuel interstate hostility, which turns domestic problems into regional and international ones. Given the religious basis of so much of South Asian politics, domestic communal violence has serious international implications which make the divide between domestic and international affairs difficult to distinguish. In this respect Third World regionalism has a dimension which is no longer so salient in the West where communal violence is usually absent. In South Asia communalism is primary, with nations created to reflect these community differences. The development of modernity has not brought a tolerance of other cultures. How such a tolerance can be achieved is critical for fostering peace in South Asia.

SAARC is not in a good position to facilitate this grassroots reconciliation as it is partly composed of 'enemy states' whose intervention in communal relations would be suspect to those involved in conflict. Rather, the organization would be more effective in assisting from a distance perhaps by funding non-governmental organizations (NGOs) which have developed credibility in improving communal relations. Such funding could however make these NGOs targets of criticism and even attack as recipients of funds indirectly provided by hostile states. Local government organizations or non-belligerent donors could provide more legitimate funding support. In South Asia cultural activities have been traditionally used for partisan party purposes. Nevertheless, there is no reason why such activities cannot be used in non-partisan ways for communal reconciliation under the sponsorship of national governments and private agencies.

Military Security Regimes

Despite the fact that India and Pakistan have fought three wars, during most of the time a tacit military security agreement existed between the two countries. The costs of a prolonged conflict that would be necessary for an outright victory led to implicit acceptance of the status quo even while it was convenient for states to deny this understanding. However, while the development of a nuclear capability by India and Pakistan makes the dangers of inadvertent conflict much greater, at the same time it presents opportunities for de-escalation and reduced military expenditures.

The need for a formalized security regime has thus been recognized and become the subject of on-going negotiations.[32] The development of nuclear weapons gives an assurance that each side can inflict unacceptable damage to the other, making a cost-effective military victory impossible. This capability ensures state survival, but can lead to greater damage from an escalation of conflict. India by allowing Pakistan to develop its capability without taking military action implicitly accepted this development, later formalized in the agreement between Pakistan and India not to attack each other's nuclear installations.

South Asia is not a totally isolated region and China's military capability would prevent a radical reduction in India's capability even with a Pakistani settlement.[33] The de-escalation of military confrontation must therefore include China as well. The nuclear capabilities of all three nations do provide opportunities for conventional force reductions in the subcontinent, which would assist in the reconciliation and economic development process. The April 1991 agreements between India and Pakistan providing for advance notification of troop movements, military aircraft landing rights, and prevention of airspace violations mark significant advances in confidence-building measures for conventional forces.[34] However, as these agreements were reached while border security forces were exchanging fire and troops were being killed, it reveals only a limited interest in de-escalating the conflict.

In addition to the alleviation of interstate rivalries, it may be possible in the long term to arrange joint military operations for regional security. The Indian military intervention in the Maldives to prevent a coup was accepted by external powers as positive. In future it may be possible to undertake such operations jointly with regional forces.

South Asian foreign military alliances have no consistent ideological foundation since they were formed through the historical imperatives of the cold war. This should permit the future de-internationalization of South Asian regional conflicts, thereby providing greater opportunities for conflict management. The domestic sources of conflict mean that regional rather than international interventions offer the most durable solutions.

Arms control is not the most suitable endeavour for SAARC as China is not in the organization. Major arms reductions must involve China since India has legitimate security concerns with its northern neighbour. A tripartite understanding between India, China and Pakistan would permit a significant reduction in defence expenditures in South Asia. Further, these can be complemented by bilateral arrangements with smaller neighbouring South Asian states.

SAARC as a Conflict-resolution Institution

In common with most other regional organizations, SAARC was founded on the basis of unanimity among its seven members. This prevents any state being isolated and outvoted by the other members, while helping to ensure that the possibility of defections from the system is minimized. As SAARC was founded only in 1985, programme implementation is still in the initial stages. Nevertheless, the range and scope of planned activities is impressive and could facilitate a general process of tension reduction. For instance, the creation of a 200,000-tonne food security reserve, though small in South Asian regional terms, offers the beginnings of a programme which could prevent future famines, just as India's own buffer stock prevented famine during its worst drought in a century.

However, the fundamental question that remains is whether institution building really reduces tensions as the functionalists claim. While such institutions undoubtedly create vested bureaucratic interests in cooperation, these may be created without any foundation in their societies and may have little or no influence on the decision-making process. The resources they absorb may not be commensurate with the cooperative tasks they perform. The social and development activities, while they may be effective in their own right, probably have little influence on communal relations or declarations of war. Those who benefit may not have any links with decision-makers, or even appreciate the advantages of reconciliation.[35]

SAARC as an institution of communal reconciliation can only play a modernizing secular function, yet the difficulties in achieving this should not be underestimated. 'Why should the guardians of tradition cooperate in its destruction?'[36] Appeals to communal organizations are unrealistic, yet public debate on religion is an acutely sensitive area for a multinational regional organization to

enter, even though this is the area in which cooperation or conflict will ultimately be determined. Which institutions and programmes can achieve demobilization of conflictual religion is
difficult to predict. Significantly, the worst communal violence
has recently been in urban centres, indicating that it may be the
trauma of modernization rather than rural tradition that is the
basis of communalism. Traditions have been interpreted in a
modern political context that will not vanish with development.
'The very rapid and sweeping advances in industrialization will
not lessen the conflicts and tensions but, rather, will exacerbate
them. The geographical areas of conflict have been the most
modern cities—Bombay, Indore, Ahmedabad, and Jamshedpur
—not the rural hinterlands.'[37] Europe experienced the Wars of
Religion for a 100 years from 1560 till the Peace of Westphalia
brought an end to religion as a major source of conflict in
Europe. Avoiding similar experiences in South Asia is critical for
international peace.

Given its own limitations as a multinational institution, SAARC's
contribution to the peace process should be targeted for maximum impact. Its most readily realizable role is in inter-elite reconciliation. Summit meetings of foreign ministers and heads of
state, and professional conferences, which are already being
undertaken, provide forums for negotiation and mutual appreciation of opposing views. The limited scale of these small group
gatherings makes the endeavour financially feasible for SAARC
as well as rewarding in terms of conflict management. Gatherings
for the sharing of ideas can also provide forums for the beginning
of regional integration schemes, particularly in areas such as economic development and resource sharing. SAARC, however, is
least equipped to deal with the fundamental cause of the conflict,
namely, politicized religion, because this has a domestic dimension which leaves prime responsibility with the nation-state.
NGOs would be best equipped to deal with this educational
process as governments have often limited legitimacy even with
their own people.

SAARC has already made considerable progress in the inter-
elite communication process. However, the structural integration
of national economies has made no headway due to vested interests in various states and fear of unequal benefits. In future this
must be a major endeavour if SAARC is to begin the institutionalization of shared regional interests.

External Input

The conflicts of South Asia are domestically rather than externally driven, making a post-cold war foreign resolution of hostilities inoperable, even if foreign influence can prevent some of the most negative consequences. The South Asian states have sought external allies in their regional disputes and proved remarkably resistant to the outside interventions that were perceived to be against their national interests. Though India's size and relatively autonomous economic base have provided it with the greatest autonomy, Pakistan has likewise been able to resist all foreign pressure against nuclear weapons development. In essence the South Asian states appear to have used their foreign backers for their own power enhancement rather than allowed themselves to be used as mere pawns in the cold war. Foreign powers therefore have less influence than in most other parts of the Third World. India receives 0.6 per cent of its gross national product (GNP) from foreign aid, providing the donors with limited leverage. Though Bangladesh receives 5.8 per cent of GNP from overseas development assistance, the resulting influence of donors over the weaker South Asian states provides limited opportunities for regional conflict reduction.[38]

In contrast with many Third World regional organizations which are created and supported with the assistance of major western powers, SAARC has avoided this foreign association. 'Whereas there has hardly ever been a major ASEAN meeting which has not conjointly had, in the antechamber, the presence of some of the major western powers', SAARC has 'stuck more closely to a non-aligned course.'[39] This relative autonomy from foreign powers makes influencing the organization more difficult, yet it can facilitate the regional reconciliation process through direct interactions among members.

As regional economic integration is often seen as a zero-sum game, creating positive benefits for the region as a whole could be facilitated by linking aid programmes to regional integration projects. This underwriting of regional integration by the international donor community could turn a marginal economic proposition into one in which all would receive critical benefits. The Colombo Plan in which Canada and other nations participated in the 1950s was an early example of this approach in South Asia.[40]

Subsequent aid efforts have tended to be on a bilateral between donor and recipient governments. The creation of SAARC will provide opportunities for new aid initiatives that could facilitate regional development planning in such areas as water resources. The encouragement of regional cooperation by the Carter administration during the formative years of SAARC indicates that external support can be forthcoming.[41] The development programmes of South Asian states provide opportunities for international organizations such as the International Monetary Fund (IMF) and World Bank to assist regional organizations in multilateral endeavours. SAARC considered collaboration with UNICEF which is an indication that multilateral organizations may be viewed as less threatening than major foreign powers. The tying of development funding to economically and environmentally sustainable projects can be extended to the selection of projects that offer opportunities for conflict resolution. The regional integrative aspect of proposed aid projects has hardly been touched on in the aid literature, though international aid can be an important asset in conflict resolution.[42] Since aid can alleviate or exacerbate regional disparities, its location and function in regional and communal conflicts is critical to developmental success. The collapse of the development aid effort in Sri Lanka is indicative of the vulnerability of economic development to military conflict.

Conflict or Cooperation?

The renewed interest in regionalism in the post-cold war era can benefit from the lessons of many previous Third World failures. Regional organizations cannot be expected to resolve all conflictual issues, nor should they be intended to do so. They should undertake only those endeavours for which they can have a built-in or foreseeable advantage over other institutions. SAARC's role in this process can be important but it is unlikely to be fundamental as the problems of ethnicity are not amenable to regional solutions given their domestic imperatives. Nevertheless, institutions are more easily dealt with than cultural values, which are extremely difficult to mould. SAARC therefore does offer an instrument for reconciliation in the subcontinent. However, it is

unlikely to be decisive. If it did not exist, other channels for reconciliation would be utilized if the need arose. Although being in
place gives it a decided advantage, SAARC is unlikely to be able
to create the desire for reconciliation in the subcontinent.

SAARC's creation of forums for negotiation within ruling elites
is a step in the right direction. However, ultimately, it is in civil
society that South Asian conflicts will find their resolution. As
long as democracy exists there will be a tendency for political
elites to reflect the sentiments of civil society, and for this reason
their reconciliation is only as permanent as the electorate that
puts them in place. If reconciliation does not exist in the population, the antagonisms will be reflected in the election of communal leaders. Though these leaders may be subject to foreign
influence, they will be primarily influenced by their electorate,
which may not give them a great deal of room for reconciliation.
In this sense democracy is not always conducive to communal
harmony. It is perhaps for this reason that foreign powers often
prefer negotiation with elites who are not subject to frequent
removal through elections. However, as the Soviet experience
indicates, even undemocratic regimes are ultimately influenced
by civil society. This influence can be prevented from removing
regimes only if it is based on an ethnic group with sufficient control over the state. For this reason national armies are often ethnically based, but too tight a control can lead to secessionist
movements and thus further weaken state influence.

The best recipe for avoiding a concentration of power would
appear to be ethnically diverse states. In South Asia, however,
only India meets this criterion, which is probably a major reason
for the longevity of its democracy. Since the other states lack this
built-in diversity, only a lessening of central state power is likely
to give minorities a fair share of state resources. In this respect a
growth of regional governance would provide minorities with
greater access to resources and political influence. To the extent
that unification of the subcontinent takes place, the diversity will
strengthen those currently without influence on their national
governments. However, because these minorities lack influence
there is no motivation for governments to pursue reconciliation.
It is difficult to see how one can get around this obstacle, given
the politics of the region.

Though it is fairly clear that the people of South Asia would be better off with reconciliation rather than the legacy of conflict that pervades the region, there are significant forces opposing it. Partition of the subcontinent is a suboptimal solution to the ethnic divisions of the region, but conflict continues because there are both the popular sentiments of nationalism and interests that oppose cooperation. Nation-states are excellent social engineers, creating elites where none may have existed, or marginalizing others considered too influential. The creation of Pakistan and Bangladesh fostered business and state elites which would now stand to lose by any significant decrease in national state power. Though the other states are not post-colonial creations, the influence of various business and state elites has been equally enhanced to the extent that they can influence their governments. These groups are bound to place strict limits on how far the reduction in barriers between states is allowed to proceed.

These barriers are significant in the business sector where existing business elites have used their control over the state to enhance their wealth and influence. The reduction in trade barriers for all but the most internationally competitive industries would threaten the survival of these indigenous business interests, which can be expected to use their not-inconsiderable influence to prevent it. The extent to which Indian business houses were able to prevent foreign competition is an example of this, but such cases can be found in other states as well.

This is not to say that there are not business sectors that see themselves gaining markets in neighbouring countries. However, as these are generally located in India, their influence on neighbouring state policies is non-existent. Consumer groups would certainly benefit from the relaxation of trade barriers, but as these groups are even less organized than their counterparts in the West, their influence on the state is negligible.

Perhaps the most influential groups are to be found amongst the ethnic groups themselves. Many are divided by national borders and are keenly interested in visiting relations in neighbouring states. The difficulties involved in doing this are well known. Muslims and Untouchables have significant groups in each other's states. These minority populations, however, are often used by politicians to create conflict in the region. As communal violence quickly brings action against minorities in neighbouring states, which creates a spiral of violence, these divisions continue to fuel communal discord decades after partition, which was supposed to resolve such problems. Instead, it has transformed what was a domestic conflict into an international one.

The search for sources of reconciliation has indicated that the forces in its favour are weak even though the benefits of cooperation for the peoples of the subcontinent are considerable. The issue of reconciling a non-antagonistic ethnic identity with human rights for other groups has never been adequately resolved in South Asia. That the rest of the world has not done much better is indicative of how intractable and universal this problem is.

REFERENCES

1. S.D. Muni, 'South Asian Regional Cooperation: Evolution and Prospects', *IDSA Journal*, Vol. 19, No. 1, July–September 1986, p. 122.
2. William T. Tow, *Subregional Security Cooperation in the Third World* (Boulder, Colorado: Lynne Rienner Publishers, 1990), pp. 7–8.
3. Pran Chopra, 'SAARC and ASEAN: Comparative Analysis of Structures and Aims', in Bhabani Sen Gupta (ed.), *SAARC–ASEAN: Prospects and Problems of Inter-regional Cooperation* (Delhi: South Asian Publishers, 1988), p. 22.
4. Barry Buzan, 'A Framework for Regional Security Analysis', in Barry Buzan and Gowher Rizvi (eds), *South Asian Insecurity and the Great Powers* (London: Macmillan, 1986), p. 7.
5. Kanti Prasad Bajpai, 'The Origins of Association in South Asia: SAARC 1979–1989', (unpublished Ph.D. dissertation, University of Illinois at Urbana-Champaign, 1990), p. 259.
6. Inis L. Claude, Jr., *Swords into Plowshares: The Problems and Progress of International Organization* (New York: Random House, 5th edition, 1971), pp. 378–407.
7. Janice Gross Stein, 'Detection and Defection: Security "Regimes" and the Management of International Conflict', *International Journal*, Vol. XL, No. 4, Autumn 1985, p. 601.
8. World Bank, *World Development Report 1995*, (New York: Oxford University Press, 1995), p. 210.
9. United Nations Development Programme, *Human Development Report 1995*, New York: Oxford University Press, 1995, p. 187.
10. Buzan, 'A Framework for Regional Security Analysis' (n. 4 above), p. 15.
11. Mohammed Ayoob, 'The Primacy of the Political: South Asian Regional Cooperation (SARC) in Comparative Perspective', *Asian Survey*, Vol. 25, No. 4, April 1985, p. 455.
12. Tow, *Subregional Security* (n. 2 above), pp. 89–125.
13. Muni, 'South Asian Regional Cooperation' (n. 1 above), p. 135; Gowher Rizvi, 'The Role of the Smaller States in the South Asian Complex', in Barry Buzan and Gowher Rizvi (eds), *South Asian Insecurity*, (n. 4 above), p. 130.

14. Ernst B. Haas, 'The Uniting of Europe and the Uniting of Latin America', *Journal of Common Market Studies*, Vol. 5, No. 4, June 1967, pp. 315–43; Lynn Krieger Mytelka, 'Fiscal Politics and Regional Redistribution: Bargaining Strategies in Asymmetrical Integrative Systems', *Journal of Conflict Resolution*, Vol. 19, No. 1, March 1975, pp. 138–60.

15. J.S. Nye, 'Patterns and Catalysts in Regional Integration', *International Organization*, Vol. 19, No. 4, Autumn 1965, pp. 870–84; W. Andrew Axline, 'The Comparative Analysis of Regional Cooperation Among Developing Countries', (Paper presented at the Fifteenth World Congress of the International Political Science Association, 21–25 July 1991, Buenos Aires).

16. W. Andrew Axline, 'Regional Co-operation and National Security: External Forces in Caribbean Integration', *Journal of Common Market Studies*, Vol. 27, No. 1, September 1988, pp. 1–25; Lynn Krieger Mytelka, 'The Salience of Gains in Third-World Integrative Systems', *World Politics*, Vol. 25, No. 2, January 1973, pp. 236–50.

17. Bela Balassa and Ardy Stoutjesdijk, 'Economic Integration Among Developing Countries', *Journal of Common Market Studies*, Vol. 14, No. 1, September 1975, pp. 37–55.

18. John W. Sloan, 'The Strategy of Developmental Regionalism: Benefits, Distribution, Obstacles, and Capabilities', *Journal of Common Market Studies*, Vol. 10, No. 2, December 1971, pp. 138–62.

19. W. Andrew Axline, 'Regional Co-operation and National Security: External Forces in Caribbean Integration', *Journal of Common Market Studies*, Vol. 27, No. 1, September 1988, p. 4.

20. Krishnalekha Sood, *Trade and Economic Development: India, Pakistan and Bangladesh* (New Delhi: Sage Publications, 1989), p. 206.

21. Eric Gonsalves, 'An Agenda for the Next Decade', *South Asia Journal*, Vol. 1, No. 1, July–September 1987, p. 23.

22. Sood, *Trade and Economic Development: India, Pakistan and Bangladesh* (n. 20 above), p. 202; Mahmudul Anam and Syed Sajjadur Rahman, 'Economic Integration in South Asia: An Exploratory Analysis in Trade, Investment and Finance', *Journal of Developing Societies*, Vol. 7, No. 1, January–April, 1991, p. 146.

23. Arun Bose, *India's Social Crisis* (Delhi: Oxford University Press, 1989), p. 2.

24. Javeed Alam, 'Political Articulation of Mass Consciousness in Present-day India', in Zoya Hasan, S.N. Jha and Rasheeduddin Khan (eds), *The State, Political Processes, and Identity: Reflections on Modern India* (New Delhi: Sage Publications, 1989), p. 243.

25. Urmila Phadnis, *Ethnicity and Nation-building in South Asia* (New Delhi: Sage Publications, 1989), p. 243.

26. Paul R. Brass, 'Elite Groups, Symbol Manipulation and Ethnic Identity Among the Muslims of South Asia', in David Taylor and Malcolm Yapp (eds), *Political Identity in South Asia* (London: Curzon Press Ltd, 1979), p. 35.

27. Ainslie T. Embree, *Utopias in Conflict: Religion and Nationalism in Modern India* (Berkeley: University of California Press, 1990), p. 2.

28. Ibid., p. 14.

29. Bruce Matthews, 'Sinhala Cultural and Buddhist Patriotic Organizations in Contemporary Sri Lanka', *Pacific Affairs*, Vol. 61, No. 4, Winter 1988–89, p. 624.

30. Lynn Krieger Mytelka, 'The Salience of Gains in Third World Integrative Systems', *World Politics*, Vol. 25, No. 2, January 1973, p. 237.
31. Buzan, 'A Framework for Regional Security Analysis' (n. 4 above), p. 10.
32. Stein, 'Detection and Defection' (n. 7 above), pp. 612, 624.
33. Mohammed Ayoob, 'India in South Asia: The Quest for Regional Predominance', *World Policy Journal*, Vol. 7, No. 1, pp. 107–33; Paul George, 'Indian Naval Expansion' (Ottawa: Canadian Institute for International Peace and Security, Working Paper 32, February 1991), p. 5; K. Subrahmanyam, *India's Security: The North and North-East Dimension* (London: The Centre for Security and Conflict Studies, Conflict Studies 215, October 1988), p. 1.
34. Foreign Broadcast Information Service, South Asia, NES-91-067, 8 April 1991, from Delhi Domestic Service in English, 6 April 1991.
35. Claude, *Swords into Plowshares* (n. 6 above), p. 385.
36. Embree, *Utopias in Conflict* (n. 27 above), p. 42.
37. Ibid., p. 53.
38. World Bank, *World Development Report 1995* (New York: Oxford University Press, 1995), p. 198.
39. Chopra, 'SAARC and ASEAN' (n. 3 above), p. 4.
40. W. Andrew Axline, 'Underdevelopment, Dependence, and Integration: The Politics of Regionalism in the Third World', *International Organizations*, Vol. 31, Nos. 1–2, 1977, pp. 83–105.
41. Muni, 'South Asian Regional Cooperation' (n. 1 above), p. 124.
42. John Siebert, *Ottawa Citizen*, 25 April 1991, p. 13.

CHAPTER 3

The State Development Impasse

Political Perception

In assessing development programmes scholars often consult a combination of ruling party members, civil servants and development beneficiaries as informants. Statistical data is collected either through their own surveys or through those of colleagues and governments. The weight given to the often conflicting evidence determines the conclusions reached. Informants inevitably have personal biases as well as restraints on their freedom of expression. Party members and civil servants must publicly defend the government position, while beneficiaries may fear their criticism will result in the withdrawal of aid.

An Untouchable is likely to have a negative attitude towards the dominant Brahminical culture, hence the alienation of a segregated population could be reflected in the research output. An upper-caste background on the other hand may create a positive outlook which is unwarranted. The overwhelming predominance of the upper castes in the scholarly community could result in an academic consensus skewed towards their perceptions.

The products of research are influenced by differing values, ideologies and personal identifications. Out-of-state scholars initially have no existing network or local cultural identification; this lends itself to greater objectivity. However, in order to complete their work they establish local contacts, and these professional contacts almost invariably flow through the upper-caste intellectual community. The out-of-state and local scholars thus tend to utilize identical contacts and have mutual interests. Local scholars may want travel assignments abroad or to present their state and government in a certain way, while visiting scholars are under considerable pressure to publish, even at the cost of adequate field research which would require use of less accessible sources.

If research is focused on an unexplored subject or a locality where an existing scholarly network does not exist, the tendency towards conformity may be avoided. Here, however, new problems arise which may be detrimental to good research because they go unrecognized. It is generally acknowledged that researchers enter a field with preconceptions. These are also reflected in the organizations doing development work, many of which are internationally funded and managed through local elite social workers and other development specialists. Even if the locality has not been touched by research or development agencies the researcher has a world-view different from that of the subjects of research. The researcher may not have the means to impose his/her values, but the development agency certainly does have the largesse to gain some local adherence, whether genuinely felt or not. The agency determines the development agenda, and what is good for the natives, and attempts to gain local commitment to it. The development priorities having already been set by the agency headquarters, the project selection is generally a formality. The new clients generally adhere to the prevailing line in public before any visitors who come to inspect the project. They are expected not to approach other development agencies that provide alternative services to the new patron.[1] Except at the village level, the development agency is almost inevitably staffed by members of the rural and urban elites. These are in turn linked to international agencies from which their funding, or a significant part of it, often originates. To obtain this funding applications must be worded according to the guidelines of the international (meaning western) agency. There are thus two levels of adherence, that of the villagers and that of the national NGO leadership. Whatever their personal views, both must adhere to the prevailing line in interaction with visiting foreigners and inspectors, or risk withdrawal of funding. Villagers are aware of what is really happening to the money at the local level, and so may some of the national NGO leadership, but if, as is normally the case, the published guidelines are not completely followed, the discrepancy is not dwelt upon.

The guidelines of the development agencies are developed in the West according to the perceptions prevalent there of what development requires, with little or no village-level input. These follow the latest trends in development thinking, which are generally abandoned after some time as they almost invariably fail to have the desired impact. The current needs have been determined in distant western capitals to be, among other priorities, sustainable development and women's empowerment. The problem is that villagers do not see their own problems in this way, so NGOs need to educate them according to these guidelines since they are better aware of what is good for the villagers even if the villagers do not realize it themselves. An example of this can be seen in the priority given in recent years to women's issues, which have predictably been taken up by Third World NGOs receiving funds from the First World. This reflects the salience of the feminist agenda in the West which is deemed appropriate to transfer to the Third World. However, what is appropriate for relatively privileged western women is not necessarily a high priority for poor Indian women. A doctoral student, Maxine Kay Weisgrau, has observed how this transference of a western agenda was carried out at a tribal village in Rajasthan.

At one point during this [feminist NGO] lecture a village woman spoke out. She said that her problems were not caused by being a woman. She said that her husband doesn't exploit her, nor do other men in her village. Her exploitation was from Rajputs and landlords…. I discussed these events, and my observations of them, with several NGO directors and workers during fieldwork. One individual remarked that the government seems to be supporting programs with a feminist ideology as a way of diverting attention from the more explosive issues of caste-based and class-based exploitation. Allowing a feminist message to be preached, this individual observed, is a way of organizing women and giving them a politically safe rallying point from the perspective of the social and political establishment without directly confronting more potentially explosive issues of caste, class and religious exploitation. Although I cannot state with any confidence that this is the intention, either overt or unconscious, of government strategy, my observations of the interaction between social workers and rural villagers, each articulating a different world view, would bear out this individual's observations.[2]

It is doubtful that anyone in the Indian government has thought through a feminist agenda as a counter-policy to caste analysis, but there is no doubt that the Indian government has adopted women's development issues in conformity with international donor interests and a domestic women's lobby. This is also the case with the environmental movement, which plays a double-edged role as promoter of aboriginal rights within a conservationist framework that aboriginal people do not put into practice or perceive in these terms.[3]

Although the ideology that perceives environmental conflict in terms of sustainability is external to adivasi consciousness, it is employed strategically by the movement in the valley to gain the sympathy of urban supporters. The discourse of the general theory of development does not allow people to speak for themselves; it tends to be deaf to people's own understanding of their predicament. This is problematic because it slights the other, equally valid concerns of adivasis which answer to a different logic—of patriarchy, caste, honour. These areas of politics which are autonomous from development tend to be marginalised, even though, ironically, they come closest to constituting truly 'indigenous' 'alternative political culture'.[4]

This projection of development agency, feminist, and environmentalist values and policies onto villagers is also undertaken by researchers who write the culture of other peoples in their own ideological terms. This results in

a refusal to acknowledge the insurgent as the subject of his own history. For once a peasant rebellion has been assimilated to the career of the Raj, the Nation or the People, it becomes easy for the historian to abdicate the responsibility he has of exploring and describing the consciousness specific to that rebellion and be content to ascribe to it a transcendental consciousness.[5]

Thus the people are portrayed as the researcher sees them rather than the way they see themselves or the way they really are. Since they cannot write their own culture or history for lack of education and resources, there need be no counterview to the distortions that may arise in the literature, and the outside world comes to see them the way the researcher sees them.

The difficulty of interpretation is compounded if access to the community is restricted or circumscribed in particular ways. This primarily happens on account of government restrictions on access to the country. 'The government of India does not permit research in strategic areas or on sensitive regional, political and social themes.'[6] In the words of Michael Brecher, the founder of the Shastri Indo-Canadian Institute:

> The restrictions imposed by the Government of India on permissible topics are inconsistent with the principle of an open society and, as such, a deviation from behaviour towards foreign scholars during the 1950s and 1960s, as I can testify from my own odyssey as a student of India. Indeed, as a colleague remarked recently, it is doubtful if any topic which I researched in India during those two decades would have been approved by Indian authorities in the 1970s and 1980s.[7]

However, the fact that India is an open society makes it possible to do unapproved research on sensitive topics. I was never challenged by anyone about whether I had permission to study Indian communism or tribal policy. It is possible to conduct research in the big cities without attracting the attention of the monitoring authorities, but a foreign scholar living in an Indian village is invariably going to be noticed by the state. To do research in West Bengal villages, according to a foreign professor, requires not only Government of India permission, but the permission of the ruling Communist Party-Marxist (CPM). This has important implications for the type of research undertaken. Not only does an innocuous topic have to be chosen for official purposes, but any critical analysis will not go unnoticed by the CPM. While a doctoral student may be able to do research and write critically afterwards, if one wants to gain repeat access to the rural areas there is an incentive to tone down the criticism. Thus anyone with career ambitions and who sees the state as more than a one-shot research endeavour should avoid negative statements. I had a scholar tell me after a lecture I gave that he did not disagree with my empirical findings, but in his subsequent published work praised the Left Front performance. One cannot have it both ways, but I suspect that the printed word as the opinion of record is likely to be the less honest under the circumstances. This creates the danger of 'feel good' publications praising developmental efforts and avoiding the really sensitive topics. This applies not only to academics but to development consultants as well. According to the Field Director of the Andean Programme for International Voluntary Services:

> There have been projects by the thousand but few have produced anything worthy of note. Objectives are routinely revised or abandoned; project directors come and go and are seldom, if ever, held to account for their actions; and the projects themselves invariably grind to a halt the moment support is removed. Self-reliance, the watchword and yardstick of the development agencies for so long, has become little more than a myth—widely held, but a myth all the same.
>
> Along with all this spectacular non-achievement has arisen a phenomenon of equally dubious character, that of the 'independent evaluation' which often takes the form of a silent pact in which the aid agency and the 'independent evaluator' are partners. The evaluator must seem to be independent so as to avoid accusations of partiality, and yet at the same time he knows only too well that if he oversteps the mark and says anything too damaging he is unlikely to be invited back and his company may have to fold. A conspiracy to avoid seeing what is taking place affects a good many of the agencies, therefore; and as a general rule the greater the resources and the more prestigious the agency, the greater is the collusion between evaluator and agency.
>
> Not many people are willing to wade through tomes of jargon-filled reports—which cost a fortune to produce and lie gathering dust on forgotten shelves—and then go back to the project site to see for themselves. Certainly no one in a head office located a few thousand miles away. In the main, they are only too happy to believe in the myths that the evaluator peddles.

There is no way the massive expenditure on aid can be justified in terms of the results achieved. Its impact has only ever been small-scale and piecemeal, and usually takes a decade at least to show through, if then. Of more direct benefit to the countries concerned are the cash and the employment that the aid agencies bring to the local economy. The governments know this, of course, and one suspects that this is the reason why they accede so readily to the request of an ever increasing number of agencies to come and set up shop. Well motivated and sincere the majority of them may be, but ingenuous also and soon, without realizing it, most of them will be acting out the same absurd charade that has come to characterize aid everywhere.[8]

While working in Ecuador as a consultant for the Canadian Foreign Ministry I had the opportunity to visit their Canada Fund programme for indigenous villagers. Despite the public rhetoric in the meetings with villagers about how the aid was benefiting them, we were surreptitiously informed that the credit loans were going to the better-off members of the community while the poorer ones received little of it. Thus the aid was fostering divisions and eroding the cohesion of indigenous communities. When I informed an Andean specialist about this, I was told that in Peru the Shining Path guerrillas had been destroying development projects in indigenous villages. This was being decried by the development agencies as the ultra-leftism of Luddite terrorists, but in fact this action found approval or indifference from many indigenous people because of the divisive and skewed benefits the aid was having in indigenous communities. The aid agencies never did fathom the reality of what their projects were doing to the villagers. Nor were the social scientists able to predict the uprisings, except in the few cases where the social scientists were Shining Path members.[9] When I mentioned my village experience to a co-consultant and suggested informing the funders, I was told that the Fund was actually much better than its major counterpart, the Canadian International Development Agency (CIDA), which had become so bureaucratized that smaller organizations and communities could not even access it. The creation of the Canada Fund had been a way of permitting greater access by smaller groups, and in the larger perspective was a progressive force in the aid community.

As some academics who make positive evaluations of the West Bengal experience are consultants with development agencies, it raises questions about the integrity of the academic consultancy process. There is more money in studying successes than failures. The scholar Harold Innis in the 1950s decried the growing connection of academics and universities with the state and private sector as an erosion of the objectivity and detachment needed for good scholarship. In the search for income and funding no one bothers much now about these questions, but the creation of linkages between local government and/or development agencies and academics raises questions about the veracity of the research. This is particularly the case with the untraceable villages that are studied by politically motivated scholars on behalf of committed development agencies and governments. State-level documents can at least be checked for typing errors in figures, but village studies fall in that area of unverifiable and unreproducible results. Avoidance of unpleasant controversial realities is seen in such issues as the segregation of Untouchables, which few of these scholars have ever mentioned as being a village issue. This is a bit like studying the old south in rural America and not mentioning that the blacks were segregated. This would not be acceptable in contemporary American studies, but similar issues pass unnoticed in almost all West Bengal studies. G.K. Lieten in his work on Left Front performance deals with caste in several pages of his books on West Bengal[10] but never asks why the Left Front in nearly two decades of office never launched a campaign against segregation, or how it has ended up preserving it longer than the South African apartheid regime it hypocritically criticized.

While not giving offence is a smart career move at the national, state and village levels, criticism is likely to prevent research at all these levels. Doctoral students can therefore do honest work on the assumption that they will be leaving the field—which is unlikely to happen voluntarily, given the work commitment—or write in a way that enables and facilitates continued access after their publications have been read. Too explicit a defence of the Communist party line is likely to lead to informal comments on the academic grapevine of being close to the party, as has happened to a number of West Bengal specialists. This presents credibility problems if the empirical data cannot be produced to support these claims of progressive governance. On the other hand, too much criticism, whether backed by empirical evidence or not, can preclude repeat access. In these circumstances the middle ground is safest on account of the need to maintain academic credibility and for career enhancement along with repeat access to the villages. This does not mean that a middle position is any closer to reality, which theoretically can be anywhere along the critical spectrum, but it does facilitate the presentation of the pros and cons and, most importantly, gives the appearance of objectivity and therefore enhanced credibility. At the other extreme of the spectrum, which is most critical of the regime, it becomes unclear whether the critique is ultra-Communist or anti-Communist, leftist or rightist, with both labels being applied to the same people in the absence of any knowledge of their politics.[11]

The South Asian field has a very large domestic component which, while resenting the greater funding of foreign scholars, has the advantage of continuous on-the-spot access which visiting scholars lack. Ideologically, however, there is not much difference between them with scholars in South Asia and abroad supporting each other through funding and reciprocal visits. As Marshall Sahlins observed in his critique of Gananath Obeyesekere, 'Indo-European speakers of South Asia are historically more closely related to native Western anthropologists than they are to Hawaiians'.[12] South Asia does have significant input into the western analysis of South Asia through students and professors studying and visiting abroad and perhaps more importantly through the Indian diaspora. When I first went to Oxford University I was surprised at Indian students explaining how they got their scholarships on merit, when I simply took this for granted and wondered why they bothered mentioning it at all. As I came to know the system better, I realized that it was through influence that many of the scholarships were obtained. In some cases it was political connections that facilitated the scholarships, but even when it was on a more personal level they still projected the views of Indian elites. The opposition to affirmative action from some in this group struck me as hypocritical. The black American Ellis Cose points out the double standard as it exists in an American context similar to India's:

A young white man, a Harvard student ... was not only troubled but choleric at the very notion that 'unqualified minorities' would dare to demand preferential treatment. Why, he wanted to know, couldn't they compete like everyone else? Why should hardworking whites like himself be pushed aside for second-rate affirmative action hires? His tirade went on for quite a while, and he became more indignant by the second as he conjured up one injustice after another. When the young man paused to catch his breath, I took the occasion to observe that it seemed more than a bit hypocritical of him to rage on about preferential treatment. A person of modest intellect, he had gotten into Harvard largely on the basis of family connections. His first summer internship, with the White House, had been arranged by a family member. His second, with the World Bank, had been similarly arranged. Thanks to his nice internships and Harvard degree, he had been promised a coveted slot in a major company's executive training programme. In short, he was already well on his way to a distinguished career—a career made possible by preferential treatment. My words seemed not to register, and that did not surprise me. Clearly he had never thought of himself as a beneficiary of special treatment, and no doubt never will. Nor is it likely that either his colleagues or his superiors would be inclined to look down on him as an undeserving incompetent who got ahead on the basis of unfair advantage and was keeping better-qualified people out of work.[13]

Nor is this disparity restricted to questions of race and class. One Oxford University professor told me that in the five faculty selection committees he had been on, the most outstanding candidate was never chosen. Someone in the selection process always used influence to swing the decision in his or her personal interest, though taking care to disguise it till after the selection. This natural selection of the best-connected is universal, and can only be corrected through outside intervention by the state. Academic selection on the basis of connections has served South Asian elites well right across the political spectrum. As a result, except for a few isolated voices, the truly fundamental questions that challenge South Asian self-perceptions are rarely raised.

An example of this can be seen in the way in which South Asian villages are perceived and analyzed. Questions are predetermined to leave out the more embarrassing and critical attributes and their situations sanitized in a way that permits return access and ensures academic kudos. Issues of village exploitation and oppression are often presented in a way that distorts reality. The portrayal of such things in the movie *Bandit Queen* rarely find an equivalent presentation in social science literature.

To meet social science criteria empirical evidence is required to back up findings. In this respect village studies are unique in the social sciences in that their empirical evidence is unverifiable. Though the basis of anthropology, village studies by a range of social scientists use that most convenient cover, the anonymous village. Ostensibly to protect the identities of the informants, this enables the social scientists to cover up their mistakes as well. I first realized this in Ecuador where, as employees of a national aboriginal Canadian NGO on an indigenous representation project funded by the Canadian Foreign Ministry, we attempted to use social scientists to access their indigenous village communities. In other countries we had used our indigenous organizational contacts to do this without difficulty. But in Ecuador we met up with the academic community and attempted access to the indigenous communities through them. By the social scientists' own admission, the communities desired development aid, and had even in one case made it a condition for their doing research there. Knowing our connections, the social scientists wanted our help to get assistance for their communities. However, when it came to visiting the communities, they raised objections. Even though we were better placed than they to get development aid, they made excuses about how the communities were not used to visiting outsiders. When I discovered the village we wanted to visit described in the Lonely Planet Tourist Guide to Ecuador with the names of local tourist guides, a social scientist said that one of the guides mentioned had a bias against tourists, and denied having known that the village was in the book.[14] In another case, a social scientist took us to the urban Indian intellectuals but asked for development aid for the village community she would not take us to see.

West Bengal

After this Ecuador experience I went back to the West Bengal studies with renewed scepticism. The Communists received their first opportunity at prolonged governance in the post-Emergency state elections of 1977, where they obtained an absolute majority in West Bengal. The Communist experiment in that state has attracted interest because the Left Front government is the longest ruling democratically elected Communist regime of any consequence in world history. Since 1977 it has governed a population which stood at 68 million in the 1991 Census. As three-quarters of the population is rural, the agrarian programmes are critically important reforms. India's state governments have jurisdiction over agrarian policies, giving them opportunities for development implementation.

The Communist reforms in West Bengal have received considerable praise in the development literature. The most detailed state-wide studies endorsing the West Bengal development programmes have been conducted by Atul Kohli (Princeton) and T.J. Nossiter (London School of Economics), but similar views have found their way into the international development literature, indicating that this is the generally accepted position.[15]

The nature of the CPM-dominated government has been a matter of debate. The CPM proclaims itself to be revolutionary Stalinist (Stalin's rather than Gorbachev's portrait was displayed at its 1989 Congress), however few outside the party give this much credence. The generally accepted academic view supported by Nossiter and Kohli is of a social democratic-type reformist regime which tries to implement change in favour of the lower classes within constitutional limits. However, dissenting from this view, one secretary of the West Bengal government claimed from his experience during a British posting that the CPM was to the right of the British Labour Party, as the latter had an orientation to the lower classes that the CPM lacked. I would argue that while there are revolutionaries within the CPM, there has been an evolution of the party, not to a social democratic position, but to that of defending dominant rural class interests.[16] A West Bengal NGO organizer supported this conclusion stating that 'the CPM did more for the poor when it was in opposition', but 'once in power, they sided more and more with the landlords'.[17] This evolution reflects changes in Indian politics and CPM institutionalization which have parallels with Robert Michels' analysis of the growth of reformism in the German Social Democratic Party.[18] The agrarian reforms are not taking place at a faster rate than in other Indian states, and there is no substantive evidence for their more successful implementation in favour of the lowest classes than occurs in non-Communist-ruled states. No significant Left Front programme can be considered a success from a lower-class perspective.

Even when some criticisms of local endeavours were made, the state-level performance of the government was often declared positive, though empirical evidence for this was not given.[19] According to Haris Gazdar, 'West Bengal can justifiably boast one of the most comprehensive [land] reforms', though in the four villages actually studied, 'the areas involved are extremely small, almost marginal', being, respectively, 0.12, 0.05, 0.05 and 0.04 per cent of total land area.[20] By this survey, my estimate that it would take the Left Front a millennium to complete land redistribution was off the mark by thousands of years. The assumption of successful programme implementation was thus maintained even when the micro-level data the authors provided did not always support this.[21] As several studies take this view, one can only speculate whether the macro-positive endorsement is for reasons of repeat research access, and the village-level results simply inconvenient contradictory data found only by reading the whole publication. More consistent were the findings of those who claimed successful local programme implementation both in their fieldwork and state-level implementation. In a lecture I gave at Brown University, Lina Fruzzetti claimed that the Left Front had performed 'miracles' in their panchayat programme, though the West Bengal Indian Administrative Service (IAS) panchayat secretary who had launched the programme told me he had put a 'lot of work' into it but it had been a 'waste of effort'.

The gap between academics and practitioners could not have been wider. Lieten is consistent in his praise of Left Front performance in both his local-level and state-level studies, though only state-level data can be verified.[22] His state-level data are selective. For instance, the table comparing land reform in different states does not include all the states and the most critical figures of land redistributed where West Bengal would look bad are not included at all.[23] The figures he does include show West Bengal with the most land declared surplus though a complete list of states using Government of India data provided by the West Bengal Land Reforms Commissioner shows it ranks 10th (Table 3.2)![24] A possible explanation for the discrepancy, though one not decipherable from the information provided, might be that zamindari land was included in the West Bengal figures. However, not all states had zamindaris and in any case this was almost entirely done under Congress regimes. Where distributed land data are provided without comparison with other states the figures are cumulative.[25] They are also cumulative for *barga* (sharecropper) recordings, so each year appears better than the last, but if separated yearly they would present a very different picture.[26] In fact, the figures for new yearly distribution and recording are relatively stagnant and it is likely that more beneficiaries of land reform are now losing their land than beneficiaries newly gaining it, though the figures for this are not kept as exhaustively as other data.

A similar analysis is not possible with Lieten's village-level data. However, according to him, the Left Front has achieved remarkable improvement in school enrolment. 'The recent progress would indicate that the coverage of all the children in the primary school-going age has been completed', with his figures indicating 98 per cent enrolment in the 6–10 age group during 1987–88.[27] Unlike the state government figures, the more definitive National Sample Survey Organization 43rd Round indicates that in that year only 42.9 per cent were attending school in rural areas (Table 3.1). This ranked 14th out of 17 states and below the national average. (For urban areas the 63 per cent attendance ranked 14th out of 17 states.)

Though Nossiter and Kohli have yet to respond to the criticism, others with similar positions have done so in their reviews of my books.[28] While they reject my findings, no one has provided any empirical evidence to refute it, for the probable reason that the data do not exist. Neither has anyone come up with an interstate comparison of land reform statistics to refute the data I have provided. Although I twice published the table given to me by the West Bengal Land Reforms Commissioner (Table 3.2), no one has

TABLE 3.1

*Percentage of Children Attending School in Rural Areas 1987–88,
Age 5–9*

State	Boys	Girls	Total
Andhra Pradesh	63.3	45.2	54.3
Assam	48.6	47.8	48.2
Bihar	33.0	19.7	26.9
Gujarat	63.1	52.1	58.0
Haryana	60.2	53.8	57.4
Himachal Pradesh	73.6	63.3	68.5
Jammu and Kashmir	53.4	40.3	46.9
Karnataka	57.0	50.6	53.9
Kerala	86.9	82.8	84.8
Madhya Pradesh	43.9	26.3	35.4
Maharashtra	64.0	54.4	59.4
Orissa	55.4	44.9	50.3
Punjab	66.3	59.1	63.1
Rajasthan	47.8	25.5	37.5
Tamil Nadu	84.9	77.7	81.4
Uttar Pradesh	45.4	28.2	37.8
West Bengal	44.8	40.9	42.9
All-India	52.5	40.4	46.8

Source: Jandhyala B.G. Tilak, 'How Free is "Free" Primary Education in India?',
Economic and Political Weekly, Vol. XXXI, No. 5, 3 February 1996,
p. 278.

TABLE 3.2

*Land Reform in Indian States (in acres)**

State	Area Declared Surplus	Area Taken Possession	Area Declared Surplus but Possession Not Taken	Area Distributed	Area Distributed as Percentage of Cultivable area
Andhra Pradesh	1,014,050	456,021	558,029	331,976	0.88
Assam	450,918	376,445	74,473	373,020	5.21
Bihar	287,931	194,037	93,894	179,046	0.67
Gujarat	182,138	87,020	95,118	51,133	0.67
Haryana	30,757	22,796	7,961	22,591	0.19
Himachal Pradesh	283,994	281,403	2,591	3,335	0.12
Jammu and Kashmir	6,000	–	6,000	–	–

Table 3.2 Continued

Karnataka	296,355	152,317	144,018	115,661	0.38
Kerala	121,385	87,189	34,196	58,443	1.04
Madhya Pradesh	227,377	139,957	87,420	93,400	0.17
Maharashtra	390,040	304,884	85,156	304,894	0.62
Orissa	162,390	140,642	21,766	127,117	0.74
Punjab	27,444	15,235	12,209	14,140	0.13
Rajasthan	240,050	232,531	7,519	145,319	0.29
Tamil Nadu	94,762	89,008	5,754	77,835	0.39
Uttar Pradesh	301,561	275,226	26,341	244,208	0.51
West Bengal	182,157	126,743	55,414	80,639	0.55

Source: Government of India, Department of Rural Development, Ministry of Agriculture and Rural Development, 'Proceedings of Conference of Revenue Ministers', New Delhi, May 1985, pp. 131–33.

*West Bengal Land Reforms Act or equivalent legislation in other states.

attempted to refute my conclusions, which indicates that data not supporting their argument of successful land reform were simply ignored.

There are neither state-level data to indicate that the Left Front can be credited for the successful implementation of any programme that would not have happened without them, nor do comparisons with other states reveal an exceptional performance even with their often lacklustre results. Before attributing credit to a regime, it is necessary to show that the positive changes were the result of government policy implementation that would not have occurred under another regime. While in an election campaign we expect politicians to claim credit for fortuitous economic improvements, scholars have the responsibility to show whether the actions of the politicians they support resulted in successful outcomes. This is something none of the supporters of the Left Front have been able to do. The failure of scholars to make interstate comparisons of programmes, even assuming improvements in West Bengal, makes attribution to particular regimes difficult, since most things in society change regardless of which party is in power.[29]

The lack of any state-level empirical evidence does not appear to prevent scholars from adhering to their positions, however. Here, village-level studies are useful because one can take a favourable view without fear of anyone re-examining the village, and even if it does contradict other studies, the village study might still be accurate, since it could prove to be an exception. State-level statistics on the other hand have known collection methods, public availability, and people who can be interviewed for verification. Other statistics can contradict these and enable a degree of verification. Village studies by contrast operate in a never-never land of unverifiable and unreproducible results which must be taken on trust based on the expertise of the scholar. This does not mean that useful anecdotal information may not be forthcoming; such information is particularly useful as a teaching aid to stimulate readers bored with depersonalized analyses. However, the study of a sample anonymous village can never be verified, even if other village studies can contradict it. This, then, is a situation where one study contradicts another with only personal prejudices and hunches to suggest that one study is more accurate than another. There is even a tendency in some West Bengal literature to critically examine the village level but take good performance at the state level for granted.[30] Personal verification, however, can take place only at the micro level, and generalizations from a locality to a whole state are problematic. On the other hand, the state-level statistics required for a definitive analysis can usually not be personally verified. The best approach is to combine the two levels when an adequate body of research has been developed by the scholarly community. West Bengal would seem to have this; however, the contradictions between the studies means that little common ground has been found. I would argue that this is due to the ideological preconceptions of scholars and the contact network through which information is collected.

These perceptions, derived from too narrow a contact base, can be illustrated from positions taken by scholars of the Left Front experiment. A surprisingly common myth among urban high-caste intellectuals is that caste segregation and discrimination does not exist in West Bengal. These views have found their way into the literature and created an exaggerated impression of social change. Government school segregation continues in West Bengal to this day as village-level studies confirm.[31] On a tour of rural Bengal with a CPM cadre, I enquired of them if the Brahmin-owned restaurant we were in admitted Untouchables. Without needing to ask the staff, the reply was that they were not. The caste sentiment is such that Untouchable CPM members say that only a 'minuscule' minority in the party are free of caste prejudice. This is one of the reasons that the Left Front failed to implement de-segregation. Rabindra Ray is more accurate in stating that 'the Bengali Hindu population ... takes its religion, including caste (particularly in matters of marriage) as seriously as the rest of India. Ideas about pollution and untouchability are the same as elsewhere in India'.[32] It came to pass that untouchability outlasted apartheid, making the Untouchables the last segregated group in the world. Though I found the living conditions of non-whites under South African apartheid better than those of Untouchables in rural India, this comparison with apartheid, often found in Untouchable literature, is not mentioned in many upper-caste analyses. There are thus differences of perception not adequately represented in the academic literature.

Aside from the cultural myth that caste discrimination does not exist in West Bengal, there is the issue of ideological bias which may be at the root of much of the uncritical acceptance of Left Front-supplied performance statistics. As information sources among scholars overlap, I found out that negative statistics and reports of Left Front performance were supplied to scholars who subsequently ignored or discounted the information and published complimentary reports instead. The role of intellectual preconceptions and other personal factors in resolving cognitive dissonance would make an interesting study in itself.

The problems of data collection and judgement calls on their validity which affect all investigators. The West Bengal development literature illustrates this problem. Atul Kohli, in interviewing 60 West Bengal gram panchayat (village council) members, states:

> Because these interviews were always carried out in group situations, which included members of the local community, it was difficult for the respondents to hide the length of their party involvement, as well as their ownership of land and the mode of land use.[33]

However, the anthropologist James M. Freeman states: 'To be polite, Indian villagers often provide answers that they think the investigator wants to hear. Their replies usually bear little relation to the way they live their lives or view the world.'[34] Public statements therefore cannot be taken at face value, which has serious implications for the collection of survey data. These statistics need comparison with earlier periods and require verification through interviews with administrators familiar with the way in which these statistics were collected. When I pointed out to the West Bengal Secretary responsible for implementation of the Scheduled Castes and Tribes Special Component Plan that West Bengal had the lowest per capita expenditure in the country, he said that there was in fact no expenditure. The programme did not exist at the district level, but was confined to planning documents which referred to expenditures from other programmes not entitled to be included. These personal and political values and misleading statistics have distorted the development literature, thus leading to a frequently invalid positive analysis.

Agrarian Reform

To understand the current agrarian reform impasse in West Bengal it is necessary to examine the connections between the state CPM party ruling from Calcutta and its class base in the rural areas which enable its re-election. Though there is no perfect correlation between caste and class in Bengal, at the lowest-caste level, the Untouchables are almost invariably in the lowest class. The top-level Left Front leadership comes from the same tricaste elite that has historically dominated Bengal at the state level. The three dominant castes in undivided Bengal were composed of Brahmin (2.83 per cent), Vaidya (0.21 per cent) and Kayastha (3.04 per cent)—collectively 6.08 per cent of the population. Though partition increased their proportion, they are far outnumbered by the Untouchables, who comprise 22 per cent of the West Bengal population. Five per cent are composed of tribal people, and the remainder of intermediate castes and Muslims. According to Atul Kohli, 95.4 per cent members of the Left Front cabinet were from the tricaste elite, with a solitary Muslim making up the remainder.[35] This need not be significant if the cabinet is willing to implement programmes in favour of the lower classes; however, it does illustrate the narrow caste origins of the Bengali elite. This tricaste state elite is largely urban based and generally does not dominate the rural areas. The dominant rural castes are often only of intermediate status in the ritual hierarchy, and not numerous or geographically centred enough to form a political caste base. As various castes are dominant in different districts and villages, the caste politicization that is electorally profitable in other states would be difficult to achieve. They have, however, been organized by the CPM on issues which have attracted similar castes in other states to mobilize in conservative movements. The mobilization of the rural elite provides the CPM with easy access to the village community as well as a relatively well-educated and prosperous class base. It has been argued that while the biggest landlords supported the Congress party, the Communists by mobilizing the more numerous class just below them permanently undercut the Congress landlord base, thereby promoting a middle class which became politically dominant.[36] This analysis has historical merit, but since the Left Front has come to power many Congress supporters have switched allegiance to the CPM. This may therefore now be too neat a formulation. But there is no doubt that the CPM has been able to achieve the objective of a multiclass alliance in which no group or class is excluded.[37] The inclusion of all classes implies that no significant programmes for socio-economic changes in favour of the lower classes can be undertaken as they would threaten the dominant landed elite.

Most of my data for analysis of programmes for agrarian reform have been presented elsewhere, but a critique of the literature provides an indication of the differences in interpretation.[38] There is a fundamental difficulty in determining how much programme implementation can be credited to the Left Front and how different a Congress government implementation might have been. The election of the Left Front in 1977 was contemporaneous with the launching of a number of rural development and poverty alleviation programmes which all state governments were obliged to implement. Being in power, the Left Front could take the credit for these programmes, since the beneficiaries were unaware that the same programmes were being implemented elsewhere too. Since the villagers were too isolated to make anything but a historical comparison, the Left Front could take credit for central government-funded programmes.[39]

The Left Front's agrarian reforms have received fulsome praise in the development literature though the reforms are in fact minimal and similar to those of other states. In support of the general view of their success, Jean Dreze and Amartya Sen state that 'the change in the balance of power in the rural society of West Bengal in favour of the poorer sections of the population, largely as a result of left-wing activist movements, has certainly resulted in a much greater participation of the poor in poverty alleviation programmes'.[40] Paul Brass states that Communist parties have been 'more serious about and more effective in implementing measures of agrarian reform such as land ceilings and land redistribution and programmes for the poor to provide them with employment opportunities and income producing assets'.[41] James Manor is equally affirmative, when he states that

A Communist government in West Bengal has entrenched itself in rural areas—an historic achievement—by providing land reform, major efforts in literacy and public health, and an impressive de-centralisation of power that gives disadvantaged groups in small arenas some control over their own destiny.[42]

In fact, neither the health nor literacy programmes of West Bengal have been particularly impressive when compared with those of other states. Though both programmes have provided rural employment for party supporters, standards have often been poor. An interstate comparison of health expenditure indicates that West Bengal is not exceptional in its outlay.[43] 'There are hospitals, but sincerely speaking, their doors are closed for the poor, despite being free. Poor people do not get a chance of admission without negotiating, without manipulating and paying black money.'[40] The Left Front proved completely ineffectual in changing this situation. As for education, enrolment under the Left Front increased at the same rate as under the previous Congress government, although as one of nine 'educationally backward' states in India, West Bengal has a lot of catching up to do. With little growth in Untouchable and tribal enrolment, however, the gap between the education of the lower and higher castes has widened. Given the prejudice Untouchables face in school and the necessity of having to work for a living, the widening gap is hardly surprising. The proportion of Untouchables attending classes 1–5 is the third worst of 20 Indian states.[45] According to

Myron Weiner, 'the Communist government of West Bengal is no more committed to the enforcement of child-labor laws or compulsory-education laws than the Congress-dominated conservative state of Bihar next door.'[46]

Manor's claim that the panchayats give the lower classes more control over their destiny is endorsed by Brass. He argues that because there has been a 'displacement of the dominant landed classes by smaller landholders, and teachers and social workers, it has been possible to use the village panchayats for the implementation of agrarian reforms'.[47] However, in a tour of the rural areas with the West Bengal panchayat secretary we found that the same class which had been exploiting the lower classes for centuries continued to dominate the panchayats. While some may have diversified their occupations and business interests, and there was the inevitable upward and downward mobility over generations, the only lower-class panchayat council members tended to be those nominated by these elites to fill the Scheduled Caste quota. Furthermore, they had used the largesse supplied by the government for projects of interest to the elite community members rather than for the benefit of the lower classes. While the poorest sections were neglected, the dominant elite established their own interests with the acquiescence of the Communist leadership and the support of the local party membership. The ideological work and consciousness raising which could have been done only by the party was never undertaken. The work of political education in the villages was neglected by the Communists, and the administrators could do nothing about this as it was beyond their jurisdiction. It is now questionable whether these new vested interests can be removed. The West Bengal panchayat secretary said that the concept had been good but the Communists had failed to follow through. Without land redistribution or some other resource transfer that provides a less elite-dependent livelihood for the poor, decentralization cannot bring empowerment to the lower classes.

In a detailed study of West Bengal reforms, Atul Kohli has described these as impressive in their redistribution for the poorer classes.[48] In endorsing this view, T.J. Nossiter states: 'To the Marxists, Kohli gives an A–, to Urs a B, and to Janata a straight D, conclusions from which few scholars would dissent.'[49] This interstate comparison is confirmed in a report to the Club of Rome which notes that while the Indian government's Integrated Rural Development Programme (IRDP) 'is often accused of favouring the better-off farmers and above all of filling the pockets of civil servants', the West Bengal Left Front government 'has carried out a genuine land reform, by distributing to the share-croppers title deeds for the lands they were working'.[50]

This praise of the sharecropper registration campaign is shared by Kohli:

> Less than 60,000 sharecroppers were registered over the last three decades in West Bengal. In about five years, however, the CPM regime has succeeded in registering over 1.2 million bargadars. Compared to the past performance of the Congress and other governments in the area, therefore, the CPM's current success is spectacular.[51]

Nossiter is equally effusive, describing this as a 'truly remarkable accomplishment.'[52]

> These steps culminated in the celebrated 'Operation Barga' in 1978, an effective campaign to register sharecroppers officially. Prior to 1977 only some 275,000 sharecroppers had bucked the rural power structure and registered. By December 1984 as many as 1.3 million of the estimated 2 million West Bengal sharecroppers—96 per cent of all 'tenants'—were recorded.[53]

It should be pointed out that though there are an estimated 3.3 million bargadars the government has lowered its own estimate to 2 million thereby appearing to achieve a better performance.[54] While an equal number of sharecroppers (1.3 million) were registered by a previous land settlement operation in 1962–65 under the Congress government,[55] the Left Front's repetition of the earlier Congress performance may have been detrimental to the poorest classes. In trying to register as many sharecroppers as quickly as possible, those with the greatest Left Front political influence got registered, often at the expense of legitimate sharecroppers who lost their tenancy rights and could not get them back since no appeals were to be considered.

As no updated record of landholdings was available, the junior officials had to go into the field and depend on local knowledge of the landownership. Under pressure from superiors to fulfil targets, the officials did their recordings in a summary fashion and often had to rely on the local Left Front cadres to select the appropriate barga beneficiaries. As a result, a large number of legitimate sharecroppers were not recorded and Left Front supporters recorded in their place. The local bureaucrats were intimidated into accepting the Left Front barga applicants as this was the easiest method and the most beneficial to their own career prospects. As a result, a lot of injustices were done to legitimate sharecroppers. One senior IAS officer, who had complaints of improper recording investigated and found the complaints justified, tried to get the land reform officials to review the cases. The officials however had been instructed that reviews of cases were not to be entertained and there was nothing they could do. As a result of this lack of appeal, the plaintiffs went to court. This resulted in a backlog of cases that will continue into the twenty-first century. The injustices resulting from Operation Barga are not likely to be quickly if ever rectified, and in that sense the delay alone represents an injustice.[56] A more prudent and just strategy would have been to conduct a fresh land settlement survey, and thereby avoid official overdependence on the local Communist party bosses in the selection of beneficiaries; but this would have left less room for Communist party patronage.

Whatever the patronage, the results were not necessarily all they were claimed to be. A survey of 14 West Bengal villages found that even among the recorded bargadars the legally stipulated three-quarter crop share was being observed more in the breach. Only one of the 11 villages, where share proportions were specifically mentioned, applied the three-quarter share even though all these villages had recorded bargadars.[57] Furthermore, a 1985 survey by the West Bengal government Land Reforms Office in Burdwan District (covering 10 per cent of the district) found that '11.22 per cent of the recorded bargadars have been thrown out of possession by one way or the other'.[58] If this is the case for what is arguably Bengal's strongest Communist district, then the state picture could be one in which more *recorded* sharecroppers were being evicted than were the sharecroppers being newly recorded. As the objectives of Operation Barga were (*a*) to prevent eviction through recorded tenancy and (*b*) to ensure three-quarter crop share, it is clear that in both respects the programme failed. If the programme had achieved anything at all, it may have consolidated the hold of the big sharecropper-landowners who leased in land from smaller land-holders who would now not have the resources and political influence to prevent their land being effectively lost to bigger recorded sharecropper-landowners.

Though West Bengal's Land Reforms Commissioner considered the tenancy programme to have failed, the World Bank's *1990 World Development Report* claimed that West Bengal's tenancy reforms had been 'successful'.[59] The World Bank's 1990 *Report* states that the West Bengal tenancy rights are inheritable, but only the richer and more influential sharecroppers are likely to be able to inherit anything as even many living recorded share-croppers are unable to retain rights to their land. If one examines the considerable number of fraudulently recorded tenants, recorded tenants who lost their land anyway, and the nearly two-thirds who were never recorded, as well as the majority who appear not to have got the legally stipulated crop shares, then the World Bank's claim of programme success is dubious. The World Bank's sources and its criteria for success are not specified in its *Report*, but if the West Bengal programme is a model of success, one wonders how many other models of successful development would stand up to critical scrutiny.

The Left Front land redistribution has also been claimed as a successful programme. According to Nossiter:

> The Left Front ministries' record on land redistribution is indubitably impressive, particularly when compared with other states in India. Some 4.4 million acres were 'vested' (expropriated and held) in government nationwide. Of this West Bengal accounted for 1.2 million acres of which 800,000 acres have been redistributed to the landless (Election Manifesto of the LF, 1987).[60]

This acceptance of the land reform statistics of the Left Front is surprising since it is well known among both the land reform officials in charge of redistribution and scholars of the subject that these figures are the result of inappropriately including redistribution figures from the Estates Acquisition Act (1,049,221 acres till 1985) with those of the Land Reforms Act (184,049). As only the Land Reforms Act is comparable with land reforms in other states, including the Estate Acquisition Act figures for zamindaris which did not exist in many other states, gives a misleading impression. 'The performance of West Bengal with respect to ceiling laws cannot, therefore, be regarded as extraordinary'.[61] Though a Left Front government annual publication continues to make the claim that Bengal has vested one-sixth of the all-India total and distributed one-fifth, the same publication admits that only about 200,000 acres have been vested over the 12 years of Communist rule, the majority of land having been vested by previous Congress regimes.[62] As the 200,000 acres vested under Communist rule are only .92 per cent of the total state area and 1.2 per cent of the cultivable area, Nossiter's claim that 'the LF ministries' record on land redistribution is indubitably impressive' is open to doubt.[63] The West Bengal government blames this poor record on central government delays in giving presidential assent to land reform legislation and on previous Marxist-dominated governments having already distributed land in the 1967 to 1969 period. It neglects to mention that in this period peasants were encouraged by the Communists to seize the land themselves without waiting for approval. It is a sign of the the CPM's change from its early revolutionary phase of the 1960s that the state bureaucracy is now left to do the work while peasant movements are discouraged. Even when legislation awaiting central government approval is delayed, giving time to 'unscrupulous' landowners 'to formulate strategy to evade the new ceiling provisions',[64] no mass movement is contemplated.

Lloyd and Susanne Rudolph argue that the end of CPM land reforms is not due to the influence of elite class interests but to the gradual disappearance of rural class differences through previously successful redistribution. 'Its pattern of landholding has been confined to so narrow a range that polarization no longer seems possible. The 87 per cent of West Bengal's cultivators who hold less than 2 hectares (about 5 acres) control 87 per cent of the cultivated land.'[65] In fact, the 87 per cent of cultivators with less than five acres do not control 87 per cent of the land as claimed, but only 56 per cent; the remaining 13 per cent control the remaining 44 per cent of cultivable land.[66] The National Sample Survey indicates even less equality, with the top 9.7 per cent of households owning over five acres controlling 47 per cent of the land, and the bottom 47 per cent owning 2.5 per cent of the land.[67] Furthermore, 45 per cent of agriculturists are landless agricultural labourers.[68] Thus the top 13 per cent own nearly half the cultivable land, while nearly half the agricultural population own nothing at all, having to work instead as labourers. Between these two polarized groups there is a middle class of cultivators who, depending on their holding size, work for themselves, as well as hire themselves out or hire others. The rural class structure is thus deeply and irreconcilably divided at its two extremes. If one followed the CPM's original policy of confiscating all land of those with over the recommended limit, such as the five-acre middle peasant limit recommended by former CPM General Secretary P. Sundarayya, it would be possible to provide enough land from the 13 per cent of owners to benefit or not affect 87 per cent of the cultivators. As this population already lives off the land as well as supplies food to the non-agricultural population, an equitable distribution of .37 acres per rural person, despite its small size, would benefit the majority of agriculturists.[69] With sufficient inputs it could increase agricultural labour income severalfold, as indicated by the West Bengal government's flyer distributed to the peasantry.[70] The flyer also says that the ownership of even a small acreage can mean the difference between hunger and self-sufficiency. The small size of landholdings therefore does not necessarily lead to the improvement of class relations as implied by Lloyd and Susanne Rudolph. When one considers the existence of the officially acknowledged bogus land transfers, the inequalities are in fact even greater than these surveys record.

In short, the classes have not disappeared, but what has happened is that elite classes have consolidated their position in the Communist movement and prevented further Left Front reform moves, as interviews with government programme administrators confirm. Operation Barga was ended not because of a lack of deserving bargadars, but because the Left Front's influential sharecropper supporters were already recorded and further work would threaten those already in possession of land. Hence, it was stalled by Communist politicians in deference to their elite-base interests, though less than half the bargadars had been recorded and a minuscule proportion of the land redistributed.[71]

In contrast to the land-grab movements of Communist peasants during the Marxist governments of the 1960s, the present Left Front government ruling since 1977 has done practically nothing. According to CPM Central Committee member Biplab Dasgupta:

> During the brief United Front rule by the left-wing parties in 1967 and 1969–70, the village level committees of poor peasants and landless labourers helped to identify such *benami* land (that is land held illegally in excess of the permitted limit), took over 300,000 acres of such land and distributed it among the landless. While the legality of such action was disputable there was no denying the effectiveness of bringing about a change in the land relations in rural West Bengal. The beneficiaries of such populist land reform formed the hard core of the support which the Left Front received during the 1977 and 1982 elections.[72]

Thus, 19 months of Communist rule in the 1960s achieved more through peasant land seizures than it had in 12 years since 1977 (300,000 acres versus 80,000 distributed till 1985). As this represents only 1.8 per cent and .55 per cent of cultivable land, the distribution of 2.35 per cent of land under all Communist governments does not indicate significant land reform. The redistribution can only be described as cosmetic, and in fact neither Congress nor Communist governments have carried out significant land reform since the abolition of zamindari.

> With these land ceiling measures, and the abolition of landlordism and intermediaries, the power in the countryside was transferred to small landlords and rich peasants.... Their needs and priorities became, to the administrators and policy-makers, the needs and priorities of the village population as a whole.[73]

Though Biplab Dasgupta refers here to the pre-Communist period, the limited land redistribution since then indicates that the elite class position has remained unchanged. There are indications of the opportunist members in this class supporting the Left Front parties, though no reliable Party–class membership survey exists. However, a class breakdown of the West Bengal peasant

Krishak Sabha sessions of 1982, 1986 and 1989 indicate only 8.48, 6.58 and 7.46 per cent agricultural labourer delegates, respectively. As Dwaipayan Bhattacharyya has observed:

> This meant that the labourer, as a class, was scarcely represented in the leadership of the Sabha even though he was acclaimed as the backbone of the organization and, along with the poor peasant, the 'basis of peasant unity'. The irony didn't end here. Instead of appreciating this problem as one of enabling the agricultural labourer to have greater control and a larger say in the organizational matters of the Sabha, the Sabha's first reflection was that the lack of suitable agricultural labourers' representation had created the problem of putting across the right views of its middle-class leadership.[74]

As the rest of the country is no better than Bengal in redistribution, the all-India land reform effort also appears to be mediocre. The downsizing of reported landholdings is largely the result of generational subdivision and bogus transfers rather than state intervention.

Kohli and Nossiter, in specifically examining and then praising the West Bengal land reform, do not point out its insignificance in terms of total cultivable land. Kohli specifically mentions the percentage of cultivable land redistributed for the other two states he examined (Karnataka 0.2 per cent and Uttar Pradesh 0.7 per cent), thereby proving their poor land redistribution performance, but the West Bengal figure is not given.[75] The redistribution in 12 years of only 0.55 per cent of cultivable land makes the claim of the Left Front's 'spectacular', 'indubitably impressive', and 'truly remarkable accomplishment' in land reform untenable.[76] It will take the Left Front a millennium at its present redistribution rate to distribute land above the five acres originally advocated by the CPM.

Though radical land redistribution might lead to violence, central government intervention, and disruption of urban food supply, even moderate reforms and social class issues have been avoided. The Left Front backtracked on introducing progressive agricultural taxation for the surplus-producing farmers whose influence was sufficient to get the Left Front to reduce their taxes instead.[77] The well-documented Communist restriction of urban labour militancy was replicated in the less publicized control over agricultural labourer activity.[78] This resulted in West Bengal having the lowest relative agricultural real wages for male labourers of any Indian state though they are the fourth most productive and therefore in a position to obtain more income.[79] While Communists' reluctance to create an independent yeomanry through radical land redistribution would be understandable given its possible conservative implications, they could have accepted the existing property divisions and endeavoured to improve the position of the agricultural proletariat within it. Instead, they tried to control the labour movement within a multiclass alliance dominated by rural elite interests. According to one agricultural labourer: 'We joined the CPI(M) with many hopes. But it seems we only tagged along fruitlessly to their processions and meetings. We did not get any benefit. We have no hopes of getting any benefit from anyone. Even the panchayat could not do anything.'[80] Kirsten Westergaard cites one case where the CPM panchayat Chairman was dismissed for leading a successful strike of agricultural labourers for higher wages. This alienated the 'middle peasants' who used agricultural labour and it also went against the CPM's line of supporting these propertied interests.[81] Though West Bengal has officially no bonded labourers, the National Sample Survey gives the state the fourth highest number (21,600) in India.[82]

These failures were admitted by the Burdwan District Committee of the CPM in an internal party document, which the CPM leadership subsequently withdrew from internal party circulation.

> The Left Front government has not been able to meet the aspirations of the people.... People feel that even the limited powers at the disposal of the Left Front government have not been properly used. It will not be an exaggeration to say that procrastination and misuse in the administration are on the increase. In areas like education, health, transport, irrigation works, labour, electricity, local self-government, police administration and High Court which are all closely connected with the people, the role of the government has no impact on the masses. Even the progressive measures like taking over vested land and cancellation of illegal pattas (records of rights), barga recording ... all undertaken for the good of the people have

not been properly implemented. There is considerable slackness and corrupt practices are followed in the implementation of these social programs by the government which bring in their own complications. As a result instead of getting appreciation from the people it is creating discontent.... For example, the mentality of teaching a lesson by stopping the work of domestic help, personal enmity or to settle scores, falsely recording rights of sharecroppers, opportunist attitudes in fixing the right share of the crop to the sharecropper ... are cases in point.[83]

From being a mobilizer of labour under the Communist governments of the 1960s the Left Front became a controller of its labour movement on behalf of the urban and rural elites whose investments and vote blocs it sought to attract. It is for this reason that West Bengal has a mediocre record of reform despite having an avowedly radical Communist government.

The Impasse

That the Left Front programmes failed to achieve social change or more significant lower-class benefits than were available elsewhere in India should no longer be in doubt. At a private social gathering of top West Bengal IAS officers I attended, a secretary of the West Bengal government asked his colleagues if they could think of a single successful Left Front programme. None of them had any suggestions even though they themselves were in charge of the programmes. According to a secretary of the Indian government from the West Bengal IAS cadre, the Left Front experiment had set the left movement in India back by 50 years. These IAS officers had been in charge of all the major reforms but found their efforts thwarted by Communist ministers intent on promoting the interests of their elite constituents. Though this criticism might be dismissed as the traditional conservative civil service attitude towards Communists, in fact these secretaries and commissioners were generally of leftist inclination and had worked hard for radical reform implementation only to be blocked by Communist ministers who feared that these would go too far. While the urban IAS officers had nothing to lose by promoting radical reform, the Communist ministers having gained a rural party base through the dominant rural elite, were not inclined to jeopardize it by undertaking action detrimental to local power structures. Similar criticism was also prevalent within the CPM itself, and it is to these party and civil service sources that one must go to find out what is really going on. Despite their obligatory public praise of Left Front performance, many veteran Communists have serious misgivings about its policy implementation. Even the number two minister in the state government, Benoy Chowdury, complained about corruption in his party, which he refused to deny when questioned by the press, though the party and the chief minister denied it.[84] According to the CPM Burdwan District Committee document:

> The state ministers in charge of different departments are not conversant with their work and do not take the necessary initiative in implementing the social schemes under their charge. They are seen to rely more on bureaucracy. The ministers are seen to have taken a detached view and have got some hazy ideas about their responsibilities. All these have clouded the minds of the people and the Left Front is losing ground. Only the group of people who are deeply committed to the Leftist ideology through hard struggle over the years stand by the Party, the others are not impressed with the performance of the Left Front government.... There is some thinking among the Party at different levels that the petty bourgeois mentality and aberrations have only affected the Party workers at the lower levels. There is no basis for such thinking. Apart from the lower levels, even the tested leadership is not free from this. If we have to fight this menace, we must start from the top.[85]

Such a purge of the leadership is difficult to foresee, as the new members are generally more opportunist than the older Communists. The trend could therefore be towards greater conservatism rather than radicalization. The split in the opposition vote between Congress and the Bharatiya Janata Party (BJP) should enable continued Left Front re-election, but growth appears less likely. 'The Communists, who in the early years of independence appeared credible challengers of the system, have been tamed, divided, and co-opted.'[86]

Unfortunately, many of the scholars have missed the internal party debate on such problems and been misled by Left Front propaganda, thereby creating an inaccurate and misleading literature on the Left Front performance. The scholarly community is likely to be the last group to acknowledge what happened. It does not speak well of development studies that this position should have been accepted so uncritically when privately both the administrative and party cadre were willing to state what was happening, and did so in a number of cases. Furthermore the Indian research material is by Third World standards relatively accessible and plentiful. One can only wonder how much of the massive Third World development literature really represents the ground realities, and how much has reflected the ideology of the social scientists and their unquestioning acceptance of official statistics. Though one cannot generalize from the experience of one state, it does raise serious questions about the standard of the literature. Certainly more informed critiques of development literature and agencies are required for a better understanding of development implementation.

There are also fundamental questions about why a Communist government with significant financial and manpower resources achieved so little on behalf of the lower classes. According to a West Bengal government secretary, despite 80 per cent of the state budget being spent on employee salaries, work output was poor. Some of this money might have been better spent on development reforms, yet it was employee interests that represent the top priority for the Left Front. Though manufacturing output in 1984–85 was at the same level as when the Left Front came to power in 1977, West Bengal fell from second to fifth place among Indian states. Productivity and social change were constrained by the class and interest groups the Left Front had come to represent.

There are deep cultural reasons why the Left Front failed in its programmes, despite the efforts of many individuals to improve the conditions of the lower classes. Fundamentally, the dominant and influential elements in society were just not bothered about such improvements. According to Myron Weiner: 'These beliefs are closely tied to religious notions and to the premises that underlie India's hierarchical caste system.... Even those who profess to be secular and who reject the caste system are imbued with values of status that are deeply imbedded in Indian culture.'[87]

As the first Untouchable elected to the Bengal Legislative Council stated in the 1922 budget debate:

So far as mere sweet words are concerned, I admit that from the highest rulers of the province to the so-called Leagues, everyone shows sympathy with the condition of the backward classes. But when the time for practical action comes, all sympathy evaporates.[88]

Unfortunately, this is as true now as it was then. Given the cultural conditions and disparities of power it is difficult to foresee a change in this situation.

REFERENCES

1. Maxine Kay Weisgrau, 'The Social and Political Relations of Development: NGOs and Adivasi Bhils in Rural Rajasthan' (Ph.D. thesis, Columbia University, New York, 1993), p. 255.
2. Ibid., pp. 272–73.
3. Amita Baviskar, 'Development, Nature and Resistance: The Case of Bhilala Tribals in the Narmada Valley' (Ph.D. thesis, Cornell University, Ithaca, 1992), p. 283.
4. Ibid., pp. 288–89.
5. Ranajit Guha, 'The Prose of Counter-Insurgency', in Ranajit Guha and Gayatri Chakravorty Spivak (eds), *Selected Subaltern Studies* (New York: Oxford University Press, 1988), p. 82.
6. Shastri Indo-Canadian Institute, *Programme Guide 1995–1996*, p. 6.
7. Michael Brecher, 'India and Canada: Origins and Assessment of the Shastri Institute', in Arthur G. Rubinoff (ed.), *Canada and South Asia: Political and Strategic Relations* (Centre for Asian Studies, Toronto: University of Toronto, 1992), p. 96.
8. Richard Poole, *The Inca Smiled: The Growing Pains of an Aid Worker in Ecuador* (Oxford: One World, 1993), pp. 259–60.
9. Orin Starn, 'Missing the Revolution: Anthropologists and the War in Peru', in George E. Marcus (ed.), *Rereading Cultural Anthropology* (Durham: Duke University Press, 1992), pp. 152–80.
10. G.K. Lieten, *Continuity and Change in Rural West Bengal* (New Delhi: Sage Publications, 1992) and *Development, Devolution and Democracy—Village Discourse in West Bengal* (New Delhi: Sage Publications, 1996).
11. John Harris, 'What is Happening in Rural West Bengal? Agrarian Reform, Growth and Distribution', *Economic and Political Weekly*, Vol. XXVIII, No. 24, 12 June 1993, p. 1238.
12. Marshall Sahlins, *How 'Natives' Think: About Captain Cook, For Example* (Chicago: The University of Chicago Press, 1995), p. 4.

13. Ellis Cose, *The Rage of a Privileged Class* (New York: Harper Collins, 1995), p. 111.
14. Rob Rachowiecki, *Ecuador & the Galapagos Islands—A Travel Survival Kit* (Hawthorn, Vic, Australia: Lonely Planet Publications, 1992), p. 296.
15. Atul Kohli, *The State and Poverty in India: The Politics of Reform* (Cambridge: Cambridge University Press, 1987); T.J. Nossiter, *Marxist State Governments in India* (London: Pinter Publishers, 1988).
16. Ross Mallick, *Indian Communism: Opposition, Collaboration, and Institutionalization* (Delhi: Oxford University Press, 1993).
17. John Stackhouse, 'Labourers Fight for Rights in West Bengal', *The Globe and Mail*, 30 December 1996, p. A8.
18. Robert Michels, *Political Parties* (New York: Collier Books, 1962).
19. Cathy Newsmith. 'Gender, Trees, and Fuel: Social Forestry in West Bengal, India', *Human Organization*, Vol. 50, No. 4, Winter 1991, pp. 337–48.
20. Haris Gazdar, 'Rural Poverty, Public Policy and Social Change: Some Findings from Surveys of Six Villages' (WIDER Working Papers, WP 98, May 1992), pp. 1, 30, 59.
21. Kohli, *The State and Poverty in India* (n. 15 above).
22. G.K. Lieten, *Continuity and Change* (n. 10 above).
23. Ibid., Table 4.1, p. 129.
24. Ross Mallick, *Development Policy of a Communist Government: West Bengal Since 1977* (Cambridge: Cambridge University Press, 1993), p. 46.
25. G.K. Lieten, *Continuity and Change* (n. 10 above), p. 137.
26. Ibid., p. 159.
27. Ibid., p. 75.
28. Subrata Kumar Mitra, 'Book Review', *The Journal of Commonwealth & Comparative Politics*, Vol. 33, No. 2, July 1995, pp. 293–95. In the oddest criticism, Mitra takes my own data to support conclusions I had reached and then claims this data proved my conclusions are wrong, which seems to indicate he may not have read the book very carefully (p. 294); A. Haroon Akram-Lodhi, 'Book Review', *Journal of Peasant Studies*, Vol. 22, No. 2, January 1995, pp. 369–73.
29. G.K. Lieten, 'Land Reforms at Centre Stage: The Evidence on West Bengal', *Development and Change*, Vol. 27, No. 1, January 1996, pp. 111–30.
30. John Echeverri-Gent, 'Politics Takes Command: Implementation of the National Rural Employment Program in West Bengal', Mimeo (June 1991); Neil Webster, 'Panchayati Raj and the Decentralisation of Development Planning in West Bengal: A Case Study' (Copenhagen: Centre for Development Research Project Paper 90.7, December 1990); Suraj Bandyopadhyay and D. von Eschen, 'The Impact of Politics on Rural Production and Distribution: A Comparative Study of Rural Policies and Their Implementation Under Congress and Left Front Governments in West Bengal' (paper delivered at annual meeting of the Association of Asian Studies, San Francisco, 26 March 1988); Kirsten Westergaard, 'People's Participation, Local Government and Rural Development: The Case of West Bengal' (Copenhagen: Centre for Development Research, Report No. 8, March 1986).
31. Linda C. Mayoux, 'Income Generation for Women in India: Problems and Prospects', *Development Policy Review*, Vol. 7, No.1, March 1989, p. 23;

Ronald P. Rohner and Manjusri Chaki-Sircar, *Women and Children in a Bengali Village* (Hanover, NH: University Press of New England, 1988), pp. 40–41.

32. Rabindra Ray, *The Naxalites and their Ideology* (Delhi: Oxford University Press, 1988), p. 58.

33. Kohli, *The State and Poverty in India* (n. 15 above), p. 110.

34. James M. Freeman, *Untouchable: An Indian Life History* (Stanford: Stanford University Press, 1979), p. 11.

35. Atul Kohli, 'From Elite Activism to Democratic Consolidation: The Rise of Reform Communism in West Bengal', in Francine R. Frankel and M.S.A. Rao (eds), *Dominance and State Power in Modern India Vol. II* (Delhi: Oxford University Press, 1990), pp. 374, 390.

36. Webster, 'Panchayati Raj' (n. 26 above), p. 68; Bandyopadhyay and von Eschen, 'Impact of Politics' (n. 26 above), p. S3; Echeverri-Gent, 'Politics Takes Command' (n. 26 above), p. 36.

37. E.M.S. Namboodiripad, *A Brief Critical Note on the Programme Drafts* (Delhi: Communist Party of India, 1964), pp. 6–7.

38. Mallick, *Development Policy of a Communist Government* (n. 24 above).

39. Bandyopadhyay and von Eschen, 'Impact of Politics' (n. 30 above), p. C9.

40. Jean Dreze and Amartya Sen, *Hunger and Public Action* (Oxford: Clarendon Press, 1989), p. 107.

41. Paul R. Brass, *The New Cambridge History of India, IV:I–The Politics of India Since Independence* (Cambridge: Cambridge University Press, 1990), p. 75.

42. James Manor, 'Tried, Then Abandoned: Economic Liberalisation in India', *IDS Bulletin*, Vol. 18, No. 4, 1987, p. 44.

43. World Bank, *India: Poverty, Employment, and Social Services* (Washington, DC: World Bank, 1989).

44. Dennison Berwick, 'Sacred and Profane', *The Sunday Times Magazine* (1 July 1990), p. 30.

45. Government of India, Ministry of Home Affairs, *Selected Statistics on Scheduled Castes* (Occasional Papers on Development of Scheduled Castes (2), (Delhi: Government of India Press, June 1984).

46. Myron Weiner, *The Child and the State in India* (Princeton: Princeton University Press, 1991), p. 186.

47. Brass, *The New Cambridge History of India, IV: I* (n. 41 above), p. 120.

48. Kohli, *The State and Poverty in India* (n. 15 above).

49. Nossiter, *Marxist State Governments in India* (n. 15 above), p. 171.

50. Bertrand Schneider, *The Barefoot Revolution: A Report to the Club of Rome* (London: Intermediate Technology Publications, 1988), p. 107.

51. Kohli, *The State and Poverty in India* (n. 15 above), p. 124.

52. Nossiter, *Marxist State Governments in India* (n. 15 above), p. 184.

53. Ibid., p. 139.

54. S.K. Ghosh, 'Land and Agricultural Development', in Manjula Bose (ed.), *Land Reforms in Eastern India* (Calcutta: Jadavpur University, 1981), p. 196.

55. Interview, West Bengal Land Reforms Commissioner.

56. Interview, West Bengal Land Reforms Commissioner.

57. Nripen Bandyopadhyaya, 'Evaluation of Land Reform Measures in West Bengal', Mimeo (Calcutta: Centre for Studies in Social Sciences, 1983).

58. Government of West Bengal, *Bargadars in West Bengal and an Assessment of Their Position in the Field*, Mimeo (Calcutta: West Bengal Land Reforms Office, August 1985), pp. 13–14.
59. World Bank, *World Development Report 1990* (New York: Oxford University Press, 1990), pp. 64–65.
60. Nossiter, *Marxist State Governments in India* (n. 14 above), p. 140.
61. Bandyopadhyaya, 'Evaluation of Land Reform Measures in West Bengal' (n. 57 above), p. 23.
62. Government of West Bengal, Department of Information and Cultural Affairs, *12 Years of Left Front Government* (Calcutta: Director of Information, June 1989), pp. 2–4.
63. Nossiter, *Marxist State Governments in India* (n. 15 above), p. 140.
64. Government of West Bengal, *12 Years of Left Front* (n. 62 above), p. 4.
65. Lloyd I. Rudolph and Susanne Hoeber Rudolph, *In Pursuit of Lakshmi: The Political Economy of the Indian State* (Chicago: The University of Chicago Press, 1987), p. 353.
66. Government of West Bengal, Board of Revenue and Directorate of Agriculture, *Agricultural Census 1976–77* (Calcutta: Board of Revenue and Directorate of Agriculture, 1979), p. 10.
67. Government of India, *National Sample Survey*, West Bengal No. 215, 26th Round, July 1971–September 1972 (Delhi: Ministry of Planning, 1972), p. 66.
68. James K. Boyce, 'Agricultural Growth in Bangladesh and West Bengal', (Ph.D. dissertation, Oxford University, Oxford, 1984), pp. 275, 345.
69. State Planning Board, Government of West Bengal, *Economic Review: Statistical Appendix 1989–90* (Calcutta: West Bengal Government Press, 1990); P. Sundarayya, *An Explanatory Note on the Central Committee Resolution on Certain Agrarian Issues* (Calcutta: Communist Party-Marxist, 1973).
70. Government of West Bengal, 'Adarsh Gramin Abash' (Ideal Village Habitation), leaflet reproduced in Ross Mallick, *Development Policy of a Communist Government: West Bengal since 1977* (Cambridge: Cambridge University Press, 1993), p. 162.
71. Theodor Bergmann, *Agrarian Reform in India* (New Delhi: Agricole Publishing Academy, 1984), p. 152.
72. Biplab Dasgupta, 'Some Aspects of Land Reform in West Bengal', *Land Reform: Land Settlement and Cooperatives*, No. 1/2, (1982), p. 13.
73. Ibid., p. 14.
74. Dwaipayan Bhattacharyya, 'Agrarian Reforms and the Politics of the Left in West Bengal', Ph.D. dissertation, University of Cambridge, Cambridge, March 1993), p. 90.
75. Kohli, *The State and Poverty in India* (n. 15 above), pp. 166, 215.
76. Ibid., p. 124; Nossiter, *Marxist State Governments in India* (n. 15 above), pp. 140, 171, 184.
77. Ross Mallick, 'Limits to Radical Intervention: Agricultural Taxation in West Bengal', *Development and Change*, Vol. 21, No. 1, January 1990.
78. Government of West Bengal, Department of Labour, *Labour in West Bengal*, (Calcutta: Department of Labour, 1977, 1979, 1983, 1984).
79. A.V. Jose, 'Agricultural Wages in India', *Economic and Political Weekly*, Vol. XXIII, No. 26, 25 June 1988, p. A55.

80. Westergaard, 'People's Participation, Local Government and Rural Development' (n. 30 above), p. 76.
81. Ibid., p. 74.
82. Planning Commission, Government of India, 'Report of the Working Group on the Development of Scheduled Castes During the Seventh Five Year Plan 1985–90', Mimeo (Delhi, February 1985), p. 74; National Sample Survey Organization, Government of India, *Sarvekshana*, April 1979, p. S590.
83. Communist Party of India-Marxist (CPM), Burdwan District Committee, *Shamiksha Astham Lok Sabha Nirbachan* ('Analysis of Eighth Lok Sabha Elections') (Burdwan: CPM District Committee, 28 February 1985), pp. 26–27, 31–32.
84. Subrata Nagchoudhury and Arnab Neil Sengupta, 'West Bengal: Projecting a Cleaner Face', *India Today*, 31 March 1996, pp. 88–89.
85. CPM Burdwan District Committee (1985), pp. 26–27, 31–32.
86. Mohammed Ayoob, 'The Primacy of the Political: South Asian Regional Cooperation (SARC) in Comparative Perspective', *Asian Survey*, Vol. 25, No. 4, April 1985, p. 450.
87. Weiner, *The Child and State in India* (n. 46 above), p. 6.
88. J.H. Broomfield, *Elite Conflict in a Plural Society: Twentieth-Century Bengal* (Berkeley, CA: University of California Press, 1968), p. 236.

CHAPTER 4

Decentralization and Rural Development

Decentralization has long been considered a potentially effective method for participatory development and delivery of assistance programmes. In the Third World, rural decentralization, though widely advocated, has now been recognized to have largely failed to provide improved distribution of benefits. The failures have been attributed to the entrenched interests of landed rural elites which garnered most of the benefits with the collusion of the public administration. Lack of political will at the higher levels of government enabled this corruption and maldistribution to take place.[1]

While some NGOs are recognized to have done good grass-roots work, their limited resources mean that these micro-level projects cannot be made universal, or even be easily replicated.[2] Only the state and its agencies have the resources to do this, yet the state is influenced by lobbies which are not inclined to support genuine decentralization, or even rural empowerment.

In India, the universal franchise, with the importance this gives to the rural population, has provided a powerful lobby for state provision of benefits to rural areas. However, these benefits are recognized to have been disproportionately received by the dominant rural interests. Although landed interests have naturally provided some impetus for rural decentralization, state politicians view this as a means of creating a rural power base that will be relatively impervious to central government intervention, in the event they are removed from power by President's rule.[3]

As the majority of the rural population are in the lowest classes, the universal franchise in local government would appear destined to put the poorer classes in direct and observable control of local state resources, which would be a significant counterweight to the power and largesse traditionally provided by local upper-class patrons. The reason for this transfer of power not having occurred in India has been attributed to the hierarchical nature of the Indian caste system, religious divisions, the limited resources available to the state, and the greater resources available to local elites, who have used state largesse to reinforce their own positions rather than those of their clientele. Decentralization has therefore tended to further empower either the traditional elites or the rival factions of upwardly mobile castes, who have the land resources to challenge their traditional dominance. In no case can the poor majority be said to have been significantly empowered by several decades of decentralization efforts.

The West Bengal Experiment

When the West Bengal Communists came to power in 1977 they were considered to have an opportunity to break the traditional cycle of lower-class dependency. They adopted the major recommendations of the central government's Committee on Panchayati Raj Institutions advocating development decentralization, with local elections being held for the first time on a party-slate basis.[4] Both academic and development workers saw this as having potential for relatively honest and effective aid delivery and empowerment.

> Many observers feel the CPM (Communist Party-Marxist) has a realistic chance of bringing about genuine reform of the local governments in the West Bengal countryside. The party is probably the best disciplined in India, has obviously made its new rural thrust its highest priority for the next five years, and has enormous incentive to succeed.... Should the CPM be able to demonstrate that it can rule effectively and bring about meaningful reform at the local level in the West Bengal countryside, its appeal to the downtrodden in most Indian states would be considerably enhanced.[5]

This experiment appeared to have great potential for success, as a Communist government could be expected to override the rural vested interests and use its rural cadre organization to ensure that not only was development aid actually delivered, but that it got to those most in need. Where previously panchayat elections were held on the basis of individual nominations, now for the first time official party slates would compete against each other, formally bringing party politics to village government. The village panchayats could give the Communists an organizational base from which to resist possible central government repression in the future. Decentralizing the administrative apparatus would make it more difficult for the central government to impose President's rule effectively, as much of the state powers would rest in Communist-controlled village organizations which, if self-supporting, could not be readily supplanted. As control of the village meant effective control of the state in electoral terms, no party could rule democratically without eliminating the Communist organization in the villages. These partisan political objectives had important implications for the restructuring of Bengal politics.

The 36-point programme of the Left Front in the 1977 assembly election stated that 'elections to the panchayats should be held immediately on the system of proportional representation with measures to be taken to confer more powers and resources on all local bodies'.[6] After the panchayat election during the floods at the end of 1978 the potential of the panchayats for rural reconstruction was realized in its flood relief programme. Unlike in the past, relief work undertaken through the panchayats prevented the usual rural migration to Calcutta normally associated with such natural calamities.[7] Their success in relief work prompted the Left Front to allocate more resources and responsibility to the panchayats.

Though the concept was promising and the public was told that the panchayats would receive greater power and more financial resources, their success as an agency of rural transformation would depend on the type of people elected to the village panchayats and the direction the Left Front gave these bodies.

The 1978 panchayat election gave the Left Front an overwhelming mandate, but the nomination of the Left Front's candidates was rather hastily and haphazardly done (Table 4.1).[8] Though the panchayat election was held in June 1978, a full year after the Left Front came to power, the Left Front, including the powerful CPM, lacked the cadre to nominate experienced party members to most of the posts. The CPM had only 38,889 members in 1978,

TABLE 4.1
West Bengal Panchayat Election Results

Gram Panchayats	1978	1983	1988
CPM	29,105	24,405	33,859
RSP	1,678	1,241	1,573
FB	1,539	1,084	1,400
CPI	825	716	889
Congress (S)	580	–	–
BJP	–	34	35
Janata	5	44	20
Congress (I)	4,535	14,733	12,229
Independents	9,436	3,443	2,426
Panchayat Samiti			
CPM	5,596	5,115	6,528
RSP	353	232	278
CPI	132	96	117
Congress (S)	105	–	–
BJP			3
Janata	2	12	5
Congress (I)	623	2,541	1,692
Independents	1,323	435	251
Zilla Parishad			
CPM	488	453	516
RSP	31	14	24
FB	44	28	18
CPI	5	–	9
Congress (S)	4	–	–
BJP	–	–	–
Janata	–	–	–
Congress (I)	22	149	51
Independents/Others	53	22	10

Source: Kalipada Basu, *West Bengal Economy: Past, Present, and Future* (Calcutta: Firma KLM Private Ltd, 1989), p. 25.

10,000 having joined since the return of the Left Front to power in 1977.[9]

In the selection the local influence rather than political consciousness of the candidates was often the prime consideration, and many relatives of CPM members were chosen as party candidates.[10] In the scramble to get nominations from the ruling state parties many influentials and even former Congressmen jumped on the Communist bandwagon and succeeded in obtaining seats.[11] Some of the traditional Communist supporters who were left out of the nominations were disgruntled by their own exclusion. The divisions among the Left Front partners resulted in their contesting against each other in about 6,000 seats.[12]

An independent survey by the National Institute of Rural Development in Hyderabad of one gram panchayat in each of the districts of Nadia, Midnapore and Jalpaiguri found the educational level of panchayat members 'high enough to justify appreciation of the voters' judgement. There is no illiterate' panchayat member.[13] Forty-seven per cent were farmers, 24 per cent professionals, 22 per cent businessmen and 4 per cent service holders.[14] Only one person was a labourer, indicating that it was the village middle and elite classes which controlled these panchayats. The study found that while the scheduled (Untouchable) castes and tribes continued their traditional occupations, the upper castes which had dominated during the zamindari period had now branched out from their landed base into the services and professions where 'their traditional literary skills, higher educational levels, and better linkages with urban areas (an aspect of the *bhadralok* syndrome) must have stood them in good stead'.[15] It was this occupational and educational elite which controlled the panchayat government in these villages.

A sample survey of 100 village panchayats by the Development and Planning Department of the West Bengal government found a similar occupational and educational distribution.[16] Only 4.8 per cent of the panchayat members were landless labourers and 1.8 per cent sharecroppers, though 44.28 per cent of agriculturists in Bengal were landless labourers (Table 4.2).[17] Over half were owner cultivators, 71 per cent with less than five acres of land (Table 4.3).[18]

The dominance of the relatively well-educated section of the village community in the panchayat was confirmed by the survey. The education of 78 per cent of members was between the primary and higher secondary levels, while 14 per cent were graduates. With only 8 per cent below primary graduation level, the underrepresentation of the illiterates, who form 67.03 per cent of West Bengal's rural population but 1 per cent of panchayat members, was marked (Table 4.4).[19] In spite of this, on the basis of the above survey the West Bengal Left Front government con-

TABLE 4.2

Distribution of Gram Panchayat Members by Occupation

Occupation	Number	Percentage
Owner cultivators	743	50.7
Teachers	206	14.0
Unemployed	110	7.5
Landless labourers	70	4.8
Sharecroppers	26	1.8
Artisans	23	1.6
Shopowners	20	1.4
Technical workers	19	1.3
Doctors	16	1.1
Tailors	8	0.6
Students	8	0.6
Fishermen	6	0.4
Others	211	14.4
Total	1,466	100.0

Source: Government of West Bengal, Department of Panchayats and Community Development, *The Working of Panchayat System in West Bengal: A Review of Main Events and Activities* (March 1980), pp. 42–43. From Survey of 100 Gram Panchayats.

cluded that 'judging by the evidence of this survey the members of the panchayats by a significant majority, can be taken to represent the interests of the poorer sections in villages'.[20] Given the class composition of contemporary Bengal villages this would

TABLE 4.3

Landholdings of Owner Cultivator Gram Panchayat Members

Acres	Percentage of Distribution
Below 2	42.9
2–5	28.2
5–8	13.0
8–10	8.1
Over 10	7.8
Total	100.0

Source: Government of West Bengal, Department of Panchayats and Community Development, *The Working of Panchayat System in West Bengal: A Review of Main Events and Activities* (March 1980), pp. 42–43. From Survey of 100 Gram Panchayats.

TABLE 4.4

Distribution of Gram Panchayat Members by Education

Education Standard	Number	Percentage
Non-literate	10	1
Just read and write	57	4
Below primary	49	3
Primary	214	14
Middle level	499	34
High/Higher secondary	436	30
Graduate level	161	11
Postgraduate	30	2
Technical degree	10	1
Total	1,466	100

Source: Government of West Bengal, Department of Panchayats and Community Development, *The Working of Panchayat System in West Bengal: A Review of Main Events and Activities* (March 1980), p. 42. From Survey of 100 Gram Panchayats.

appear to be something of a distortion, the opposite being closer to the truth. Using the same government statistics, Roy Choudhury argues that the panchayats are dominated by 'the same old class of rural vested interests including moneylenders'.[21] 'Fifty-one per cent belong to the landowning classes; the rest are classified as "others", but are themselves linked with landed interests.'[22] He refers to the Land Reforms Commissioner, D. Bandyopadhyay, as claiming that only 6.54 per cent of panchayat members belong to the rural poor.[23]

From a sample of 60 gram panchayat members Atul Kohli takes an intermediate position that 'institutional power has, at least for now, been transferred from the hands of the dominant propertied groups to a lower middle stratum'.[24] As with all surveys that attempt to determine class landholdings, underestimation of holdings by landowners tends to place them in a class lower than is actually the case. In Kohli's survey, 8.3 per cent of agriculturist gram panchayat members had less than two acres, 69 per cent 2–5 acres, 19.4 per cent 6–10 acres and 2.8 per cent over 10 acres of land. Yet in this group none used only family labour on their land, 83.3 per cent hired labour and 16.7 per cent used sharecroppers. This indicates that these panchayat members were probably more prosperous than the survey responses indicate.

While reporting the use of outside labour was presumably considered safe, landholdings were under reported. The stated small size of holdings indicates that at least some would more efficiently use family rather than hired labour. Underreporting of landholdings from fear of confiscation is more clearly revealed in an International Labour Organization (ILO) survey in West Bengal, where listing and agriculture schedules of leased lands revealed a close correlation of 4,645 and 4,436 acres of leased in land but only 1,408 and 312 acres of leased out land. As the figures of leased in and leased out land should be identical, landowners clearly understated their ownership.[25] For this reason in-depth village studies are better able to reveal the true picture than large interview sample surveys by transitory outsiders, particularly on topics as sensitive as landownership and political affiliations.[26] Such studies indicate that Communist leadership is rather more elitist than the lower middle-class composition revealed by sample surveys.

Whatever the differences in class composition, there are similarities with the class–caste composition under the previous Congress government. A 1974 village study of panchayat leadership in Hooghly district showed that leadership in the anchal and gram panchayats was 25 and 11 per cent rich (holding over 15 acres), 50 and 56 per cent upper middle class (7–15 acres) and 21 and 25 per cent middle class (2–7 acres), respectively. There were no positions held below this level except for an 11 per cent landless share in the gram panchayat. In caste composition, the anchal and gram panchayats were composed respectively of 25 and 11 per cent high caste, 50 and 67 per cent dominant agriculturist caste, and 25 and 22 per cent other middle castes. There were no members outside these categories.[27] According to the 1977 Davis study, even though government requirements for ward representatives gave the low castes three of nine seats, the members were nominees of the dominant faction on whom they were dependent.[28] Thus class–caste composition alone can often disguise the political controls exercised by the dominant elite over lower-class members who are their nominees. The Communist government exacerbated this tendency by changing the law to make appointments of scheduled castes, tribes' members and women by the state government dependent on the nominees recommended by the local panchayats, thereby increasing the control of the locally dominant faction.[29] Thus, even this small proportion can be assumed to represent some poor scheduled caste and tribe members nominated by the richer landowners to fill the reserved quota and, therefore, cannot automatically be assumed to represent the interests of their class, as they are indebted to and under the influence of the richer landowners.

Even if it is accepted that the panchayats are composed of the middle strata of village society, their interests do not coincide with those of the poorer sections of the villages. The heavy bias towards small propertied owners, and the gross underrepresentation of the landless, however, was expected, given the middle-peasant and rural middle-class dominance in the CPM rural membership. As the question of the landless organizing and representing themselves through the panchayats did not arise on account of their token membership in the panchayats, it was up to the rural middle class to represent their interests. Since according to panchayat and party officials, 60–70 per cent of the CPM's own gram panchayat appointees have no grasp of leftist theory, their ideological commitment to leftist mobilization of the poorest classes was limited. In tours with government officials to a number of panchayats, the relative prosperity of members was obvious from their appearance, while most of their projects were of dubious value for the lower classes. In one of the meetings with a gram panchayat, the elected members all assured me that they were landless agricultural labourers. The local government official who had arranged the meeting however indicated that this was not the case. Nevertheless, it revealed an understanding of whom they were supposed to represent and they could hardly be blamed for trying to misrepresent themselves to a foreigner. The meeting was cut short by the CPM guide who suggested that I talk to the party leadership as local village panchayat leaders did not have a good understanding of the programme objectives.

While the rural propertied classes failed to represent the poorest classes effectively, the poorest classes themselves were often unable or unwilling to assert themselves politically, making the task of the Communists more difficult. Their lack of education, indebtedness to the propertied classes, and their strenuous preoccupation with making a living gave the propertied and middle classes a significant political advantage. The organizers who came from outside the poorer classes were often unsuited to being their spokespersons and found greater affinity and ease of mobilization among the rural middle class.[30]

While in 1977 only Rs 0.08 per capita was spent through the panchayats, over the next three years per capita annual expenditure was over Rs 10 for the rural population. From 1979 to 1981, Rs 3 billion were routed through the panchayats by government departments, a substantial sum considering the neglect of the panchayats under the Congress government and the limitations of an annual state budget of about Rs 10 billion.[31] By the end of the five-year term in June 1983, Rs six billion had been distributed through the panchayats.[32] The major project assigned to the gram panchayats by the Relief and Welfare Department was the Food for Work Programme, with food and funds supplied by the central government. From 15 December 1980 this was replaced by the National Rural Employment Programme (NREP).[33] The Rural Reconstruction Programme of the Relief and Welfare Department and the Rural Works Programme of the Development and Planning Department, both financed by the central government, created 56.63 million person-days of employment in 1978–79, reaching 70 million by December 1979.[34] If spread over all four million farm labourers in West Bengal, this represented 17.5 person-days per capita. Considering that agricultural labourers are without work at least seven months, or 210 days, a year, the programme was inadequate.[35] Though the minimum wage was fixed at Rs 8.10 per day, the Food for Work Programme paid only slightly over Rs 4 in both food and cash per day. However, as the labour was utilized in the off-season, this exceeded the prevailing local wage rates. But these labourers were better off than those in some other states where corruption was rampant. An IAS officer from Bengal who visited a Food for Work Programme in another state found that the recipients were not even aware that there was a food component to the payment, as the programme administrators had misappropriated it.

The Final Report of the Programme Evaluation Organization of the Planning Commission found shortcomings in the Food for Work Programme. In taking a sample based on one good district and one average district in 10 states, including the districts of Burdwan (good) and Nadia (average), in West Bengal, this positively biased survey found that West Bengal had created the highest number of person-days in both years of the programme covering 1977–79.[36] However, this was due in part to cheap labour paid below the West Bengal government's own legal minimum wage. As six districts in other states paid the legal wage and five paid above it, the eight districts, including the two in West Bengal, paying below were in a minority. In Nadia the programme had a positive effect on market wage rates, but in Burdwan it had no effect. The 40 beneficiaries interviewed were unanimous that the wages were insufficient to meet daily requirements, as compared with 12 out of 40 in Nadia. Half of the Nadia beneficiaries interviewed found the wages above prevailing market rates while 35 of 40 from Burdwan found them below. The programme contributed only a 5.6 per cent and 8.4 per cent increase in employment to its beneficiaries in Burdwan and Nadia, respectively. The responses of beneficiaries indicated that the quality of foodgrains distributed in the two districts was worse than in the other states, 33.75 per cent in West Bengal compared with 14.6 per cent in the whole survey. Half the Burdwan respondents found the grain mixed with sweepings, as did two of 40 in Nadia, where two others found it stone ridden.[37] In one block in Nadia the investigators found that

> although checks were officially applied at every stage still malpractices like false entries of names in the muster rolls, insufficient work than prescribed were reported by the local people. Even if some workers did not work up to the prescribed extent, they managed to get the certificate of satisfactory work. It was also reported that at times the modified Ration Shop dealer supplied very bad quality of wheat. It was doubted that the dealer sold out the actual foodgrains in the open market and distributed the worst quality of grains purchased at lower prices.[38]

In Burdwan on the other hand, in distribution of foodgrains 'there was no scope for malpractice as it was done in the presence of panchayat members and other villagers, including rival political party members'.[39] Under the conditions of the programme, foodgrains supplied free to the state had to be matched by a specified cash component provided by the state government. During 1977–78 West Bengal was the only state not to match the additional sum required, making the Rs 20,301,000 shortfall recoverable from the state government by the central Ministry of Rural Reconstruction.[40]

A World Bank-commissioned study by the Institute for Financial Management and Research found that the implementation of the NREP in West Bengal had been 'perhaps the best' of all the Indian states and union territories.[41] However, its own statistics in the report indicated that West Bengal had the third highest amount of allocated but unutilized funds and foodgrains in the country, totalling Rs 182,622,000 as of April 1981, and the second highest amount of unutilized grains and funds, of Rs 258,738,000, by April 1982. Despite the considerable funds and grain available, employment generation was only 40–60 per cent in 1981–82 of what it had been in 1980–81. During 1980–81 employed beneficiaries in West Bengal received 20–40 days of work—which fell in the following financial year to less than 20 days—which the report considered 'very unsatisfactory'.[42]

The study dealt in detail with the implementation of the Integrated Rural Development Programme (IRDP) in four states, including West Bengal. Unlike the implementation of the NREP in West Bengal, the IRDP came in for serious criticism. West Bengal achieved just 18.6 per cent of its target in the first year and 33.5 per cent in the second. 'This achievement rate was the lowest of all the states in the country.'[43] Less than 5 per cent of the target group was covered.[44] Investment per family was the lowest in India, and 'declined disturbingly', from Rs 1,287 in 1980–81 to Rs 941 in 1981–82. The subsidy of Rs 314 was the lowest of all the states and territories. The low level of assistance was due to West Bengal spending less than envisioned in the IRDP guidelines, 13.39 per cent in 1980–81 and only 10.5 per cent in the following year. The reason was that 'the Centre released very small sums to West Bengal in both years', that is, 5.02 per cent and 3.96 per cent of central allocations in the two years, respectively. 'The blame for the poor Central release is apparently to be laid at the door of implementing authorities of the IRDP and the administrative machinery of the State.'[45] Between 1977–78 and 1980–81, Rs 80 million out of an admissible outlay of Rs 90 million had been left unutilized. 'The Government of India after reviewing this expenditure trend decided not to make any allocation for the two years 1980–81 and 1981–82.' Though this may have been justifiable, political motivation of the newly elected Congress government cannot be ruled out. The study however concludes that 'compared to what the state got from the Centre for the years 1980–81 and 1981–82, it has done well', spending about 530 per cent of what the centre allocated to it. 'Nevertheless, in absolute terms, the performance of West Bengal in the first two years is poor', 'much below the national average in all aspects of the IRDP.'[46] The study attributes this to the state government channelling the programme through the panchayats rather than the state bureaucracy, as was done in other states.

As the object of the programme was to assist families below the poverty line, the state government argued that the lower-level bureaucracy showed favouritism in giving aid to the better-off classes or at best to those already near the poverty line, where the additional subsidy would allow them to cross the poverty line and thereby enable the administrators to claim success in achieving their targets for removing poverty in recipient families.[47] The West Bengal government felt that the target groups should be the poorest families who would receive smaller subsidies which they would be better able to utilize in sustainable projects rather than the more expensive ones that were beyond their resources and expertise to sustain after termination of the aid.[48] The vested interests who had received this aid from the administration in the past could be bypassed by giving the aid for distribution by the panchayats, who as local elected representatives would be best able to select recipients and administer the programme. Commercial banks supported the West Bengal government position, since distribution through the panchayats would give them fewer accounts to deal with and greater collateral than individual poor families could provide.[49] This approach, however, was not acceptable to the central government and 'the disagreement between the two Governments persisted for four years, beginning with 1977–78, and threw the implementation of the IRDP in disarray in the State. Consequently, very little was done in assisting the poor families or utilizing the national funds made available to the State.'[50]

In accordance with the state government policy

the Panchayats were given comprehensive powers for implementing the IRDP, and Government officials at the block

level were made completely subservient to them. The West
Bengal Government feared that if bureaucracy is given more
powers and the Panchayats become subservient to it, there
would be a collusion between bureaucracy and vested interests and the benefits would be cornered by the well-off rural
families through wrong identification.... Hence neutralizing
the bureaucracy was felt to be absolutely essential for ensuring that the benefits would go to the most needy.[51]

As the panchayats were under Left Front control, while the
bureaucracy was nominally independent, it was politically expedient to distribute aid through the panchayats where it could be
used to create political goodwill for the Communists. It could
also enable the distribution of development aid as political
patronage. This might have been the real reason for the disagreement between the state and central governments over distribution channels.

When aid was distributed through the panchayats numerous
problems arose. For instance, one senior West Bengal government official who happened to look at the files of IRDP beneficiaries was surprised to find that the flocks of goats were dying of
disease or accidents. On investigation it was found that the beneficiaries would take the flocks along with the subsidy, and then
sell the flocks and bribe the veterinarians to give false death cer-
tificates, and with this collect the insurance money. They were
thus better off than if they had kept the flocks as the programme
intended, without having to do any work or entail any risk. This
was not the most fraudulent case, however. On a visit to Maharashtra which has a strong panchayat system, but where IRDP
beneficiaries were chosen by local schoolteachers, I found that
not only the schoolteachers, but the local village officials and
moneylenders too were beneficiaries of the IRDP. When bank officials complained that the schoolteachers were ineligible, they
recorded their spouses instead. The local administration considered the IRDP their least successful development endeavour.

The World Bank-commissioned study noted various problems
in West Bengal:

The village Panchayats lacked administrative expertise, and
found the task of decision making tough. Since the bureaucracy

was prevented from taking any part in the Panchayats' activities as a matter of policy, the implementation of anti-poverty programmes ground to a halt. Besides, the Panchayats in the State were entrusted with many other activities and made responsible for implementing a variety of schemes and programmes. Under the burden of these numerous responsibilities, lack of bureaucratic support, communication gap, etc., the whole setup nearly collapsed. No decisions could be made, no activities could be undertaken and no programme was implemented. This explains the poor performance of the State in IRDP.[52]

A total of 18,000 loan applications for IRDP families were pending with Bengal banks in 1982–83, and performance in that year was less than 50 per cent of target. Only one district exceeded the target, while four achieved over 75 per cent of the target and six were unsatisfactory.[53]

The panchayats' priorities were often misconceived or oriented to benefiting the richer sections. The larger share of funds went to infrastructure development mainly through road and building construction, which created off-season employment for agricultural labour but contributed little to the poorest sections.[54] Programmes of direct relevance to the landless tended to be ignored, with agricultural labourers receiving remuneration of food and wages only. The panchayats generally gave low priority to minor irrigation works, which could have been made more productive. Though West Bengal has over 1.1 million ponds and tanks, the Food for Work Programme did insufficient work to make these water resources effective. In other works, such as embankment repair after the 1978 floods, the repairs were unsatisfactory. The Left Front Irrigation Minister, Provash Chandra Roy, complained that most repairs were useless and would have to be redone. The same was often said regarding buildings and roads.[55]

The programme tended to reflect the demands of the rural middle class represented in the panchayats. Through the CPM-dominated panchayats they were able to consolidate their political and economic control of the villages and create new vested interests opposed to the interests of the landless. The new vested interests undoubtedly represent a less prosperous and more numerous class than the zamindars of the colonial period or *jotedars* of the post-independence Congress party, but often they are just a different faction of the same class.

Socially the leftist leadership in rural areas are connected with the rural power structure by kinship and affinity; they were not strangers elevated to power. Often the family struggle took a political shape and often it was within the rural power elite a struggle for power between two relatives.[56]

A Board of Revenue publication for government officials notes the difficulties involved in trying to benefit the poor through panchayats.

The Zilla and Panchayat Samitis are filled with rural elite—the larger surplus farmers and the leaders of dominant lineage or patronage groups....

Far from establishing or introducing a territorially based structure at odds with traditional village power relations, the administrative system at its lowest level becomes an instrument of the traditional village power relations. As a result of this capture of the local system by the rural elite, their interests, and not those of the average farmer, or those proclaimed by the national government, continue to dominate the rural scene....

If attempts to create an effective administrative structure independent of the local elite have thus foundered, most government programmes to directly promote rural development have met with a similar fate....

Government attempts to impose outside organisation and direction have for the most part been taken over by traditional forces, which have diverted them to their own ends.[57]

Given the vested interests represented in the panchayats, the aim of the panchayat programme of distributing benefits to the lowest strata of society would face a formidable obstacle, which could only be overcome if the political parties ensured that local organizations directed the resources in an appropriate manner. The Board of Revenue handbook concluded that 'it will need strong political and social will in the Panchayati Raj structure to bend these opposing forces into making available the bulk of the social product to those that are in most need.'[58] The administrators of the panchayat programme, however, found this political will lacking in the Left Front government. They complained that they had to do everything in the panchayat programme, while the Left Front claimed all the credit but did little to fulfil its role. While the poorest sections were neglected, the middle peasants established their own interests with the acquiescence of the Communist leadership and support of the local party membership. The leftist administrators regretted that the ideological work and consciousness raising which could be done only by the party was never undertaken. The work of political education in the villages was neglected by the Communists, and the administrators could do nothing about this as it was beyond their jurisdiction. As a result the panchayats could not be an effective organ of support in the event of repression. A small minority of about 5 per cent of the panchayats are even believed to have misappropriated funds.

Corruption often had the backing of leftist political parties at different levels. It is now questionable whether these new vested interests can be removed. Even if they are not given party tickets they can run as independents, using their local following and patronage resources. If there is changing of panchayat members at the party nomination, the party may find the panchayat moving out of their control. At the outset it would have been possible to correct these defects. Despite repeated warnings from the bureaucracy, they were left alone to carry out the work without complementary support from the leftists. What might have been an asset to the leftist struggle is in danger of becoming a liability to the Communists, due to lack of party work in the villages. Now, if resources are not continually allocated to the panchayats it will create opposition to the leftist government from the vested interests of the panchayat, but if the funds are given or increased, the patronage and entrenchment of these interests will also increase. The CPM Chief Minister of West Bengal, Jyoti Basu, noted with disappointment that

Those supporters of ours from whom we expected so much have not come up to expectation. The sincere application and selfless will which may solve many of the problems, we have not been able to notice in some important matters....

That political consciousness which should have been expanded or implemented has not taken place.... I cannot say that in the state we have been able to achieve noticeable progress in controlling and ending corruption. We have to keep a vigilant eye on party workers and supporters conscious that before the ruling party there is a great temptation.... From the point of view of our party and its organization it is essential to maintain a clean image and we attach great importance to this work.[59]

The degree to which the Left Front has retained a clean image and delivered improved services to the rural areas through the panchayats has been a matter of on-going debate. The most cynical view is that it merely enables corruption and patronage to spread from the urban to the rural areas. This equalizes urban–rural disparities and integrates the rural elite in the party patronage network. According to Kalipada Basu, in this view 'if corruption cannot be stopped let it be distributed in rural areas also. Wealth was so long concentrated in city and town areas, let it be distributed in the villages through the process of corruption.'[60] The literature analyzing the West Bengal panchayat experiment has reached vastly divergent conclusions. Those who argue that empowerment of the poor has been achieved include Kohli and Lieten, while Webster and Echeverri-Gent claim that the power is in the hands of a new politically assertive middle class.[61] Bandhopadhyay, von Eschen, and Westergaard are less sanguine about a genuine power transfer, and argue that the old classes retain their economic resources and some continuing share of political influence.[62] This is a wide spectrum for what should be an empirically verifiable conclusion. Since these are village-level micro studies, it could be argued that they represent the full range of villages, where different classes have gained control. However, with some exceptions, the social and economic conditions do not appear to have been so different as to result in such divergent conclusions. While at the state level it is clear that land reforms and education enrolment increases have been no better under the Communist than the Congress regime, there has been new development aid since the Communists came to power. This has been credited to the Communists when in fact it was being simultaneously offered as part of central government programmes in all other Indian states as well. Though the electorate may give the credit to the Communists for this new delivery, credit is only due if their performance is better than that in other states. This is something the micro-level studies in West Bengal cannot address without parallel studies from other states.

The changes that studies of West Bengal attribute to the intervention of the Left Front also appear to be taking place in other parts of the country under different regimes. If this is the case, the Left Front may therefore be the political beneficiary of socio-economic improvement without being the cause of these changes. A more likely candidate for credit may be the civil service which exists in all states, with politicians playing peripheral or merely enabling roles. That there have been significant changes in class relations in other parts of India is indicated by Marguerite S. Robinson's study of Andhra Pradesh, where there was a sea change in class relations between 1969 and 1981, despite the lack of any land redistribution. Here, development assistance by state and central government interventions eroded the power of local elites even in the absence of land reform.[63] Thus, what has been observed in West Bengal appears from various studies to be part of a national trend for which undue credit may have been attributed to leftist parties.[64] Echeverri-Gent finds the strength of the West Bengal CPM to have contributed to party clientelism and patronage-dispensing that can be remedied through recourse to popular elections which remove corrupt officials.[65] Distribution of aid through the panchayats, however, has led to delays in implementation which have given West Bengal the worst record in utilization for at least one major programme as Table 4.5 indicates.

The premise even of critiques of Left Front programmes is that power has devolved to a new middle class. Echeverri-Gent suggests it is analogous to the 'backward classes' in other parts of India who found allegiance with non-leftist caste-based parties, which was not possible in West Bengal because of the diffused caste identities there. The leftist political parties were therefore able to mobilize without a caste appeal in opposition to the traditional elite.[66]

The question remains, however, as to where the old elite went. They did not give up their land, as there has been no significant land reform for over a generation. The elite, if questioned in surveys, can try to pass themselves off as the more politically

TABLE 4.5

National Rural Employment Programme as a Percentage of Resources Available Annually by State

State	1981–82	1982–83	1983–84	1985–86	1986–87	1987–88	1988–89	Average 1981–89
Andhra Pradesh	72.9	73.3	70.1	101.2	91.6	77.1	108.0	84.9
Assam	50.1	63.6	47.4	67.3	102.6	67.2	67.3	66.5
Bihar	52.1	70.2	65.1	97.3	83.7	106.2	106.0	82.9
Gujarat	39.8	76.1	96.0	73.9	85.4	112.6	85.2	81.3
Haryana	74.9	72.8	77.2	102.0	97.6	88.9	104.5	88.3
Jammu & Kashmir	83.1	65.7	80.4	67.5	87.4	109.8	93.1	83.9
Karnataka	57.1	73.2	75.1	90.5	65.4	90.8	117.8	81.4
Kerala	96.7	72.2	76.7	81.7	106.0	74.6	119.0	89.6
Madhya Pradesh	100.0	93.0	84.9	71.6	101.3	94.2	112.8	94.0
Maharashtra	100.0	52.7	60.8	100.3	104.9	94.8	78.8	84.6
Orissa	61.1	48.4	46.6	106.8	103.5	93.1	127.8	83.9
Punjab	100.0	94.0	98.3	100.0	100.0	81.7	94.9	95.6
Rajasthan	74.3	72.2	71.6	83.6	103.6	111.2	92.1	86.9
Tamil Nadu	71.6	84.9	90.3	88.7	112.0	84.9	130.5	94.7
Uttar Pradesh	67.8	73.3	78.1	98.6	85.3	73.3	123.9	85.6
West Bengal	42.8	62.8	66.1	72.3	114.0	87.0	74.4	74.2
Average for all states	71.5	71.8	74.0	87.7	96.5	90.5	102.3	84.9

Source: John Echeverri-Gent, 'Public Participation and Poverty Alleviation: The Experience of Reform Communists in India's West Bengal', *World Development*, Vol. 20, No. 10, October 1992, p. 1408.

expedient new middle class. Greater resources, education and contacts enabled them to diversify into salaried employment and business. This diversification enables them to appear in surveys as separate from the old elite, bereft of landed property, which appears in the names of relatives, dead and alive. In fact, detailed analysis of much of the elected panchayat leadership would probably reveal familial contacts with the old elite. This does not mean that upwardly mobile backward castes have not used their control over some landed property to move into dominant positions. Communist party membership can assist in this process, and both old and new elites, or their family members, have undoubtedly used party membership as a lever to occupy leading positions in local panchayats. The problem is that none of the surveys are detailed enough to differentiate between the new and the old elites and the family relationships between the two. New dominant classes may just be the descendants of the old elite whose property was subdivided and scattered into smaller holdings over generations. Just as the urban elite originated from zamindari landed property in the colonial period, the rural politically dominant middle classes may have come from the poorer relations of the old elite who left for the cities. A genealogical chart of this linkage would only be practical at the level of at most a handful of villages, making generalizations difficult. A caste and class analysis of the dominant rural elite and how it is represented through the panchayats is therefore impossible to do at present.

Lieten, however, makes a case in his sample that while initially the panchayats elected from among the elite, they have now moved to a lower-class membership. Repeated elections over time have increased the proportion of Scheduled Castes and Scheduled Tribes in the panchayats to the point that it matches their proportion of the population, which was not the case before, or even at the beginning of the Left Front government.[67] Even with economic inequality political power has been achieved. Few others are claiming such empowerment of the lower classes, but it is logical that where elites are not prosperous or are narrowly based, the numerical predominance of the lower classes will lead to the election of poor candidates. Their newly obtained control of state largesse will enable them to acquire a relative autonomy from the economically dominant elites. However, the lack of confirmation from other surveys may indicate that this sample is exceptional, and the proportion in this category cannot be estimated. Though Kohli states that disciplined reformist parties are the most effective impetus for implementing change in rural India, Echeverri-Gent is less sanguine about CPM dominance being conducive to lower-class empowerment, noting the tendencies to anti-democratic behaviour and corruption in single-party dominant states. The extent to which the CPM has been a free rider on changes that would have occurred anyway and on development programmes also available in other states is difficult to determine. Unlike in other states, however, it has ensured its control over the distribution of largesse, and marginalized its Congress opponents whose fractious infighting has been extremely fortuitous for the Communists.

If one accepts the consensus that power has been transferred to a newly politically dominant rural middle class with the electoral support of the lower classes, the question must be raised as to the benefits this provides the poor. It is not apparent that it produces any benefits, and most probably makes further changes for their own class benefit more difficult. Small elites are easier to remove politically than broad-based ones. However, prosperous small elites can make more economic and wage concessions to the poorest classes than middle classes that operate with less resources and lower profit margins. Hence, the retention of a small prosperous elite which provides credit guarantees against famine is arguably more advantageous to the poor than a numerous middle class which must pursue its own interests to the exclusion of others. The Communists may have facilitated this process, which makes lower-class empowerment more difficult. Only a series of detailed micro-level studies can determine this. The issue, however, has hardly been raised in this literature.

Since property redistribution has been insignificant, economic improvements for the poor will have to come from state programmes. That these programmes are inadequate for the scale of the problem of poverty alleviation is universally recognized. Even the most enthusiastic exponent of the panchayat programme, Lieten, admits that the funding 'amounts remain meagre (Rs 150 per capita per year for the state as a whole). All programmes which look attractive on paper—since they are allocated large sums—when broken down to the units of implementation, are confronted with far too little money'.[68] However, his figures are from projected planning expenditures. If one looks at these figures on the ground and deducts the non-developmental administrative and non-beneficiary expenditures, the amount that reaches intended beneficiaries is a fraction of the total.

A gram panchayat in Hooghly District had expenditures of Rs 236,000 but Rs 69,500 was spent on employee salaries, and only Rs 77,000 on development work. That worked out to a per capita expenditure of Rs 4.40 (about 12 cents), which is an insignificant part of even a poor Indian's annual income.[69] Neil Webster's study of panchayats provides detailed revenue receipts for two gram panchayats but the lack of full expenditure lists makes a breakdown of administrative and developmental expenditures impossible. However, even if all revenues are divided by total population, the per capita revenue for the years 1983–84 to 1987–88 is Rs 11.34, Rs 9.55, Rs 14.52, Rs 21.15 and Rs 24.93, respectively, for Kanpur II, and Rs 15.35 and Rs 13.18 for the Saldya gram panchayat in the years 1986–87 and 1987–88.[70] Webster concludes that

> by retreating from the prosecution of class politics within the agrarian society and moving towards consensual politics within the villages, the static class relations within the villages can combine with the economically dependent position of the panchayats for funds from above [the government] to make the panchayats somewhat vulnerable political institutions, susceptible to being hijacked from within, or undermined from above, by those whose fundamental interests lie opposed to the poor peasants and agricultural labourers.[71]

Given the lack of adequate government funding and property redistribution, the panchayats are largely irrelevant to empowerment of the poor. If the number of poor are divided by the funds distributed it is clear that the funding is inadequate for any meaningful economic changes. Thus, even if the poor were elected to office, shortage of funds would prevent them from achieving any great measure of independence from the landed classes. Therefore, in development terms, panchayats cannot be said to provide an economically significant benefit, or even a relative economic autonomy from the landed rural elite. Without some means of independent livelihood, labour, as Adam Smith argued, will be at a disadvantage in the struggle with their employers. The state which might act as a coercive force on behalf of labour under the present government follows a conciliation policy between classes. Echeverri-Gent's 'findings differ with those who find the CPI(M) regime to be a captive of "its landlord base" and the "dominant elite" (Mallick, 1990, p. 157; 1991). They also diverge from those who stress the dedication of the CPI(M) to the uplift of the rural poor (Kohli, 1987; Nossiter, 1988, pp. 137–143)'.[72] This stance between two opposing positions does not indicate where panchayats have provided more than palliatives to the poor or aid sufficient to alter class relations. Without state resources adequate to create autonomous livelihoods for the poor, economic dependency remains unaltered by the panchayats. In the face of this, panchayat elections must be a rather insignificant activity. Even if a consciousness-raising takes place through the electoral process, it is doubtful if this can provide any benefits to the poor who are unable to alter their dependency relationship with the rural elite. The Left Front government by refusing to confront the rural elite, and even promoting their class interests through lowering their agricultural taxation, have instead pursued their elite interests. The poor by contrast have received enough largesse to maintain the Communist vote base. Though aid is also offered in other states by different parties, this is not appreciated by the poor who are in no position to make a comparative analysis. Only redistribution of rural assets, most likely through land redistribution or at least by progressive agricultural taxation, can alter their situation. That neither policy was undertaken does represent an elite landed class interest, and there is no way to avoid this conclusion, however much it conflicts with the Communist self-image and reputation.

Bhabani Sen Gupta's book on the CPM published in 1979 has a chapter devoted to a sympathetic examination of the organization and work of the 'Red Panchayats'.[73] By 1982, however, the author's perspective has changed. 'The CPM in West Bengal has, in fact, no concrete plans to take the peasantry through the Panchayats to a higher level of mobilisation for political or development purposes. Hence the stagnation of the Panchayat system.'[74]

Atul Kohli comes to a more positive conclusion:

The CPM's organizational arrangements allow it to penetrate the countryside without being captured by the propertied groups. In part because of the democratic-centralist nature of the party organization and in part because of the carefully reorganized local government, the CPM can now reach the lower peasantry without landlord mediation. This feature of the CPM distinguishes it from all other organized political alternatives in India. It allows the regime to channel some developmental resources directly to the rural poor, as well as to mobilize them for occasionally fulfilling reformist goals.[75]

This contradicts the conclusions of almost all independent observers of the panchayat programme. However, Kohli's conclusion that 'the CPM has moved away from a revolutionary to a reformist orientation' would find general agreement, and the panchayat experience in West Bengal is indicative of this general tendency.[76]

The deficit financing that had helped fund the panchayat development programme placed financial strictures on state governments. Whereas the Left Front spent Rs 430 million and distributed 150,000 tonnes of foodgrain under the Food for Work and rural works programmes in 1978–79, central government cutbacks resulted in only Rs 140 million and 15,000 tonnes of foodgrain being distributed in 1983–84.[77] The unevenness of the aid flows points to the dependence of the whole process on central government funding. The programmes formally continued, but the panchayats never achieved any financial self-sufficiency. Though the Communists had succeeded to a certain extent in devolving political power in the villages to the next lower rung of the more numerous middle-class elements and consolidated their position, they had not increased the bargaining power of the lowest classes to any appreciable degree. Thus, by bringing a numerically stronger landed and professional middle class to a dominant position in village life, further mobilization and radicalization of the lower classes may become a more difficult task for the party. Though the Communists' conception was for an alliance of the middle and lower classes, there is no evidence that this would have furthered the interests of the lower classes whom the middle class panchayat members supposedly represent. They are possibly more efficient and honest than their counterparts in other states, but they do not represent a qualitative or revolutionary break with traditional methods of operation. The failure of the panchayats to deliver the goods to those most in need reflects the failure of the Left Front government in general to alter the balance of power in rural Bengal in favour of the lower classes. In the event that the Left Front is defeated in an election or removed by the central government, the panchayats will be unable and unwilling to put up resistance to a new state government.

The Communist government's failure to shift political power to the lower classes has important implications for the possibilities of radical change in India. There is little doubt that the mainstream Indian Communist parties are at an impasse, observable particularly in West Bengal where the movement is now on the decline. In the face of its inability to change economic relations, the Communist government's attempts at political change in favour of the lower classes have failed. Without the power to implement radical agrarian reform that would be needed to break the dependence of the lower classes on the dominant landowners, political emancipation of the lower classes is impossible. The reformist tendencies inherent in depending on a middle-class landed elite to lead the peasant movement, and the constitutional restraints of operating in a democracy, led the movement in directions the Communists had not originally intended or initially desired. The failure was inherent in the constraints that the Communists had to operate under, and therefore raises the question of what is possible within the Indian political system.

If the most radical national party in India controlling a state government did not break the political control of the propertied rural classes, the possibilities for radical change at the state level within the Indian constitutional system appear to depend on new political coalitions. There is no evidence so far that universal franchise and political democracy will enable the dominance of the middle and upper rural classes over political and economic power to be broken. Even coalitions of lower- and middle-class elements which the Communists succeeded in organizing in West Bengal did not result in significant economic and political change in favour of the lowest classes.

The Communists in effect made a compromise with the landed rural elite, similar to that made by its Congress predecessors. According to Geoffrey Hawthorn, this political bargain that the largely urban and middle-class Congress Party made with landlords in the late 1930s and cemented at independence, in which, in return for the crucial rural vote, and notwithstanding its stated commitment to structural reforms to raise agricultural production and redress inequalities in the countryside, the party agreed not to disturb the rural status quo (including the level of agricultural taxation).[78]

was to be replicated by the Communists a half century later in West Bengal. This is not as unusual as it might seem, for few land reforms have been undertaken without the intervention of foreign conquering powers. This was seen in East Asia in the American post-War occupation of Japan and the Kuomintang (KMT) occupation of Taiwan. The exception to this rule has been under Communist regimes which in every other country made radical land reforms. Though Indian Communists lack the power of a national government, their failure even to raise agricultural taxes, and choosing to lower them instead, is indicative of their fundamental transformation by society. How a Communist party leadership came to such an impasse is a reflection of Indian politics and society as a whole. Like the Congress elite before it, the Communist elite who came from the same class/caste group, sought radical change through their own particular ideologies. But this process of political mass mobilization incorporated groups lower down and outside the ideological paradigms of the elite. Like the Indian state, which Sudipta Kaviraj characterizes as having 'to find its personnel, especially at lower levels, from groups who did not inhabit the modernist discourse', the Congress and Communists had to utilize human resources with which they were in fundamental disagreement. 'Since major government policies have their final point of implementation very low down in the bureaucracy, they are reinterpreted beyond recognition.'[79] From this it has been concluded by a number of observers that

there seems to be some incompatibility between the institutional logic of democratic forms and the logic of popular mobilization. The more one part of the democratic ideal is realized the more the other part is undermined. The paradox, to put it in the way in which T.N. Madan has done recently, is that if Indian politics becomes genuinely democratic in the sense of coming into line with what the majority of ordinary Indians would consider reasonable, it will become less democratic in the sense of conforming to the principles of a secular, democratic state acceptable to the early nationalist elite.[80]

However, no one has a good idea of what ordinary Indians really think, given the paucity of opinion polls, and since they are hardly likely to be of one mind, what a genuine popular democracy would look like in India is problematic. The reactions to job reservations, for instance, are elite reactions rather than the reactions of most of the ordinary Indians. In fact, political mobilization hardly touches the genuine poor, though many relatively privileged groups like to characterize themselves as of the people. Democratization beyond the current rural and urban elite manipulation may be more egalitarian, though it could also be more communal. The paradox is that no one knows which way this democratization process will lead. One observer in a retrospective analysis of the Soviet Union referred to social scientists in the West as producing 'nonsense on stilts'. 'It is hard to believe that the Moonies got it right when the CIA, Brookings, RAND, Harvard, Columbia and the rest got it wrong.'[81] Though the openness of Indian society probably precludes the grossest of errors, the predictive power of Indian studies is negligible. Few social scientists have much feel for what is going on at the grassroots in civil society, and without this understanding prediction is problematic. This lack of feel for civil society, and the paucity of accurate empirical village-level analysis makes for the wide range of interpretations on the decentralization experiment in India. Hence, it is hardly surprising that so much of the analysis gets it wrong.

Why this is so is not difficult to discern. I was confronted by this problem when invited to a conference in Calcutta on agrarian change in Bengal because, as the organizer put it, I was the only one who would be taking such a position on the Left Front. As my position was similar to that of many civil servants, and even party members who had been my informants, being the sole dissident seemed an unusual position to be in. Government officials and party members are bound by regulations not to deviate too far from government and party lines, but greater independence should be possible from academics. In fact, the latter tend to follow official thinking to such an extent that they are of little use even to the policy-makers and implementers themselves. The West Bengal Land Reforms Commissioner in giving me data from the Communists' traditional stronghold of Burdwan, which showed that more recorded sharecroppers were losing their land than were likely to be newly recorded, indicated that this sample survey had caused surprise in some government circles. The implication of the survey was that if even in this model district the land reform effort was coming to nothing, the true picture in the rest of the state was worse, and the whole land reform effort was a fraud. Hence, an analysis of who was losing their land might enable the people in charge of the programme to introduce remedial action. This was something the micro-level studies which were subsequently undertaken by academics might have pointed to.

Since then I have been looking in vain for any data on land loss which would indicate whether land reform is making any difference at all. What one finds are data collected at great expense to taxpayers but of no conceivable use to anyone except those trying to get tenure and promotion points. The studies of the villages have become so politically correct that even the people in charge of implementation cannot get the information they need to improve the programmes. No one bothers to inquire whether land reform beneficiaries retain their land or lose it to money-lenders and landlords. This is something scholars doing micro-level studies have an obligation to investigate if they are going to proclaim success in their villages. It seems unlikely that, given the nature of rural society, this question could have totally escaped their attention or not have occurred to them at all. Hence, silence on this issue is significant. If indeed beneficiaries do not retain their land, it throws the whole effort into disrepute, and to expose it could make repeat access to the villages more difficult. At some stage a conscious or unconscious decision was likely to have been made to exclude this question from study. This amounts to a cover-up of rural realities. It is like the Chinese Communist secret police clearing out the people and dressing their own agents up as peasants and street vendors so that when Mao's entourage went by they would feel that everything was normal.[82] Scholars project to their audiences the realities they want to expose, and often neglect to mention the evidence that counters their argument. The academic selection of topics and data can result in distortion just as surely as the Chinese secret police dressing up to mislead Mao about country life. What emerges is a sanitized version of reality, which can tell more about the mindset of authors than the society they are describing. One of the better-known examples is Clifford Geertz, who fails to mention the massacre of hundreds of thousands of Communists around him while he studied Indonesia, and in the process is alleged to have got what he did write about Java wrong, thus combining questionable morality with poor scholarship.[83] While this interpretation is still a matter of scholarly dispute, there is little doubt now that Margaret Mead was misled in her interpretation of Samoan society.[84] Unless fraudulent activities are studied, government will not be fully informed of the extent of the problems, and will be unlikely either to make its own studies or to rectify the problems. With this type of analysis everyone gets to believe their own propaganda, and academic writing becomes a more sophisticated type of group thinking.

Such lopsided reporting would be virtually impossible in other social science fields. In reality, land reform operates in a cycle of redistribution and land loss over time, while the academic studies portray it as a linear progression of cumulative redistribution to beneficiaries with no subsequent losses mentioned. When what in reality is a cyclical pattern is portrayed only in the context of gains, the result is deceptive. If governments released only positive statistics from the business cycle, or businesses reported only profits but never their losses they would quickly be discredited. However, since positive results are good for obtaining funding and there are limited career opportunities in examining failed programmes, there are reasons for omitting probing questions.

Though India represents an extreme form of village oppression, the role of rural areas in academic writing has a western heritage as well.

While the American intellectual tradition has often disparaged urbanism, to most intellectuals throughout history the city has been the scene of individual liberation rather than anonymous repression. Local politics have often been pictured as dominated by grasping oligarchies, not by the equality-minded citizens' councils of eco-radical rhetoric. Significantly, anti-rural intellectual sentiments were stronger in an era when small-town and village life was fresh in most writers' memories; rural romanticization, in contrast, has flowered in recent years among writers who have grown up in comfortable suburbs, completely lacking direct experience of the small-scale social milieu.[85]

The western infatuation with village life, whether in the ecological or town hall democratic variety, finds resonance in the Gandhian tradition, which also distorts Indian realities. Changing the intellectuals' view of rural life to a perception of how poor people live it is no small task, given the intellectual myths that surround it.

REFERENCES

1. David C. Korten, 'Community Organization and Rural Development: A Learning Process Approach', *Public Administration Review*, Vol. 40, No. 5, September/October 1980, p. 480; Mukul Sanwal, 'The Implementation of Decentralization: A Case Study of District Planning in Agra District, Uttar Pradesh, India', *Public Administration and Development*, Vol. 7, No. 4, 1987, p. 394.
2. Bertrand Schneider, *The Barefoot Revolution: A Report to the Club of Rome* (London: Intermediate Technology Publications, 1988).
3. Richard Slater and John Watson, 'Democratic Decentralization or Local Government Reform in Karnataka', *Public Administration and Development*, Vol. 9, No. 2, April–May 1989.
4. *Report of the Committee on Panchayati Raj Institutions* (Delhi: Government of India, Ministry of Agriculture and Irrigation, Department of Rural Development, August 1978).
5. Marcus Franda, *India's Rural Development* (Bloomington: Indiana University Press, 1979), pp. 142–43.
6. Anjali Ghosh, *Peaceful Transition in Power: A Study of Marxist Political Strategies in West Bengal 1967–1977* (Calcutta: Firma KLM, 1981), p. C-40.
7. West Bengal, Directorate of Panchayats, *Panchayat in West Bengal* (Calcutta: Directorate of Panchayats, 1981), p. 14.
8. M. Shivian, K.B. Srivastava and A.C. Jena, *Panchayati Raj Election in West Bengal, 1978: A Study in Institution Building for Rural Development* (Hyderabad: National Institute of Rural Development, 1980), p. 134.
9. Communist Party of India (Marxist), *Reports and Resolution on Organization*, Salkia Plenum, 27–31 December 1978 (Delhi: Communist Party of India [Marxist], 1979), pp. 12, 49.

10. Shivian et al., *Panchayati Raj Election* (n. 8 above), p. 51; Bhabani Sen Gupta, *CPI-M: Promises, Prospects, Problems* (Delhi: Young Asia Publications, 1979), p. 137.

11. Communist Party of India (Marxist), West Bengal State Conference, 27 December 1981–1 January 1982, *Rajnaitik-Sangathanik Report* ('Political-Organizational Report') (Calcutta: West Bengal State Committee, Communist Party of India [Marxist], March 1982), p. 91; Shivian et al., *Panchayati Raj Election* (n. 8 above), p. 51.

12. Shivian et al., *Panchayati Raj Election* (n. 8 above), p. 136.

13. Ibid., p. 51.

14. Ibid., pp. 116–17.

15. Ibid., p. 127.

16. *The Working of Panchayat System in West Bengal* (Calcutta: Department of Panchayats and Community Development, March 1980), pp. 42–43.

17. Ajit Kumar Ghose, 'Agrarian Reform in West Bengal', World Employment Program Research Working Paper (Geneva: International Labour Organization, May 1980), p. 8.

18. *The Working of Panchayat System in West Bengal* (n. 8 above), pp. 42–43.

19. Government of India, Registrar General and Census Commissioner, *Census of India, 1981, Provisional Population Totals: Workers and Non-Workers*, Series 1, Paper 3 (Delhi: Government of India Press, 1981), p. 177.

20. Government of West Bengal, *Economic Review 1980–81* (Alipore: West Bengal Government Press, 1981), p. 21.

21. P. Roy Choudhury, 'Land Reforms: Promises and Fulfilment', *Economic and Political Weekly*, Vol. XV, No. 52, 27 December 1980, p. 2173.

22. Ibid.

23. Ibid.

24. Atul Kohli, 'Parliamentary Communism and Agrarian Reform', *Asian Survey*, Vol. XXIII, No. 7, July 1983, p. 794.

25. Tares Maitra, *Expansion of Employment Through Local Resource Mobilization*, (Bangkok: Asian Employment Program, International Labour Organization, 1982), p. 9.

26. Marvin Davis, *Rank and Rivalry*, (Cambridge: Cambridge University Press, 1983), pp. 184–85; Swasti Mitter, *Peasant Movements in West Bengal*, (Cambridge: Department of Land Economy, 1977), p. 55.

27. Rajatasubhra Mukhopadhyay, 'Resource Distribution and Power Structure: A Case Study of a West Bengal Village', *The Eastern Anthropologist*, Vol. 35, No. 1, January–March 1982, p. 70.

28. Davis, *Rank and Rivalry* (n. 26 above), p. 185.

29. Government of West Bengal, Legislative Department, *The West Bengal Panchayat Act, 1973* as modified up to November 1980 (Alipore: West Bengal Government Press, 1980), p. 96, Section 210.

30. T.M. Vinod Kumar and Jatin De, *Basic Needs and the Provision of Government Services: An Areas Study of Ranaghat Block in West Bengal* (Geneva: International Labour Organization, World Employment Program Working Paper, February 1980), p. 21.

31. B.C. Mukherji, 'The Impact of Panchayats on Socio-Economic Development of Rural Bengal', in *Panchayats in West Bengal from 1978–79 to 1980–81: A*

Review (Calcutta: Department of Panchayats and Community Development, Government of West Bengal, January 1982), p. 13.

32. Sumanta Sen, 'Grassroots Power', *India Today*, 15 June 1983, p. 50.

33. *Panchayats in West Bengal from 1978–79 to 1980–81: A Review* (Calcutta: Department of Panchayats and Community Development, Government of West Bengal, January 1982), p. 53.

34. West Bengal, Directorate of Panchayats, *Panchayats in West Bengal* (Calcutta: Director of Panchayats, 1981), p. 53.

35. Roy Choudhury, 'Land Reforms' (n. 21 above), p. 2173.

36. Government of India, Programme Evaluation Organization, Planning Commission, *Evaluation of Food for Work Programme: Final Report* (Delhi: Government of India Press, 1981), pp. 2, 56.

37. Ibid., pp. 29, 41, 77, 69, 65.

38. Ibid., p. 16.

39. Ibid., p. 16.

40. Ibid., p. 22.

41. Institute for Financial Management and Research, *An Economic Assessment of Poverty Eradication and Rural Unemployment Alleviation Programmes and their Prospects* (Madras: Institute for Financial Management and Research, April 1984), Part III, p. 463.

42. Ibid., pp. 447, 444, 455–56.

43. Ibid., Part I, p. 150.

44. K. Sundaram and Suresh D. Tendulkar, *Integrated Rural Development Programme in India* (Kuala Lumpur: The Asian and Pacific Development Centre, May 1984), p. 27.

45. Institute for Financial Management and Research, *Economic Assessment* (n. 41 above), p. 151.

46. Ibid.

47. Ibid., p. 154.

48. K. Sundaram and Suresh D. Tendulkar, *Integrated Rural Development* (n. 44 above), p. 49; Institute for Financial Management and Research, *Economic Assessment* (n. 41 above), Part I, p. 158.

49. Ibid., p. 153.

50. Ibid., p. 153.

51. Ibid., p. 154.

52. Ibid., pp. 154–56.

53. Ibid., p. 160.

54. Government of West Bengal, Department of Panchayats and Community Development, *The Working of Panchayat System in West Bengal, A Review of Main Events and Activities* (Calcutta: Department of Panchayats and Community Development, March 1980), p. 37.

55. Roy Choudhury, 'Land Reforms' (n. 21 above), p. 2173.

56. Ranjit Kumar Gupta, *Agrarian West Bengal: Three Field Studies* (Calcutta: Institute of Social Research and Applied Anthropology, August 1977), p. 45.

57. West Bengal, Board of Revenue, *Dynamics of the Rural Situation in West Bengal* (Calcutta: West Bengal Government Press, 1979), p. 20.

58. Ibid., p. 17.

59. Jyoti Basu, 'Tin Bachar Bamfront Sarkar Parichalanar Aviggyata Samparke Kichhu Baktyavba' ('Something to Say Regarding the Experience of Running the Left Front Government for the last Three Years'), *Deshhitaishee*, Annual Puja Issue 1980, pp. 19, 23.

60. Kalipada Basu, *West Bengal Economy: Past, Present, and Future* (Calcutta: Firma KLM, 1989), p. 249.

61. Neil Webster, 'Panchayati Raj in West Bengal: Popular Participation for the People or the Party?', *Development and Change*, Vol. 23, No. 4, 1992, pp. 129–63.

62. Suraj Bandhopadhyay and Donald von Eschen, 'The Impact of Politics on Rural Production and Distribution: A Comparative Study of Rural Policies and the Implementation Under Congress and Left Front Governments in West Bengal, India', Paper delivered at the annual meetings of the Association for Asian Studies (26 March 1988); Kristan Westergaard, *People's Participation, Local Government and Rural Development: The Case of West Bengal, India* (Copenhagen: Centre for Development Research, 1986).

63. Marguerite S. Robinson, *Local Politics: The Law of the Fishes* (Delhi: Oxford University Press, 1988), p. 272.

64. Miriam Sharma, *The Politics of Inequality: Competition and Control in an Indian Village* (University of Hawaii Press, 1978), p. 162; Gilbert Etienne, *India's Changing Rural Scene: 1963–1979*, (Delhi: Oxford University Press, 1982).

65. John Echeverri-Gent, 'Public Participation and Poverty Alleviation: The Experience of Reform Communists in India's West Bengal', *World Development*, Vol. 20, No. 10, October 1992, p. 1414.

66. Ibid., p. 1411.

67. G.K. Lieten, 'Panchayat Leaders in a West Bengal District', *Economic and Political Weekly*, Vol. XXIII, No. 40, 1 October 1988, pp. 2069–73; 'Caste, Gender and Class in Panchayats: Case of Barddhaman, West Bengal', *Economic and Political Weekly*, Vol. XXVII, No. 29, 18 July 1992, pp. 1567–74.

68. Lieten, 'Panchayat Leaders in a West Bengal District' (n. 67 above), p. 2069.

69. Basu, *West Bengal Economy* (n. 60 above), p. 248.

70. Neil Webster, *Panchayati Raj and the Decentralization of Development Planning in West Bengal* (Copenhagen: Centre for Development Research, December 1990), pp. 49–50, 164–65, 167.

71. Ibid., p. 147.

72. Echeverri-Gent, 'Public Participation and Poverty Alleviation' (n. 65 above).

73. Sen Gupta, *CPI-M: Promises, Prospects, Problems* (n. 10 above), pp. 118–39.

74. Bhabani Sen Gupta, 'Time to Take Stock', *India Today*, 31 December 1982, p. 115.

75. Atul Kohli, 'Parliamentary Communism and Agrarian Reform', *Asian Survey*, Vol. 33, No. 7, July 1983, p. 806.

76. Ibid., p. 805.

77. S.K., 'Diminishing Returns from Blaming Centre', *Economic and Political Weekly*, Vol. XX, No. 15, 13 April 1985, p. 633.

78. Geoffrey Hawthorn, '"Waiting for a Text?": Comparing Third World Politics', in James Manor (ed.), *Rethinking Third World Politics* (Harlow, Essex: Longman, 1991), p. 35.

79. Sudipta Kaviraj, 'On State, Society and Discourse in India', in James Manor (ed.) *Rethinking Third World Politics* (Harlow, Essex: Longman, 1991), p. 91.
80. Ibid., p. 93.
81. Peter Rutland, 'Sovietology: Notes for a Post-Mortem', *The National Interest*, No. 31, Spring 1993, p. 111.
82. Li Zhisui, *The Private Life of Chairman Mao: The Memoirs of Mao's Personal Physician* (New: York: Random House, 1994), p. 129.
83. C.W. Watson, 'Autobiography, Anthropology and the Experience of Indonesia', in Judith Okely and Helen Callaway (eds), *Anthropology and Autobiography* (London: Routledge, 1992), pp. 134–35.
84. Derek Freeman, 'Fooled in Paradise', *The Times Higher Education Supplement*, 27 December 1996, p. 19.
85. Martin W. Lewis, *Green Delusions* (Durham: Duke University Press, 1992), p. 91.

CHAPTER 5

Managing Ethnicity

Governments in South Asia have been following divergent strategies for dealing with ethnic movements, but all states in varying degrees fail to satisfy minority groups. A comparative analysis of the ethnic policies of governments reveals that the problems have remained for the most part unresolved. If the democratization process currently under way in the subcontinent is to be institutionalized an effective ethnic accommodation policy is imperative.

Ethnicity, like nationalism, seems to defy scientific rationality, yet most of humanity believes in it. Some people are more committed to it than others, but few can deny some emotional attachment to one of these categories or both. Nations need not have an ethnic identity and ethnic identities may not become politicized to the point of demanding nationhood. Most states survive with numerous significant ethnic groups, yet such nations usually face demands from ethnic groups that remain unfulfilled. How a state manages ethnicity depends on its perception of these ethnic demands. At root this depends on whether a particular ethnic identity is considered legitimate in its own right, or a manipulation by interested parties.

The nature of ethnicity has been a controversial issue in academic literature. Ethnic identity varies and even changes from one historical period to another, as ethnicities are transformed by different issues and ideologies. Ethnicity exists in some form whether or not it is politicized, and in this sense it is an 'objective' identification. When these marks of identification are utilized in a political movement ethnic boundaries are determined and an ideology formulated. Language identities can be changed by the state, given sufficient time and power, while religious conversion is more difficult to implement and racial identification impossible to alter. Though most people have an ethnic identity, the objective criteria may be of no importance politically. However, other identifications may have significance even if this is not recognized by its members. Class exploitation can be objective regardless of the perceptions of the participants, while ethnicity has no social significance until it is recognized as significant by participants.[1]

Creating Ethnicity

The process of recognizing a shared identity is part of the nation-building process. It may have taken place over centuries, as in Europe, or during a few years of anti-colonial struggle. In the Third World it is in some way linked to the colonial experience, with the ethnic groups as resisters or collaborators of the colonial regime. In South Asia, which experienced a long colonial intrusion, the British government has often been seen as the initiator and promoter of ethnicity.

The extent to which the colonial power was the creator or merely the manipulator of earlier divisions varies from case to case. It has been argued that even in the nineteenth century Hindus and Muslims 'were separate religious communities predisposed towards, if not necessarily pre-ordained as, separate national groups'.[2] While one view attributes greater significance to religious differences, others see the process as more open to manipulation. That the creation of Pakistan only became probable shortly before independence supports the position that partition was not inevitable, while the persistence of the two communities through the centuries points to the futility of attempting assimilation. 'The Whig interpretation of history—of judging the past from hindsight and concluding that anti-Congress feeling had made Muslims a nation by 1939' in one view is considered erroneous, thereby leaving the creation of Pakistan to a series of historical accidents.[3] The extent to which British concessions of such things as separate Muslim electorates was a means of fostering ethnicity or simply appealing to existing valued collaborators is a matter of ongoing debate.[4] These concessions can be seen as inadvertently having led to the creation of Pakistan, or simply as a reaction to contemporary exigencies with no historical inevitability.

If ethnicity will inevitably become politicized, a state that fails to promote or at least tolerate its expression loses its legitimacy to govern, making secession morally justifiable. The failure of states to tolerate this right has repeatedly led to civil wars, which before the break up of the Soviet bloc tended to be won by the central government. The two most prevalent identifications are religion and language, which are sometimes adhered to by the same group, but usually the overlaps are far from perfect. Pakistan was created as a religiously defined state, but it broke up over linguistically defined ethnicity, which continues to threaten the present truncated state. A theocracy, once created, seems to have difficulty maintaining itself if it rules a multiethnic society. Common religion alone is insufficient to hold a nation together if there are other ethnically relevant political differences. Afghanistan and Pakistan are examples of states where a common religion has never resulted in national reconciliation. At the same time, dominant religious majorities are rarely tolerant of other religious practices, as in the case of Pakistan and Sri Lanka. Religion as a nation-building tool seems to be of dubious value after the religious community has taken state office, however effective it may have been in the struggle to seize power.

Those who adhere to a class analysis tend to regard ethnicity as being designed by ethnic elites to persuade gullible people into following them. That achieving state power benefits leaders more than followers is seen as part of the hollowness of such ethnic claims. However, those leaders who believed in a class analysis behaved no better than ethnic rivals when they took state power. The 'iron law of oligarchy' showed no ideological barrier when it came to amassing the privileges of office.[5] The reversion of the Soviet bloc to ethnicity indicates the weakness of even prolonged national integration efforts in the face of historical ethnic identities. The traditional western scholarly perception that modernity would bring secularization has ceased to exist, but the alternative paradigms lack a consensus.[6] The detailed empirical work needed to lay the groundwork for generalizable paradigms is either insufficient, or too controversial to be taken as definitive. The data are particularly weak when it comes to grassroots understanding of ethnic identity among followers who are often illiterate and inaccessible to scholars. The work focuses on the leadership, whose human rights abuses and personal acquisitions tend to discredit the movement.[7] However, these leaders could not inspire a following without having some identity or issue in common with their constituency. Though it may appear bogus to outsiders, these identities need to be understood for the popular support they provide. These beliefs and the leaders who promote them are easiest to criticize when they are opposing one's own values or identity. Few politicians, however, can claim not to have used some sort of ethnic or national identification to create a following in whatever society they are from.

South Asia is a rich field for the study of ethnic movements. Many movements have risen and subsided, or in some cases continued on newly found issues. One such transformation was that of the non-Brahmin movement of Madras Presidency during the colonial period which, on achieving dominance, was eventually transformed into a linguistic movement against the Hindi north.[8]

In DMK Tamil politics, it would seem that the way to succeed is to adopt rhetorical positions which are untenable in the light of all the available evidence, abandon them as soon as they have done their job and provided the means of achieving office; adopt new positions which are precisely the reverse of the old ones, and use power to reduce economic growth and general levels of development. If this is done blatantly and rapidly enough, it brings massive popularity and what amounts to a virtual hegemony over the state-level political process and discourse.[9]

This cynical view of ethnic politics could arguably be relevant with variations for any movement that takes state power. The Tamil case, however, is particularly interesting for the transformations in ideological justification and symbols that have occurred in its history. In this respect the central governments first of the British and then of the Congress party were managers of the situation rather than instigators. 'The British were able to direct the anti-modern protests of the Dravidian ideology away from themselves and on to the Indian National Congress', thus serving as an obstacle to the independence struggle.[10] This movement was eventually accommodated by the Congress party through the creation of a linguistically based Tamil Nadu and the abandonment of any attempt to impose Hindi on the state. This did not provide much, however, for the lower caste/classes, who were excluded as beneficiaries.[11]

While ethnic movements promoting linguistic issues can be accommodated within the political system, class-oriented movements can be more difficult to co-opt. In India the Communist movement was either successfully co-opted or repressed and is no longer a threat. For the most part it became an effective support for the existing system. This movement was led by and represented relatively privileged elements in society who could also be accommodated with trade union concessions and a share of government power at the state level. In other South Asian nations similar movements have frequently been effectively suppressed by their governments. The growth of the Communist movement in Nepal indicates that the Indian experience has possibilities of replication elsewhere in the subcontinent.

Class and religion combine in the most unambiguous way in the Untouchable emancipation movement. The few Untouchable leaders who have acquired some education and attempted to lead their castes are sometimes seen by social scientists as manipulative in their resorting to a caste identity to mobilize followers. Even if class issues are a component of their demands, their movements are perceived as being motivated for career advancement through the mobilization of a caste following.[12] These tendencies are probably inherent in any political movement that achieves some measure of success. For the Scheduled Castes, however, benefits can accrue only through access to the state, since the resources of the community are insignificant. The community does not have an indigenous business class to fund the movement, as is the case with most ethnic groups. The movement received support indirectly from Christian missionaries and the colonial state. The more co-optive role of the post-colonial state and the decline in foreign missionary endeavour had a detrimental effect on the movement. However, the Untouchable electorate has been a useful vote bloc, open to manipulation by outside groups who have sought their support. The spoils in this bargaining process—in competition with other ethnic groups—is state largesse. In India the system is in fact designed to be open to this competition. In neighbouring nations the state has been less flexible in adjusting its resources to subordinate groups, and has rather effectively been used to enhance dominant interests.

The critical role in the creation of ethnic movements is seen in the literature as played by ethnic elites. Sometimes they are a business elite, but more often they are the intellectuals and professionals of the ethnic group's middle class. As such they are seen as a modernizing influence. However, in specific cases, movements can be led by religious fundamentalists and clerics who are reacting to the traumas of modernization. Either way the elites act as mediators between their ethnic followers and the state. Though seen as manipulative, this group is usually highly committed to its identity and values. The subordinate ethnic elite may have found its attempts to join the dominant national elite frustrated and therefore sees ethnic mobilization as a way of getting its own and its group's fair share of state entitlements. It may in an extreme case opt out and demand secession.

If the ethnic elites are unable to integrate with the dominant groups of their class they may seek support in their own community. Among the educated Untouchables 'the modernists, in their alienated isolation, need the comfort and identity of their cultural heritage.... This has laid the basis for recent efforts to reassert the cultural identity of Untouchables'.[13] This forging of links between the politically aware activists thrown up by ethnic elites and the community as a whole is critical. The activist 'whole timers' can turn to extremism if their demands are not accommodated, but usually the state will try to integrate their elites, if not the activists themselves, through state patronage. The reassertion of cultural identity can breed parochialism even in western-educated elites, but this serves to reduce the distance between them and their ethnic followers. The Untouchable leader Ambedkar could afford to adopt western habits because he was sure of his popular base, whereas Gandhi used traditional symbolism to develop his. Significantly, in popular Untouchable idolatry Ambedkar continues to be portrayed in a business suit, while Gandhi appears in the traditional Indian attire. Both ethnic leaders adopted dramatically different symbolisms, yet appealed to ordinary people from very different backgrounds. The very use of traditional dress for someone not of that class could be interpreted as a sign of political calculation and ethnic affirmation. The adoption of western dress by an Untouchable was an affirmation of modernity and community upliftment and a rejection of traditional values. Clearly, leaders organize ethnic followings in different ways. The symbolic interaction with its followers reveals a movement's orientation. In the case of Gandhi it was in part an affirmation of traditional identities, for Ambedkar a socio-economic upliftment and rejection of these values.

Which values, movements and ideas are likely to dominate the political arena and emerge as winners in the course of history is determined by many variables, almost all of which are beyond the control of individual leaders. Even if a movement has greater power and influence than its leaders, it is constrained by its financial resources, class position, geographic concentration and ethnic diaspora. Ethnic leaders must seek out these valuable resources and contacts, and the intellectual and financial contributors will in part determine the policy options available to the movement.

Paralleling the mobilization of tangible resources (money, volunteers, media outlets) is the formulation of ideologies. Creating new ideologies being a formidable and long-term enterprise, usually old values and traditions are resurrected, albeit in the contemporary cultural context. The ideologies cover the full range of political beliefs from fascist to communist. Usually, rival parties of a wide range of ideologies compete for ethnic groups, utilizing different symbols and versions of group history. Some explicitly appeal to one facet of ethnic identity, while others choose some foreign model or identity which has been idealized and made appropriate for transplanting on their soil. The interaction of ideologies with ethnic values can produce some unusual adaptations to local conditions. Many of the world ideologies and religions have an egalitarian streak that is hard to find in their local practices.

Perhaps the most prevalent acculturation in South Asia has been the adaptation of religion to the caste system, with Islam, Sikhism and Sinhalese Buddhism adopting aspects of the Hindu caste system. This is indicative of how ethnic movements acquire values to fit existing conditions. In the case of political ideologies, this is particularly observable in the adaptation of communism to national values and interests. Even within nations such as India, different regions can acquire an ideology in different ways through the establishment of political bases among varied ethnic groups. Communism in Kerala and West Bengal though led by the same Communist party has developed from different castes.

While in Kerala it developed in part out of lower-caste movements, in West Bengal it developed from the dissatisfaction of the traditional tricaste elite, whose class orientation and values it has never transcended. Thus communism in West Bengal has become the ideology of an elite suffering from perceived relative deprivation, compared both to other ethnic groups and to their own past status. The Communist ideology becomes less important than the ethnic identity of a small group purporting to represent the people. The ideology justifies their right to rule on behalf of people who have no leadership role in the process.[14]

All ethnic parties when they take power are expected to provide tangible benefits, and will be judged by their followers accordingly. The seizure of state power offers the opportunity for major redistribution in ways that were non-existent before. However, the state cannot help everyone equally, and a let-down soon follows. Before the seizure of power, when the state is not accessible to the ethnic movement, the government may actively seek to emasculate the movement in various co-optive or repressive ways, or even promote rivals to undermine it. Though the state can rarely create an ethnic group, it has powerful tools to politicize symbolic identities in new and often unforeseen ways. In India, the unforeseen consequences of state manipulation of ethnicity can be found in the initial Congress support of the Sikh religious extremists as a way of undermining the more moderate Akali Dal, which was the main rival to Congress in the state.[15] This support may have strengthened the extremists against the moderate constitutionalist opponents of Congress. The Indian government was even more directly involved in the arming of the Tamil Tigers in Sri Lanka, giving the Tamils the capacity to launch a civil war on a scale not otherwise conceivable. The historical irony is that the Congress government's manipulations of ethnicity directly contributed to the assassinations of those partly responsible for promoting extremist ethnicity, Indira Gandhi and Rajiv Gandhi. On the Pakistani side, the arming of the more fundamentalist Islamic Afghan guerrillas by General Zia gave them a strength they could not have otherwise had. These attempts at destabilization of neighbouring governments can have unpredictable and even fatal results for those who promote extremist ethnicity to further party and national interests.

Though India is currently facing secessionist threats, it must be recognized that it also achieved considerable progress in accommodating autonomist demands. The creation of linguistic states in the 1950s and occasionally thereafter has enabled an accommodation of interests for ethnic elites through redistribution of largesse and not inconsiderable state powers. Even revolutionary parties such as the Communists have been accommodated and co-opted with the concession of allowing them to remain in power at the state level. At the same time, the centre has maintained the right to intervene and dismiss state governments, and retained a large measure of control on financial and economic development disbursements.

While minorities exist in each state, they retain influence in their home state governments as well as in some local electoral districts. The most threatened minority are the Muslims but other groups have also been killed in communal violence. Despite this violence, the warnings of systemic disintegration have been continually disproved. Though ethnic interests have to a certain extent been conceded through the creation of ethnic or linguistic states, the same cannot be said for other human rights demands. Segregation has no more than formally ended for Untouchables, while Muslims and Backward Castes have never attained their proportional share of government posts. Land reform has remained a dead letter since the abolition of zamindari. Devolution of power to the state governments makes land reform even less likely, as landed interests seem better able to exert their influence at the state level.[16] The benefits from ethnic concessions have largely been garnered by elites and not brought major improvements for the lower classes. Conceding ethnic demands led to disillusionment once state power was achieved, but not to have granted them might have exacerbated conflict. These demands could only be viable when there was an ethnic-majority area that could be given statehood. The Untouchables, Muslims and tribals, whose populations generally lack a majority location, cannot hope to attain statehood, and thus they remain relatively underrepresented minorities without access to state power similar to that of the linguistic ethnic majorities. That these groups may also be part of the same linguistic majority does not negate their separate rights as non-linguistic minorities. The concession of linguistic ethnic rights by the centre, but not equal rights to other categories must be seen as somewhat arbitrary, even if it has practical political reasons behind it. The centre as the final arbiter of rights, should not negate the rights of non-linguistic groups. How these other minorities are able to get their rights represented will determine in large part the extent of democratization in South Asia.

The situation in Pakistan is illustrative of a failure to manage ethnicity through the accommodation of a linguistic redivision of states. Forcible secession enabled the creation of Bangladesh, but since then a redistribution of provincial boundaries to accommodate linguistic demands, though proposed, has never been adopted.[17] Pakistan has an ongoing nationality problem which has never been accommodated, given the control of the Punjabi community and its reluctance to concede its predominance in the government and armed forces. Though 55 per cent of the population, the Punjabi community constitutes 80 per cent of the army. The next largest, the Sindhi population, of 21 per cent, had only 1.56 per cent of government and semi-government personnel prior to Z.A. Bhutto's prime ministership.[18] The dominant military and governmental position of the Punjabis makes a major concession unlikely; hence the continued alienation of peripheral ethnic groups together constituting a near majority of the population. This parity makes domestic ethnic harmony difficult to achieve alongside economic and political ethnic disparities. By contrast the most serious dissent in India comes from Sikhs who constitute only 2 per cent of the population, and cannot therefore be considered a domestic threat of equal significance.

Every society has groups which have greater access to or even dominant control over the state. These groups in India have been described as being of the business and landlord classes, with some dispute over whether the bureaucratic elite should also be included in the dominant classes.[19] Because these groups belong to a number of ethnic groups, opposition to their dominance has never been able to coalesce against their privileged positions. Had their control been identified with one ethnic group, as with the Punjabis in Pakistan, such dominance would have been subject to more serious challenge. The influence of these groups in civil society and the state being less visible, the continued influence does not become a target for serious challenge to the existing system. When at least a partial challenge to their position in the state sector was brought by the backward class movement, the Indian government was able to concede to the demand, thereby undermining the movement. Similar challenges in Pakistan have been met with more coercion, which makes democratization and equalization of ethnic opportunity difficult to achieve. Dissatisfied minorities need resources and numbers to make their protests felt. In Sri Lanka the Tamils were a relatively small minority (18 per cent) but their former socio-economic influence and proximity to their own Tamil state in India made them a formidable challenge to the Sri Lankan state. Sri Lanka with its own limited resources relative to those of its Indian neighbour was vulnerable to a secessionist movement, just as Pakistan was in its eastern wing. When the secessionist state of Bangladesh was created, it in turn treated its own minorities badly, but they lacked the numbers and resources to mount an effective challenge to the state, or to influence it constitutionally. In this sense the nearer to parity between the dominant majority and subordinate minority, the greater the threat of violence and secession. If there is no accommodation, democratization is unlikely to become institutionalized, in a way similar to that in India.

State Ethnic Mediation

The role of the state in the creation and maintenance of ethnicity has been widely recognized.[20] The process of modernization may itself enable and foster ethnicity. Easy communications beyond the village 'little tradition' creates common wider identities. The creation of ethnically identified educated elites provides leadership both culturally and in bargaining for state recognition.[21] Every South Asian, or for that matter every Third World ethnic group, has in some way gone through this process, though the specific symbols of identity and historical development differ. What varies significantly, however, is the attitude of the state to ethnic politicization. The state may be taken over by an emerging ethnic group, or accommodate the group within its patronage network, or simply suppress it altogether. South Asian states have achieved or attempted all these strategies. Of all the South Asian states, India has been the most accommodative. Given the persistence of democracy, this is perhaps hardly surprising. Yet why did the other states of South Asia which inherited democratic institutions with decolonization not continue to be democratic, but became instead de facto dictatorships? There are obviously many factors, some unique to each case, but it is striking that India survived as a democracy where all its neighbours, and almost all developing countries, failed to maintain the democratic institutions bequeathed them by the colonial powers.

Given the problems of India, of poverty, underdevelopment, caste, language, religion, its survival as a democracy seems extraordinary, when contrasted with the failures of its neighbours. Yet the very diversity of these problems, and their failure to coalesce in a united opposition movement, prevented a seizure of national state power. Disunited, each ethnic group lacked the numbers to seize more for itself either militarily or through the ballot box. Yet these groups were not excluded from a share of state largesse, which was what many of their minimalist demands were about. If one were to point to a ruling coterie it might be the Kashmir Brahmins under the Nehru 'dynasty', but aside from obtaining a few key jobs, their numbers were insufficient to form a ruling class. The Brahmins as a whole were much more influential but linguistically divided and not organized in a single political party. They operated on personal and family contacts without pressing their own political claims. Frequently, they were outnumbered in the elite by other high castes, and electorally middle castes were usually more numerous. As for a religious identity, until the rise of the BJP no group could claim to represent the Hindu 'nation'. Even if the Hindu north could be united, the cultural and linguistic divide with the south provides a barrier to the Hindu 'majority' takeover by a Hindu movement or party.

The heterogeneity of Indian politicized ethnicity is in sharp contrast to that of its neighbours, where one ethnic group manages to dominate the state and invariably discriminate against other ethnicities. In Pakistan the Punjabis, though a minority, dominated the Bengali majority until the creation of Bangladesh. Thereafter, they represented 55 per cent of Pakistan's population, which gave them the numbers to maintain their traditional dominance. In Sri Lanka the Sinhalese, comprising a 74 per cent majority, have used their control of the state for positive discrimination against the 18 per cent Tamil minority. Significantly, the maintenance of electoral politics in both states is now possible due to the dominant group being the ethnic majority, as was not the case for Pakistan prior to the secession of Bangladesh. 'The ethnic centrality of the Punjabis has continued but the multiplicity of other groups in the centralised ethnic system has provided the dominant group a relatively greater clout and lesser vulnerability.'[22] Nevertheless, the bare majority Punjabi population makes Pakistani politics inherently unstable.

If South Asia were treated as a regional nation, then no ethnic group would be able to claim dominance, given the internal divisions of Hinduism, and partition would be a suboptimal solution for most ethnic groups. Certainly, the Muslims would have been more influential in a united India; however, that very influence might have exacerbated rather than reduced communal tensions, and politicized a Hindu identity. Thus it is not clear what effect partition has had on communal relations in the subcontinent. This raises the fundamental question of how far South Asia should be partitioned. To what extent secession is beneficial to collective and individual expression and well-being and, short of secession, how much ethnic or state autonomy should be provided to subnational groups is difficult to determine. Every partition or secession creates new minorities within the new boundaries which tends to replicate the ethnic problems rather than resolve them. Some minorities, such as Untouchables, are too dispersed to have their own territory, so a geographical partition is unfeasible. The solution lies only in the majority protection of minorities' rights. Given the strength of ethnicity in South Asia, this is extremely difficult to achieve.

The solution to problems of ethnicity as advocated by minority groups and academic sympathizers has been decentralization of power. In India the process of centralization, carried out particularly by Indira Gandhi, came to be associated with the creation of personalized rule, which was seen as detrimental to long-term national unity.[23] The dynastic aspects of this process appear to be at an end; however, the power distribution between the central and state governments is bound to be subject to on-going dispute and negotiation.

The difficulty with conceding ethnic demands is that there is no end to the problems that can arise from concessions, which may provide only temporary satisfaction to ethnic minorities. Furthermore, if an ethnic group has a territorial claim, new minority groups will invariably be created in that territory should the concessions be granted. The new majority may be just as parochial as the old one, so the division of existing states only results in suboptimal economic units with parallel bureaucracies. Thus, state subdivision may exacerbate problems. The present states of Assam and Punjab are essentially states created on linguistic lines. The new states contained minorities almost as large as, or even possibly larger—depending on how the population is categorized—than the majority community which felt threatened by these potentially dominant minorities.[24] The campaign demands of Sikhs and Assamese for greater control of their own destiny were a clear violation of the civil rights of their own state minorities, who soon became subject to terrorism and enforced flight as refugees within their own country. Concessions made before the insurgencies might have undercut militant demands, but it is far from certain that decentralization would have prevented ethnic extremism.

The best interests of minorities would therefore appear to lie in large ethnically diversified societies with strong central governments that cannot be controlled by any one ethnic group, because all lack the numbers and resources to dominate. India essentially still fulfils these criteria, despite partition and the rise of Hindu nationalism, and this has facilitated the continuance of its democratic institutions. Partition, however, created in Pakistan the demographic and military conditions favourable to Punjabi dominance, which continues to hamper its democratization. States controlled by identifiable ethnic groups have to make concessions to ensure fair treatment of other groups in order that they maintain legitimacy. Dominant ethnic groups rarely do this, and the consequences for South Asia have been civil wars with considerable loss of life and retarded economic development.

REFERENCES

1. Achin Vanaik, 'A Liberal–Pluralist Paradigm', *Economic and Political Weekly*, Vol. XXVII, No. 3, 18 January 1992, p. 95.
2. Paul R. Brass, *Ethnicity and Nationalism: Theory and Comparison* (New Delhi: Sage Publications, 1991), p. 42.
3. Anita Inder Singh, *The Origins of the Partition of India: 1936–1947* (Delhi: Oxford University Press, 1987), p. 44.
4. David Page, *Prelude to Partition: The Indian Muslims and the Imperial System of Control: 1920–1932* (Delhi: Oxford University Press, 1982), pp. 12–13.

5. Robert Michels, *Political Parties* (New York: Collier Books, 1962).
6. Saul Newman, 'Does Modernization Breed Ethnic Political Conflict?', *World Politics*, Vol. 43, No. 3, April 1991, p. 454.
7. Jyotirindra Das Gupta, 'Ethnicity, Democracy, and Development in India: Assam in a General Perspective', in Atul Kohli (ed.), *India's Democracy* (Princeton: Princeton University Press, 1988), p. 146.
8. D.A. Washbrook, 'Caste, Class and Dominance in Modern Tamil Nadu', in Francine R. Frankel and M.S.A. Rao (eds), *Dominance and State Power in Modern India: The Decline of a Social Order: Vol. 1* (Delhi: Oxford University Press, 1989), p. 230.
9. Ibid., p. 216.
10. Ibid., p. 249.
11. Ibid., pp. 260, 226–27.
12. Sekhar Bandyopadhyay, *Caste, Politics and the Raj* (Delhi: K.P. Bagchi & Co., 1990).
13. Mark Juergensmeyer, *Religion as Social Vision: The Movement Against Untouchability in 20th Century Punjab* (Berkeley: University of California Press, 1982), p. 244.
14. Atul Kohli, 'From Elite Activism to Democratic Consolidation: The Rise of Reform Communism in West Bengal', in Francine R. Frankel and M.S.A. Rao (eds), *Dominance and State Power in Modern India: Decline of a Social Order, Vol II* (Delhi: Oxford University Press, 1990), pp. 374–75.
15. Brass, *Ethnicity and Nationalism* (n. 2 above).
16. James Manor, 'How and Why Liberal and Representative Politics Emerged in India', *Political Studies*, Vol. 38, No. 1, 1990, p. 36.
17. Theodore P. Wright, Jr., 'Center–Periphery Relations and Ethnic Conflict in Pakistan: Sindhis, Muhajirs, and Punjabis', *Comparative Politics*, Vol. 23, No. 3, April 1991, p. 302.
18. Ibid., p. 304.
19. Pranab Bardhan, *The Political Economy of Development in India* (Oxford: Basil Blackwell, 1984).
20. Brass, *Ethnicity and Nationalism* (n. 2 above), p. 300.
21. Malcolm Yapp, 'Language, Religion and Political Identity: A General Framework', in David Taylor and Malcolm Yapp (eds), *Political Identity in South Asia* (London: Curzon Press, 1979), p. 17.
22. Urmila Phadnis, *Ethnicity and Nation-building in South Asia*, (New Delhi: Sage Publications, 1990), p. 48.
23. Brass, *Ethnicity and Nationalism* (n. 2 above).
24. Myron Weiner, *Sons of the Soil: Migration and Ethnic Conflict in India* (Princeton: Princeton University Press, 1978).

CHAPTER 6

Foreign Aid for Conflict Development
in Sri Lanka

No project in Sri Lanka has absorbed as many national and international resources as the Mahaweli irrigation scheme. In its conception and execution it was intended to transform part of a sparsely inhabited interior into heavily populated and irrigated cropland. As with all projects of this scale, it attracted its share of academic analysis. Big hydroelectric projects have come in for considerable criticism in recent years, and Mahaweli has been no exception.[1] The technical shortcomings were not its most salient feature. Though the contribution of foreign aid and the ensuing political entanglement in the project has been documented,[2] and the project's contribution to accentuating ethnic differences dealt with at length,[3] the role of foreign aid in contributing to ethnic conflict and the resultant civil war in Sri Lanka has hardly been mentioned.

The historical justification of the Mahaweli project goes back a millennium, to when a Sinhalese kingdom in the dry interior used elaborate irrigation techniques to settle the area. Why these settlements were abandoned is lost in history; however, modern Sinhalese nationalists have attributed it to Tamil invaders from India.[4] A more prosaic explanation may be that it was due to the spread of malaria which, until its control in recent times, prevented large-scale settlement of the interior.[5] The Tamils comprised only 19 per cent of the island population, but in the northern and eastern region they were usually the local majority. The Mahaweli project threatened to change this through the settlement of the Sinhalese in adjoining interior areas, along with the gerrymandering of constituency boundaries to give them greater representation than was proportional to their population.

Mahaweli undermined whatever ethnic balance and tranquillity existed in Sri Lanka during the late 1970s and early 1980s.

Ethnic Development

The foregoing is the generally accepted analysis of the background to the colonization scheme. The contribution of foreign aid agencies to the intensification of ethnic conflict has also been alluded to. Horowitz states: 'Ceylon Tamils have opposed the settlement of Sinhalese in the East of Sri Lanka, and the Mahaweli irrigation scheme, supported by international aid donors, is controversial because it is supposed that the scheme will attract Sinhalese colonists.'[6] Peebles, Manogaran and Tambiah have pointed to its negative consequences for ethnic relations.[7] Shanti P. Kumar states that Mahaweli reflected 'Sinhala desires of expansion into what were predominantly areas populated by Tamil-speaking people in the northern and eastern parts of the Dry Zone'.[8] However, few of the studies have analyzed the role of foreign donors in accentuating the ethnic conflict and eventual civil war in Sri Lanka. Levy notes the role of aid donors in the project despite reservations among some of them, including the then President of the World Bank, Robert McNamara.[9] Ultimately, the Sri Lankan government was able to obtain what it wanted from donors despite the apparent reservations about its economic viability and lack of preparatory analysis. This could be achieved partly through the mindset in the development community responsible for such projects, as shown in the book by Uphoff which touches on the role of ethnicity in the Sri Lankan irrigation colonization scheme. In arguing that the irrigation scheme he worked with achieved successful local participation he states that party politics was avoided, and quotes a local saying that 'water has no color' and 'putting color in water spoils it'.[10] However, he states that while the Tamils had the downstream irrigation, the upstream parts were owned by the Sinhalese, who controlled the flow to Tamils. No problems arose from the Tamils' powerlessness due to intercommunity cooperation, though Tamil areas became infiltrated by Tamil guerrillas.

Every aid project, however, is within a social and political context which if not understood can have unforeseen consequences.

The aid implications are obvious for a country where 72 per cent of the population are represented by the two main parties trying to outdo each other in the espousal of Sinhalese ethnicity. The 19 per cent Tamil population were being systematically and deliberately excluded from the state sector and educational institutions, effectively marginalizing them from the middle-class occupations in which they were previously well represented.

The Mahaweli scheme had the overt developmental function of providing irrigation for agriculture and hydroelectric power, but the hidden agenda included marginalizing the Tamil population politically and economically. Though it is unlikely that the ulterior motive has ever been put on paper, those responsible for the project almost certainly had this in mind. What is clear is that the Sri Lankan government was fully aware of its political objectives and effective in achieving the desired results. The role of the aid donors in this process is undisputed, but what is not clear is when the foreign donors became aware of how their aid was being used for 'ethnic swarming', to adapt a phrase from the Yugoslav example. The ethnic conflict in Sri Lanka was well known, having dominated post-colonial politics, but how this government project fitted in with their ethnic policy may not have become known to aid donors till later. That they would not have known at the time was argued by a development aid observer who pointed out that programmes administered by diplomats and aid workers were in the hands of generalists and technicians who handle too many projects and administrative details to occupy themselves with possible ethnic implications. 'Aid donors were not affected in their views, their thinking, and their feeling by Sri Lanka's history, its culture, its ethnic complexity, its eagerness to be truly independent.'[11] On the other hand, the Tamils certainly knew of the difficulties, and the ethnic problems were too central not to be known to those with even a superficial knowledge of the country.

What was known to members of the donor community at the time were the potential drawbacks and limited return of investment in the Mahaweli development project. Despite this the Sri Lankan government overcame all objections and obtained foreign funding, no mean achievement for a small nation of limited influence and resources. Peebles, though critical of the Tamil ethnic marginalization entailed in the project, nevertheless states:

'The successful completion of the Accelerated Mahaweli Programme can be a source of pride to Sri Lankans regardless of ethnic identity, and so can the ability of the government to pay for them largely with foreign aid.'[12]

How the Sri Lankan government succeeded in enlisting foreign government aid in its ethnic swarming policy has not emerged in the academic literature. However, the contribution of the project to the ethnic conflict in Sri Lanka has been documented by Peebles and Manogaran. Levy on a separate theme shows how the Sri Lankan government essentially manipulated the World Bank and western donors into bankrolling the project. If the sources are put together it is possible to reconstruct how Sri Lanka utilized foreign aid for ethnic swarming and thereby helped foment a civil war.

A confluence of interests between the Sri Lankan government and the western aid community certainly facilitated the project. This came about with the election of the United National Party (UNP) in 1977. Its declared policy was the liberalization of the economy through a structural adjustment policy that converged with the prevailing advice of the World Bank and western donors.[13] The reversal of the state interventionist and subsidy policy of the previous Sri Lankan Freedom Party (SLFP) government, along with the country's democratic institutions and small scale of the programmes, made Sri Lanka an ideal candidate for implementing the World Bank's structural adjustment programme at a time when such policies were far from generally accepted in the Third World, and Soviet-supported regimes seemed to be still ascendant.

Neither the Sri Lankan government nor the foreign donors were able to reduce the role of the state sector and its subsidization of social programmes and unproductive investments. The government had a clientele to satisfy through state subsidies and public sector investments such as Mahaweli. In the face of a determined government, foreign pressures had little impact, with liberalization occurring alongside increased public project investment. Though both policies were in apparent contradiction to each other, the government was able to maintain its domestic constituency while paying lip service to the policies favoured by the donors. In a country where ministers had their own projects, and little centralized direction, the inclination was to expand projects regardless of the cost overruns and macroeconomic liberalization policy. The threefold increase in foreign aid between 1978 and 1982 enabled this expansion and funded an accelerated Mahaweli programme.[14]

The idea of irrigating the interior was developed in the colonial era by nationalist Sinhalese politicians but the programme began in earnest with independence. Though it was claimed by Mahaweli project officials that colonization would reduce ethnic tensions by reducing unemployment, 'earlier colonization schemes had divided the Sinhalese majority and the Tamil minority long before either Mahaweli river development or ethnic violence accelerated'.[15]

> This resettlement of Sinhalese peasants in Tamil areas has drastically altered the ethnic composition of the Tamil districts; at least 165,670 Sinhalese were added to the population of the Northern and Eastern provinces in fewer than thirty years. This explains why the Sinhalese population increased dramatically from fewer than 46,500 in 1953 to as many as 243,000 in 1981, an increase of 424 percent. In contrast, the Tamil and Moor population increased by only 145 and 136 percent, respectively, during the same period.[16]

The official government position was that settlement should reflect the national ethnic population rather than those in the district with the inevitable ethnic swamping of the local Tamil majority that would result from this policy. However, in one settlement, 226 families were Buddhist and two Catholics, indicating that even a policy of national proportions was being observed in the breach.[17] This changing ethnic composition was accompanied by the more politically salient decrease in the representation of Tamils through the gerrymandering of constituencies, which reduced even the marginal representation they had previously had (Table 6.1).

The government colonization scheme was a project with a poor economic rate of return which could justify itself on only ethnic political grounds. Being in control of the state gave ethnic Sinhalese politicians an important power base from which to lobby aid donors, and utilize their advocacy of liberalization policies as leverage to enhance foreign aid contributions. There is a theory

TABLE 6.1

Ethnic Distribution and Parliamentary Representation in Sri Lanka, 1946–77

Ethnic Community	Population % of	Total Elected MPs	Weightage (%)
1946			
Sinhalese	4,621,507 (69.2)	68	71.0
Tamils	1,514,320 (17.3)	20	21.0
Muslims	408,823 (6.2)	6	6.3
Total	6,658,339	95	(Burghers 1)
1953			
Sinhalese	5,616,705 (69.3)	75	78.0
Tamils	1,818,801 (22.9)	13	13.6
Muslims	511,425 (6.3)	6	6.3
Total	8,097,895	95	(Burghers 1)
1971			
Sinhalese	9,146,679 (71.9)	123	81.0
Tamils	2,611,935 (20.5)	19	12.5
Muslims	853,707 (6.7)	8	5.3
Total	12,711,143	151	(Burghers 1)
1977			
Sinhalese	10,204,000 (73.3)	137	81.5
Tamils	2,644,000 (19.0)	21	12.5
Muslims	983,000 (7.0)	10	5.9
Total	14,850,000	168	

Source: Chelvadurai Manogaran, *Ethnic Conflict and Reconciliation in Sri Lanka* (Honolulu: University of Hawaii Press, 1987), p. 144.

that weaker parties who are fully committed to a project of vital interest to themselves can outbargain and negotiate more favourable terms from stronger parties for whom such projects are of marginal concern. The high level of Sri Lankan commitment and the relatively small stake foreign donors had in the country enabled a successful fund-raising effort. The Tamil minority, though having an educated middle class, had no corresponding lobby which could match the Sri Lankan state in influencing foreign donors, who were in any case not particularly disposed to heed their grievances.

What most concerned the donors was the viability of the project which, despite serious misgivings, went ahead with the backing of both the western donors and the Sri Lankan government. Shortly after the UNP came to power a delegation was sent to

Washington to obtain World Bank support for the accelerated Mahaweli scheme. The World Bank President, Robert McNamara, supported the project but cautioned against an overambitious and poorly planned implementation. While it was agreed that a review of the project would take place, this would occur simultaneously with implementation of those parts of the project that had been established as viable. According to Levy:

> Thus was born the tension between encouragement of acceleration and a caution about its wisdom that was to enable the Sri Lankans to garner support for the Mahaweli scheme largely on their own terms.... Although some donors highlighted the risks involved in the accelerated Mahaweli program there were also signs that their words of caution would not be heeded.[18]

Though the government hoped to complete the project at a cost of Rs 12 billion, within a year and a half the cost estimate doubled, to 24 billion.[19] This led to a series of budget cut-backs, but while other projects were cut back 32 per cent, the three priority projects of which Mahaweli was the largest were cut back by only 8 per cent.[20] The British, Germans and Canadians prepared feasibility studies. The Germans made their largest single project commitment with $230 million, the Canadians provided $65 million, and the Swede committed $170 million. Total foreign aid under the UNP government totalled about $4 billion, significantly higher in per capita terms than for almost any other developing country (Table 6.2). Mahaweli took up a large portion of the project aid and a substantial part of total aid disbursements (Table 6.3).

Though the rates of return on other agricultural projects were significantly higher than the 11 per cent forecast for Mahaweli, this project went ahead despite its lower projected benefits, and absorbed 49 per cent of all public investment between 1982 and 1984.[21] Mahaweli's advantage of size and visibility made it attractive to donors, who generally prefer to administer a few large projects than many small ones that are more cumbersome to manage.

What is more inexplicable is that while the donors espoused liberalization the share of gross domestic product (GDP) from public investment nearly doubled, from 6.6 per cent in 1977

TABLE 6.2

Bilateral Aid Commitments, 1978–87 (US$ million)

	1978–85	1986–87	Total
Aid Group			
Australia	38.7	1.0	39.7
Belgium	3.1	–	3.1
Canada	235.4	28.1	263.5
Denmark	14.6	6.7	21.3
EEC	88.9	13.0	101.9
Finland	31.1	18.6	49.7
France	122.1	25.7	147.8
West Germany	278.1	113.7	391.8
India	37.5	–	37.5
Italy	1.1	–	1.1
Japan	570.0	363.5	933.5
Netherlands	154.0	34.0	188.0
Norway	73.1	20.3	93.4
Sweden	206.2	41.9	248.1
Switzerland	26.3	1.8	28.1
United Kingdom	307.9	23.7	331.6
United States	583.3	58.9	642.2
Non-aid Group			
Centrally Planned Economies	43.1	–	43.1
OPEC	160.1	–	160.1
Total	2,974.6	750.9	3,725.5

Source: Gunnar M. Sorbo, Grete Brochmann, Reidar Dale, Mick Moore and Erik Whist, *Sri Lanka: Country Study and Norwegian Aid Review* (Bergen: Centre for Development Studies, University of Bergen, April 1987), pp. 190–91.

when the UNP took power to 12 per cent the following year, and continued to increase, reaching 18.4 per cent in 1980.[22] This indicates that the liberalization policy was never comprehensively followed, and was completely violated in the public investment sphere, both by the Sri Lankan government and the western donors who supposedly supported it. 'Rather than promoting the strategy that enjoyed rhetorical support, foreign aid provided the Sri Lankan government with the wherewithal to push forward with the Mahaweli scheme on a scale that worked against both liberalization and other components of public investment.'[23] The Sri Lankan government had obvious interests in promoting foreign-

TABLE 6.3

Disbursement Performance, 1978–83 (US$ million)

	Project Aid		Non-Project Aid		
	Non-Mahaweli	Mahaweli	Commodity	Food	Total
1978					
Opening Pipeline	353.7	–	98.9	12.9	465.5
Pipeline Disbursements	92.6	–	80.1	12.9	185.6
Disbursement Rate (%)	26	–	81	100	40
1979					
Opening Pipeline	443.8	11.0	187.6	3.5	645.9
Pipeline Disbursements	65.7	11.0	110.0	3.5	190.2
Disbursement Rate (%)	15	100	58	100	29
1980					
Opening Pipeline	530.5	201.4	160.1	3.5	895.5
Pipeline Disbursements	74.7	48.8	81.6	3.5	208.6
Disbursement Rate (%)	14	24	51	100	23
1981					
Opening Pipeline	801.5	240.4	130.3	4.6	1,176.8
Pipeline Disbursements	118.5	59.4	76.0	4.6	258.5
Disbursement Rate (%)	15	25	58	100	22
1982					
Opening Pipeline	947.1	539.7	139.5	7.4	1,633.7
Pipeline Disbursements	131.7	136.5	49.9	7.4	325.5
Disbursement Rate (%)	14	25	36	100	20
1983					
Opening Pipeline	890.6	506.5	132.4	36.8	1,566.3
Pipeline Disbursements	144.4	138.9	57.9	36.8	378.0
Disbursement Rate (%)	16	27	44	100	24

Table 6.3 Continued

1984					
Opening Pipeline	922.4	411.2	104.7	38.2	1,476.3
Pipeline Disbursements	199.7	148.4	65.4	35.9	449.4
Disbursement Rate (%)	22	36	63	94	30
1985					
Opening Pipeline	835.3	417.6	110.7	34.4	1,398.0
Pipeline Disbursements	212.3	144.6	73.0	26.6	456.5
Disbursement Rate (%)	25	35	66	77	33
Total Period 1978–85					
Opening Pipeline	5,724.9	2,327.8	1,064.2	141.3	9,258.2
Pipeline Disbursement	1,039.6	687.6	593.9	131.2	2,452.3
Disbursement Rate (%)	18	30	56	93	27

Source: Same as Table 6.2, p. 198.

financed public investment for 'without the aid commitments, the resources needed for an acceleration of public investment would not have been available'.[24]

What is also not clear is why the foreign donors ignored both the project's doubtful economic viability and its underlying ethnic discrimination. Reaching a firm conclusion would require access to the internal memos of several development agencies, which is not presently possible, but a hypothesis may be advanced. The western donors involved in the struggle for influence in the Third World found the return to a pro-western position in Sri Lanka, after Soviet advances in Southern Africa and Southeast Asia, an opportunity to assert the superiority of the western model. That their policy prescriptions were being less than rigidly applied on the ground by either themselves or the Sri Lankan government was never allowed to interfere with the process. As the project progressed, however, a greater discretion could have been shown. Levy notes that

> The goals of the UNP government may have had at least as much to do with directing the benefits of economic expansion

to their core Sinhalese political constituency as with pursuing some more broadly defined conception of development. The benefits of Mahaweli could readily be targeted to the regions of the country where Sinhalese were dominant; indeed, the first projects that were eliminated from the Accelerated scheme as it began to be cut back were those targeted to the Tamil-dominated Northern Provinces.[25]

At this juncture the donors could have pointed out the injustice and then insisted on an equitable distribution of benefits. However, once the project was begun and the aid committed, the initiative was with the Sri Lankan government, which got what it wanted. It attempted to maintain a favourable view of the project through control of research.

The whole attitude to research, studies and so forth, expressed in a circular of 1981, whereby the secretary general of the Mahaweli Authority demanded that researchers submit proposals approved by the authority and so forth, indicated that there was some fear that the government propaganda machine about settlement would be contradicted by those who carried out scientific research.[26]

A doctoral researcher, Ruwani Anush Jayewardene, while undertaking seemingly innocuous research on malaria incidence in the project area, noted that

The response from the Mahaweli Authority of Sri Lanka (MASL) was extremely cordial, qualified with an informal warning that I should be given all possible assistance but also, 'watched', because I was a social scientist. I was also told that prior to publishing 'it would be better to have an official from the MASL read the work'. The Ministry is extremely sensitive about information published regarding the project, I suspect largely because the project is dependent on external aid and adverse publicity could affect the flow of outside funds.[27]

This may explain the lack of data on ethnic conflict in the area despite the widely known ethnic problems in Sri Lanka.

The success of the project depended on 'massive foreign aid, continuous propaganda barrages, and creative arithmetic.... The propaganda succeeded in winning domestic and foreign support for the project, but it created further difficulties for Sinhalese–Tamil relations.'[28] Not only were the Tamil components of the irrigation projects eventually dropped, but even the transport links were made to Sinhalese areas rather than to adjacent Tamil areas.[29] Though President Jayewardene stated that the government would not alter the demography of the Tamil provinces, 'his Minister responsible for the Mahaweli River Development Scheme paid no heed to the guarantee, and it would seem that the President turned a blind eye'.[30] As a quotation from A. Jeyaratnam Wilson, who was close to the President, this is as near to pinning personal responsibility for the ethnic swarming of the project as one is likely to get. There was a lack of statesmanship in the development of the project, with party patronage considerations and political mileage overriding economic viability and improving ethnic relations.[31] Perhaps it could not have been expected to be otherwise, but foreign aid donors with no ethnic constituency to appeal to might have been expected to intervene. However, they too had their own motivations for turning a 'blind eye' to the ethnic bias of the project. A 1987 retrospective analysis of Norwegian aid to Sri Lanka noted:

> The GOSL [Government of Sri Lanka], the World Bank, the International Monetary Fund, parts of the international business community and most bilateral aid donors have in practice entered in a close and mutually reinforcing web of relationships. Because of its commitment to economic liberalization, its openness to foreign investment, and its generally pro-Western foreign policy stance, Sri Lanka has created a very favourable impression and image overseas, and has received a great deal of support. At the same time the major aid donors, especially perhaps the World Bank, have become very heavily committed to continuing to support Sri Lanka because of a strong desire to be able to exhibit its experience to other developing countries as an example of successful economic liberalization. The GOSL and its major aid donors are heavily interdependent; the latter have often felt obliged to acquiesce to economic policy measures taken by the GOSL of which they disapprove.[32]

Though foreign aid donors are often criticized for interfering in the domestic policies of Third World countries, the relationships are usually of mutual though unequal dependency. Local foreign aid staff depend on local government cooperation, and have a mutual interest in the promotion and expansion of their projects.[33] However, when projects are going badly or are skewed by corruption or ethnic preference, donors have an obligation to exert influence in a more positive direction on behalf of their own taxpayers as well as deprived local groups.

When it became obvious that Mahaweli had evolved into a blatantly biased colonization scheme, the question remains as to why the foreign donors allowed it to continue. David Gillies in a study of Canada's aid to Sri Lanka notes the Canadian government's insensitivity to ethnic and human rights problems:

> Interviews with CIDA and External Affairs officials suggest that at the planning stage virtually no attention was given to the project's impact on the fragile ethnic balance of Batticaloa district in which resettlement would occur. There is no evidence of sensitivity to human rights matters such as participation and nondiscrimination by, for example, canvassing the opinions of local Tamil politicians or ensuring that an equitable ethnic balance was inscribed into the memorandum of understanding between the two governments. CIDA seems to have uncritically accepted the government's proposed resettlement formula. Canada's unwillingness to examine the political implications of the aid project was to prove costly.[34]

Part of the reason for this lack of sensitivity may lie with the socialization of the local and visiting foreign donor staff in the project ethos, and in the society of their hosts. Uphoff's edited journals of his visits to the Sri Lankan irrigation and colonization schemes as published in book form provide an insight into the perspectives of the local aid establishment. In sifting through the bureaucratic rivalries and office politics of the aid community that are dealt with at length, I was struck by the overall acceptance of the value of the project, and the lack of understanding of the role the scheme played in national politics. The fact that the Tamils had been given the downstream plots and made strategically dependent on upstream Sinhalese farmers is not given much more than cursory attention, with no explanation of how this inequity came about in the first place. The assumption is that it is possible to do good at a local level, even when the nation as a whole descends into civil war. This is a major theme of NGO literature and a justification for the continuance of aid at the micro level in the face of macro-level development failures. The linkages and interaction between the two are, however, not generally explored or well understood, though this is critical in determining the value of an aid input. The aid workers as presented in Uphoff's work perceive themselves as achieving successful development and interethnic cooperation in the face of an escalating ethnic civil war in their project area.[35] The inherent inequity of keeping Tamil farmers dependent on upstream Sinhalese farmers for irrigation water is perceived as one of the givens in the situation. The question of what USAID and aid consultants did to give the Tamils equality of access is not raised, nor is the appropriateness of participating in such an inequitable government-sponsored project an issue. This is in itself indicative of a development view which fails to look at the macro role local projects (however effective) can play in skewed development. They may assume that they are achieving economic development but may in fact be developing conflict. This lack of understanding raises questions about the role of scholars and universities in the international donor consultancy network and their participation in development projects affecting minority rights. The alternative view that they in fact knew what was going on but chose not to write about it is even less charitable than using their ignorance as an explanation.

Another obvious reason for inaction, particularly once the project was under way, was the commercial interests involved. In Canada's case:

CIDA's pragmatic antipathy against using aid as a political lever had less to do with defending a development profile in Sri Lanka and rather more to do with its relationship with some high profile Canadian companies contracted to work on Mahaweli. CIDA officials 'spoke with disarming frankness' of the commercial contracts already negotiated with three of Canada's largest engineering firms. They had, in any case, already sunk $100 million into building the Maduru dam. CIDA saw no way for Canada 'to quietly phase down' after it had spent $100 million. With $60 million still allocated to the project and with prestigious companies 'with bags of political influence' hinting at litigation if the project stalled, CIDA wanted to proceed 'without being reckless, in order to realize the developmental potential and commercial benefits'. As one diplomat read CIDA's position, the agency 'was more concerned about the direct access of these companies to their own Minister ... and was quite unmoved by the fuss going on about human rights violations'.[36]

What Gillies only hints at here, but which is well known in Canadian government circles, is that though French Canadians comprise only about 20 per cent of the population, they comprise 56 per cent of CIDA's staff (CIDA has 2.6 per cent visible minorities compared with 4 per cent in the Federal Public Service and 9 per cent in the population[37]) and the French Canadian minister responsible for CIDA had politically important Quebec businesses to deal with. According to the opposition Reform Party MP Lee Morrison, 71 per cent of the 20 largest CIDA service contracts in 1995 went to Quebec-based companies and the two top institutional grant recipients were the Quebec universities of Laval and McGill.[38] Unlike Sri Lanka, which marginalized its Tamil minority, Canada pandered to the French Canadian minority with government largesse in the hope of creating vested interests which would oppose the secession of Quebec. It was uncertain whether this would work in the long term, and it had already created an English Canadian backlash, but having ruled out force to preserve unity, only largesse and more political concessions were possible. While Sri Lanka used sticks, Canada resorted exclusively to carrots. The irony was that while aid was being used to effectively undermine national unity in Sri Lanka, the same aid was being used to foster Canadian unity at home. Though Canadian aid to Sri Lanka was not large enough to change Canadian politics, the general use of state largesse, including the over $2 billion in overseas development assistance, was critical to the Canadian effort for national unity. Marcel Massé, then a Canadian diplomat and former and subsequent CIDA President, tried to have Sri Lankan aid made conditional on human rights adherence but 'after canvasing other donors, it became clear that conditionality was not a viable option. The Americans were opposed and the Europeans were not interested because of commercial interests or diplomatic ties.'[39]

After the civil war was well under way one of the donors, the Norwegian Ministry of Development Cooperation, commissioned a review of their development effort by a team of social scientists. The team stated that any development assistance not aimed at deliberately overthrowing a government

> provides, in one way or the other, support for the recipient government. *All* aid is to some degree *fungible* i.e. it increases the general capacity of the recipient to do as he wishes and thus in some sense has consequences beyond the sphere in which it is formally to be used.[40]

The provision of hard currency can assist in the purchase of arms. This is an extreme case, but developing favourable trade balances increases options. Decisions on whether to provide aid must take into account the nature of the recipient regimes, which could range from largely repressive all the way to nominally democratic. Sri Lanka belongs to the latter category, although it represses minorities. While humanitarian aid for war victims might be justified in most situations, the Norwegian study recommended cutting off aid in the event of non-improvement in the situation. Scandinavian countries reduced aid for government projects in favour of greater NGO funding. Canada suspended aid to the Mahaweli project pending provision for increase in Tamil settlement, a clear indication that aid donors had become aware of the project's ethnic implications.[41] Initially Canada attempted a more equitable resettlement according to the existing population proportions, but negotiations with the government were unsuccessful. According to a senior Canadian official in Sri Lanka:

> [The national formula was] a type of gerrymandering [which] heightened the sensitivity of the Oya project well beyond the local impact. [This formula] put us in a difficult position because as an aid donor you can't go around telling a recipient how its going to conduct its internal affairs, particularly over

sensitive issues, such as land resettlement. A principle of domestic jurisdiction [over internal affairs] has been our tradition. On the other hand, we weren't very happy about our money going into something that was going to cause more dissension, and, in fact, to a scheme you could argue simply wasn't fair.[42]

A Canadian External Affairs official bluntly stated: 'Why the hell were we emptying $125 million a year down a rat hole like Sri Lanka?' More diplomatically, an internal telex from the Canadian High Commission in Colombo to Ottawa stated that the Sri Lankans had accepted the aid pull-out and 'We were not left feeling we were seen by the Sri Lankans as [project] killers'.[43] In 1990 the World Bank decided to pull out of the Mahaweli scheme because according to a Bank official the project 'was just not going to fly' and had become 'an embarrassment'.[44] This indicates that the aid community had eventually become fully aware of the ethnic conflict inherent in the implementation of the project. These measures were too insignificant and too late to affect the development of the civil war, which began in earnest in 1983. In belatedly extricating itself from the project, the aid community had wasted considerable money and intensified ethnic animosities.

The aid group found itself not only unable to affect policy decisions on Mahaweli (as well as on other matters), but indeed found itself supporting a project about which it had major doubts. The evidence also supports the view that other investment projects would have contributed more (in some sense) to social welfare than even a completed Mahaweli—and certainly more than an incomplete Mahaweli. Given the context as it had evolved over the years, these alternative projects, along with modified policies, were essentially impossible. As noted, even the World Bank, said to be objective and non political, became so caught up in the situation that it, too, acquiesced. It can be argued that such a large-scale, imaginative project was important in its effect on morale and hope within the government and among the population. It may have been true that less imposing projects would not have attracted aid. This is a useful point, but it must be acknowledged that the project created tasks that could be managed less well than tasks associated with smaller, more indigenous projects.[45]

This World Bank publication is as close to self-criticism as can be found in the literature. It is a critique that reveals economic inviability and the lack of donor influence in creating what it deems appropriate policies in recipient countries. The ethnic and human rights aspects of foreign aid, however, are only marginally touched upon in the Sri Lankan development literature, which appears odd considering there are detailed academic critiques of the ethnically skewed Sinhalese colonization scheme as well as critiques on the project's economic viability and the failures of donors to influence it. In exposing the role of foreign aid in developing ethnic conflict, the lessons that can be learnt are significant for Third World projects. What is required is a new method of aid evaluation and monitoring that takes into account local ethnic and political conditions. Though Environmental Impact Assessments are now required for approval of many donor projects, ethnic and socio-political studies have generally not been done for projects in sensitive areas. There is reason to believe that these can have consequences that are as adverse as environmentally destructive schemes. Environmental pollution may be relatively easier to quantify, but the social impact of projects also requires analysis. The Mahaweli project contributed to a civil war and continued to receive funding even after the war had begun. Hence donors should stipulate genuinely independent social assessments of major projects and an ongoing monitoring of implementation and approval for any revisions. Anything short of such a measure will allow politicians to divert resources into their own community to the detriment of less advantaged groups. It appears that larger political considerations motivated the western donor community to take a more lenient view towards the Sri Lankan government than might have been the case with countries to which it was less favourably disposed. Nevertheless, a more perceptive assessment of the political situation might have led to a more rigorous enforcement by donor agencies of an ethnically neutral development implementation.

When I pointed out the need for research on the effects of NGO projects, the Executive Director of South Asia Partnership

International, Sri Lanka, was not in favour of this as the research would become dated in a changing situation.[46] The problem in opposing social science research is that it leaves a suspicion that the projects have something to hide. In reviewing their publicity literature this would indeed appear to be the case. According to one Canadian bilateral aid official, the new priority would be funding for civil society and good governance which was 'a lot cheaper than working on the Mahaweli dam disaster'.[47] However, their shift from bilateral aid for the Mahaweli Dam to NGO funding for more modest civil society work perpetuated the initial project defects. 'Over 300,000 people migrated to the dry zone assisted largely through government settlement schemes, adding to the pressure on land', which became so degraded from overuse that South Asia Partnership along with others stepped in to alleviate the problem.[48] Instead of facilitating the return of the Sinhalese settlers to their traditional homelands, they perpetuated their ethnic expansion by undertaking Canadian government-funded development work that continued the ethnic imbalance.[49] It was no wonder that Canada was able to downgrade a commitment to Mahaweli because all they were doing was moving on from one Sri Lankan government project to a new government priority necessitated by the environmental degradation caused by the previous one. That the Sri Lankans were again able to get foreign aid donors to cover the costs of a political project, despite the now widely acknowledged failure of Mahaweli, is indicative of the degree to which local national elites can mobilize aid to serve their own ethnic interests. Why the foreign NGOs did not learn from the mistakes of their own government funders and consider the ethnic interests involved in these projects remains a mystery.

The Mahaweli scheme contributed to ethnic polarization but it was hardly unique in that the whole state apparatus was involved. The Sri Lankan state succeeded brilliantly in gaining the initial complicity of foreign aid donors, after which it was too late for the donors to back out easily due to their own commercial interests in the project. Such success would have been unlikely in the present-day scenario of tightening foreign aid budgets and sensitivity to environmental concerns. However, there is not much evidence that political and ethnic issues are as actively under consideration as is warranted.

REFERENCES

1. Agrarian Research and Training Institute (ARTI), *Anuradhapura Dry Zone Agricultural Project: A Socio-Economic Study of the Project Beneficiaries* (Occasional Publication No. 40, Colombo, August 1991), p. iii; David Dunham, 'Politics and Land Settlement Schemes: The Case of Sri Lanka', *Development and Change*, Vol. 13, No. 1, January 1982, pp. 43–61; N. Serena Tennekoon, 'Rituals of Development: The Accelerated Mahaweli Development Program of Sri Lanka', *American Ethnologist*, Vol. 15, No. 2, 1988, pp. 294–310.

2. Brian Levy, 'Foreign Aid in the Making of Economic Policy in Sri Lanka, 1977–1983', *Policy Sciences*, Vol. 22, Nos.3–4, 1989, pp. 437–61.

3. Patrick Peebles, 'Colonization and Ethnic Conflict in the Dry Zone of Sri Lanka', *The Journal of Asian Studies*, Vol. 49, No. 1, February 1990, pp. 30–55.

4. Mick Moore, 'The Ideological History of the Sri Lankan Peasantry', *Modern Asian Studies*, Vol. 23, Part 1, February 1989, p. 190.

5. Peebles, 'Colonization and Ethnic Conflict' (n. 3 above), p. 33.

6. Donald L. Horowitz, *Ethnic Groups in Conflict* (Berkeley: University of California Press, 1985), p. 8.

7. Chelvadurai Manogaran, *Ethnic Conflict and Reconciliation in Sri Lanka* (Honolulu: University of Hawaii Press, 1987). p. 97; Peebles, 'Colonization and Ethnic Conflict' (n. 3 above), p. 43; Stanley Jeyaraja Tambiah, *Buddhism Betrayed? Religion, Politics, and Violence in Sri Lanka* (Chicago: The University of Chicago Press, 1992), pp. 68–70.

8. Shanti P. Kumar, 'The Mahaweli Scheme and Rural Women in Sri Lanka', in Noeleen Heyzer (ed.), *Women Farmers and Rural Change in Asia: Towards Equal Access and Participation* (Kuala Lumpur: Asian and Pacific Development Centre, 1987), pp. 220–21.

9. Levy, 'Foreign Aid in the Making of Economic Policy in Sri Lanka' (n. 2 above), p. 453.

10. Norman Uphoff, *Learning from Gal Oya* (Ithaca: Cornell University Press, 1992), p. 362.

11. Henry J. Bruton, *The Political Economy of Poverty, Equity, and Growth: Sri Lanka and Malaysia* (Oxford: Published by Oxford University Press for the World Bank, 1992), p. 138.

12. Peebles, 'Colonization and Ethnic Conflict' (n. 3 above), p. 43.

13. Surjit S. Bhalla and Paul Glewwe, 'Growth and Equity in Developing Countries: A Reinterpretation of the Sri Lankan Experience', *The World Bank Economic Review*, Vol. 1, No. 1, September, 1986, p. 36.

14. Levy, 'Foreign Aid in the Making of Economic Policy in Sri Lanka' (n. 2 above), p. 441.

15. Peebles, 'Colonization and Ethnic Conflict' (n. 3 above), p. 41.

16. Manogaran, *Ethnic Conflict and Reconciliation in Sri Lanka* (n. 7 above), p. 143.

17. Ruwani Anush Jayewardene, 'The Impact of Malaria on New Settlers in the Mahaweli Development Project, Sri Lanka' (Ph.D. dissertation, University of Connecticut, Connecticut, 1988), p. 182.

18. Levy, 'Foreign Aid in the Making of Economic Policy in Sri Lanka' (n. 2 above), p. 453.
19. Ibid., p. 447.
20. Ibid., p. 447.
21. Ibid., p. 442.
22. Ibid., p. 441.
23. Ibid., p. 438.
24. Ibid., p. 449.
25. Ibid., p. 452.
26. Shanti P. Kumar, 'The Mahaweli Scheme and Rural Women in Sri Lanka' (n. 8 above), pp. 244–45.
27. Jayewardene, 'The Impact of Malaria on New Settlers' (n. 17 above), p. 121.
28. Peebles, 'Colonization and Ethnic Conflict' (n. 3 above), p. 41.
29. Ibid., p. 43.
30. A. Jeyaratnam Wilson, *The Break-Up of Sri Lanka* (London: C. Hurst & Co., 1988), p. 143.
31. Ibid., p. 146.
32. Gunnar M. Sorbo, Grete Brochmann, Reidar Dale, Mick Moore and Erik Whist, *Sri Lanka: Country Study and Norwegian Aid Review* (Bergen: Centre for Development Studies, University of Bergen, April 1987), p. 27.
33. Brian H. Smith, *More Than Altruism: The Politics of Private Foreign Aid* (Princeton: Princeton University Press, 1990), pp. 264, 273.
34. David Gillies, 'Canadian Aid, Human Rights, and Conflict in Sri Lanka', in Robert Miller (ed.), *Aid as Peacemaker: Canadian Development Assistance and Third World Conflict* (Ottawa: Carleton University Press, 1992), p. 55.
35. Uphoff, *Learning from Gal Oya* (n. 10 above), p. 3, 11.
36. Gillies, 'Canadian Aid, Human Rights, and Conflict in Sri Lanka' (n. 34 above), pp. 58–59.
37. Prem Kumar, 'CIDA and Canada's Visible Minorities', *Policy Options*, Vol. 10, No. 7, September 1989, p. 14.
38. Juliet O'Neill, 'Bidding for Foreign-aid Contracts to Become Fairer, Quicker Process', *Ottawa Citizen*, 11 December 1966, p. A15.
39. Gillies, 'Canadian Aid, Human Rights, and Conflict in Sri Lanka' (n. 34 above), p. 59.
40. Sorbo et al., *Sri Lanka* (n. 32 above), p. 5.
41. John M. Richardson, Jr. and S.W.R. de A. Samarasinghe, 'Measuring the Economic Dimensions of Sri Lanka's Ethnic Conflict', in S.W.R. de A. Samarasinghe and Reed Coughlan (eds), *The Economic Dimensions of Ethnic Conflict* (London: Pinter Publishers, 1991), p. 204.
42. David Gillies, *Between Principle and Practice: Human Rights in North-South Relations* (Montreal: McGill-Queen's University Press, 1996), p. 122.
43. Ibid., pp. 306–307.
44. Ibid., p. 132.
45. Bruton, *Political Economy of Poverty* (n. 11 above), p. 140.
46. 'Partnerships for Civil Society', Lecture, Conference on Strengthening Civil Society, South Asia Partnership Canada, Ottawa, Canada, 3 October 1997.

47. Alison Van Rooy, Lecture at South Asia Partnership Canada conference on 'Strengthening Civil Society: Progressive Strategy or Smokescreen?' Ottawa, Canada, 2 October 1997.
48. 'Harvesting the Future? Development in Sri Lanka's Dry Zone', *Lanka Link: A Newsletter of South Asia Partnership Canada*, Summer 1997, p. 1.
49. *Sri Lanka Canada Development Fund: Annual Report 1995–1996* (Colombo, Sri Lanka, 1996).

CHAPTER 7

Pakistan: Bound to Fail?

The prominent American academic and government official Joseph Nye in his book entitled *Bound to Lead: The Changing Nature of American Power*[1] argues that America's geopolitical position made world leadership that country's destiny. Similarly, it can be argued that the situation of some countries makes their failure as nation-states inevitable. A country that would seem to fit in that category is Pakistan. Yet, after a half century of its creation it is still around, and in certain respects has outperformed neighbouring India, with which it is often unfavourably compared.

Until very late in the decolonization process, the creation of Pakistan was never a likelihood, let alone a certainty. The Muslim-majority areas which eventually became part of Pakistan had traditionally been the least supportive of the Muslim League and the impetus for Pakistan came from the Muslim-minority areas which would remain in India. The 'maimed, mutilated and motheaten Pakistan'[2] that Jinnah was ultimately forced to accept had virtually none of the resources and infrastructure needed to launch a new country. While India legally and practically inherited the old state, which made the transition relatively smooth, Pakistan had to deal with a massive transfer of personnel and a delayed and less-than-adequate transfer of financial and other resources from India. The Pakistani areas of India were more predominantly agricultural than the rest of the country and its agricultural products such as jute were manufactured in what had become neighbouring India. Divided in two by India, Pakistan seemed to represent the ultimate triumph of ideology over geography. Despite these inauspicious beginnings, in a relatively short period a new state infrastructure was created, central authority imposed on recalcitrant provinces, and a formidable military and industrial complex established which, for its size, was at least the equivalent of that of India. On the basis of per capita income Pakistan ranks ahead of India by $380 to $320, while in terms of the Purchasing Power Parity method, Pakistan's per capita income at nearly $2,000 is twice that of India's, making it arguably a de facto middle-income country.[3] However, on the United Nations Development Programme (UNDP) Human Development Index, Pakistan at 128th place is only marginally ahead of India at 134th position among states.[4] This reflects the relatively low standards of health care and education in Pakistan as compared with India. Poor social services are not necessarily an impediment to development if economically critical sectors have access to both, but in Pakistan it is not just the lower classes that have been adversely affected; middle-class groups too have difficulty pursuing developmental activities. Similarly, there is no clear correlation of development with democracy, but despite favourable growth rates when compared with India, Pakistan has not been outstanding when compared with other dictatorships.[5] This reflects the failure of ruling elites to pursue development objectives in preference to personal acquisition, despite no political necessity to undertake social service spending. According to one survey by Transparency International, a European group which monitors worldwide corruption, Pakistan is the most corrupt country in Asia.[6] This is an important cause of its developmental failure and gross financial mismanagement. With government debts of $51 billion, which is equivalent to 90 per cent of GDP or six years' export revenues, the need for reform is obvious. However, with 26 per cent of the budget being devoted to defence, there is limited scope for social development and debt repayments.[7]

No government in Pakistan has lasted out its term, and whether removed through constitutional coups or by the military directly, the end result has been much the same. The incentive of those in power to look to the short-term opportunities for aggrandizement knowing that they are unlikely to serve out their terms is not conducive to the accommodations necessary for democratic institutionalization. Indeed, it appears doubtful that the institutionalization of democracy is seriously on the agenda of either of the two major parties. 'Provincial or national, it has been widely agreed among specialists on Pakistan that its politics, no matter what regime is in power, have been dominated by a relatively

small number of landlord families.'[8] The failure to introduce progressive agricultural taxation, though similar to Indian policies,
reflects the interests of a narrower landlord class base more
directly in control of the state. On the industrial side 76.8 per cent
of all manufacturing assets are owned by 43 families.[9]

> The current crisis of the State in Pakistan has arisen out of a
> State structure in which the dominance of the military-
> bureaucratic oligarchy systematically constrained the devel-
> opment of the political process. The oligarchy devised a
> political framework which, while allowing rivalry between
> the landlords and the industrial bourgeoisie for the division
> of the economic surplus maintained the mode of appropria-
> tion of the surplus through which the existence of these
> elites could be perpetuated.[10]

If this should seem too harsh an assessment, one could take the
words of Professor Saleem M.M. Qureshi as summing up the
Pakistani dilemma.

> In less than half a century Pakistan has lost more than half of
> its population and may yet lose its very existence in a class
> and regional war.... Only Pakistan has suffered the loss of
> territory and the rejection of its conceptual raison d'être by
> its majority population.... Pakistan is perhaps a very major
> and outstanding example of the failure of nation-building,
> an example of what not to do. Pakistan today is more vulner-
> able to fissiparous and divisive pulls than it was at its birth or
> during the first year of its life. The initial enthusiasm and
> commitment has long departed, the national vision van-
> ished. What have replaced the early euphoria are narrow
> provincialism, bigoted sectarianism and petty opportunism.[11]

The central theme of academic writing on Pakistani politics has
been the military-bureaucratic dominance over civil society and
the suppression of democracy. These writings reveal a deep pessimism about the prospects for Pakistan without some innovative
statecraft. The overlay of elite perpetuation along with regional
inequality creates a particularly volatile recipe for conflict. This
was accentuated by the development of a real conflict in neigh-

bouring Afghanistan that helped break down social cohesion through the introduction of arms and drugs. With the state no longer having a monopoly over arms, and lacking the institutions for accommodation normally available in democratic states, the ground was prepared for an escalation of violence and corruption. In contrast to India, where the parliamentary system encouraged the creation of coalitions between rivals to attain power, Pakistani electoral politics was not organized for these accommodations. According to Shahid Javed Burki,

> There is a growing feeling that the country may not find the resources it needs to put its economic and political house in order.... Abandoned by the United States and largely ignored by the western world, Pakistanis seem to feel they now have to live in a singularly hostile world.[12]

In retrospect, it is difficult to see how things could have turned out differently. The alternative scenario most observers preferred was the consolidation of democratic civilian rule, along much the same lines as in India. The failure of civilian leadership to institute effective democratic governance resulted in military intervention. Civilian politicians, however, had failed long before the military intervened. It has been argued that military intervention was necessitated by the failure of politicians to reach a consensus, and the threat this posed to national survival. Hamza Alavi, in a take-off on Marx's interpretation of bonapartism, attributes the failures of various class elites to reach a consensus as necessitating this intervention.[13] However, that these elites were divided in the first place, was a reflection of their constituencies, which were by then inherently opposed to each other.

It has been a matter of speculation whether Pakistan would have been created had the terminal illness of Jinnah been known sooner, or, perhaps more interestingly, if he had survived as long as Nehru, whether democratic civilian control might have been institutionalized in those early years. Certainly Jinnah shared the westernized views of Nehru—even if he made rhetorical statements to the contrary—and his political acumen was arguably more acute. However, it would have taken extreme political dexterity for Jinnah to overcome Pakistan's unfavourable geopolitical position. That the country has been progressively unravelling almost from the time of independence is testimony to the difficulties of nation building in acutely adverse circumstances.

Though at one time some academics might have argued that the primacy of class divisions were at the heart of Pakistan's problems, a consensus would now consider ethnic diversity to be the wellspring of the country's centrifugal forces. As created in 1947, it was a recipe for disintegration. The dominant political, economic and military power of the new state was in the western half, and mostly in the Punjabi part of that, while most of the people were in the east. If democracy was to prevail, the east would have to be given control of the central state. The unwillingness of the western elite of all complexions to do this made a democratic state impossible, and for this reason even a constitution could not be introduced. From this it followed that even civilian rule would have to be undemocratic; and civilians without a popular mandate were vulnerable to overthrow by the military. For a long time most of the Third World was governed by military dictatorships without the countries themselves being threatened with disintegration, but Pakistan was different. The eastern wing was difficult to control without local consent, being geographically separate and distant, and the population too large and distinct to be co-opted or effectively repressed indefinitely. With Indian occupation the first state ended and Bangladesh was created, but this merely hastened the inevitable outcome. The Pakistani military in the east had been stretched to the limit by local insurgents with Indian backing. They were fortunate to have been able to surrender to the invading Indian army.

The end of the first Pakistani 'state' was in certain respects much less traumatic than the creation of the nation, since the government and institutions had been predominantly western all along. The fiction of two wings in one nation could be abandoned and, more importantly, for the first time there was a realistic possibility of stable democratically elected civilian government. However, the shedding of the eastern wing revealed a western wing that was subject to its own divisions along ethnic lines. Geographical contiguity made for greater coercive control, and the prospect of a successful secessionist insurgency rather remote, but the issue was still salient. Successful democratic governance would still require the consent of the various ethnic groups.

Pakistan was very different from India in having fewer major ethnic groups, which might have made for greater ease of governance, except that they were not equal in numbers or influence. The Punjabis were either a near majority or a bare majority, depending on the definition (by first language 48 per cent, by declared ethnic group 56 per cent) (Table 7.1), disproportionately controlling the military and civilian apparatus of the state, and much of the wealth besides.

TABLE 7.1

Pakistan: Population by Mother Tongue

Language	Households	Per cent of Total
Punjabi	6,051,356	48.17
Pashtu	1,651,223	13.15
Sindhi	1,478,621	11.77
Siraiki	1,235,830	9.84
Urdu	955,039	7.60
Baluchi	379,148	3.02
Hindko	305,505	2.43
Brahui	151,958	1.21
Others	353,197	2.81
Total	12,561,877	100.00

Source: S. Mahmud Ali, *The Fearful State* (London: Zed Books, 1993), p. 157.

India by contrast had no such identifiable group. The nearest to an Indian ruling group might have been the Kashmiri Brahmins, but they hardly had the numbers or base to exercise hegemony. Even the larger category, sometimes disparagingly referred to in subaltern literature as the 'Brahmin Social Order' (reduced to the acronym BSO), never existed as an organized group either in religious or political terms. Like Hinduism itself it had no organized centre or leadership. Brahmins covered the full political spectrum and even supported sharply conflicting linguistic groups. The Order's supposed ultimate defenders, the BJP, supported the installation of the country's first Untouchable chief minister and government in Uttar Pradesh, where the order might have been considered to be at its strongest. It is an order that reflects an attitude but no organization willing to espouse its position. Such an amorphous category is difficult to organize against, and no other category could remotely claim to predominate in the Indian state. The very heterogeneity of the linguistic minorities and the caste divisions within the Hindu majority have made Hindus a politically difficult category to organize collectively. The majority of Indians are Hindus but with such an amorphous category its other internal divisions become politically salient. The BSO has no identifiable class or ethnic group but is a set of dominant cultural attributes and values that pervade the whole society, including minority and subordinate groups, but because it lacks an institution or group focus it is difficult to identify or challenge. It nevertheless enables dominance through its culture, in much the same way as Foucault[14] refers to the dominant ideas that unconsciously permeate western society and perpetuate rule by particular classes. Just as 'American scholarship pursues two approaches to this history: one explores the tensions of racism, sexism, and egalitarianism in American politics; another follows the mainstream',[15] similarly, analysis of India is divided according to self-interested agendas.

In Pakistan, by contrast, because political dominance is ethnically and culturally associated with specific minorities, it can never be universal and therefore truly legitimate. This gives India a stability Pakistan is unlikely to ever attain. Despite a common religion, Pakistan proved incapable of overcoming ethnicity and culture in a unifying ideology. India's caste divisions as internal ethnic divisions cannot be secessionist in the way that Pakistan's politicized ethnicity already is. Where India's ethnicity has become secessionist its relatively peripheral position in the outlying areas of the country like Kashmir and the northeast, or as small minorities in the heartland as in Punjab, makes it less of a threat to the nation as a whole.

As if the indigenous ethnic categories in Pakistan were not enough, the founding fathers were mostly from the Muslim-minority provinces of India. Arriving as refugees in Pakistan they had the importance of being a driving force behind the nation's creation and were able to have their native Urdu adopted as the national language. Their disproportionate share of the civil and military state institutions however was not a problem as long as the locals were marginalized and were unable to fill various positions. The refugees in Karachi came to be the dominant population, creating resentment among the Sindhi population, in whose province the city is located. While Punjabi refugees could cross over the border and disappear among the locals, the distinct culture of the Muhajir refugees meant that they were unassimilated locally, and even the next indigenous generation continued this tradition. Their relative deprivation compared to their position after their nation's founding was engineered by the local Sindhi population, who felt deprived of status and positions within their own homeland. As long as the Sindhi population were marginal in politics under the military regimes this presented no threat. However, with the return of civilian rule under the first democratically elected government after the secession of East Pakistan, the Sindhis finally had an influence at the centre with their leader, Zulfiquar Ali Bhutto, who introduced a quota in the civil service for Muhajirs, reducing their proportion from a peak of 30 per cent to 20 per cent.[16] The induction of Sindhi and other political patronage appointees into the civil service was a direct threat to the Muhajirs who lacked the electoral numbers to exercise influence proportional to their share of privileges. In this they were distinct from the Punjabis who had both disproportionate influence and the votes to ensure their share of assets under electoral politics. There were also hill groups who were variously well-represented in the military regimes, such as the Pashtuns who are second only to the Punjabis in the civilian-military bureaucracy, to the often insurgent Balochs who, though repressed by both military and civilian regimes, have secessionist potential in their own right. Even the Pashtuns to the extent that they make common cause with those in Afghanistan could, depending on the political outcome there, present a secessionist threat to Pakistan. Interestingly enough, on the Kashmir question, both Sindhis and Balochs oppose the government line on integration with Pakistan, preferring self-determination.[17] There are thus serious north–south as well as east–west ethnic divisions which make centralized nation building problematic. The recommended solution of a genuine federal state with central resource transfers to alleviate regional disparities has never been attempted.

Unlike the situation in India where no single ethnic group is in a position to exercise central control and must therefore bargain for a share of the patronage, in Pakistan two ethnic groups have more than their fair share, while a third refugee group is losing the share it had. The dominance of the Punjabis in the military-civilian bureaucracy has been challenged unsuccessfully by three Bhutto-led Pakistan Peoples' Party (PPP) governments. After repeated failures at governance, the military is understandably reluctant to rule directly again. However, the absence of direct military rule does not solve the governance problems of Pakistan, which rest in civil society and are therefore beyond the control of even civilian politicians, or at least the ones who are still willing to negotiate with each other. The criminalization of politics, the use of arms and the infiltration of drug runners, arms and fundamentalists into street violence have created problems which may in time be beyond the control of the state and lead to its break up. The use of Pakistan as a base for the war in Afghanistan brought with it the refugees and armed culture from that country which have yet to go away. A million heroin addicts are a by-product of a country that has lost its sense of purpose.[18] The demoralization noted by visitors to Pakistan[19] is surprising in a country created by a messianic idea and developed in the face of a more powerful neighbour that for years was perceived as a threat to its very existence. Now that Pakistan has the bomb, that threat has receded, and the component parts have fallen with increasing violence into mutual recrimination. There have even been allegations that India has been able to foster this mutual antagonism, an indication that at least for some groups the rivalry with India is no longer of predominant interest. The PPP, though led by the Bhuttos from Sind, also has bases in the Punjab and the Northwest Frontier Province,[20] and might represent the best chance for a transethnic consensus. However, it has watered down its populist ideology and become scarcely different in its programme from the rival Punjab-based Nawaz Sharif faction of the Pakistan Muslim League (PML), which it outvoted by a mere 1.9 per cent in Pakistan's second fair election in 1993.[21] The 1997 election more than reversed this position, though whether the Muslim League will use its majority to effectively restructure Pakistani politics remains to be seen. There is nothing in its history to indicate that it will do better than the PPP in this regard.

Significantly, none of these divisions dominate the western perceptions of Pakistan, which has come to be associated with the struggle against fundamentalist Islam. Though it is a powerful force in the country, it was a distant third in the popular vote of

1993. It is an idea various politicians have had to pay lip service to and General Zia attempted to implement as a means of obtaining legitimacy for himself, but it has failed to capture the electoral support of all but a small minority. The elections of 1993 indicated just how weak the political support for the fundamentalists was, which is perhaps why they boycotted the 1977 elections. However, as an idea of what the Pakistani state should or could become it has intimidated critics and prevented a liberalization that some political leaders such as the Bhuttos might personally have preferred. In cultural terms the Bhuttos and Gandhis had more in common with each other than with their own fundamentalist opponents, though they were limited in how secular an agenda they were willing and able to promote.

The Kashmir issue is a typical example of how the elites in the two countries have been placed in untenable positions by their electorates and political elites. Both countries want the area for themselves, while the local inhabitants, as nearly as can be determined, want neither. Though self-determination is the only just solution to this seemingly intractable problem, neither side is willing to countenance it. During the cold war such attitudes were the norm, but with the break up of the Soviet bloc self-determination is no longer being denied to those people who insist on it, as in the case of Bosnia whose government has even been recognized as legitimate by the western world. Though according to an Indian analyst, Bhabani Sen Gupta, there are only about 10 people in the Indian policy-influencing circle who would countenance the secession of Kashmir, in Pakistan, Sindhi (though not the PPP) and Baluch opinion would favour it in contradiction of the official policy of annexation with Pakistan. However, since Pakistan does not control the territory it may be more flexible on this point. As any fair settlement would have to include Pakistani-occupied-Kashmir (POK), Pakistan will likely prove to be as reluctant as India to give up the territory it controls to an independent secessionist state. The divide in Pakistan on an issue that for years appeared sacrosanct is indicative of how deep ethnic differences in public opinion in Pakistan are. India, having successfully controlled the Sikh insurgency, which never had majority support, still appears determined to impose a similar military solution on Kashmir, though its human rights abuses went some way towards creating the sentiment for secession in the first place. India may have the means to continue the military option indefinitely, but it is unlikely to obtain Kashmiri public support for Indian rule by this means alone. While the Muslim areas of Kashmir are peripheral to India, which could survive its secession, the potential of secession in Pakistan extends across most of the country.

A belated programme of equalization of opportunity attempted to integrate East Pakistanis into the educational and administrative system, and this has now been extended to myriads of ethnic and occupational groups, many of which are relatively privileged, such as the military and the children of these occupational groups. 'An unintended by-product of the effectiveness of Pakistan's redistributional policies has been the exacerbation of perceptions of inequities between ethnoregional groups.'[22] If this is the case, it is difficult to see what state action can be used to resolve ethnic disparities without further politicizing and exacerbating them. However, to the extent that the PPP and PML are able to transcend their regional bases, which is partly the case, national political parties may be able to make the compromises required to keep the country together.

Despite stepping down from formal leadership of Pakistan, the military remain a power behind the scenes, though internal differences have recently kept them from unanimously pursuing an agenda outside their group interests. However, these group interests are formidable and the political economy of Pakistan's defence establishment exerts an influence that no politician has successfully curbed. The last politician who seriously attempted to do so, Z.A. Bhutto, was hanged by General Zia, the very officer he had appointed to support him against a possible military coup. The Pakistani military unlike their Indian counterparts, who generally pursue traditional military occupations, are heavily involved in big business, and in this respect more closely follow the Latin American tradition.[23] This does not mean that the Indian military do not have perquisites such as free food and medical facilities, but they are surpassed by their Pakistani counterparts who have developed major business interests as well, something unthinkable for the Indian military which lacks institutional investment portfolios. Defence expenditure is widely considered a major drain on the national budget. Likewise, the Pakistani bureaucracy enjoy a standard of living and power that far exceeds that of their Indian counterparts, whose income and power have been steadily eroded by inflation and ministerial authority. As an example, in the colonial period a middle-level provincial officer could afford to send his children for university education to Britain, but by the end of the Indian Civil Service (ICS) in the late 1970s, even the highest paid officers could not afford to send their children abroad without private means. I recently talked to one Indian UN official who was offered the post of secretary to the Indian government. His response was that the government would have to pay his bills, which was impossible. His salary would have been less than the rent on his daughter's small apartment in Bombay. The wife of the head of one central government agency complained to me that after her husband retires and they leave their government house they would have difficulty in making ends meet. When even the highest echelons of government service have such difficulties, a state faces the problem of maintaining bureaucratic integrity. Yet there are academics who see bureaucrats as part of a ruling-class triumvirate along with politicians and big business, when in fact the bureaucracy has long since been subordinated to the politicians and by extension to the electoral process. The fact that a civil service cannot even get its pay indexed or adjusted to inflation, as in some other countries or for that matter even in sectors of the Indian unionized working class, reveals that it does not have much influence over government policy. That the judiciary was finally able to bring some politicians to book in India only served to contrast its differences with Pakistan where similar demands went unheeded, except when these were politically useful to those in office.

In Pakistan the civilian-military bureaucracy really does have power. Pakistani military officers undertake a modern equivalent of the Grand Tour, visiting the capitals of the western world as part of an annual outing with no apparent business except public relations. For their Indian counterparts excursions on this scale for no apparent official purpose are quite inconceivable, as it would be the politicians who would undertake such events. This is merely one aspect of what is in fact a rather corrupt patronage system in Pakistan which enables such things as distribution of cheap land to military officers so that they can resell it at market price. Though this corruption may not have reached the level of that in some African countries where the military is essentially parasitic rather than developmental, it closely resembles the Latin American officer corps which amasses corporations and privileges as the self-identified developmental vanguard of the nation. Until these sectors can be effectively brought under elected civilian control, democracy cannot be considered institutionalized in Pakistan. In this respect Pakistan is still dealing with issues of democracy which have long since been resolved in India.

On the principle of self-determination and the right of secession, however, both Pakistan and India are wedded to the old concept of absolute state sovereignty with or without the consent of minorities. India has been innovative in granting autonomy and even statehood to particularly vocal groups, but on the question of self-determination it has been as adamant as Pakistan. Though self-determination is finding increasing acceptance in the world, and the human rights abuses associated with maintaining territorial integrity are no longer considered acceptable, the lack of effective human rights enforcement mechanisms means that both Pakistan and India have a relatively free hand in suppressing minorities. However, this should not distract attention from the fact that India's and Pakistan's policy-making elites in their adherence to territorial integrity are somewhat out of step with current thinking. They often have an exaggerated view of the importance of South Asia in world affairs, and the foreign conspiracies that are supposedly being hatched by western democracies to destabilize them. As a Pakistani general pointed out to a sceptical Western diplomat, one in seven persons in the world is Indian. Coming from an Indian that might have been a boast, but to the general it was a threat. From this fear of a larger neighbour stems the need for a defence budget that is proportionately more than twice (7 per cent of GNP) that of India, and the apprehension that any concession to regional autonomy is a prelude to disintegration.[24] However, this is a problem Pakistan will have to face. By virtue of its size and heterogeneity India may be able to combat a couple of regional insurgencies indefinitely, but given its smaller size and more volatile ethnic combination Pakistan may someday find this beyond its coercive resources. Even today most of India's infantry is said to be active in putting down local insurgencies. Pakistan has so far avoided such a draining commitment, but its potential to deal with it is more limited and the likelihood of facing it in the future even more probable. Islamic ideology whether of a fundamentalist or social democratic variety is unlikely to be able to replace an already mobilized ethnicity. The last attempt at it, by General Zia, was a failure.[25] The PPP governments have resorted to repression in Karachi and elsewhere but this may ultimately prove equally unsuccessful.

At the heart of the Pakistani dilemma is finding its role in the modern world. Its founder was scarcely different from his former colleagues in the Congress party. 'Jinnah was a thoroughly secular and this-worldly man, a completely eclectic individual for whom there were no dietary taboos.... He knew little or nothing about either Islam as a religion or Islam as a civilization.'[26] As the only unifying theme for the new nation it was natural that the concept of an Islamic state and what it should embody would come to dominate the nation-building agenda. Though it helped spawn the most fundamentalist of regimes in Afghanistan, Pakistan itself had a much more ambiguous relationship with the outside world, with both modernist and fundamentalist camps vying for influence over state policy. While the United States remained its major patron during the cold war, its culture and undemocratic institutions made it unattractive to western scholars despite the realpolitik behind their governments' support of the regime. According to Professor Qureshi,

> Pakistan's anti-Indian preoccupation has had no echo in the United States for the simple reason that, in Washington's perspective, India is eight times larger than Pakistan, it has democratic and secular politics with which the US can identify more easily than with Pakistan's Islam-oriented and autocratic politics.... Consequently, when foreign aid for Pakistan is under consideration in the US Congress, there is virtually no Pakistani lobby, no important American scholars or famous journalists to speak for Pakistan or advocate Pakistan's cause. On the contrary, there are numerous Indophiles and friends of Israel within the American intellectual community who are eager to volunteer their expert service and advice about the dangers of the American aid to Pakistan either for India or for Israel or both.[27]

Issues such as the death sentence on a Christian child for defiling Islam do not play well in the western media, and with American scholars such as Samuel Huntington talking about a civilizational clash with the Islamic world,[28] the West may be losing sight of the more modernizing elements in Pakistani civil society that do not catch media attention but nevertheless exist.

Without technologically advanced and powerful western allies, Pakistan has recently had to rely on lesser powers with limited interest in sustaining its competition with India. While its nuclear umbrella will preserve it from destruction by India, it is in danger of losing the economic and technological battle with its neighbour, and imploding from its own internal ethnic and political contradictions. This has not prevented some from attempting to resurrect a democratic national project, but the rot may have gone too far for the system to cleanse itself, in a way that Indian democracy still seems capable of doing. The landslide majority for Nawaz Sharif in the 1997 general elections was described as a last chance for Pakistan to avoid joining the 'ranks of Asia's failed states'.[29] Even if the country survives, successful development and democratization will prove more difficult to achieve. Without resolution of the fundamental problems facing the country, Pakistan will turn itself into a political and economic backwater in fairly short order.

The contrasts between Indian and Pakistani politics have been downplayed by Ayesha Jalal in favour of emphasis on the identical roots of authoritarianism in the two countries.[30] The process and outcomes, however, were significantly different. The bureaucratic-military dominance in Pakistan resulted from the necessity of establishing a new state, practically from scratch in the face of local resistance. India inherited the ICS, which provided a ready-made structure for governance, while the Congress party facilitated the institutionalization of democratic party politics without the necessity of military intervention. Despite the unfavourable beginnings of Pakistan, military takeover occurred only after the state had been effectively established, and was a result of the failure of politicians and other members of the elite to make the accommodations that would have enabled a constitution to be drawn up over which all parties could be in agreement. The colonial legacy was common to both countries, but the Indian constitution maintained a complex series of concessions, including those to marginalized groups that served to integrate them with the democratic process.[31] The Pakistani elite consistently failed to grant concessions to minorities or the Bengali majority, because they realized that they could not have democracy and retain power for themselves, so dictatorship of the bureaucratic and finally the military variety was essential to their retaining power. Democracy could only be established after the secession of Bangladesh enabled West Pakistani dominance to continue through the electoral system for the first time. However, by then the military-bureaucratic dictatorship had already been well established and proved unwilling to restrict its influence within democratic norms. With the growth of violent dissent, the Pakistani military has a continuing motivation not to restrain itself. The Indian elite at independence faced no such threat to their rule, and democracy represented the best way of negotiating and managing governance with the diverse minority groups.

The current failure of Pakistan had its genesis shortly after independence when the West Pakistanis failed to concede majority rule to East Pakistan. They might have maintained a unitary state by devolving power in a confederation in which both East Pakistan and West Pakistan retained real power in their respective wings. The West Pakistanis refused this assuming they could control the whole nation under their own minority dominance.[32] Their justification for undemocratic leadership also came from viewing Bengalis as following a degraded version of Islam as practised by lower caste converts.[33] This sense of cultural and religious superiority was brought home to me by the comment of an Oxford student from a leading Muslim Congress family who referred to a group as not belonging to the type of Muslims who had converted from the Namasudra community, thereby indicating their superior status and culture. Though his grandfather had been president of India, his father a central government minister, and he himself later became a union minister, the derogatory attitude towards Bengali Muslims was common to both Muslim Congress and Muslim League leaders. Among those who had chosen to flee to Pakistan rather than remain in India the attitude of superiority was probably accentuated. West Pakistan's imposition of Urdu and other attempts to denigrate Bengali culture were justified as a means to upgrade the Islamic culture of East Pakistan to its own standards. The civilizing mission helped justify the imposition of West Pakistani civilian and military dictatorship over the whole nation, which democracy would have prevented through Bengali majority rule. When East Pakistan was lost through the West Pakistanis' own lack of respect for democracy and Bengali culture, West Pakistan introduced democracy for itself for the first time. However, with a legacy of dictatorship well established, the temptation to have the military and its sponsors intervene when things did not go the way the military wanted proved irresistible. A generation has now grown up not knowing a united Pakistan, but the legacy of that period of dictatorship continues to work itself out in the failures of democracy to become institutionalized. Rather than looking to colonial legacies to place the blame on foreigners, or denying that there is any real difference between India and Pakistan, given their common authoritarian tendencies, it is important to recognize how the cultural attitudes and political interests of elites served to immiserate the country. That these proved exceptionally destructive in Pakistan, while Indian democratization continues to surmount these tendencies, reflects the volatile ethnic mix Pakistan inherited and the failure of its leadership to accommodate this diversity.

Intellectual elites who view regimes according to their own freedom of self-expression naturally portray Pakistan negatively in comparison to India. Nevertheless, it needs to be recognized that regime differences have little perceptible effect on much of the population, and at the lower levels perhaps none at all. The threats from lower-class empowerment need to be differentiated from those coming from elites. While Indian democracy is sometimes seen to be threatened by the inclusion of previously excluded groups, much of this analysis is by elites who find the extension of democracy to the lower classes and castes undesirable, for it threatens their intellectual perceptions and positions. This is all the more so in Pakistan where there is limited input from civil society in institutions of state power, making for greater instability and violent conflict. If Pakistan is willing to abandon a strong central state in favour of devolution to the provinces some of the crisis can be defused, but it would require the elites to redefine themselves and not see the ethnic and regionalist forces as nation destroying, but as part of a radical reinterpretation of the meaning of Pakistan. The democratization of Pakistan may bring about this devolution, but without it, it is difficult to see how the state can abandon its tradition of constitutional coups and military takeovers. Alan Whaites argues that this process of democratization through the growth of the middle-class civil society and its associations is already far advanced, and has implicitly rendered academic analysis based on ethnic bureaucratic-military dominance dated.

> The neglect of Pakistan's evolving society has threatened to stereo-type Pakistan as a static state stuck in a continuing cycle of military and feudal government. The 'geopolitical and demographic' context approach to Pakistani politics has led to macro-analysis in which the internal politics of the country, placed within its wider context, is reduced to an elite orientated evolution of political interaction.... This context centred discussion and its elite centred view of politics has engendered a pessimism which fails to address the tremendous changes within the social fabric of Pakistan during the last forty years.[34]

The empirical evidence for this change is presented through the growth in media outlets and non-governmental organizations. Scholars of the subcontinent often neglect to analyze changes in civil society due to the lack of an adequately diverse range of contacts. The fact that in both India and Pakistan the state is under attack is itself a reflection of this activism in civil society. However, that previously dominant elites find themselves under threat and resorting to repression, while significant, does not necessarily alter the way the state is run or who runs it. The influence of middle-class civil society is still not a determinant in Pakistan despite the growth of its associations and media. That Alan Whaites, as Policy and Research Manager for the Christian NGO World Vision, should view the society from the perspective of an NGO is understandable, but the influence of the organizations he refers to on the state appears fairly negligible. That these organizations are being funded by international aid organizations also raises the question as to the extent of their grassroots support being exaggerated for fund-raising purposes, and how much of it would survive in the absence of foreign funding. 'This theoretical labelling of the Pakistani state and the concentration on the apparent power of the state's military arm has obscured the more subtle forces which have gradually transformed the relationship between Pakistani state and society.'[35] The difficulty with analysis of changes in civil society is that they can be so subtle as to be easily misinterpreted. Demands for democratization may simply be inter-elite rivalries with those temporarily out of power mobilizing their following in anticipation of their return to office. In the absence of a series of critical victories of the civil over the military, and of ethnic minorities over the dominant elite, these changes in civil society may not change methods of governance or negate earlier elite-oriented analyses. The frustration in civil society could, however, result in a polarization similar to that which occurred prior to the secession of Bangladesh.

REFERENCES

1. Joseph Nye, *Bound to Lead: The Changing Nature of American Power* (New York: Basic Books, 1991).
2. Jinnah's address to the All-India Muslim League (AIML) Council at Lahore, 30 July 1944 quoted in Ayesha Jalal, *The State of Martial Rule: The Origins of Pakistan's Political Economy of Defense* (Cambridge: Cambridge University Press, 1990), p. 19.
3. Shahid Javed Burki, 'Pakistan's Economy in the Year 2000: Two Possible Scenarios', in J. Henry Korson (ed.), *Contemporary Problems of Pakistan* (Boulder: Westview Press, 1993). pp. 4–5.
4. United Nations Development Programme, *Human Development Report 1995* (New York: Oxford University Press, 1995), p. 157.
5. Mahmood Monshipouri and Amjad Samuel, 'Development and Democracy in Pakistan', *Asian Survey*, Vol. 35, No. 11, November 1995, p. 988.
6. *The Economist*, 15–21 June 1996, p. 37.
7. *The Economist*, 21 December 1996, p. 44.
8. Theodore P. Wright Jr., 'Can There be a Melting Pot in Pakistan? Interprovincial Marriage and National Integration', *Contemporary South Asia*, Vol. 3, No. 2, 1994, p. 131.
9. Akmal Hussain, 'The Crisis of State Power in Pakistan: Militarization and Dependence', in Ponna Wignaraja and Akmal Hussain (eds), *The Challenge in South Asia: Development, Democracy and Regional Cooperation* (New Delhi: Sage Publications, 1989), p. 222.
10. Ibid., p. 235.
11. Saleem M.M. Qureshi, 'Regionalism, Ethnic Conflict and Islam in Pakistan: Impact on Foreign Policy', in Hafeez Malik (ed.), *Dilemmas of National Security and Cooperation in India and Pakistan* (London: St Martin's Press, 1993), pp. 230–31.

12. Burki, 'Pakistan's Economy in the Year 2000' (n. 2 above), pp. 2–3.
13. Akmal Hussain, *Strategic Issues in Pakistan's Economic Policy* (Lahore: Progressive Publishers, 1988), p. 354.
14. Graham Burchell et al. (eds), *The Foucault Effect: Studies in Governmentality* (Chicago: The University of Chicago Press, 1991).
15. Jacqueline Stevens, 'Beyond Tocqueville, Please!', *American Political Science Review*, Vol. 89, No. 4, December 1995, p. 990.
16. Yunas Samad, 'The Military and Democracy in Pakistan', *Contemporary South Asia*, Vol. 3, No. 3, 1994, p. 193.
17. Mehtab Ali Shah, 'The Kashmir Problem: A View From Four Provinces of Pakistan', *Contemporary South Asia*, Vol. 4, No. 1, March 1995, pp. 103–12.
18. Marvin G. Weinbaum, 'The Impact and Legacy of the Afghan Refugees in Pakistan', in J. Henry Korson (ed.), *Contemporary Problems of Pakistan*, (Boulder: Westview Press, 1993), p. 135.
19. Burki, 'Pakistan's Economy in the Year 2000' (n. 3 above), p. 1.
20. Shah, 'The Kashmir Problem' (n. 17 above), p. 107.
21. Andrew R. Wilder, 'Changing Patterns of Punjab Politics in Pakistan: National Assembly Election Results, 1988 and 1993', *Asian Survey*, Vol. 35, No. 4, April 1995, p. 378.
22. Charles H. Kennedy, 'Policies of Redistributional Preference in Pakistan', in Neil Nevitte and Charles H. Kennedy (eds), *Ethnic Preference and Public Policy in Developing States* (Boulder, Colorado: Lynne Rienner Publishers, 1986), p. 87.
23. Ayesha Jalal, *Democracy and Authoritarianism in South Asia*, (Cambridge: Cambridge University Press, 1995), p. 143.
24. Robert E. Looney, 'Pakistani Defence Expenditures and the Macroeconomy: Alternative Strategies to the Year 2000', *Contemporary South Asia*, Vol. 4, No. 3, 1995, p. 331.
25. Urmila Phadnis, *Ethnicity and Nation-building in South Asia* (New Delhi: Sage Publications, 1989), p. 105.
26. Qureshi, 'Regionalism, Ethnic Conflict and Islam in Pakistan' (n. 11 above), pp. 234–35.
27. Ibid., p. 246.
28. Samuel P. Huntington, 'The Clash of Civilizations', *Foreign Affairs*, Vol. 72, No. 3, Summer 1993.
29. 'Last Chance in Pakistan', *The Economist*, 8–14 February 1997, p. 22.
30. Jalal, *Democracy and Authoritarianism* (n. 23 above),p.249.
31. Asthma Barlas, *Democracy, Nationalism and Communalism: The Colonial Legacy in South Asia* (Boulder: Westview Press, 1995).
32. Richard Sisson and Leo E. Rose, *War and Secession: Pakistan, India, and the Creation of Bangladesh* (Berkeley: University of California Press, 1990), p. 10.
33. Ibid., p. 9.
34. Alan Whaites, 'The State and Civil Society in Pakistan', *Contemporary South Asia*, Vol. 4, No. 3, p. 230.
35. Ibid., p. 240.

CHAPTER 8

Minorities in Bangladesh

There are two major minority groups in Bangladesh, the largely Untouchable Hindus and the tribal peoples of the Chittagong Hill Tracts. There is very little literature on the Hindus and rather more on the guerrilla war being conducted between the tribals and the Bangladesh government. Why the one should have attracted more attention than the other can be surmised by the respective circumstances of the two groups. While the Hindus are almost certainly being discriminated against, they are not being killed, and the communal violence has in recent years not equalled that of neighbouring India. The tribals on the other hand are being decimated by ethnic cleansing that has forced many to become refugees in India. As this has been done with the complicity of western governments and their aid agencies, it has brought their plight to the attention of international human rights organizations, which were largely ineffective in getting western donors to influence Bangladesh policies, but did publish some literature on the subject of tribal minorities.

Hindus in a Muslim State

By far the largest minority in Bangladesh are the Hindus. Historically they were the majority, but the conversion of many low-caste and Untouchable Hindus to Islam changed this forever. That the vast majority of Muslims are of the same ancestry as their Hindu neighbours with whom they reside in the same communities indicates that there is little cultural difference between the two groups in the secular sphere. However, as Islam found more appeal in the lower castes, their conversion meant that there was a tendency for the Muslims to be tenants and the Hindus to be landlords. Most of the larger landowners were Hindus, and the greater proclivity of Hindus for western education led in time to their dominance in modern professions and the colonial administration as well. This group came to lead the independence struggle in Bengal, but found little response from the Muslim and lower-caste population in the state, which also began to organize in their own interests and in opposition to Hindu dominance. The struggle between the higher-caste Hindus and the Muslims soon tended to supersede the anti-colonial struggle as the determinant issue in a provincial politics where religion and class made for different interpretations of who the main opponent should be. Table 8.1 indicates the caste and religious disparities which made for different political perspectives.

TABLE 8.1

Caste and Economic Differentiation in Rural Bengal

	High Castes	Intermediate	Muslims	Untouchables	Santals
Literate (%)	50	33	18	4	3
Landless Families (%)	18	13	25	87	92
Average Assets (rupees)	2,823	1,528	1,083	73	76
Average Value of Land (rupees)	2,220	1,340	1,098	38	39
Average Annual Income (rupees)	436	236	172	84	76

Source: Joya Chatterji, *Bengal Divided* (Cambridge: Cambridge University Press, 1994), p. 37, citing Hashim Amir Ali, *Modern Review*, Vol. 56, 1–16, July–December 1934, pp. 42–43.

The Muslims were a bare majority, 54 per cent, in 1931, though relegated in a communal award to 47.8 per cent of the seats, while the Hindus, 44 per cent, got even less, with 32 per cent.[1] However, 10 of the 80 Hindu seats went to Untouchables who generally sided with the Muslims, effectively putting the Hindu-dominated Congress party in the opposition benches of Bengal from the 1920s till partition of the state between Hindu India and Muslim Pakistan enabled them to stage a comeback in the western part of the province. The alliance between the Untouchables and Muslims in governing coalitions amounted to a class alliance against the economic dominance of the Hindu landed class which provincial legislation attempted to undermine through land reform and other legislation. Faced with this loss of provincial power the Hindu community turned from implicit to increasingly explicit communal demands. The Hindu version of history has been that Muslims initiated communal killings in Calcutta to force partition of the province and independence for Pakistan, thereby destroying the Congress view of a united secular democratic India. However, in a ground-breaking work by Joya Chatterji, it is made clear that partition had come to be the favoured position not only of the Hindu communalists, once Hindu dominance was lost, but the preferred option of the Congress and the vast majority of Hindus in Bengal.

> The United Bengal Plan was never more than a pipe dream. Even as Gandhi gave his conditional approval to the plan to keep Bengal united, he was forced to withdraw his support, since, as he later confessed, his colleagues on the [Congress] Working Committee had 'taken him to task for supporting Sarat Babu's move'.... Even Nehru and Patel, so often at odds, saw eye to eye on this matter.[2]

According to Joya Chatterji,

> Hindus in West Bengal had decided to plump for a Hindu state of their own rather than continuing to live under the premiership of a notoriously unreliable Muslim, and the Hindus of East Bengal were already reconciled to the bitter fact that they had to pack up their belongings and flee to the west.[3]

Unlike the situation in the Punjab where the transfer of population was about equal so that the refugees could occupy abandoned property, in Bengal more Hindus fled to India than Muslims to Pakistan, leaving the Indian government with an added population. This refugee group was not a representative cross-section of the Hindu minority in East Bengal. The Untouchable leaders had opposed partition, perhaps because it would mean the loss of the balance of power between caste Hindus and Muslims that they were likely to hold in a united Bengal. When partition became inevitable they sided with Pakistan as the Muslims had been their allies in government coalitions and they expected more equitable treatment from them. The early inclusion of an Untouchable in the Pakistan cabinet indicated that this was a fair assumption, and in any case the best organized Untouchable movement fell within the area of Pakistan. In retrospect, there is some feeling in the Untouchable community that their leaders should have organized a complete withdrawal of their people to India, just as the Sikhs did in the Punjab; however, at the time it was not obvious which country would preserve its democratic traditions, and migration is always more difficult than staying where you are, particularly when you lack the resources to move easily.

The caste Hindus were in a very different position. As the dominant landed and professional elite in Bengal, their land holdings were probably untenable and, given the violence of the period, their lives were under a potential threat that made departure much more desirable. They had the funding and education to start afresh relatively quickly in West Bengal, and also the family connections to make a fairly rapid adjustment. As Calcutta was the metropole for Bengal, many in this class already had property or relatives there.

> Even progressives among the Hindu bhadralok responded in reactionary outrage and pique at becoming a 'minority'— with its connotations of secondariness. Having ridden on the backs of a deprived and degraded Muslim and Namasudra society, they were not well situated to welcome any movement towards social equality and politico-economic reform, neither were they able to prevent a dismantling of the privileges of status and wealth they had presumed to be 'naturally' theirs. Escape to West Bengal seemed the only way to 'keep face'—avoid assimilation and humiliation by those they had considered their social inferiors.[4]

With Hindu landlords and moneylenders having difficulty collecting their dues, a livelihood for many of them was obviously coming to an end.[5] For them flight was the most obvious option but the Untouchables chose for the most part to stay behind. In explaining the difference an Untouchable refugee stated:

'All the Muslims had to do was wave a stick at the babus and
they ran away, they had to break our heads before they
could make us leave.' He laughed derisively and informed
me that after the partition, during time of unrest, the caste
Hindus forgot their prejudice and took shelter in the Namasudra enclaves. These were the same people who had not so
long ago addressed them arrogantly as charaler po or 'son of
an untouchable' and bathed if so much as their shadows
crossed. Now they were eager to embrace them as 'brothers'.[6]

The differential flight patterns of the caste-Hindu elite and the
Untouchables meant that East Pakistan came to be denuded of its
traditional Hindu elite, while the poorer castes and classes for the
most part remained behind. Soon Untouchables outnumbered all
other Hindus (both Backward and Forward Castes) combined.

Of the Hindus who remained behind the caste Hindus continued their opposition towards the new Pakistani government,
while some Untouchable leaders joined it. However, now that
the Muslims had achieved partition they were no longer in need
of Untouchable allies, and communal riots which continued after
partition increasingly targeted the remaining largely Untouchable
Hindu population. In the face of these atrocities and the West
Pakistani dominance, the Untouchable minister in the Pakistan
cabinet J.N. Mandal fled his office for India, tendering his resignation to the Pakistani prime minister in words that summarized
both the Untouchable and Bengali Muslim position.

After anxious and prolonged thought I have come to the
conclusion that Pakistan is no place for Indians to live in and
that their future is darkened by the ominous shadow of conversion or liquidation. The bulk of the upper class Hindus
and politically conscious scheduled castes have left East
Bengal. These Hindus who will continue to stay in the
accursed province and for that matter in Pakistan will, I am
afraid, by gradual stages and in a planned manner be either
converted to Islam or completely exterminated....

And what about the Muslims who are outside the charmed
circle of the League rulers and their corrupt and inefficient
bureaucracy? There is hardly anything called civil liberty in
Pakistan.... East Bengal has been transformed into a colony

of the western belt of Pakistan, although it contained a population which is larger than that of all the units of Pakistan put together. It is a pale ineffective adjunct of Karachi doing the latter's bidding and carrying out its orders. East Bengal Muslims in their enthusiasm wanted bread and they have by the mysterious working of the Islamic State and the Shariat got stone instead from arid deserts of Sind and the Punjab.[7]

The end of Untouchable–Muslim cooperation led to a greater unity among the Hindu population represented by the remaining Hindu leaders as the Scheduled Castes moved away from their former ally in the ruling Muslim League and set up alliances with their old enemies in the Congress.[8] During and shortly after partition most of the refugees were from the Hindu elites, but with most of the caste Hindus gone, continued communal feeling resulted in more of the middle and lower castes departing.[9]

However, in the face of West Pakistani dominance, Muslim Bengali nationalism soon arose and found common cause against it with the Hindu minority. Much of the property left by the departing Hindu elite had been seized by non-Bengali Muslim refugees from India who identified with West Pakistan. Attempts to impose Urdu and West Pakistani values led to East Pakistani resentment and the defeat of the Muslim League in 1954. From then till the imposition of overt military dictatorship in 1958 a series of coalition governments enabled the Hindu minority to have significant influence and even on occasion the balance of power in the formation of governments. 'In this brief period there were five governments at the centre. East Bengal had three governments and was under governor's rule for nearly two years. This situation gave the minorities a unique chance to "fish in troubled waters" and to maximize their interest.'[10] According to one Muslim,

The ministry is now at the complete mercy of the Hindu members, even though they represent only 12 per cent of the population. The exploited Muslim peasants of East Pakistan supported the movement for Pakistan in the hope that domination by the Hindu minority would come to an end, but today political instability in East Pakistan has given the

Hindu members undue predominance in the Province's affairs.[11]

They used this power to try and prevent the more blatant manifestations of Islamization and to protect minority constitutional rights. Though they failed to prevent some Islamic provisions, they were able to get equal rights placed in the constitution and laws. At that time they were elected under separate Hindu constituencies representing 23 per cent of the seats, a figure greater than their share of the population after the flight of so many refugees. Though the Congress had opposed separate electorates before independence, with partition the Hindus in East Pakistan had the most to gain electorally from the maintenance of a separate electoral roll, as their votes would not be swamped by the Muslim majority. However, despite this electoral logic the Hindus were adamant that there be a common secular electoral roll, because they feared that a separate electorate would make them more exposed to Muslim attack. In what amounted to a form of political submerging, they succeeded in obtaining a common electoral roll which virtually wiped out their presence in parliaments and higher elected bodies. Such was their fear of Muslim backlash that they forfeited their last remaining hold on political power. Henceforth, they could expect only about 3 per cent of the seats as opposed to the 23 per cent they had previously been allotted under a separate electorate. As a result of this marginalization under the joint electorate, by the late 1960s Untouchables again began demanding a separate electorate or, failing that, a separate state or province for themselves.[12]

After the imposition of military dictatorship in 1958 the Hindus were subjected to increased discrimination and repression by the government, but they found common cause with Muslim fellow Bengalis in the struggle against West Pakistani military rule. The common religious identity that was the raison d'être for Pakistan was lost in the east through repressive West Pakistani cultural, political and economic policies that left the Bengali population almost totally alienated from the union with Pakistan. With the outbreak of civil war in East Pakistan, 90 per cent of the 10 million refugees who fled to India were Hindus fearful of the genocide allegedly being conducted by the Pakistan army.[13] However, the independence struggle was predominantly secular and the forces of secularism were never as strong as during the Bangladesh independence struggle. With the Awami League leader in a Pakistani jail, the leader of the government in exile, Tajuddin Ahmed, assumed a strong secular position that was characterized variously as pro-India, pro-Soviet and 'anti-western'.[14] However, on his return Sheikh Mujibur Rahman rescinded the previous secular policy banning Quranic recitations and Islamic greetings on state TV and radio, though the ban on the pro-Pakistani religious parties continued. The Awami League period is often seen as secular, but Mujibur Rahman did introduce Islamic prayers into secular government occasions, and the period only appears secular when compared with subsequent military regimes. In fact, each subsequent regime has felt it necessary to be even more Islamic than its predecessors. The Zia regime changed the secular constitution by including 'absolute trust and faith in the Almighty Allah', and attempted to bring Muslim fundamentalists on side without itself being branded fundamentalist or anti-minority.[15] However, the abolition of constitutional secularism convinced the minorities that the Bangladeshi military had ideas similar to those of their former Pakistani colleagues, though there was nothing that could be done about it. Unlike Zia who had been a leader of the independence war, General Ershad had spent the war as an army officer in West Pakistan as part of a group of Bengali officers whose sympathies with the liberation struggle were sometimes suspect. In his attempt to obtain legitimacy for his military regime he promised to introduce Sharia law, though he did so only in a limited formal sense. He amended the constitution in 1988 to state: 'The state religion of the Republic is Islam, but other religions may be practiced in peace and harmony in the Republic.'[16] The issue gave Ershad the opportunity to appease the fundamentalists and the Middle East states, while creating divisions in the opposition between secularists and fundamentalists, both of whom had reason to dislike his rule.

With the return of democracy and the rule of the wife of General Zia, the more secular Awami League was relegated to the opposition along with the fundamentalists, both of whom united in a parliamentary boycott to bring down the government. The anti-fundamentalist writings and alleged statements of Taslima Nasrin provided the government with the opportunity to split the opposition between secularists and fundamentalists by bringing charges of blasphemy against her.[17] This ultimately did not succeed in fragmenting the opposition, but did point to the continued salience of religion as a mobilizing tool which could be brought against the secularist Muslims and the more vulnerable minorities. Even though the implementation of Sharia law was avoided, no regime has ever moved in a decisively secular direction. Thus, while the move to Islamization may be halted for a time, the long-term trend seems to be towards greater Islamic identity. Like their Pakistani military counterparts, they perceive that stirring up religious sentiment in support of their regime may pay political dividends. However, this did not prove effective and the policies never got overwhelming support. In fact, Bangladeshi Islam has often been compared to the less fundamentalist interpretations of Indonesia, where Islam is poorly and inaccurately understood at the grassroots, and laced with indigenous cultural representations which do not make for the fanatical adherence to the doctrine found in the Middle East. Middle East states have attempted to remedy this by providing foreign aid, though at 6 per cent of the total Bangladeshi receipts they are a tiny fraction of what the West provides. Remittances from Bangladeshis in the Middle East may in fact be more significant, but trade continues to be more oriented to the non-Islamic world.[18]

The return of democracy has not brought increased electoral representation to the Hindu community. In the 1973 elections only 3.3 per cent of the seats were won by Hindus, and they all belonged to the ruling Awami League.[19]

A greater threat to the community in the longer term is its gradual decrease relative to the Muslim population, whose higher birth rate will contribute to a relatively smaller Hindu percentage of the population as has been occurring since long before independence (Table 8.2).

As a percentage of the population, which has an influence on the numbers that can be elected, the relative decrease in the Hindu population is more dramatic (Table 8.3).

Even projecting for a lower Hindu birth rate, 'as many as 1.7 million Hindus "disappeared" from the Bangladesh population during the 1981–1991 period, presumably through surreptitious migration to India'.[20] After the destruction of the mosque at Ayodhya, violence against Hindus in Bangladesh reached 'unprecedented proportions, spawning a fourth wave of emigration,

TABLE 8.2

Growth Rate of Hindus and Muslims, 1901–61 Censuses

	1901–11	1921	1931	1941	1951	1961
Muslims	11%	7%	9%	19%	9%	27%
	(21,202)	(22,646)	(24,731)	(29,509)	(32,227)	(40,890)
Hindus	4%	2%	3%	12%	– 21%	2%
	(9,952)	(10,166)	(10,453)	(11,747)	(9,239)	(9,890)

Source: Muhammad Ghulam Kabir, *Minority Politics in Bangladesh* (Delhi: Vikas Publishing House, 1980), p. 6.

TABLE 8.3

Percentage of Population by Religious Group in East Bengal, 1901–91

Year	Muslims	Hindus	Others
1901	66.1	33.0	0.9
1911	67.2	31.5	1.3
1921	68.1	30.6	1.3
1931	69.5	29.4	1.2
1941	70.3	28.0	1.8
1951	76.9	22.0	1.1
1961		18.4	
1981		12.1	
1991		10.5	

Sources: Muhammad Ghulam Kabir, *Minority Politics in Bangladesh* (Delhi: Vikas Publishing House, 1980), p. 6; Partha S. Ghosh, 'Bangladesh at the Crossroads', *Asian Survey*, Vol. 33, No. 7, July 1993, p. 699; Harry Blair,'Civil Society, Democratic Development and International Donors: A Case Study from Bangladesh', Paper presented at the annual meeting of the American Political Science Association, New York City, 1–4 September 1994, p. 19.

although smaller in magnitude and duration than its predecessors'.[21] However, unlike India, where over a thousand people were killed, in Bangladesh there were no fatalities and about 70 injuries.[22] Some of the migration may be more economically driven, given the greater number of Bangladeshi Muslim migrants who travel to India as well. This has become an issue the BJP has taken up both on account of the migrants and the higher birth rate of the resident Muslim population. In Bangladesh by contrast, the population of the Hindus is in decline relative to their Muslim neighbours', and may be in absolute decline due to economic and politically motivated migration to India. Since those who are left behind are likely to be of the poorest classes and increasingly composed of Untouchables, the best they can hope for is benign neglect. That I was unable to find a reference to any book-length treatment of Bangladeshi Hindus is an indication of the lack of public policy and academic interest in them.[23] With the departure of the educated elite the community is at a disadvantage in getting its concerns internationalized or studied.

Chittagong Hill Tracts

If the Bangladeshi Hindus are likely to disappear as a result of conversion and emigration, the Chittagong Hill peoples face the prospect of permanent refugee status or at best minority status through ethnic swamping in their own homeland. Paradoxically, the Chittagong Hill Tracts (CHT) along with Khulna district were tribal and Hindu-majority areas, respectively, and therefore should never have been given to Pakistan. The Hill Tracts should have been awarded to India as a tribal area, but the British allegedly wanted to help their close allies, the Sikhs, who were a large minority in a Muslim-majority district in Punjab. Rather than award the district to Pakistan they gave it to India, and instead gave the Chittagong Hill Tracts to Pakistan, though it had 98 per cent tribal Buddhist and Christian population.[24]

> The inclusion of the CHT with Pakistan met severe opposition from the native leaders. They wanted to join India and kept the Indian national flag hoisted for ten days. Finally, some indigenous leaders, among them was Sneha Kumar Chakma, fled to India when the Pakistani Army arrived.[25]

Had it been rightfully awarded to India the area would likely have been a tribal-run state similar to the other tribal states in northeast India, though as these also have insurgencies and non-tribal immigration, it is unlikely to have been peaceful under Indian rule. However, the award to Pakistan undoubtedly made things worse for the tribals, whose population declined in the face of state-sponsored or state-tolerated Bengali migration. The Bengalis comprised 9.1 per cent of the population in 1951, 17.7 per cent in 1961, 33 per cent in 1981, and by some reports now equal or outnumber the tribal population of about 600,000 (Table 8.4).[26]

TABLE 8.4

Population of Chittagong Hill Tracts by Ethnicity, 1872–1981

Ethnic Group	1872	1901	1951	1974	1981
Bengali (Muslim)	1,097	8,762	26,150	1,35,673	3,04,873
Chakma (Buddhism)	28,097	44,392	1,24,762	–	2,12,577
Marma (Buddhism)	22,060	34,706	65,889	–	1,22,734
Tripura (Hindu)	8,100	23,341	37,246	–	54,375
Mro (Animism)	2,378	10,540	16,121	–	17,811
Tanchangya (Animism)	–	–	8,313	–	17,696
Bawm (Christian)	305	696	977	–	5,733
Reang (Animism)	–	–	1,011	–	4,011
Pankhua (Christian)	177	241	627	–	2,278
Kheyang (Buddhism)	306	416	1,300	–	1,422
Khumi (Animism)	534	1,053	1,951	–	1,188
Lushei (Christian)	–	678	3,341	–	1,041
Chak (Buddhism)	–	–	–	–	910
Total Population	63,054	1,24,762	2,87,688	5,08,199	7,46,649
Total Native	61,957	1,16,000	2,61,538	3,72,526	4,41,776
% of Total Population	*98.26*	*92.63*	*90.91*	*73.30*	*59.16*
Total Bengali	1,097	8,762	26,150	1,35,673	3,04,873
% of Total Population	*1.73*	*0.67*	*9.08*	*26.29*	*40.83*
Density per km²	4	9	22	39	57

Sources: Aditya Kumar Dewan, 'Class and Ethnicity in the Hills of Bangladesh' (Ph.D. thesis, McGill University, October 1990), p. 48; religious affiliation from S. Mahmud Ali, *The Fearful State* (London: Zed Books, 1993), p. 166.

The situation gradually deteriorated for the tribals as ethnic Bengalis infiltrated the region. While Pakistan was united, the distant rulers in West Pakistan did not view the Chittagong Hill Tracts as a high political and development priority, and the economic and political neglect of the east was reflected in the Hill Tracts. In retrospect this period under Pakistani rule was relatively benign. The Pakistani government did not actively promote Bengali settlement in the area though the infiltration and local-level state support for Bengalis existed. The leading cause of tribal displacement during the Pakistan era was foreign aid which, as in Sri Lanka, altered the ethnic composition of the local population. The Kaptai Dam project, funded by the US Agency for International Development, displaced as many as 96,000 tribals. Most of the compensation money never reached the tribals.

The natives, during Pakistani rule, never faced forced eviction or any physical threat (such as beating, torture, killings,
etc.) from the non-natives and the Chakma Chief had always
friendly relations with the Pakistani authorities. As a result,
the natives never revolted or took up arms against the Pakistani Government in spite of destruction caused by the
hydro-dam.[27]

During the Bangladesh independence war some of the chiefs
sided with Pakistan, and the Bengali perception was that the
tribals had sided with Pakistan and were therefore collaborators.
Native youth were recruited into the Civil Armed Forces by the
Pakistani army against the Bangladeshi guerrillas, but in general
the tribal population remained neutral in the conflict.[28] This was
in marked contrast to the Hindus, who had been the worst suffer-
ers of Pakistani repression. After the defeat of Pakistan the Bangladesh guerrillas killed as many as 400 tribals for alleged
collaboration.

Arbitary arrests, intimidation, threats, ransom demands, extortion, harassment, beatings, bribes and other unlawful activities were carried out by the Bangladesh law enforcement
agencies throughout the CHT during the first few years after
the independence of Bangladesh. These gross human rights
violations were the immediate cause for the rise, growth and
birth of the Shanti Bahini, the main guerrilla force, and the
formation of Parbattya Chattagram Jana Sanghati Samittee
(PCJSS), the main political party of the indigenous people.[29]

The Bengali secessionist movement, with Indian assistance and
invasion, achieved independence in 1971, but then hypocritically
turned around and denied the right of secession to the tribals in
their own homeland.

It is ironic that the Bangladesh elite, whose own right to
self-determination was obtained in armed struggle against
Pakistani/Punjabi repression, should fail to respond in some
conciliatory way toward Chittagong claims. But after all, elites
elsewhere, once in charge of governments, have forgotten
their own struggles and have used the tools of repression
borrowed from their former adversaries.[30]

A Bangladeshi scholar told me of the censure he received for raising human rights questions about tribal policy. At a seminar on 'Tribal Cultures in Bangladesh' at Rajshahi University, a Bengali scholar, who advocated tribal autonomy, was

> severely criticized for his views and accused of acting on the instruction of American agents, i.e. the CIA (this is because the seminar was funded and organized by the Ford Foundation). In the middle of his presentation, one scholar of Rajshahi University (who is known as a progressive Marxist) made an attempt to assault the sympathetic scholar physically (fortunately he was stopped by others) and also he shouted at him loudly. Finally, normalcy was restored in the seminar room by the intervention of a moderate senior scholar.[31]

Shortly after independence Pakistani intelligence services began supporting tribal insurgents in Indian Nagaland and later Mizoram.[32] India in turn supported the Chittagong Hill tribes against Pakistan. After Bangladesh was created this was stopped as amicable relations were established between the two neighbouring countries. After a military coup in Bangladesh, relations deteriorated and both governments started supporting tribal insurgencies in each other's territory, while publicly denying that they were doing so. Whatever purposes the wars served for the Indian and Bangladesh governments and insurgents, the civilian population has been badly affected. No substantive empowerment has been achieved in Bangladesh, and the district council autonomy implemented by Bangladesh is alleged by the insurgents not to have provided tangible benefits.[33] Fifty-seven thousand tribals took refuge in India where they provided a base for the insurgents and an expense for the Indian government.[34] This migration was the result of the atrocities and massacres conducted by the Bangladesh army, police, paramilitary forces and Bengali settlers. By this ethnic cleansing, settlements and cleared land were made available for Bengali settlement, and a refugee problem created for the Indian government.

However, as relations between India and Bangladesh improved, it was agreed that the refugees should return to their homes, and pressure was exerted for negotiations between Bangladesh and the insurgents, which continued inconclusively for seven rounds before a peace agreement was signed on 2 December 1997.[35] In preparation for the return of refugees, a joint Indian and refugee delegation visited the Chittagong Hill Tracts with the permission of the government of Bangladesh, and returned with a report of land confiscation, continued confinement in cluster villages (forcefully relocated tribal settlements similar to the strategic hamlets in Vietnam and the concentration camps in the Boer War), destruction of Buddhist temples, forced conversion to Islam, and the continuous Bengali settlement on tribal lands.[36] Despite this the Indian government pressed strenuously for their repatriation, cutting back on their relief supplies and threatening to stop the supplies if they did not return.[37] Though the government of Bangladesh like the Indian government restricts access of independent observers to tribal frontier areas, and generally denies atrocities, reports from various sources indicate the authenticity of the atrocities.[38]

The government of India is somewhat more open to investigation than that of Bangladesh since incidents are more likely to be reported in the press. A judicial inquiry commissioned by the Supreme Court confirmed a mass rape of tribal women in Tripura state despite a cover up by the army and the state government.[39] A negotiated settlement is now extremely difficult as the removal of Bengali settlements will be vehemently opposed in Tripura, India and the Chittagong Hill Tracts. The construction of the Kaptai Dam flooded 40 per cent of cultivable lands. A Canadian consultancy report by Forrestal Inc. led to forest projects that caused further land alienation.[40] These environmental refugees left for India, where they now live as stateless persons in Arunachal Pradesh.[41] Though this state has been mentioned by scholars, such as Christoph von Furer-Haimendorf, as a model for tribal empowerment and development, they have not been sympathetic to the cause of other tribal peoples. Local tribals led by the All-Arunachal Pradesh Students Union with the support of the Congress chief minister threatened violence to drive out the 70,000 Chakma refugees living in the state since 1964. This resulted in 15,000 Chakma tribals fleeing to the state of Assam, which issued shoot-at-sight orders to prevent further flight.[42] Those who remained in Arunachal Pradesh built defences for protection against attacks by 'indigenous' tribals.

In the Chittagong Hill Tracts the numerically dominant and more educationally and economically advanced Chakmas predominate in the tribal opposition. The guerrillas have been so bitterly divided among themselves that they have killed a number of fellow members over strategy and in power struggles which led to the assassination of their top leader. Many of those who lost in the power struggle surrendered to the Bangladesh government, which offered an amnesty.[43] The guerrillas have attempted their own ethnic cleansing by attacking Bengali settlements in tribal areas. On 31 May 1984 they attacked a Bengali settlement with automatic weapons, killing 105 new settlers. In retaliation the army and settlers killed about 300 men, women and children, and burned villages, causing the flight of 18,000 tribals to Mizoram state in India.[44] Amnesty International reported that on 10 April 1992 a tribal cluster village was attacked by the army and Bengali settlers in retaliation for the killing of a Bengali youth. The villagers were locked in their homes and burned alive with the loss of 1,000–1,200 lives. This resulted in the flight of 1,000 tribals to refugee camps in India and 5,000 to hiding in the forest.[45] Since independent on-the-spot investigations of human rights abuses in Bangladesh and India are not generally permitted, the government's admission of only 13 deaths is highly unreliable.

The division between the plains people who drove the tribals into the hills hundreds of years ago, and are now encroaching on even these tribal areas, represents a major fault line in north-eastern South Asia that has spawned several on-going tribal insurgencies. The plains areas have suffered from overpopulation and the resultant environmental degradation and this has motivated settlement in forested tribal areas. This encroachment fosters tribal armed resistance which is facilitated by the neighbouring hostile states attempting to destabilize each other. The opportunity to acquire land makes the risk of death at the hands of tribal guerrillas appear worthwhile to Bengali settlers who are inadequately armed to protect themselves, but too poor to find an equivalent opportunity in non-tribal areas. The refugee population is destabilizing for India, which has tribal insurgencies of its own. The CHT refugees in Tripura live in a state that till independence was predominantly tribal but was flooded by Bengali refugees after partition. The fear of local tribal insurgents from the Tripura National Volunteers making common cause with the CHT refugees has prompted the Indian government to isolate the camps and attempt to repatriate the refugees to Bangladesh.[46] Since India has not signed the 1951 Convention and 1967 Protocol Relating to the Status of Refugees, the United Nations High Commission for Refugees (UNHCR) does not have access to the camps and no international protection exists for the refugees and little NGO aid is received.[47] As most of the insurgent areas and states are out of bounds to foreigners, little in the way of independently verifiable information is obtainable.

In a country where neither the military regimes nor the short-term democratic governments have shown genuine sympathy towards aboriginal rights, only pressure from external aid donors upon Bangladesh, which receives 9 per cent of its GNP from them, will make any difference. With a civil society preoccupied with other problems, no internal pressure for aboriginal empowerment is likely to be forthcoming. As there were only 807 college and university graduates as of 1983 and the total overseas Chakmas number only 137 (Table 8.5), there is a limited Chittagong Hill Tracts aboriginal diaspora to influence foreign governments.

By contrast the total Indian diaspora numbers 10 million, with an income equal to that of all the 800 million-plus Indians put together. This kind of diaspora can have a major impact on both domestic economic and political orientations. Even relatively small groups such as the Sri Lankan Tamils can bankroll an insurgency from abroad and mobilize major demonstrations in foreign

TABLE 8.5
Population of Overseas Chakmas

Country	Estimated Number
France	75
Canada	15
United Kingdom	10
Thailand	15
West Germany	4
Sweden	8
East Europe	10
Total	137

Source: Aditya Kumar Dewan, 'Class and Ethnicity in the Hills of Bangladesh' (Ph.D. thesis, McGill University, Montreal, October 1990), p. 352.

capitals. The Sikhs, with the assistance of their considerable diaspora, were able to give the much more powerful Indian state
some difficulties despite being only 2 per cent of the Indian
population and having minority support within the Punjab.

Pressure brought an end to the official policy of Bengali resettlement, and India offered to assist in repatriation, but it appears
that the Chakmas might have lost majority status in their own district for ever. Though foreign donors inadvertently contributed to
the alienation of tribal homelands, the publicity surrounding the
Chakma struggle appears to have made the aid community more
sensitive to the effects its aid might be having. The political climate in the West towards environmentally unsound development projects makes similar projects less likely in the future. Aid
agencies, however, do not seem to have used their influence on
the government of Bangladesh to change its policies towards the
Chittagong Hill Tracts.

> The CHT remain under military rule till to date even though
> military rule was lifted in other parts of Bangladesh since the
> overthrow of the General Mohammad Ershad (President of
> Bangladesh) in 1991. Reports of massacres, torture, rape,
> forced relocation of indigenous peoples and counter insur-
> gencies continued to flow out of the CHT through various
> channels.... Similarly, the flow of aid from overseas to Bang-
> ladesh has not been diminished or stopped ... and the Gov-
> ernment of Bangladesh continues, until today, to use aid
> money for the so-called development project in the Chitta-
> gong Hill Tracts.[48]

The signing of a peace agreement in December 1997 may mark
the end of the insurgency and enable the tribals to gain a degree
of control over their homelands. But since much of the opposition is against the agreement, the final outcome is yet to be determined.

REFERENCES

1. Joya Chatterji, *Bengal Divided: Hindu Communalism and Partition, 1932–1947* (Cambridge: Cambridge University Press, 1994), p. 20.
2. Ibid., p. 260.
3. Ibid., p. 263.

4. Nilanjana Chatterjee, 'Midnight's Unwanted Children: East Bengali Refugees and the Politics of Rehabilitation' (Ph.D. dissertation. Brown University, Providence, May 1992), p. 73.
5. Ibid., p. 68.
6. Ibid., p. 65.
7. J.N. Mandal's Letter of Resignation to the Prime Minister of Pakistan, 9 October 1950, in Muhammad Ghulam Kabir, *Minority Politics in Bangladesh* (Delhi: Vikas Publishing House, 1980), pp. 150–51.
8. Ibid., p. 39.
9. Ibid., p. 15.
10. Ibid., p. 45.
11. Ibid., p. 61.
12. Yuri V. Gankovsky, 'The Social Structure of Society in the People's Republic of Bangladesh', *Asian Survey*, Vol. 14, No. 3, March 1974, p. 228.
13. Syed Aziz-al Ahsan, 'Islamization of the State in a Dualistic Culture: The Case of Bangladesh' (Ph.D. thesis, McGill University, Montreal, October 1990), p. 142.
14. Ibid., p. 137.
15. Ibid., p. 178.
16. Ibid., p. 227.
17. Ali Riaz, 'Taslima Nasrin: Breaking the Structured Silence', *Bulletin of Concerned Asian Scholars*, Vol. 27, No. 1, 1995, p. 24.
18. Ahsan, 'Islamization of the State in a Dualistic Culture' (n. 13 above), p. 269.
19. Kabir, *Minority Politics in Bangladesh* (n. 7 above), p. 89.
20. Harry Blair, 'Civil Society, Democratic Development and International Donors: A Case Study from Bangladesh', Paper presented at the annual meeting of the American Political Science Association, New York City, 1–4 September 1994, p. 19.
21. Sharat G. Lin and Madan C. Paul, 'Bangladesh Migrants in Delhi: Social Insecurity, State Power, and Captive Vote Banks', *Bulletin of Concerned Asian Scholars*, Vol. 27, No. 1, 1995, p. 7.
22. Partha S. Ghosh, 'Bangladesh at the Crossroads: Religion and Politics', *Asian Survey*, Vol. 33, No. 7, July 1993, p. 706.
23. Muhammad Ghulam Kabir's book *Minority Politics in Bangladesh* is exclusively about the East Pakistan period.
24. S. Mahmud Ali, *The Fearful State: Power, People and Internal War in South Asia* (London: Zed Books, 1993), p. 176.
25. Aditya Kumar Dewan, 'Class and Ethnicity in the Hills of Bangladesh' (Ph.D. thesis, McGill University, Montreal, October 1990), p. 178.
26. Buddhadeb Chaudhuri, 'Ethnic Conflict in the Chittagong Hill Tracts of Bangladesh', in S.W.R. de A. Samarasinghe and Reed Coughlan (eds), *Economic Dimensions of Ethnic Conflict: International Perspectives* (London: Pinter Publishers, 1991), p. 140.
27. Dewan, 'Class and Ethnicity in the Hills of Bangladesh' (n. 25 above), p. 185.
28. Ibid., pp. 401–02.
29. Ibid., p. 193.
30. Akram H. Chowdhury, 'Self-Determination, the Chittagong and Bangladesh', in David P. Forsythe (ed.), *Human Rights and Development*, (New York: St Martin's Press, 1989), p. 300.

31. Dewan, 'Class and Ethnicity in the Hills of Bangladesh' (n. 25 above), p. 395.
32. Mahmud Ali, *The Fearful State* (n. 24 above), pp. 181–82, 187.
33. Ramendu Shekhar Dewan, 'A Report on the Fifth Round of the Dialogue Held Between the Bangladesh Government Commission and the Jana Samhati Samiti', 18 September 1993, at Khagrachari Circuit House, pp. 1–2.
34. Survival International, 'Violation of Human Rights and Fundamental Freedoms in the Chittagong Hill Tracts, Bangladesh', Commission on Human Rights: Sub-Commission on the Prevention of Discrimination and Protection of Minorities, 45th Session, 2–27 August 1993, Agenda Item 6.
35. South Asia Human Rights Documentation Centre, 'The Jumma Refugees: Post Script as Prologue', C-16/2, DDA Flats, Saket, New Delhi 110017, 1 June 1994, p. 2; Zaglul A. Chowdhury, 'Dhaka, tribal leaders sign pact', *The Times of India*, 3 December 1997.
36. *Report on the Visit of Jumma Refugee Team to Chittagong Hill Tracts*, Bangladesh, 19–23 September 1993, (South Tripura, India: Chittagong Hill Tracts Jumma Refugees Welfare Association, Takumbari Relief Camp, P.O. Dumburnagar [Jatanbari]).
37. South Asia Human Rights Documentation Centre, 'No Secure Refuge' (Delhi: South Asia Human Rights Documentation Centre, 14 February 1994), p. 3.
38. International Labour Organization, 80th Session, 1993, Report III (Part 4A), *Report of the Committee of Experts on the Application of Conventions and Recommendations* (Geneva: International Labour Office, 1993), C. 107, pp. 308–10.
39. Amnesty International, *Appeal: 1992 India Campaign*, 'Mass Rape of Tribal Women in Ujan Maidan Village, West Tripura', (London: Amnesty International, 1992), p. 3; in comparison, 'Despite some sporadic affirmative action policies for Adivasis [tribals], the policies endorsed in India have not been implemented to nearly the same extent in Bangladesh.' Father Timm, Minority Rights Group.
40. Mahmud Ali, *The Fearful State* (n. 24 above), pp. 179–80.
41. Father R.W. Timm, *The Adivasis of Bangladesh*, London: Minority Rights Group International Report, December 1991, 92/1, p. 12.
42. Almas Alam, *South Asia Newsweek*, 25 September and 9 October 1994, CFMT Television, Ottawa, Canada.
43. Mahmud Ali, *The Fearful State* (n. 24 above), p. 192.
44. Dewan, 'Class and Ethnicity in the Hills of Bangladesh' (n. 25 above), pp. 296–98.
45. Shin-Wha Lee, 'Environmental Change, Refugees, and Conflict in the Third World: A Framework for Inquiry Applied to Case Studies of Sudan and Bangladesh' (Ph.D. thesis, University of Maryland, College Park, 1994), p. 297.
46. Ibid., p. 311.
47. Ibid., pp. 310–11.
48. Dewan, 'International Development and Indigenous Peoples in the Chittagong Hill Tracts in Bangladesh', Paper presented at the Annual Meeting of the Canadian Association for the Study of International Development, Learned Societies Conference held at the University of Quebec, Montreal, 4–6 June 1995, pp. 10–11.

CHAPTER 9

Tribal Self-determination

There has been an on-going debate from at least the eighteenth century as to whether tribal peoples should be assimilated or their culture preserved. At the present stage in the discussion the consensus falls between the two schools of thought. It is generally agreed that acculturation is inevitable; however, the indigenous people themselves should have control over the pace and nature of the developmental process. The difficulty is that indigenous people the world over rarely have a significant degree of control over their destiny. Many societies have simply marginalized them and they have spent much time in futile attempts to prevent encroachment on their traditional lands, to which they rarely have legal title. Even when they are legally entitled to protection, as in India, the laws are observed in the breach.

Part of the solution lies in better law enforcement, but on account of police corruption and the nature of the lower-level bureaucracy, this has usually been more of a hindrance to justice for aboriginal peoples. Even with proper enforcement the results are likely to ameliorate rather than solve aboriginal problems.

Since development and acculturation are inevitable, the problem is one of retaining the most appropriate and valuable aspects of tribal culture while introducing, in as non-traumatic a form as possible, developmental changes that will enable tribal peoples to survive in the modern world. The environment in which this development must take place in South Asia is particularly hostile to tribal empowerment. The dominant South Asian Muslim and Hindu cultures are antithetical to some of the more emancipatory tenets of modernity. Islam has in its practice been repressive towards women, while Hinduism has exploited the lower castes. Even religions such as Christianity, Islam, Sikhism and Sri Lankan

Buddhism have adopted some of the prejudices of Hinduism despite the more emancipatory aspects of their own original tenets. The impact of this Hindu influence has been devastating. It is generally believed that the Untouchable castes were aboriginal peoples whose conquest resulted in their exploitation and acculturation within Hinduism, to the point where a separate cultural identity is problematic and their origins are lost to history. It is significant that the dominant Hindu society considers this process a positive development, and feels threatened by any of these groups converting to more emancipatory religions.

Tribal peoples on the other hand still retain much of their culture though even here there is great variation, with some groups having lost their languages to regionally dominant groups. The dominant groups in the plains of South Asia have been gradually imposing their cultural taboos on tribal peoples in a particularly negative way. For instance, the attempts by dominant Hindu groups to prevent the eating of beef by tribals, when successful, are likely to lead to an inferior diet. In fact, the more regressive aspects of Hindu culture are being imposed on tribal groups by the most culturally unenlightened elements in Hindu society at a time when these values are being abandoned by urban middle-class Hindus.

At the village level this social differentiation is manifested in varying levels of segregation. According to a World Bank study,

the non-SC/ST [Scheduled Caste/Scheduled Tribe] people often do not want their children to eat food cooked by a lower caste helper. There appears to be slightly less proscription if the food is cooked by a Scheduled Tribe AWW [community worker] (but this evidence is not conclusive). No conclusive evidence was found of antipathy between the Scheduled castes and tribal people either, although a Scheduled Caste AWW and some officials reported that tribal people will not partake of food cooked by Scheduled Caste workers/helpers....

Both in Bihar and M.P., workshop participants confirmed that the situation of Scheduled Caste people is often worse than that of Scheduled Tribes. They are often poorer, and are exposed to caste biases even at the anganwadis [Integrated

Child Development Services delivery centre] (e.g. 'separate lines' for feeding).[1]

As Tribals come in contact with upper-caste cultural values, the attempts to assert superiority over other groups can have deleterious cultural and political effects.

It is paradoxical that in many areas where tribes are exposed to the influence of caste Hindus just those features of Hindu society which modern India strives to discard are newly introduced among populations to which they had hitherto been foreign. Thus, not only the prejudice against certain occupations such as leather working and butchering, but also dietary taboos, child marriage, and restrictions on the remarriage of widows and divorcees are gaining a foothold among the hill- and jungle-folk at a time when they are losing ground in the larger urban centres. This development is almost inevitable as long as throughout rural India compliance with puritanical precepts of Hindu morality remains the principal criterion of social respectability.[2]

The result of this process is likely to be the creation of new groups of Untouchables rather than the elevation of the tribal peoples to a higher level in the modernization process. 'In South India many primitive jungle tribes became low caste and untouchable when assimilated within the caste system.'[3] The traditional tribal practices are in fact superior to the local Hindu folk traditions in many cases and the adoption of Hindu values is a regressive process that will be psychologically traumatic. The adoption of Christianity, which is more emancipatory than Hinduism, posed a threat to the Hindu-dominated nation-state.[4] The struggle for the religious allegiance of tribals has been corrosive for tribal cultures, a fact which is now recognized by the major European Christian denominations, though this is not an issue in Hindu and Muslim theology.

In countries where Christianity is a minority religion, church members are often seen by tribal peoples as among the few allies they possess and the official state religions are seen as oppressive because they represent the dominant culture. In

India, for example, Hindu organizations are now promoting policies of Sanskritization in order to assimilate animist scheduled tribes.[5]

Retaining the many positive aspects of indigenous culture, while assimilating the skills and education required by industrialized society, is difficult, and few if any indigenous peoples have accomplished it. In South Asia the Indian tribal-dominated border states have come closest to the ideal. Arunachal Pradesh is being seen as a model in this regard.[6] However, the British colonial 'inner line' policy of excluding immigration and its pursuance for security reasons by the independent Indian government deserves the primary credit. As a general tribal policy it has not been well implemented elsewhere. In the plains the policies have been more systematically violated by locally dominant groups, with only sporadic opposition from higher levels of government.

Conceptual Redefinition

While the alienation of tribal land is beyond dispute, there is division on whether this represents simply the dominance of local landed interests or is part of a hidden agenda of the dominant society as a whole. The argument that it is merely the local interests that are responsible can be advanced by the state and national governments which have a considerable bureaucracy and legally binding statutes to prevent exploitation. That these laws are routinely violated and ineffectually enforced is pointed out by critics as proof of the lack of serious intent of the state. According to the former Dhanbad MP A.K. Roy, these tribal areas represent 'internal colonies' being exploited by the dominant powers in Indian society.[7] This reflects the concept of tribal areas as a 'fourth world' within the Third World which utilizes their natural resources.

Third World colonialism has replaced European colonialism as the principal global force that tries to subjugate indigenous peoples and their ancient nations.... Invasion and occupation of indigenous nations once done by foreign white expansionist powers are now done by foreign brown expansionist powers. The majority of these artificial Third World states can only be maintained by the invasion and physical incorporation of lands and resources of hundreds of indigenous nations. What is called 'economic development' is the annexation at gun point of other peoples' economies. What is called 'nation-building' is actually state expansion by *nation-destroying*.[8]

'Any movement which questions this presumed identity between the people-nation and the state-representing-the-nation is denied the status of legitimate politics.'[9] Seen from this perspective, Third World governments are not legitimate representatives of indigenous minorities, making resistance and rebellion by indigenous 'nations' legitimate forms of expression. This is essentially subversive of the political ethos fostered by Third World governments and the non-aligned movement, which seek to project themselves as representative of poor people in their countries. Once the nation-state is no longer considered legitimate, acts of subversion and rebellion are justified.

From this perspective indigenous peoples become nations in their own right. However, this does not determine who will represent these nations, because indigenous groups are usually as divided among themselves as is the outside dominant society. The standard criticism of indigenous movements is that they represent indigenous middle-class elites who are no more representative of their own society than are outsiders. These ethnic elites utilize their claim to represent their people to garner the lion's share of the benefits that the state provides indigenous groups. While this is a legitimate criticism, there are no other more authentic representatives of indigenous people than these ethnic elites. Traditional leaders may be more representative, where they still exist, but they are often uncomprehending of the wider world and lack the skills needed for negotiating with the state.

In the early 1990s India had all the appearances of being on the verge of a Hindu fundamentalist revolution that would remove the secular forces from power. Four states had already been taken over by the Hindu fundamentalists and the central government appeared likely to fall to religious sectarians. Then, in state elections, all but one of the Hindu revivalist governments were defeated by opposition parties. New social forces representing lower castes presented a challenge to both Hindu fundamentalists and secular parties. This new social force which took power in India's most populous and politically important state of Uttar Pradesh and extended its influence in other states, represented a coalition primarily of Untouchables, 'backward castes' and other minorities. It was the first time such a political combination had taken state power and it represented a sea change in the organization of Indian politics. Seen from their lower-caste perspective, the Hindu revivalists, while politically opposed to the secular Congress and Communist parties, were from identical dominant upper-caste backgrounds. The lower castes had never before taken power in their own interests on such a scale. By mobilizing the majority of the Hindu population that were from non-elite castes they would prevent the Hindu revivalists from taking power. While this was welcomed by the secular forces, it represented a threat to them as well, for now caste had become an organized social category that was politically mobilizable in its own interest. India had always been ruled by a small caste elite of various political parties and persuasions, dependent on the 'vote banks' of the lower castes and other minorities that made up the majority of India's population. The dominant Congress party had always counted on these communities to vote for its secular policies in return for protection of their religious and minority rights and privileges. With the formation of new political coalitions of parties representing lower castes and religious minorities, new ethnic and caste elites could take the political initiative.[10]

Indigenous Peoples' Diversity

The politicized ethnic groups included India's tribal population, the largest in the world, representing 67.75 million people, or 8.08 per cent of the Indian population.[11] Though it is too early to determine how their empowerment will work itself out in relations with the rest of society, tribal movements will undoubtedly have the opportunity of forming powerful combinations with other minority groups which could control state and central governments. These opportunities have yet to be realized, but the building blocks for such coalitions are being put in place. They represent perhaps the best possibility for the reconciliation of tribals with the dominant society. These new social forces for the most part have been a long time in formation, though they have only recently come to state power. The tribal movements have the longest antecedents, having resisted Aryan invaders in prere-corded history, and in various phases opposed subsequent waves of invaders to the present day. It is generally considered that Untouchables were tribal peoples who were enslaved and assimilated into the Hindu caste system, while those original inhabitants who escaped or successfully resisted domination by the invaders are the ancestors of the tribal peoples of today. The tribal population is often depicted as unassimilated, but tribals in fact represent a continuum from peoples who have retained their own culture to those who have essentially lost their own lan-guages and culture but retain a nominally separate ethnic identity. While both tribals and Untouchables can be considered indige-nous, those who came to be assimilated into the caste hierarchy are designated as Untouchable. This has led to political divisions over who is indigenous. Untouchables and tribals both consider themselves indigenous, but the upper-caste-dominated Indian government accurately claims that documentary proof of the identity of the original inhabitants of India is impossible to ob-tain. The tribals are also reluctant to accept the indigenous claim of Untouchables because of their assimilation of Hindu culture.

> Many dalit [Untouchable] 'organic intellectuals' are con-vinced that they too are indigenous and would like in prin-ciple to be accepted immediately. Such an approach can result in further splits because there can be competition among the various groups for power and leadership. The tribals being a small minority may be outnumbered. Moreover, in many areas the dikus [outsider exploiters] have used the dalits as their agents in exploiting the tribals. 'Organic intellectuals' may think in terms of a regional, national and even a global approach and may not always take the field reality into con-sideration. That may be one reason why there is less enthu-siasm among the tribal leaders on this question than among the dalits. This difference may also be two different sides of a search for an identity viz. the tribals trying to re-assert theirs when it is under attack and the dalits attempting to

attain a new one. All these aspects have to be taken into account and non-tribals should only support this search without pushing the issue beyond a point. It certainly is an ideal, but it has to be balanced with the field reality.[12]

Since Untouchables outnumber tribals two to one, they have an electoral clout that tribals lack, making alliances with them particularly important in achieving empowerment. The tribals, however, have populations concentrated in a few areas. This gives them opportunities for regional autonomy and secessionist movements which the scattered minority Scheduled Caste population lacks. The differences between Scheduled Castes and Scheduled Tribes in culture and living standards are not as distinguishable as is commonly thought. For instance, most plains tribals have abandoned shifting cultivation for the sedentary agriculture of their Hindu neighbours, and many tribals speak only the regional languages rather than their indigenous one. Nevertheless, all tribals have an ethnic identity separate from their Untouchable neighbours. Most of them have languages of their own and customs and traditions that separate them from other peoples. They are generally divided between those in the plains of peninsular India and the hill tribes of the Himalayas and northeast India. While the latter have for the most part achieved statehood, those in the plains do not control their state governments and partly as a result of that are considered more economically backward. This division of the tribal community between plains and hills has presented an insurmountable obstacle to joint tribal political action, which could have brought considerable pressure to bear on the Indian political system. A national-level attempt to politically combine all tribals with Untouchables and other minorities has never been made. The Indian Council of Indigenous and Tribal Peoples (ICITP) states: 'Dalits are our co-sufferers. Dalit organizations and individuals are invited as observers which will be enlisted under a separate Dalit Register. Such observers can also speak if permitted by the Chair but they cannot vote.'[13] In the words of one ICITP official, 'Let there be clear understanding—that ICITP would support Dalit movement on the Dalit platform and don't get mixed up with Tribal movement in [the] present Indian context.'[14] Though the tribal leaders are often accused of being unrepresentative of their own grassroots communities, they are adamant about excluding Dalits from equal participation because of their tribes' perceived cultural differences. However, the reality on the ground is that some tribes and lower castes are little different from each other in culture, having the same language and similar histories. The political distinction is made less on the basis of cultural difference than from fear of domination by the more numerous Dalits. However, the leadership of both groups often have more in common with each other than with their own grassroots supporters. The differences may represent the protection of turf rather than culture, and certainly these divisions have prevented any political unity in practice. While Dalits have tended to include the tribals and Untouchables as part of the 200 million indigenous peoples, the tribals have tended to see themselves alone as indigenous, with Dalits having lost that claim through cultural assimilation.[15]

> The ideology of 'tribalism', [is] a mechanism through which the indigenous elite is precisely the most vocal adivasi sector in proclaiming its 'tribal' identity. The 'tribalist' ideology permitted the adivasi elite to enter the political arena and dominate certain fields like that of education, for instance, through the channels provided by the missions, also promoting the tribal construct. The adivasi elite's self-definition as 'tribal' helps push underground the class affiliations, privileges and ambitions of its members, and contributes to present social conflict in Jharkhand only in terms of ethnic confrontations.[16]

Criticism of the tribal intellectual elite as unrepresentative is also relevant in the development field. 'The tribal elites tended to take away all the benefits of development programmes, leaving the vast majority of backward tribals untouched.'[17] This view is common among administrators concerned with tribal affairs. A representative of the National Commission for Scheduled Castes and Scheduled Tribes felt that reservation should be discontinued after a couple of generations to encourage equality of tribal access, though this is not official policy. However, given the underfulfilment of the existing quota, such a policy would only reduce total representation, since there is as yet no intra-tribal competition for places (Table 9.1).

TABLE 9.1

*Actual and Prescribed (bracketed) Percentage of Scheduled Tribe
Recruitment in Central and State Administration
(Class I are higher ranking officers)*

State	Class I	Class II	Class III	Class IV
Andhra Pradesh	(14)	(14)	(14)	(14)
Arunachal Pradesh	(45)	(45)	(45)	(45)
Assam	(12)	(12)	(12)	(12)
Bihar	(10)	(10)	(10)	(10)
Gujarat	2.3 (14)	3.2 (14)	9.1 (14)	17.8 (14)
Haryana	No information provided			
Himachal Pradesh	4.2 (7.5)	3.6 (7.5)	3.4 (5)	4.7 (5)
Jammu and Kashmir	No information provided			
Karnataka	(3)	(3)	(3)	(3)
Kerala	(2)	(2)	(2)	(2)
Madhya Pradesh	(18)	5.15 (18)	14.5 (20)	19.3 (20)
Maharashtra	1.3 (7)	2.1 (7)	3.8 (7)	4.9 (7)
Manipur	(7.5)	(7.5)	(2)	(2)
Meghalaya	(40)	(40)	(40)	(40)
Nagaland	(45)	(45)	(45)	(45)
Orissa	0.23 (24)	0.77 (24)	5.78 (24)	8.73 (24)
Punjab	No information provided			
Rajasthan	2 (12)	3 (12)	3.5 (12)	6 (12)
Tamil Nadu	(18)	0.8 (18)	0.7 (18)	0.6 (18)
Tripura	(29)	(29)	(29)	(29)
Uttar Pradesh	0.4 (2)	0.25 (2)	0.25 (2)	0.72 (2)
West Bengal	0.35 (5)	0.54 (5)	1.89 (5)	(5)
Central Government	1.01 (7.5)	1.25 (7.5)	3.55 (7.5)	4.78 (7.5)

Source: Government of India, *Report of the Commission for Scheduled Castes
and Scheduled Tribes: Second Report April 1979–March 1980,* (Delhi: Government
of India Press, 1981), pp. 274–75.

Not a few tribals are also dissatisfied with the conduct of their
educated tribal elite, though this does not usually enter the published record. In this respect they are no different from other
elites who have the opportunity of preferential access to resources
and patronage. It has however led to dissatisfaction in the ranks
of the tribal movement between intellectual leaders with outside
connections and local followers.

The standard view presented by Furer-Haimendorf is one of
oppression and exploitation of the plains tribals, while the hill
tribals through control of their own states obtain development
and education on their own terms.[18] According to the central

government's Commissioner for Scheduled Castes and Scheduled Tribes,

> The present state of the tribal people in the North-East and in middle India [i.e., plains], which was almost the same in the beginning of this century, presents a striking contrast which is largely relatable to the place of education in the scheme of development in the two regions. In the North-East education preceded development of their economy which continues even to this day at the pre-agricultural stage. But in middle India economic development took precedence over education which has remained neglected. Whereas tribal people in the North-East are now ready for a leap forward in development based on the resources which have remained under their command, those in middle India have fallen prey to the adverse processes of development and are facing disorganization, many of them having been rendered resourceless.[19]

The gains in tribal-controlled states have presented new problems which are no closer to being resolved than those of the plains tribals. Whereas plains tribals have been exploited for their cheap labour or through confiscation of their land and natural resources, the achievement of state power for most of the hill tribes has prevented the more egregious forms of exploitation by outsiders. Statehood has presented its own problems, however. One of the main demands for state support and avenues for individual advancement is education. With the rapid spread of education in tribal states, the educated youth have only the state sector for employment, given the low level of private sector development activity that has been attracted to these isolated areas. The government, however, though expanding during the period when the tribal states were being created, is now facing budget cutbacks from accumulated deficits. As a result, the state will no longer absorb the educated tribal unemployment, which can create social problems of its own. Since most tribal states have armed insurgencies under way these problems cannot be ignored by the tribal state leadership and the central government. The central government's Commissioner for Scheduled Castes and Scheduled Tribes points to the social problems this creates.

Even though all educated youth in principle have equal opportunity with regard to employment, the opportunities for the SC and ST youth cannot be said to be really the same at least for some more time unless there are specific reservations in their favour. There is a big differential in their preparedness for open competition not only in terms of quality of education but also the social background and other support which matter in getting employment.... Members of SCs and STs can look forward to only employment in the public sector which is now saturated and whose pace of growth is also slow.... In fact, this provides one of the biggest motive forces for demands for establishment of smaller politico-administrative units. It is obvious that this cannot be continued indefinitely and contradictions are bound to arise sooner than later. This is already happening, e.g. in *Bihar* where the tribal population is large and the new opportunities for the educated youth cannot be found in the tertiary sector.[20]

Jharkhand Movement

The creation of aboriginal states has created new indigenous state elites, while the spread of education has increased political awareness. However, it is not clear where tribal people can go with this. For an ethnic population without a capital or entrepreneurial base, development means to some extent the entry of other Indians into tribal areas. But in areas such as the plains where this has happened extensively, outsiders have come to dominate not only the economy but local politics as well. This is clearly seen in the Jharkhand movement, the most persistent attempt by plains tribals to create their own state. Though the hill tribes have been granted several states, no tribal state exists in the plains despite most of the tribal population residing there. The failure of the Jharkhand movement to achieve statehood is a reflection of the opposition of the state governments who would have to abandon territory for its formation. It is also a reflection of divisions in the movement, and the immigration that has now left the tribals as a minority group within their own Jharkhand region. Attempts to create common agendas with local non-tribals for the promotion of Jharkhand statehood have been only partly successful.[21] No united movement has arisen, yet the popular demand for Jharkhand among the tribal people and the indigenous peoples shows no sign of decreasing.

While touring the Jharkhand region in Bihar it was found that there was popular sentiment in favour of Jharkhand among the tribals but also a cultural gap between this sentiment and the leadership of the movement organized around its advocacy. As one of the oldest movements in the country and by far the most important tribal movement, the progression and frustrations are indicative of the problems faced by both Indian tribal and foreign indigenous movements for emancipation.

In the eighteenth and nineteenth centuries there was a series of revolts in 1780, 1831, 1855, and finally in 1899 of tribal peoples against the encroachment of British colonialism.[22] These revivalist movements were replaced in the 1920s by modernist Christian-dominated movements, most prominently led by an Oxford-educated Christian tribal leader, Jaipal Singh. He eventually joined the Congress ministry after independence, thereby effectively undermining the Jharkhand movement.[23] This movement parallels the experience of the Scheduled Caste movement in what one writer sees as a betrayal of mass interests in favour of the ethnic elite's class interests.

> When the colonial government began to patronise such movements, their leaders also started forgetting the masses and got involved in a politics of backwardness. They now merely used the depressed socio-economic condition of their communities for obtaining some concessions that could hardly benefit the entire community. The masses, still hoping for a better world and having much less faith in the high caste Hindu nationalists, continued to support their caste leaders, but certainly not with the same keen enthusiasm as before. As a result, such lower caste movements could not ultimately crystallize into a distinct alternative political force and these parallel streams were eventually captured or appropriated by the dominant nationalist mainstream when an end to colonial rule seemed imminent and there was the need for new political alignments.[24]

This phase ended with the integration of tribal political leaders into the Congress party and the eventual erosion of their legitimacy within the tribal movement. In recent years there has been a resurgence of ethnic tribal politics outside the patronage of the state, but within the democratic political system. Tribal politicization had led to an understanding of the need for pan-tribal unity, as the British colonial census and the majority electoral system pointed to the importance of numbers and the existence of ethnic identity. This was accompanied by the reservation or affirmative action policy which offered immediate individual benefits for tribal identification.[25] The colonial state has often been blamed for manufacturing ethnicity, but the identity was already there; the colonial system merely opened up the possibility for organization on a previously unknown scale. While the late-colonial system did promote this as an attempt at 'divide and rule', the independent government continued the system, and in recent years has greatly expanded it under pressure from new ethnic elites. That this is more than a British legacy and is part of a global phenomenon is indicated by the spread of affirmative action programmes for minorities throughout the western world. The Indian state under pressure from significant sections of the electorate has been the main force behind this move. It has thus created a tribal middle class and the bureaucracy and states to support it. It also created a backlash from traditional non-tribal elites, but the programmes still expanded rather than contracted.

The tribal peoples had a majority population in the Jharkhand area which gave them in the late-colonial period a reasonable expectation of eventual statehood, given a colonial regime that was generally sympathetic to tribal emancipation. Gradually, immigration resulted in the relegation of tribals to a minority status in their own areas. The movement's orientation has also undergone a transformation.

> From being a struggle of tribal masses to preserve, strengthen and assert their distinct ethnic culture, identity, values, history and independence, the Jharkhand movement in the course of its long existence has slowly but steadily been transformed into a movement for the 'development' of the tribals much along the same path as that of their non-tribal neighbours. This is the first ideological victory of the dominant communities over the tribals within the movement.[26]

From being a majority community, the tribals have been relegated to a minority position, which has made political alliances with local non-tribals essential for electoral success. As a result the distinctive cultures of the tribals have been downplayed in favour of class alliances and regionalist movements against exploitation by outsiders.

> At the level of political practice it is advised that unity of the people of the entire 'backward area' would strengthen the movement or more directly that the movement would not succeed unless it wins over the support of the non-tribals. Ethnicity is the idiom of the tribals while regionalism is that of the dominant communities and the movement is definitely moving in the direction of regionalism.[27]

The difficulty for a tribal movement which hopes to achieve some measure of local autonomy, if not statehood, is profound. The need to obtain allies compels the tribal movement to limit the divisive issue of ethnicity in favour of the common cause regionalism offers. How a tribal ethnic identity can be retained in this coalition is by no means clear. The argument that the indigenous leadership by adopting the developmental mode transfers the grounds of discourse to the outsiders' paradigm, begs the question of how a genuine tribal development can be achieved, given the low level of development that has hitherto existed in tribal communities. The obvious option of abandoning development altogether is no longer realistic since the people themselves want modern goods and services.[28] Without development the tribals are doomed to what has come to be considered poverty (though it has only in the modern age been recognized as such), while the promotion of ethnicity relegates them to political oblivion. The tribal leadership has attempted to overcome these barriers by promoting development under its own control and political power through strategic alliances with non-tribals. The extent to which the ethnic cultural revival has suffered as a result is open to debate. Certainly, there is a large gap between the tribal leadership and the masses, with no widely recognized leader or party to give the movement a clear direction. This is in part because indigenous peoples are divided culturally and politically along a number of tribal ethnic lines, and further divided between Christians and non-Christians both among the tribal leadership, and to perhaps a lesser extent among followers. Religion is an area of contest in India, with the Hindus attempting to convert tribals or at least undermine the efforts of Christians to do so. By the 1960s,

Kartick Oraon, a Hindu version of Jaipal Singh, with Western education and experience, emerged as a reaction against the Christian domination of the tribal scene. He was against the special privileges enjoyed by the Christian tribals under the Constitution of India, as the Christians were in a better position vis-a-vis the non-Christians in educational and other fields.[29]

From the early 1960s to the early 1970s,

the non-Christians overwhelmingly took the side of the ruling Congress party and a small section of them even joined the Janasangh [the party of the Hindu fundamentalists]. On the other hand, whereas one section of the church (particularly the Roman Catholic) supported the establishment, and thus countered the attack of the non-Christians, the rest especially the German Lutheran Mission, remained loyal to the Jharkhand party. There was thus a deep vacuum in ideology within the leadership in the Jharkhand movement. Ethnic rivalry, religious conflicts and inter-party competition (among the Congress, the Janasangh and the Jharkhand parties) absolutely disrupted the mobilization of the people inviting pessimism and degradation for them.[30]

With an ethnic movement politically divided along religious lines, the cross-cutting allegiances made political unity impossible. The movement was repeatedly undermined by defections of leaders and followers to the ruling party, most notably by Jaipal Singh to the Congress party. On a more subtle level, tribals with education could secure government jobs which, however, precluded political activity. A new phase of the movement began in 1973 with the Jharkhand Mukti Morcha in which common cause was made with radical Marxist parties that had bases among the working class and non-tribal agriculturists, but these were alliances of convenience rather than a heartfelt political conversion.

Before the newly emerging ideology could crystallise and take an acceptable shape the two-pronged tactics of the state, for example, terrorism and domestication of the leaders, broke its backbone.... The colonising forces gained back their dominance. Both the set[s] of leaders, 'green' and 'red' were rejected by the people. The 'domesticated' 'green' and the sectarian 'red' blamed each other and later on, both blamed the people for their failure.[31]

Internally divided and spread over four states, all of whose governments are opposed to separation, the movement faces seemingly insurmountable obstacles. The concession of district councils in tribal areas is possible, but with tribals now in a minority position in the Jharkhand region it is difficult to see what additional benefits this will bring. While the assertion of a tribal identity is present, it is far from clear what this means in terms of empowerment, particularly in a poor country where the state largesse for ethnic development promotion is limited, and may decrease with structural adjustment. At a time when job reservations are being extended to most of the population, even while the public sector is not expanding, the relative position of tribals as beneficiaries of these affirmative action programmes could be diminished in favour of larger and more politically influential groups.[32]

In conjunction with a limited capability of the state to achieve social engineering comes a new concept of community empowerment in both India and the West. In the case of tribal populations this is seen as a return to traditional tribal authority and learning to achieve empowerment. According to the Commissioner for Scheduled Castes and Scheduled Tribes,

Good government is no substitute for self-government is a universal principle accepted in all civil societies. In the case of tribal areas where the tradition of self-management is still in vogue, self-governance is also the best bet for good government. A major contributing factor for lack of peace and tranquillity in tribal areas is the waning authority of the community, interference by exotic agencies even in matters concerning their day-to-day life and their growing dependence on others in matters such as right over land and access to other resources. Since the community life in tribal areas is still vibrant and capable of managing its internal affairs it will be in the general interest of the people and their well-being if their authority is not allowed to get eroded. It will also help in engendering a sense of self-confidence amongst the people to face the new challenges from all sides and maintenance of their proverbial idyllic milieu.[33]

The Commissioner concludes from this that 'as large an area as possible should be brought within the purview of specially constituted local institutions. These institutions should be responsible to the people of the village and *not* to any higher authority either in the administration or even formal representative institutions.'[34]

This approach of preserving or reconstituting traditional community authority, however, is not without its problems. In one village assembly we attended, there was a total absence of women, because the male participants considered the subjects under discussion to be outside their area of interest. Non-tribal observers to the Indian Council of Indigenous and Tribal Peoples 1993 General Assembly noted that 'many tribal movements too are male dominated, with women's participation being minimal'.[35] The participation of women may be in contradiction of certain local customs, but most governments and activists would insist upon their involvement. Such reconstitution of traditional institutions is today usually a government-sponsored imposition, and how this is to achieve local legitimacy while maintaining a social reform orientation local participants may reject is by no means clear. In one area of Jharkhand that we visited, the modern facilities built by the Young Men's Christian Association (YMCA) had been bombed while a nearby government microwave tower had been destroyed by the tribals. However well intentioned these development endeavours may be, they were perceived as a threat to the tribal peoples. Without a clear political movement with a leadership that can deliver a local following, such acts of resistance to externally imposed development will continue. One Christian tribal organization, Vikas Maitri, which has attempted to combine tribal culture with development, notes that in

drawing a dichotomy between tradition and modernity no effort is being made to build from what the people have in their society and culture.... In the traditional social system of the tribals there are some inherent qualities which can be constructively used for building a just society. Some of these qualities are the spirit of cooperation and mutual obligation, community solidarity, sense of general equality and partnership among all, sense of equal partnership between men and women, honesty, sincerity, doing one's duty silently, democratic procedures for dealing with common affairs with emphasis on consensus, dignity of physical labour, etc. Innovative programmes could be based on these elements of tribal culture and values to the extent they prove to be compatible with development. While adopting such an approach to development Vikas Maitri does not intend either to eulogise or to romanticise the tribal tradition as a golden era. We fully realise that there are certain tribal values and attitudes which impede development, but we are also convinced that there are definitely some other types of values and attitudes which can contribute to developing a just society. We also believe that some so-called negative values and attitudes can be used for constructive work, if appropriate strategies are adopted. Our emphasis is on refining the traditional institutions and value in such a way that they can cope with the changing society or on giving them new meaning and make them function for the greater good of the society.[36]

The social engineering being attempted with tribal peoples in India and elsewhere presents particular problems. Despite over a century of missionary education in the Jharkhand region, tribal peoples have not developed an entrepreneurial base, and have remained at most salaried government employees. The development which occurred was undertaken by outsiders. Exposure to western education alone was not enough to launch the developmental process. The development that has occurred has been skewed towards tribal elites. According to an ILO study,

By giving privileges to the tribal leaders, the British administrators not only introduced a degree of stratification in tribal society which did not exist before, but also created tribal elites who themselves exploited the tribal people and were later to do so to a much greater degree when in free India massive investment was made in tribal development.[37]

Ironically, affirmative action may have increased tribal differentiation.[38]

Notwithstanding a lack of funding for such policies, positive discrimination has secured many benefits for the tribal populations of independent India. Ironically, too, it has served to fortify an emerging tribal middle class, for it is this group which monopolises most of the benefits on offer. Again, this tends to undermine the ideology of undifferentiated tribal communities upon which tribal policy is based, and from which a traditional tribal politics derives.[39]

According to Sajal Basu,

The positive achievements of the movement in the sphere of language, [and] identity have been hijacked by the activities of its leaders who carry on their squabbles and personal fortune making. The erosion in the movement caused by the performance of its leaders may be due to lack of ideological consistency and weak organizational network. Due to this, the movement could never reach a take off stage, not to speak of nationality formation.[40]

Though in recent years the religious divide in the movement between Christian and non-Christian has declined, the entrance of Marxist trade unions

may have catered to the needs of mining and industrial labour in the area, and made a headway into non-tribal groups, but intrusion of diverging ideological trends only added further confusion to the movement. The import of class-caste-ethnicity issues, debate on nationality as a category, language and religion, etc., have all been mixed up. The movement and the groups were soon destined to be in disarray.[41]

What has maintained the movement over 50 years despite its failure to achieve political power has been its 'civilizational base' as expressed 'in oral folklore, participatory cultural forms, caste-free social structure, naturalistic religious pursuit', in other words, the culture of tribal peoples which has persisted despite the multiple defections and divisions in the organized movement.[42] From this base new parties and tendencies will continue to arise, and some day may achieve a measure of local empowerment, and just possibly statehood.[43]

If this is to be achieved the leadership will have to resist accepting subordinate positions in ruling parties and be more effective in mobilizing a mass base.

Above all, the role of other national parties in the region has effectively paralysed the Jharkhand movement. They have ended a mass support for themselves and their ideologies in the Jharkhand area. They have recruited tribes in their parties and allotted them their party tickets to fight elections. Congress and Janata and previously also Jan Sangh and Raja Kamakhya Narain's Janata Party played a dominant role in this regard.[44]

Significantly, when we toured the tribal areas of Jharkhand we found even the Hindu communalist BJP had found support among tribal people, despite what would appear to be an ideology antithetical to tribal culture. By the end of 1994 the Congress central government was offering home rule to the Jharkhand areas of Bihar state, which was ruled by an opposition party opposed to this policy. The centre threatened to invoke the constitutional powers under the Fifth Schedule to overrule the state government on this issue. This rather transparent attempt to win tribal and regionalist support before state elections reflects the persistence of the Jharkhand demands, and the movement's dependence on ruling party politics.[45]

Land Alienation and Rehabilitation

Tribal peoples once controlled large tracts of India in the late-colonial period. Despite legislation to prevent loss of land to moneylenders and landowners, the alienation has been continuing. While much of the land alienation is at the instigation of local moneylenders and landlords in violation of statutes, the state has on occasion been involved in this process as well. The leasing of forest land to private logging companies and construction of hydroelectric dams have been the major causes of state-sponsored land confiscation.[46] In effect, land can be taken by the state whenever it is deemed by the government to be in the national interest. While this is a universal practice, in South Asia the compensation system is inadequate at best and often non-existent. The Narmada Dam project has been particularly controversial from both an environmental and ethical standpoint.[47] This in itself represents an important break with the past when such practices were taken for granted. That the World Bank was eventually pressured to withdraw funding is indicative that the era of uncritical development implementation by governments is now over. This will not prevent the continued erosion of tribal lands which continues in both government and private sector projects, but it does indicate to government that the environmental and indigenous movement can no longer be ignored. Even if governments choose to ignore the protests, international lending agencies will be pressured to withhold funds by indigenous and international NGOs. The World Bank's decision to withhold further funding for Narmada points to a new awareness of the adverse effects development can have on tribal peoples.

According to the central government's Commission for Scheduled Castes and Scheduled Tribes,

> Almost in all States, laws have been passed prohibiting alienation of tribal lands to non-tribals.... In Bihar, 52,127 cases involving an area of 76,411 acres have been registered and in 27,454 cases the decision is in favour of restoration of land to the tribals. The area in question is 32,636 acres. Getting this type of decision from the government is one thing, but actual restoration of land is quite another. As a matter of fact, only 1774 acres have been actually physically restored to the tribals.
>
> In West Bengal, the land restored is [a] mere 1681 acres, in Madhya Pradesh 1500 acres and in Orissa 889 acres. In the face of a situation where very large areas have passed hands from the tribals to the non-tribals, the progress of work is rather dismal.[48]

Though the government has become active in restoring land to tribals, we do not know to what extent it will succeed, because most non-tribals are economically well off and are employing lawyers to defend their cases, while the tribals have no documents in their possession to prove their claim to the land and do not have the economic resources to employ lawyers to defend their cases.[49]

Though the Working Group notes that all but one major state has passed laws safeguarding tribal land interests 'despite the laws, however, the tribals' land continues to pass out of their hands'.[50] This alienation was done, according to a study by the Department of Rural Development, through land sale in almost 40 per cent of cases, 25 per cent for public purposes, 25 per cent by mortgage or lease and the remaining 10 per cent through other modes. Eighty per cent of the acquisition in private cases went to non-tribal people.[51] The study found that the tribals were generally unaware of the laws protecting them. Only 1 per cent of tribals in MP, 4 per cent in Rajasthan and 18 per cent in Tripura were aware of the laws.[52] According to the Working Group,

Even in States where awareness is more, the tribals' poverty and the cumbersome process of law prevented recourse to the legal process. The laws contain certain inherent deficiencies such as the absence of a machinery to initiate suo-moto action, the general period of limitation of 12 years for adverse possession, lack of a provision against relinquishment, lack of a provision against trespass and lack of a provision against collusive or fraudulent transfers. The legal process suffers from delays, several stages of appeals and revisions and administrative delays in disposal of cases. Absence of free legal aid to the contesting tribals is often a constraint. Much of the tribal areas continue to be unsurveyed or partly surveyed and lack of updated land records prevents quick action. In certain States, even after orders are passed in the tribals' favour, the law requires them to approach the competent authority again with an Execution Petition, setting in motion another round of litigation. The law does not prescribe a time limit for physical restoration of the land to the tribals from the issue of orders.[53]

Private encroachments of tribal land are accompanied by government expropriations to make way for development projects.

This is particularly adverse in the case of dam construction which frequently results in the flooding of the forested areas tribals inhabit.[54] According to the Report of the Working Group on Development and Welfare of Scheduled Tribes, during the Eighth Five-Year Plan (1990–1995),

> Out of the 16.94 lakhs [1,694,000] persons displaced by 110 projects studied, about 8.14 lakhs [814,000] persons displaced are tribals. The number of displaced tribals is, however, likely to be much more than this, if we take into account the total number of development projects executed so far. The rehabilitation of the displaced tribals is a serious problem which has not received due attention. In States like Madhya Pradesh and Maharashtra which have made acts/regulations for rehabilitation of displaced persons, including tribals, provisions have remained on paper only. The Working Group felt that absence of a national policy for rehabilitation of displaced tribals has been the chief reason for the present state of affairs. The Working Group felt that various guidelines have, no doubt, been issued from time to time regarding rehabilitation of the displaced persons including tribals, the latest by the Bureau of Public Enterprises in February, 1986. But these have remained only a pious declaration of intention and have remained on paper only.[55]

The traditional economy of shifting cultivation is now undertaken by only 12 per cent of tribals.[56] The erosion of the traditional economy has produced a marked decline in nutritional standards. According to a World Bank report,

> The nutritional literature on tribal people holds that the most primitive tribes who subsist on natural resources which have not been interfered with by the 'outside world' are better fed and have better nutritional status than other tribal or non-tribal people. Where natural resources have been exploited and are declining, groups which were dependent on them demonstrate worsening nutritional status.[57]

This deterioration has been worsened by the assimilation of traditional Hindu vegetarian dietary preferences. According to the Commissioner for Scheduled Castes and Scheduled Tribes,

The small tribal communities, which were entirely dependent on forests, have not been able to face the challenge of the changing situation. Many of them have almost disappeared. Moreover, a few communities, which are still surviving in the forests, are being forced to move out. Their rights are not recorded. Therefore, they cannot hope, let alone claim, a sympathetic hearing. On the other hand the resources from which they have been making a living are dwindling in the face of growing pressure from more stronger communities or the government itself. In this way tribal communities got dispersed and they have ceased to exist as communities. Similarly, in many areas the economy of the shifting cultivators has collapsed. Only those shifting cultivators have survived, who did not come under pressure of the outside system.[58]

The implication of this is that nature preserves would have to be created that would allow the ecosystem and the tribal population to exist according to traditional lifestyles. The need and usefulness of involving tribals in forest development has now been recognized. According to the Government of Maharashtra's Report of the Sub-Committee for the Indepth Study of the Various Schemes Under Tribal Sub-Plan of 1992,

> It is observed that there are confrontations between the forest department and the tribals. The tribals perceive the forest department as merely [a] controlling and a punishing authority. There is a potential of rejuvenating, and conserving the vanishing forests by winning the confidence of the tribals. This would also motivate them for participation in the programme and would also generate a source of employment for the tribals. There is a need to systematically tap the potential of minor forest produce and it would certainly contribute as a source of income for the tribals. The Committee is firmly of the opinion that this is a major drawback in the prevalent Tribal Sub-Plan.[59]

At least 600,000 people are estimated to have been removed to make way for national parks and wildlife sanctuaries and 400,000 of these have not been rehabilitated.[60] In a country where a third of the population suffers from malnutrition and grows by 12 million a year the pressure on land and resources is difficult to accomodate. Settled cultivation, which most plains tribals have adopted, however, represents a change of lifestyle to some extent. The introduction of settled agriculture implies greater entry into the cash economy and the intrusion of state institutions. Only the northeast tribal majority states have managed this transition under their own auspices.

They can take their own decisions. Moreover, the system of self-governance at the village level is still continuing in these areas. The people still enjoy full rights over all the resources and the land within their respective territories. Therefore, they are in a position to prevail upon others to agree to their proposition.[61]

However, this incorporation of development has uneven effects.

The emerging tribal elites are generally educated and acculturated; and, in most cases, are estranged from their 'backward' brethren in different proportion. They move in the direction of emulation of the pattern of culture of the people of the higher state of the wider society, although it leads to the impairment of their ethnic solidarity.[62]

The need for community control of the development process to moderate the inevitable class and cultural differentiation that results from it places the tribal movement in a conflictual position. In the northeastern states, tribals control their own destiny to a large extent, but the need for employment and education, and the lack of rapid enough development create social pressures. In the plains the total lack of control has meant land alienation, increased poverty and exploitation. With marginalization and reduction to a minority status, the creation of a tribal state is no longer likely, but greater influence at the state level, and district council control by tribals, as has happened in Darjeeling district of West Bengal, is possible. This compromise, while less than what has already been achieved in the northeast, would provide a large measure of protection to tribal interests without driving out the non-tribal population who have the skills and investment needed for development activities.

The tribal movement is so divided between hill and plains tribes and along many smaller ethnic, religious and political lines that the ICITP was not formed until 1987.[63] Even then there was criticism that the hill tribes were underrepresented, and the Jharkhand movement had an inordinate representation in this national body. 'Tribal peoples outside Chotanagpur have by and large kept aloof from the organization, which could have become an All India organization of the tribals of India.'[64] As the tribal hill states have access to greater government resources than the plains tribals, the failure of the state governments in northeast India to take national leadership of the tribal movement must be seen as primarily their own responsibility, and a reflection on the internal divisions of the Indian tribal movement between autonomist plains tribals and oft-times secessionist hill tribals. While the plains tribals advocate more autonomy within the Indian union, with which they are integrated to a large degree, the hill tribes of the northeast tend towards secession and independence. Being less tied to India and situated on international boundaries, they regard this as a viable option in a way not open to plains tribes.[65]

According to one observer,

Perhaps the most crucial prerequisite for tribal developments is to curb severely the power of the non-tribal moneylenders, landlords and traders that control the tribal economy. However, since the political organizers for the centre and centre-right parties that are likely to control any government under the present political system come from this class it is highly unlikely that this basic change will ever be made. The laws exist, but no government that wants to remain in power can afford to implement them.[66]

According to another observer,

Given...the fact that political support for the Government of India derives fundamentally from those social classes which most profit from the exploitation of tribal people, it is hardly surprising that tribal development remains for the most part an unconscionable sham. From their inception right to the present time, it has been recognized that developmental programme benefits for tribals 'did not flow to the tribal communities. They only strengthened the exploitative elements.'[67]

Since these two writings were published, however, major changes have occurred in Indian politics. Traditional elites are finding access to universities increasingly difficult as reservations make them accessible to lower castes and tribals. The World Bank had to withdraw its loan to the Narmada Dam project after international pressure. It is now recognized in government circles that tribals need to be involved in environmental conservation, and the failure to do so can lead to the types of politically uncomfortable protest that marked the Narmada Dam project. The assertion of minorities and the lower classes in the electoral system is proving to be an important and growing counterweight to the influence and financial power of large corporations that bankroll the major political parties.

Government-sponsored Development

Since independence, state commitment to tribal development has significantly increased. 'From the first to fourth plans the investment in tribal areas was meagre.'[68] Since the launching of the Tribal Sub-Plan (TSP) in the Fifth Plan period there has been a significant increase in funding (Table 9.2).

With the Seventh Plan, the percentage of proposed outlay (7.22) was almost as much as the percentage of tribals (7.76 per

TABLE 9.2
Plan Funding for Tribal Development Programmes

Plan Period	Total Plan Outlay	Tribal Development Programme (Rs million)	%
1st	1,960	19.33	1.0
2nd	4,672	42.92	0.9
3rd	8,577	50.53	0.6
1966–99	6,756	32.32	0.5
4th	15,902	75.00	0.5
5th	39,322	1,067.27	2.71
6th	97,500	5,535.50	5.47
7th	180,000	13,000.00	7.22

Source: Government of India, *Report of the Commission for Scheduled Castes and Scheduled Tribes: Eighth Report, April 1985–March 1986* (Delhi: Government of India Press, 1988), p. 70.

cent) in the 1981 Census which the Commission for Scheduled Castes and Scheduled Tribes found 'very heartening'.[69] The actual expenditures were even higher, at 8.39 per cent in 1985–86 and 8.68 per cent in 1986–87, anticipated expenditures at 9.52 per cent in 1987–88 and 9.67 per cent in 1988–89 (Table 9.3).

TABLE 9.3
Tribal State Plan Expenditures (Rs crores)

Year/Period	State Plan	Flow to TSP	% of TSP to State Plan
7th Plan Projection	70,317.00	5,988.85	8.51
1985–86 (Actual)	11,630.85	975.76	8.39
1986–87 (Actual)	13,782.12	1,196.68	8.68
1987–88 (Anticip)	14,800.99	1,408.92	9.52
1988–89 (Anticip)	17,432.50	1,685.80	9.67
Total of first 4 years of 7th Plan	57,646.46	5,269.60	9.14

Source: Government of India, Ministry of Welfare, *Report of Working Group on Development and Welfare of Scheduled Tribes During Eighth Five-Year Plan, 1990–95,* (Delhi: Ministry of Welfare, Government of India, 1989), p. 15.

In per capita terms the shift has been from underfunding tribals to giving them more than the general share (Table 9.4).

TABLE 9.4
Per Capita Investment on General and Tribal Populations during various Five Years Plans

Plan Period	General	Scheduled Tribes (Rs per capita)
1st	38	10.43
2nd	51	22.47
3rd	94	16.96
1966–69	68	10.84
4th	145	21.01
5th	345	278.71
6th	891	1,045.12

Source: Government of India, *Report of the Commission for Scheduled Castes and Scheduled Tribes: Eighth Report April 1985–March 1986* (Delhi: Government of India Press, 1988), p. 70.

However, quantitative distribution does not indicate how much actually benefits the tribal people. Indian government reports are frank about shortcomings in this regard.

The per capita investment in respect of Scheduled Tribes is not a very clear indicator of the fact that the money invested has actually benefited the tribals. There is strong indication that due to poor infrastructure, comparatively heavy investment on development of administrative structure, leakages and other related factors, the real benefit of the investments made in the tribal areas has not been of the desired level. The Commission would recommend that keeping in view the poor economic status of the tribals, the per capita investment for them should be of a much higher order than that of the general population.[70]

Further, increased funding, given the admitted leakages and inappropriate development, will not necessarily improve the tribals' lot.

There has been too much emphasis on quantitative investments rather than qualitative achievements. As a result, even when over-all percentage of investments under Tribal sub-Plan have shown positive signs of increase during every plan period, the ground results do not reflect the achievements. Beneficiary oriented schemes have received a much less share in almost all the years. An analysis of investments during the first four years of the Seventh Five Year Plan has revealed that beneficiary oriented schemes may not have received more than 20% of the total outlay under TSP during Seventh Five Year Plan. It is a matter of concern that this has been the state of affairs despite an increasing emphasis in every successive plan period on states to quantify more and more for the beneficiary oriented schemes.

Tribal sub-Plan is a plan within the State plan and therefore draws outlays from different sectors. The present bias in favour of infrastructure development schemes is resulting in an exaggerated and notional flow to Tribal sub-Plan. Quantification under Tribal State Plan (TSP) are presently made under the general plan schemes of different Departments as percentages of the outlay without any careful look at the relevance of the schemes to tribal areas and without any assessment of the likely flow of physical benefits to tribals. The Working Group felt that in the sectoral fragmentation of

Tribal sub-Plan, the schemes under which quantification are made do not reflect the felt needs of the tribals, and, therefore, these do not create the desired impact....

The investments in tribal areas, however well planned and however massive these may be, will only add to the miseries of tribal people if they are not provided proper protection umbrella. The Working Group, therefore, felt that there was a strong concomitant need for stringent implementation of protective laws to ensure that the benefits of economic development are not taken away from the tribals. The loopholes in the existing laws should be plugged forthwith and, if possible, a Central model law on prevention of alienation of tribal land, should be framed.[71]

The Commissioner for Scheduled Castes and Scheduled Tribes is even more blunt in his assessment of the TSP implementation.

The quantification of funds under the TSP continues to be notional in quite a few cases and schemes that cannot be legitimately shown as flow to the TSP are actually shown as such. The detailed planning and exercise that are necessary on the part of each developmental Department to quantify the flow to the TSP realistically are seldom undertaken.[72]

The Commissioner after a survey of eight states which received central government funding under the Special Central Assistance (SCA) scheme reported that '*The total unutilized amount in these eight States according to the preliminary investigation is of the order of Rs 236.75 crores*', indicating that when money is available for tribal development it is not fully utilized. Even the money that is provided does not necessarily benefit the tribals according to the Commissioner.

The overall outlays for the TSP do not indicate the nature of investments in the area which are beneficial to the tribal people. It appears that all the States are not using a common frame notwithstanding the fact that the Sub-Plan exercises are now more than a decade old. Major and medium irrigation projects, power and large industries are the most obvious examples in which more often than not investment results in a severe backlash for tribal people and benefits may accrue partly to the area but not to the people. Power projects may be located in tribal areas but benefits go to the State as a whole. In some States, therefore, major and medium irrigation projects and power are not included in the Tribal Sub-Plan outlays. In some cases a *pro rata* share of these projects is credited to the Sub-Plan based on the quantum of benefits likely to accrue to the Sub-Plan areas. But in some States no such consideration appears to weigh with them and the entire outlay on such projects is reflected in the Sub-Plan which highly inflates the figure of investments for tribal development without meaning much in real sense or even having adverse effects, as stated earlier.

In such a mixed affair the performance based on overall outlays and expenditure is misleading. Moreover, the heavy investment infrastructural programmes involving big contracts prove to be large sponges which absorb whatever comes in their way. The inevitable draw is on vital programmes like education, health and agriculture which are even otherwise difficult to operate and the strain on resources caused by such capital intensive projects becomes a convenient alibi for non-action.[73]

Nevertheless, not all failures can be blamed on programmes. The traditional exploitation of tribals by outsiders has left a legacy of tribal mistrust that makes well-intentioned programmes more difficult to implement.

During the Sixth Plan all the TSP documents did not contain references to the part to be played by the financial institutions. However, it was assumed that around Rs 800 crores would be the contribution of financial institutions in tribal programmes. Thus, on the whole, institutional finance has not so far emerged as a strong financial support to tribal development programmes. The reservation in the matter on the part of the tribal is understandable as he has had the bad experience of moneylenders who charged him exorbitant rates of interest and made him indebted. In many cases alienation of lands and even bondage can be traced back to taking loans from moneylenders. Thus, there is a general reluctance

to get entangled in schemes involving a loan element. Till
the requisite degree of enlightenment and awareness among
tribals is reached we will have to go carefully for those
schemes linked with loan element. It will have to be ensured
that schemes involving loan component do not deteriorate
the economic condition of the tribals.[74]

The Working Group summed up the shortfalls in the implementation of the tribal programme.

States have, no doubt, enacted protective laws to provide
protection to tribals from exploitation by non-tribals. But in
actual implementation, this has not received priority. There
are still instances reported by states of tribal lands passing
into the hands of non-tribals despite the existence of these
laws. The moneylenders in tribal areas have been charging
higher rates of interest and the tribal indebtedness to them
continues, although the extent of indebtedness varies from
State to State. LAMPS [Large Size Multipurpose Cooperative
Societies] have not been able to substitute the money lend-
ers as viable credit agencies. In the area of marketing of
tribal produce the price realised by tribals has improved to
an extent in respect of certain items with the intervention of
the State Tribal Cooperative Marketing Corporations/Federa-
tions, but it is still less than the market price. In the non-
nationalised items, the private traders have continued to
exploit the tribals.[75]

National overviews by government agencies can only hint at
the problem tribals face in obtaining the benefits planners and
development agencies have assigned to them. For this, village-
level studies are required though their micro-level results make
generalization difficult. However one study of tribal displacement and rehabilitation by the Indian Social Institute found the
corruption that was alluded to in the previous government
reports all too evident, even in the receipt of compensation benefits the tribals were legally entitled to receive. As Table 9.5 suggests, every development offer can have a price for receipt.
     The well-known corruption and inefficiency of the Indian bureau-
cracy presents a dilemma for development agencies involved in

TABLE 9.5
Bribes Paid to Officials for Compensation and Facilities

Project	Officials				Purpose				
	LAO	BDO	Proj	Total	Job	Comp	House	NA	Total
Thermal Power			1	1				1	1
Fertilizer Plant									
Coal Mine			5	5		1	3	1	5
Crocodile Farm									
Aluminium			4	4	3		1		4
Aluminium	8	4	4	16		16			16
Bauxite									
Major Dam (multipurpose)									
Dam Power	4		3	7		3	4		7
Dam Irrig	5		2	7		5	2		7
Total	17	4	19	40	3	28	10	2	40

Note: LAO = Land Acquisition Officer, BDO = Block Development Officer, Proj. = Project Officer, Comp. = Compensation

Source: Walter Fernandes and S. Anthony Raj, *Development, Displacement and Rehabilitation in the Tribal Areas of Orissa* (Delhi: Indian Social Institute, 1992), p. 97.

tribal development. Though India has ratified the ILO Convention 107, but not the less assimilationist 169, the ILO's Report to the Committee of Experts noted that the report requested from the Indian government was not received. 'It hopes that in its next report the Government will make every effort to provide detailed information, and that it will submit a report in time for the Committee to examine it fully before its session begins.'[76] The Report found that NGOs considered that the government 'has not taken any positive action to guarantee appropriate compensation for displaced persons in accordance with *Article 12 of the Convention*'.[77] The World Bank-commissioned report by Bradford Morse on the Narmada project which stated that ILO 107 was not being implemented despite India's ratification of the convention was to contribute to World Bank withdrawal of funding.[78] Agencies involved in tribal work are regularly monitored and have had their mail opened by Indian intelligence agencies. Those who stick to development work and avoid political involvement can operate. Some such as UN agencies are required by their statutes to work only with host governments. Since this leads to corruption and inefficiency, tribal development programmes by UN agencies are being funded through Indian government departments which pass on the money to NGOs for implementation. The UN tribal project funding of NGOs through the Indian government offers opportunities for tribal beneficiaries to receive large-scale funding while avoiding the problems of dealing with corrupt local government officials. Although some NGOs exploit tribals for their own benefit, the funding agencies can over time monitor and evaluate the programmes to weed out the less successful operations. However, this can be a long process and mistakes are made. A senior diplomat at a western mission in Delhi recommended that we visit the non-tribal leader of a tribal development agency that had received significant foreign funding. On further investigation we found the man who had received an OBE (Order of the British Empire) for his work among tribals was a practising pederast. A film crew sent to do a publicity film for the organization found that the local tribal beneficiaries called him a 'thief'; so this comment had to be edited out of the film. The scene of tribal children working also had to be omitted as it looked too much like a sweatshop.

An established reputation among donor agencies and effective networking for foreign funding can contribute to a lack of independent evaluation of what is going on in tribal development projects. The existing networks often reflect old programmes, which may have lost their dynamism, and neglect new organizations with greater grassroots capability but fewer contacts in the capital. Development staff are too few to adequately evaluate large funding projects at the village level. Yet the trend is to decentralize aid operations to the local area. In the Indian context, this often puts more power and resources in the hands of those most directly involved in exploiting the poor. To avoid this problem, development agencies need to have grassroots intelligence about programme recipients which, on account of the prejudices and cultural barriers, can be difficult to determine, particularly when programmes reach a scale that precludes micro-level monitoring. With corrupt low-level government officials and exploitative moneylenders and landlords, the tribal population is vulnerable to exploitation from both the state and the private sector. The laws in place for their protection often tend to be observed in the breach. On account of their minority status, the tribals are unlikely to overcome these problems, but without active pressure on the political system their participation will be minimal. It is a mark of tribal alienation that the ICITP told the UN Working Group on Indigenous Peoples in 1990 that 'Our Indigenous Peoples are fighting for their right of self-determination, not necessarily in the colonial situation of a foreign power, but against the internal colonial situation created by the dominant groups of our own country, which is even more exploitative, suppressive and oppressive than the foreign rulers'.[79] Though encouraging steps are being taken, not least of them by the Indian government in increasing allotment to tribals, greater efficiency and elimination of corruption will be required for effective implementation. This is not beyond the realm of possibility, but ultimately the tribal peoples will have to resolve their internal contradictions themselves if permanent solutions are to be found.

Tribal Cooperation

Unity among tribes has not lasted long. Each tribe has promoted its own interests, but failed to unite with others. The principal divide has been between the hill tribes in the frontier and those in the plains. As a result of factors such as missionary activity, limited outsider settlement, and government security imperatives, the hill tribes have been better placed to demand and receive government concessions, including statehood. This has not been obtained by plains tribals who are generally a minority even in their own areas. Only 13 districts have tribal majorities, and Madhya Pradesh and Orissa, with 22 per cent tribal population, have the largest minority tribal population.[80] The Jharkhand movement for a plains tribal state has not made significant headway to date, and even if achieved, would leave out many plains tribals and include many non-tribals within a newly created state.

This is the dilemma of any ethnically based political entity. It only creates new minorities within its borders who in turn agitate against discrimination. The creation of ethnic boundaries may permit the rise to dominance of subordinate ethnic groups and the marginalization of dominant ones, but this creates new injustices.

While the inner-line policy certainly made possible the rise of a tribal middle class and political elite and general developmental improvements, the restrictions on the travel of 'outsider Indians' is at the very least incongruous in a democracy. However, when the alternative is the swamping of an indigenous culture, this is perhaps justifiable. If it can be justified for security reasons in the northeast then it should also apply for humanitarian reasons to the tribal people in the plains. That this has not happened is a reflection in part of the dominance of local landed and moneylending interests, as well as the interests of resource-extracting companies.

While the creation of states in the plains may not be realistic in the face of the resistance of existing state governments to partition, a reserve or system of district-level autonomy may be possible. Hundreds of lives were lost in the West Bengal government's repression of the Gorkhaland movement in Darjeeling before a compromise involving local autonomy was reached. In the northeast the central government did impose tribal states through the partition of Assam, overruling the objections of the Assam government. Similar arrangements are legally possible in the plains. The creation of linguistic states during the 1950s is generally seen as resolving a number of destabilizing issues that were endangering national unity at the time.

Such protected enclaves, districts and states, however, will not be achieved without a movement that transcends tribal ethnic boundaries and will probably require support from other ethnic groups and interests as well. The failure of existing hill states to press more effectively for protection of the plains tribals is a reflection of the ethnic atomization of Indian politics. Their protection, however, cannot be entrusted to the locally dominant elites which control state governments. Only the centre can impose local autonomy for tribal peoples. At the very least the tribal peoples must control sufficient state power to prevent the locally dominant landed interests from alienating their land. While there are already laws to prevent this, local-level administration has proved unable and often unwilling to implement them.

The administration is unlikely to change its attitude unless it is severed from locally dominant commercial interests and classes. Without local tribal empowerment and the prevention of encroachment, such a change is unlikely, since the administration itself is often involved in the exploitation through kickbacks from contractors or even outright extortion of tribals. However, turning over power to local elected panchayats is not the best solution as long as there are non-indigenous dominant elites. According to the most prominent authority on tribal India,

> As early as 1963, the Commissioner for Scheduled Castes and Tribes expressed in his report for the year 1962–63 the fear that, due to the existing pattern of concentration of social and economic power in the hands of a dominant section of the population, democratic decentralization may lead to a more extensive exploitation of the scheduled tribes. This apprehension was fully justified, for recent experiences have shown that the panchayat samiti and zilla parishad, which in some states took over the functions of the former district officers, were dragging their feet in the implementation of tribal welfare schemes, for the simple reason that their leading members belonged to the very classes which traditionally profited from the exploitation of tribes. By diluting the powers of civil servants, who alone were likely to safeguard the interests of the tribals, decentralization certainly did more harm than good to the tribal cause.[81]

Civil servants may on occasion provide some redress to tribals caught between dominant landed and moneylending village elites and corrupt bottom-rung officials, but without transfer of local powers to the tribals themselves, justice cannot be achieved. Such powers can only be provided by the state and national governments which have not been forthcoming in this regard. While the creation of hill states has precluded some of the worst effects of outsider exploitation, nothing of consequence has been done to arrest the erosion of tribal human rights in the plains. For this, a sea change in the administration of the country as a whole is required, which only a democratization movement in society is likely to bring about. There is evidence of this in the rise of grass-roots movements, and the increasing inclination to vote out corrupt or ineffective governments. Whether the hill states and the plains tribals can make common cause to press for implementation of legislation could be critical in improving the lot of tribal peoples in India. However, their ethnic diversity makes such a unity of purpose problematic.

228/*Development, Ethnicity and Human Rights in South Asia*

This is the difficulty of ethnic identity; it can divide or unite people, depending on the criteria selected and the goals articulated. According to an indigenous peoples human rights advocate,

Allegations of ethnic divisiveness, backwardness or separatism are often used by governments as cloaks for exploitation, authoritarianism and hegemonic privilege.... Nowadays, in many parts of the world, people are resorting to their ethnicity as a sort of civil rights movement, to achieve the equality of treatment which had previously been denied them in the name of modernization.[82]

Ethnicity has also been used to oppress others. While few would deny the right of tribals to assert their rights to cultural survival, the concept of ethnic identity is by its nature exclusive as well as inclusive, and this creates disunity among even like-minded tribal peoples which hinders their emancipation. It is therefore a mistake to place too high a premium on the retention of traditional practices which are counterproductive in modern society. The context in which ethnic identity should be preserved and promoted by the state and civil libertarians is a matter of on-going debate, but its promotion is fraught with the danger of intolerance of others.

Tribals are seen as preservers of a lost way of life and therefore retain in some circles something of the 'noble savage' aura. Their relegation to the bottom of the class hierarchy makes it impossible for them to act out the more repressive aspects of ethnic identity. However, in promoting their emancipation, the regressive tendencies within any ethnic movement need to be taken into account.

REFERENCES

1. Meera Chatterjee, *ICDS Service Delivery Among Tribal Populations in Bihar and Madhya Pradesh* (New Delhi: World Bank, October 1992), pp. 35, 58.
2. Christoph von Furer-Haimendorf, *Tribes of India: The Struggle for Survival* (Berkeley: University of California Press, 1982), p. 319.
3. Ibid., p. 189.
4. Julian Burger, *Report from the Frontier: The State of the World's Indigenous Peoples* (London: Zed Books, 1987), p. 275.

5. Ibid., p. 275.
6. Ibid.
7. Arun Sinha, *Against the Few: Struggles of India's Rural Poor* (London: Zed Books, 1991), p. 185.
8. Bernard Nietschmann, 'Third World Colonial Expansion: Indonesia, Disguised Invasion of Indigenous Nations', in John H. Bodley (ed.), *Tribal Peoples and Development Issues: A Global Overview* (Mountain View, California: Mayfield Publishing Company, 1988), p. 192.
9. Partha Chatterjee, *Nationalist Thought and the Colonial World: A Derivative Discourse* (London: Zed Books, 1986), p. 168.
10. Kancha Ilaiah, 'BSP and Caste as Ideology', *Economic and Political Weekly*, Vol. 29, No. 12, 19 March 1994, pp. 668–69.
11. Government of India, 'Primary Census Abstract for Scheduled Castes and Scheduled Tribes', Paper 1 of 1993, *Census of India 1991*, Registrar General and Census Commissioner, India (Delhi: Government of India Press, 1993), p. 6.
12. Walter Fernandes, 'Meetings of Non-tribal Observers During the General Assembly', Indian Council of Indigenous and Tribal Peoples, 15–20 November 1993, New Delhi, unpublished typescript, p. 3.
13. Draft: A First Call to Convene an All India National Central Assembly of all the Ethnic Indigenous and Tribal Groups, 30 November 1992. p. 3.
14. Ibid., p. 3.
15. Shahataj, 'Dalits: Indigenous Peoples of India', in *Proceedings of the First Asian Indigenous Women's Conference Sharing Commonalities and Diversities: Forging Unity Towards Indigenous Women's Empowerment* (Teachers' Camp, Cordillera Region, Philippines, 24–30 January 1993), p. 21.
16. Susana B.C. Devalle, *Discourses of Ethnicity, Culture and Protest in Jharkhand* (New Delhi: Sage Publications, 1992), p. 154.
17. M.M.K. Wali, *Tribal People in India*, (Geneva: International Labour Organization, 1993), p. 29.
18. Furer-Haimendorf, *Tribes of India* (n. 2 above).
19. Government of India, *Report of the Commissioner for Scheduled Castes and Scheduled Tribes: Twentyeighth Report 1986–87* (Delhi: Government of India Press, 1988) p. 35.
20. Ibid., pp. 76–77.
21. Boniface Minz, 'The Jharkhand Movement', in Walter Fernandes (ed.), *National Development and Tribal Deprivation* (Delhi: Indian Social Institute, 1992), p. 365.
22. Government of India, *Report of the Commissioner for Scheduled Castes and Scheduled Tribes: Twentyseventh Report, 1979–81, Part I* (Delhi: Government of India Press, 1982), p. 11.
23. Arunabha Ghosh, 'Probing the Jharkhand Question', *Economic and Political Weekly*, May 4, Vol. 26, No. 18, 4 May 1991, pp. 1175–76.
24. Sekhar Bandopadhyay, 'A Peasant Caste in Protest: The Namasudras of Eastern Bengal 1872–1945', in Suranjan Das and Sekhar Bandopadhyay (eds), *Caste and Communal Politics in South Asia* (Calcutta: K.P. Bagchi & Company, 1993), p. 147.

25. Mahesh Gavaskar, 'Bahujans as Vanguards: BSP and BMS in Maharashtra Politics', *Economic and Political Weekly*, Vol. XXIX, Nos. 16–17, 16–23 April 1994, p. 895.
26. A.L. Raj, 'Ideology and Hegemony in Jharkhand Movement', *Economic and Political Weekly*, Vol. XXVII, No. 5, 1 February 1992, p. 201.
27. Ibid., p. 201.
28. Nirmal Minz, 'Identity of Tribals in India', in Walter Fernandes (ed.), *The Indigenous Question: In Search for an Identity* (Delhi: Indian Social Institute), p. 31.
29. Ghosh, 'Probing the Jharkhand Question' (n. 23 above), p. 1176.
30. S. Bosu Mullick, 'Jharkhand Movement Through Time', *Religion and Society*, Vol. 38, September–December 1991; also in p. 164 Susana B.C. Devalle, *Discourses of Ethnicity* (n. 16 above), P. 164.
31. Bosu Mullick, 'Jharkhand Movement Through Time' (n. 30 above), p. 60.
32. Bharat Dogra, 'Mandal Commission: Will Tribal Interests Suffer?', *Economic and Political Weekly*, Vol. XXV, No. 39, 29 September 1990, p. 2187.
33. Government of India, *Report of the Commissioner for Scheduled Castes and Scheduled Tribes* (n. 19 above), p. 114.
34. Ibid.
35. Fernandes, 'Meetings of Non-tribal Observers During the General Assembly' (n. 12 above).
36. Dominic Bara and Boniface Minz, *Towards Building a Self-Reliant Tribal Community: Vikas Maitri Approach to Development* (Ranchi: Vikas Maitri, 1981), pp. 10–11.
37. Wali, 'Tribal People in India' (n. 17 above), p. 27.
38. Myron Weiner, *Sons of the Soil: Migration and Ethnic Conflict in India* (Delhi: Oxford University Press, 1988), p. 199.
39. Stuart Corbridge, 'Ousting Singbronga: The Struggle for India's Jharkhand', in Peter Robb (ed.), *Dalit Movements and the Meaning of Labour in India* (Delhi: Oxford University Press, 1993), p. 136.
40. Sajal Basu, *Jharkhand Movement: Ethnicity and Cultural Silence* (Shimla: Indian Institute of Advanced Study, 1994), pp. 44–45.
41. Ibid., p. 64.
42. Ibid., p. 41.
43. B.P. Keshari, 'Development of Political Organizations in Chotanagpur', in S. Bosu Mullick (ed.), *Cultural Chotanagpur: Unity in Diversity* (Delhi: Uppal Publishing House, 1991), p. 132.
44. A.K. Jha, 'Jharkhand Politics of Bihar: Paradigm of Non-Performance', in S. Narayan (ed.), *Jharkhand Movement: Origin and Evolution* (Delhi: Inter-India Publications, 1992).
45. *South Asian Newsweek*, CFMT Television, Ottawa, 11 September 1994.
46. Robert S. Anderson and Walter Huber, *The Hour of the Fox: Tropical Forests, the World Bank, and Indigenous People in Central India* (Seattle: University of Washington Press, 1988).
47. John R. Wood, 'Sardar Sarovar Under Siege: The World Bank and India's Narmada River Dam Projects', Paper presented at Learneds Conference, Canadian Asian Studies Association, Carleton University, Ottawa, 10 June 1993; Raymond F. Mikesell and Lawrence F. Williams, *International Banks and the*

Environment (San Francisco: Sierra Club Books, 1992), pp. 87, 91; The Editors, 'Withdraw from Sardar Sarovar, Now', *The Ecologist*, Vol. 22, No. 5, September–October 1992, pp. 218–20.

48. Government of India, *Report of the Commission for Scheduled Castes and Scheduled Tribes: Fifth Report*, April 1982–March 1983 (New Delhi: Government of India Press, 1984), p. 21.
49. Furer-Haimendorf, *Tribes of India* (n. 2 above), p. 285.
50. Government of India, Ministry of Welfare *Report of the Working Group on Development and Welfare of Scheduled Tribes During Eighth Five-Year Plan, 1990–95*, (Delhi: Ministry of Welfare, Government of India, 1989), p. 35.
51. Ibid., p. 35.
52. Ibid., p. 35.
53. Ibid., p. 35.
54. Enakshi Ganguly Thukral (ed.), *Big Dams, Displaced People* (New Delhi: Sage Publications 1992), p. 8.
55. Government of India, *Report of the Working Group* (n. 50 above), p. 43.
56. J.J. Roy Burman, 'Shifting Cultivation: A Need for Reappraisal', in *Report of National Seminar on Contemporary Tribal Economy in India*, 1989, Jigyanau Tribal Research Centre, New Delhi, p. 66.
57. Chatterjee, *ICDS Service Delivery* (n. 1 above). p. 15.
58. Government of India, *Report of the Commissioner for Scheduled Castes and Scheduled Tribes: Twentyninth Report, 1987–89* (Faridabad: Government of India Press, 1990), p. 275.
59. N.P. Bhanage, *Tribal Commissions and Committees in India* (Bombay: Himalaya Publishing House, 1993), p. 424.
60. Walter Fernandes, J.C. Das and Sam Rao, 'Displacement and Rehabilitation: An Estimate of Extent and Prospects', in Walter Fernandes and Enakshi Ganguly Thukral (eds), *Development, Displacement and Rehabilitation* (Delhi: Indian Social Institute, 1989), p. 78.
61. Government of India, *Report of the Commissioner for Scheduled Castes and Scheduled Tribes: Twentyninth Report* (n. 58 above), p. 289
62. N.K. Behura, 'Santal Sub-Nationalism and New Identity: The Orissa Situation', in Buddhadeb Chaudhuri (ed.), *Ethnopolitics and Identity Crisis* (Delhi: M.C. Mittal, 1992), p. 445.
63. Declaration Adopted, 19 October 1987 for constituting ICITP; Roy Burman, 'Indigenous People and Their Quest for Justice', in ibid., p. 10.
64. B.K. Roy Burman, Letter to Professor Kisku, the then General Secretary ICITP, 21 January 1993, p. 3.
65. Ghanshyam Shah, *Social Movements in India: A Review of the Literature* (New Delhi: Sage Publications, 1990), p. 95; Surajit Sinha, 'Tribal Solidarity Movements in India: A Review', in K. Suresh Singh (ed.), *Tribal Situation in India* (Shimla: Indian Institute of Advanced Study, 1972), p. 410.
66. Steve Jones, 'Tribal Underdevelopment in India', *Development and Change*, Vol. 9, No. 1, January 1978, p. 48.
67. Anderson and Huber, *The Hour of the Fox* (n. 46 above), p. 127, quote from Ajit Raizada, *Tribal Development in Madhya Pradesh: A Planning Perspective* (Delhi: Inter-India Publications, 1984), p. 40.

68. Government of India, *Report of the Commission for Scheduled Castes and Scheduled Tribes: Eighth Report, April 1985–March 1986* (Delhi: Government of India Press, 1988), p. 70.
69. Ibid.
70. Ibid., p. 71.
71. *Report of the Working Group* (n. 50 above), pp. 4–6.
72. *Report of the Commissioner for Scheduled Castes and Scheduled Tribes: Twentyeighth Report* (n. 19 above), p. 363.
73. Ibid., p. 379.
74. Ibid., p. 382.
75. *Report of the Working Group* (n. 50 above), p. 4.
76. International Labour Organization, *Report of the Committee of Experts on the Application of Conventions and Recommendations: General Report and Observations Concerning Particular Countries,* 80th Session, 1993, International Labour Conference, Report III (Part 4A), p. 312.
77. Ibid., p. 313.
78. Ibid., p. 312; Commentary, 'Sardar Sarovar Project: Review of Resettlement and Rehabilitation in Maharashtra', *Economic and Political Weekly,* Vol. XXVIII, No. 34, 21 August 1993, p. 1705.
79. United Nations Working Group on Indigenous Peoples, 8th Session, July 31, 1990, Agenda Item 5, p. 4.
80. Sachchidananda, 'Patterns of Political-Economic Change Among Tribals in Middle India', in Francine R. Frankel and M.S.A. Rao (eds), *Dominance and State Power in Modern India,* Vol. II (Delhi: Oxford University Press, 1990), p. 279.
81. Furer-Haimendorf (n. 2 above), p. 320.
82. David Maybury-Lewis, 'A Special Sort of Pleading: Anthropology at the Service of Ethnic Groups', in John H. Bodley (ed.), *Tribal Peoples and Development Issues: A Global Overview* (Mountain View, California: Mayfield Publishing Company, 1988), p. 378.

CHAPTER 10

Untouchable Emancipation

Congress and the Colonial State

Comparative British and post-colonial policy analysis on the emancipation of India's Untouchables reveals how different state strategies can determine the development of social movements. Despite Untouchables representing 2.6 per cent of the world's population and 16 per cent of India's people, the failure to implement the official abolition of untouchability makes this group the last segregated population in the world with the ending of South African apartheid. Both the British colonial government and the independent Indian government attempted to improve the lot of Untouchables with only modest success. A comparison of the ethnic policies of the British and Congress governments reveals the role of state policy in political mobilization and the effect alternative strategies of state support can have on subordinate populations. It is argued that the colonial strategy, despite its limitations, was more conducive to the political emancipation of Untouchables than was the Congress policy of co-option.

The differences between two historical periods, the late-colonial and the post-colonial era, might make a comparison inappropriate. However, there is no sharp division between the two periods with regard to Untouchable emancipation strategies, as both the colonial government and the Congress party formulated alternative approaches early on in the colonial independence struggle, which the Indian government continues to implement to this day. These alternative strategies sought the emancipation of Untouchables in directions conducive to the maintenance of state control over this potentially subversive population. The two state policies differed in the degree of autonomy that officially encouraged mobilization would support, the British offering more latitude than the independent Congress government. This paradoxical situation, where a colonial government offers more encouragement to ethnic emancipation than the independent government, reflects the values and support bases of the two regimes.

There is a tendency to see the post-colonial governments as inherently more progressive and modern than colonial governments, which may be the case in many policy areas, but it cannot be assumed in every instance. Some groups undoubtedly had more to gain from decolonization than others, but with traditionally suppressed groups such as Untouchables the post-colonial record is not good. There has been a retreat from the state promotion of ethnicity following independence.

A number of strategies were pursued in executing the nation-building design. The colonial pattern of avid classification largely ceased; indeed, the state frequently sought to replace ethnic categories by those based on territory.... Thus the overly exuberant celebration of ethnicity is viewed with suspicion by the state. A number have forbidden the formation of ethnic associations, which were generally tolerated by the colonial state.... That politicized ethnicity is a potential—and potent—threat to the nation-building mission has been a prime factor in the widespread adoption of single-party or military formulas of governance, where open political competition is averted.[1]

Though independent India has not discouraged ethnic politics, the state's accommodation of it has not brought the emancipation of Untouchables. Any comparison favourable to the colonial power goes against nationalist scholarship, but this 'pro-British' view is commonly held by Untouchables old enough to have experienced both regimes.

Although Communist Party members denounce Western imperialism in their speeches, the A.D.'s [Untouchables] I met in Thanjavur showed little or no antagonism to the British.... Some think that British people were more opposed to the caste system than are their Congress Party rulers, for they knew of individual British businessmen in the coast towns who paid no heed to caste distinctions, while they know of the Congress Party only through their landlords.[2]

This is a view shared by the Untouchable elite. When I asked a Scheduled Caste ICS officer whether it was better working under the British than the Indians, his silence brought laughter from subordinate government officials who guessed the answer he dared not give publicly. The ICS officer later privately said that though the Indians were more oriented to development, in terms of merit and justice the British were better.

Such views point to differing perceptions of colonial rule among Untouchables which are inadequately represented in the literature on the independence struggle. It will be argued that this view is more historically accurate than the prevailing scholarship on the subject of Untouchable emancipation, which either takes the Congress party view or avoids an explicit historical comparison on a politically sensitive subject. The sensitivity is indicated by the frequent prohibition on research into untouchability imposed on foreign scholars.

Both the British and Congress attempts at Untouchable emancipation were impositions on traditional Indian society, motivated by the British and western-influenced Indian elite attempting to break a centuries-old view of Hindu society. The gap between the British and westernized Indians attempting social reform and the mass of Indian people made change particularly difficult. These elites attempted reform of the caste system relatively late in the colonial period, the British having earlier largely accepted caste prohibitions as inherent to the society they governed.

The delay in the British attempts at Untouchable emancipation has often been attributed to the need to 'divide and rule' in the face of a nationalist mobilization. In fact the modern sense of Hinduism as an entity is even attributed to western scholarship constructing an identity from what had been localized beliefs. The caste system had long been in existence but it became a modern political category for mobilization only through the operation of British census takers and ethnographers who constructed an identity which was subsequently accepted by the participants.[3] This ascription of caste mobilization to British machinations, though common in the literature, at times suggests a near conspiracy of colonial policy to create identities in pursuit of state control over the population. The fact of the matter is that these identities were already there, but communication barriers, which hinder interaction beyond the village, rapidly eroded with colonial rule. Modernization inevitably resulted in the formation of larger identities and their politicization, over which the colonial state had only limited influence. The politicization of ethnicity during modernization was inevitable given the beliefs of traditional society, but the reaction of the state might have had a significant influence on the direction these movements took.

Scholars, by blaming British census enumerators rather than the oppression inherent in the caste system, place the responsibility for the current state of affairs on colonialism rather than their own national culture. Had the caste system not existed the British could not have enumerated it or helped politicize it. Caste and communalism were indigenous creations which the British could only manipulate, not invent or significantly change. If caste and communalism raises negative aspects the intellectual elite dislike, they need to examine their own culture to find fault rather than serve a nationalist project by finding a 'foreign hand' in British colonial manipulation. The nationalist project assumes the benefits of an anti-colonial struggle, but these were hard to find for the Scheduled Castes and Tribes. While tribals may have lost their independence through colonial conquest, for Untouchables colonialism was a relatively liberating experience, however limited the opportunities for emancipation it offered. The differential impact of colonialism on subaltern emancipation needs to recognized for the opportunities it provided rather than being condemned according to the nationalist agenda of scholars. While anti-colonialism may reflect the interests of the high-caste intellectual elite, we cannot assume it was of equal benefit to all sections of society.

People can only be mobilized on grounds they can identity with, and if caste mobilized them it was because they already identified with it. One suspects that scholars' attribution of caste manipulation to colonialism serves the contemporary political purpose of delegitimizing caste and communal beliefs in favour of the nationalist project they wish to impose on the disaffected, who have difficulty identifying with such nationalist abstractions of their historical oppressors. Until scholars are willing to

acknowledge these cultural defects and not favour their nationalist agenda over caste and communal identities, they will fail to
understand how the majority of South Asians feel. Like nationalism, caste and communalism have their negative aspects; however, to rank one set of values over another is to impose a belief
system on people with different values and perceptions. Since
these peoples lack the access to media and academic publications for their own perspectives, they are subject to misrepresentation by others who place them within an alien discourse they
may be unaware of or hostile to.

The colonial state's promotion of Untouchable interests was a
decidedly late colonial concern and essentially a twentieth-
century phenomenon. The first step in this direction was the
Christian missionary movement in the nineteenth century which
created an awareness of a modern alternative to the caste system.
At the same time, western-influenced Hindu social reformers of
the Brahmo Samaj and Arya Samaj attempted to modify Hinduism by incorporating humanistic values that would enable the
continuance of Hinduism without the negative consequences of
the caste system. This approach formed the basis of the Congress
strategy of Untouchable emancipation: of integrating Untouchables within a reformed Hindu system devoid of its social
stigmas. However, this reformed Hinduism as advocated by intellectuals was rarely followed in practice.[4]

The creation of a minuscule educated Untouchable elite
through Christian missionary educational institutions provided
the leadership for the first mobilization of Untouchables in modern politics. The missionaries and colonial state however
approached this mobilization differently from the Hindu nationalists of the Congress party. The colonial state was willing to
accept the politicization of Untouchables with an identity separate from the Hindus, while the nationalists saw their emancipation as integrative with the Hindu nationalist agenda. The
removal of social stigmas would create the conditions for this integration. However, the Untouchable elite saw their position and
that of their caste differently from the role the nationalists perceived for them. While the nationalists saw independence as the
primary goal, the Untouchables saw political emancipation from
traditional Hinduism as the objective to be achieved with or without
independence. It was a goal the British seemed more sympathetic

to than the Congress party. This was because untouchability was more than just a social stigma; it was a class system that entrenched economic exploitation which would not be removed through social or religious reform. This was the essential difference between the Untouchable leadership and the Congress party. Though the Untouchables saw themselves as both economically and socially exploited, Congress expected them to maintain their traditional economic position while removing the social stigma that came with their occupations. In this sense the Untouchable leaders were more radical than the Congress leadership were prepared to be. The British proved more willing to promote these radical leaders than did the Congress party; hence the alienation of the Untouchables from the independence struggle, and their functional role in the maintenance of colonial rule.[5]

The British could tolerate radical ethnicity more easily than the Congress party because, being a foreign power, they were less dependent on local elites for the maintenance of their rule. They could manipulate a wider range of conflictual social groups as they did not have a nation-building programme or identity to foster. Congress by contrast could not rely on a foreign power base and had to depend on indigenous sources of support. The gradual extension of the franchise under British rule played both ways: incorporating Untouchables as a significant potential vote bloc and power base, while at the same time giving the rural elite a greater opportunity to thwart reform by westernized Congress leaders.

The Poona Pact

The conflict resulted in a confrontation which was ultimately resolved through the Poona Pact between Mahatma Gandhi and the Untouchable leader Dr Ambedkar in 1932. The subsequently revised tenets of that Pact continue to be in effect today, hence this event is critical to the present condition of the Untouchables in India. As part of an on-going devolution of power to Indians the British were prepared to grant a separate representation to Untouchables as they had previously given to Muslims. This concession would have given the Untouchables an independent power base in proportion to their population which could be critical in the event that coalitions were required to form govern-ments. Gandhi clearly saw the threat this presented to upper-caste Congress dominance and went on a fast unto death to prevent its implementation. Gandhi's role was critical in that other Congress leaders such as Nehru saw it as peripheral to the independence struggle.[6] However, Gandhi placed greater impor-tance on the untouchability issue than any other Congress leader, either before or since then, and was unwilling to see the creation of Untouchables as a political entity independent of mainstream Hindu Congress politics. He placed the struggle against the social stigma of untouchability near the top of his personal agenda, though it had always been of minor interest to other nationalists. At the same time, he was unwilling to change the caste system through agrarian reform or anything that would politically eman-cipate the Untouchables. Though in practical effect his fast was to prevent the political emancipation of Untouchables, it is more often than not portrayed in history as a fast for their emancipa-tion.[7] Mulk Raj Anand's novel *Untouchable* portrays it thus, while the movie *Gandhi* omits it entirely, possibly because it cannot be accurately portrayed in a progressive light. Paradoxically, the leader who did the most to put the problem on the Indian nation-alist agenda, did more to prevent its resolution than anyone else.[8]

The compromise Gandhi forced on Ambedkar was subsequently changed by Congress leaders when they found that their own nominees were not getting elected. The resulting policy enabled Untouchables to be elected by the general population in re-served seats allocated to them by the government, from where, as a minority in each constituency, they would be dependent on the higher castes to elect them. This system was tailor-made to create Untouchable dependency on the higher-caste electorate. At the same time, this enabled the most subservient Untouch-ables nominated by the higher castes to obtain elected office. The Pact thus followed the Congress pattern as a model of politi-cal accommodation and co-option. As an electoral minority in each constituency, Untouchables with an independent political base would have found it virtually impossible to be elected except in unusually divided multicandidate elections.

The willingness of the British to grant a separate electorate was meant to both emancipate the Untouchables and separate them from the Congress party, and thus hinder the independence movement. This offer followed an affirmative action programme of job and educational reservations, which pre-dated similar programmes in America by several decades. These programmes which were implemented under colonial rule were also resisted by many Congress party supporters, though as a minor concession to a minority not yet able to take full advantage of it, this did not meet the resistance the separate electorate received.

The Post-colonial State

Independence brought the opportunity to abolish reservation of seats and affirmative action programmes; however, these have continued to the present day. The trend was for an extension rather than contraction of benefits, as more groups sought inclusion for job reservations. These included groups of 'Backward Castes', who were frequently the dominant rural castes.

The Untouchable leader Ambedkar, long an opponent of Gandhi and the Congress party, was made the law minister responsible for drafting the Indian constitution, which officially abolished untouchability. Though he soon resigned over the slow pace of reform under the Nehru government, the affirmative action programmes, which were initially considered time-bound, were repeatedly extended and expanded.

The difficulty was that the Congress party had less autonomy for action against dominant rural castes than the British colonial power. As the years passed its autonomy was further eroded, as it became more dependent on the rural elite to deliver the votes at election time. Though in the first years of independence the intermediary rights of zamindars were abolished, no further land reform of any significance was ever undertaken. Had the Nehru government implemented land reform in the immediate post-independence period, an empowerment of the poor might have been possible. However, the landed base of the rural Congress was already developing in the colonial period, and the degree of state autonomy in this regard is questionable.

Paradoxically, the universal franchise reduced the autonomy of the state from its rural elite class base, while it gave the vote to the Untouchables. The pressures of the higher-caste landed elite and the Untouchable vote bloc both prevented socio-economic reform and made the incorporation of the Untouchables within the Congress system imperative. Congress accommodation and co-option after independence followed the classic Congress strategy of absorbing or accommodating dissent within the political system. In this there was a qualitative difference from the colonial state. While the latter could foster independent organization and politicization of the Untouchables in conflict with the dominant castes, which better served to undermine the independence struggle, such autonomy, while democratically permissible, was discouraged by the Congress system. The Poona Pact was the linchpin in this accommodation process. Since the Congress party had a plurality of votes, it could nominate its own favoured Untouchable candidates for reserved seats and have the higher-caste majority elect them to power. Independent Untouchable organizations, such as those led by Ambedkar, with only a minority vote in each constituency were immediately marginalized by electoral politics. In states such as Bengal and the Punjab where the colonial divisions between Hindus and Muslims enabled the Untouchables to obtain power as an anti-Congress coalition partner with Muslims, partition effectively ended significant Untouchable political influence.[9] However, a 16 per cent Untouchable population was an auxiliary constituency the Congress could ignore only at its own electoral peril. Concessions to the aspirant Untouchable middle class effectively incorporated many of them. The concessions were a continuance of colonial preferential policies, aimed not at property redistribution, which threatened dominant rural interests, but at the creation of an Untouchable middle class through education, job and electoral reservation. The problem with affirmative action was that by definition it could only help a minuscule minority. Essentially an urban class, this group had limited contacts and influence to improve the lot of fellow Untouchable caste members. They had no influence whatsoever in implementing rural desegregation.

The difference between the colonial and post-colonial state was exemplified in the two dominant Untouchable leaders, Ambedkar during the colonial period and Jagjivan Ram under the Congress government. The resignation of Ambedkar from the central cabinet marked the end of any attempt at systemic change within the ruling Congress party. His marginalization thereafter ended any pretensions to political power the Untouchables might have had outside the ruling party. Even the influence of Ambedkar's conversion to Buddhism as a way of shedding untouchability did not extend much beyond his own caste, the Mahar. The rise to prominence of Jagjivan Ram, however, was not reflective of leadership in the traditional sense, since unlike Ambedkar he did not mobilize the Untouchables in any signifi-cant way.[10] The only national leader to have any claim to inde-pendence was Ambedkar, but he cannot be said to have politically survived the transition to independence despite his role in draft-ing the Indian constitution. Along with him the Untouchables' role in politics has remained marginal in independent India. In retrospect, Gandhi's fast to prevent the British concession of a separate electorate was critical in preventing Untouchable eman-cipation, though none of those involved could have predicted the longevity of its consequences.

The implementation of affirmative action has produced an Untouchable middle class which was non-existent at the turn of the century and minuscule at independence. The post-colonial expansion of education has not brought rural desegregation or curtailment of exploitation and human rights abuses. Though the share of Untouchables in the state sector has increased, in no state is the job quota for Untouchables in non-traditional occupa-tions anywhere near full. There has been considerable debate in India as to whether affirmative action, by creating a middle class, achieves benefits for the mass of Untouchables. While the bene-fits to the Untouchable community are indeed limited to a small minority, benefits to the community as a whole cannot be achieved without property redistribution, which is anathema to dominant rural interests. Even segregation of public places in rural India has remained unchanged by constitutional abolition of untouchability. It is difficult to see how anything beyond affirmative action will be tolerated by the dominant interests in contemporary India. In fact, the limitations of affirmative action are what make it acceptable to elites, who are hardly threatened by it. Only when reservation was extended to Backward Castes, a larger and more politically influential category of the middle castes, did the traditional elite object strenuously.

India and the World

Though the segregation of Untouchables in rural India has remained unchanged for hundreds of years, significant changes in rest of the world seem to make their continued segregation untenable. The problem is that there is no Indian constituency with sufficient influence to implement desegregation. Though the Indian state is highly interventionist in other spheres, there are practical limits to its influence. State institutions and communications reach remote villages, but changing the lifestyles in rural areas is a formidable task. This difficulty is exacerbated by the caste spectrum being more of a continuum than a sharply defined ranking. Each caste attempts to improve its status in competition with its rivals through acquiring wealth and other attributes of higher castes. This applies to Untouchables as well as to the higher castes, there being no inevitable unity between castes at any level in the hierarchy. Castes thus have opportunities over time and generations to improve their ritual status and become recognized as superior to their rivals. While every 'peasant has someone's boot on his neck, many have the concurrent satisfaction of stepping on someone else's face. Inequality, the bane of the hierarchical society, is also its chief delight'.[11]

This segregation, towards which the Indian government has been apathetic for over half a century, is unlikely to change in the foreseeable future. The question of foreign influence in human rights implementation thus comes to the fore. Foreign pressure for democratization has achieved some success in the Third World, but such instances in Latin America and Africa were comparatively straightforward. Once single-party rule and repression were stopped, groups quickly mobilized to create a competitive political environment. In India, the democratization process has been institutionalized. Untouchable social segregation, however, is not a state-sponsored activity, unlike apartheid, and therefore cannot be changed by administrative fiat. State coercion alone can change it in the short term. The alternative approach of changing cultural values through education could take generations, if it occurs at all. Traditional India has proved remarkably adaptable in accepting integration of public facilities in urban areas, yet repudiating it back in the villages, where Untouchables can be personally identified. Even among the westernized urban elite, segregation in marriage continues virtually unchanged.[12]

The major obstacle to integration remains with the dominant interest groups influencing the Indian states. Rural landed interests oppose desegregation and even westernized urban elites are not particularly concerned with the problem. The commitment to such social change has not increased despite the creation of a new urban middle class, which continues caste practices in private life. This class is also generally opposed to foreign pressure for human rights implementation.

With the extinction of the Soviet Union, India can no longer play off the superpowers against each other, and its own debt crisis has made it much more vulnerable to foreign pressure. The IMF and World Bank structural adjustment programmes have been accepted as necessary by the Indian government. However, many in the elite had already recognized the necessity of these reforms and foreign pressure came as an additional source of influence on politicians to implement long-sought changes. There was thus an important domestic constituency for structural adjustment that is not as evident in the human rights field.

The Indian government has been more resistant to 'foreign interference' in its human rights problems than to structural adjustments which provide opportunities for economic recovery and development. At the 1991 Commonwealth Prime Ministers' Conference in Harare, Canada proposed tying foreign aid to human rights, which India's then Prime Minister Narasimha Rao opposed. Though Indian officials will sometimes publicly acknowledge failure on the social front, in their official position they continue to insist on non-interference in internal Indian affairs. Although foreign pressure for democratization and human rights has had some successes, these have usually been with weak states dependent on foreign aid, while large relatively autarchic economies such as India and China have proved resistant to foreign influence on human rights. Since India receives less than 0.7 per cent of its GNP in foreign aid, this leverage is necessarily limited.[13]

From the perspective of northern donors, however, gross human rights abuses such as those in India may become increasingly difficult to tolerate alongside foreign aid programmes. The tying of aid to human rights also serves to justify curtailment of aid to the Third World or its diversion to the former Soviet bloc. The tying of aid is particularly problematic in India's case, given its democratic institutions and the social rather than state sponsorship of segregation.

Such changes in lifestyle unlike state policy require the reforming of cultural values. However, traditional Indian cultural values have continued despite significant industrialization.[14] The wife burnings for more dowry are indicative of the adaptation of traditional values to modern consumerism. Untouchable segregation can survive shared urban public transport. Hinduism has a ritual for purification from pollution resulting from such situations of inevitable proximity. Desegregation of public facilities is therefore not beyond the pale of implementation, though it remains elusive in the villages.

Such reforms frequently require a lobby to influence the state and society in the direction of change. However, no significant lobby exists either in India or abroad. Overseas middle-class Hindus are overwhelmingly from dominant castes, and the few that are not are too preoccupied with establishing themselves to be effective as a lobby group. Untouchables, as the lowest caste in Indian society, almost inevitably form the lowest class in modern India, and in this position are too poor to promote demands or finance movements. International refugee migration is a middle-class prerogative, as the destitute lack the mobility to easily escape their situation or even their villages. As the poorest class, they have therefore no one to promote their interests except the Indian state and foreign aid agencies, neither of which has this group as a 'top' priority. The fact of the matter is that international causes require an influential lobby to support them. This is usually provided by an indigenous or exiled middle-class ethnic group. The correlation of untouchability with lower-class occupations contributes to making the issue. despite the scale of the problem, a forgotten cause, notwithstanding the increased international interest in human rights. The disinclination to interfere in foreign cultures and the domestic policies of sovereign states has further hampered action on the issue. However, the Japanese suggestion of tying aid to control of Indian defence expenditures indicates that measures to increasingly limit national sovereignty may in due course extend to Indian human rights concerns.

Constitutional Remodelling

Among the 'secular' Indian elite and the academic community there is no attempt to justify segregation, and in this sense westernized concepts of equality have replaced pre-colonial values. However, these groups have no significant influence on rural culture. While the caste system is seen as morally indefensible, thereby indicating a westernized view of caste, solutions are sought in class terms for Marxist scholars, or in ritual integration with Hinduism for nationalists. Both groups tend to see the Indian national ideology as legitimate and ethnic particularism as a 'false consciousness' that must be raised to a higher level of national and/or class awareness.[15] This view has been challenged, as ethnicity and casteism have proved resistant to secularization. There is now a greater understanding of the need to recognize the legitimacy of popular culture.[16] The colonial roots of the politicization, however, continue to make contemporary ethnic struggles appear in the literature as colonial legacies, and therefore illegitimate in a post-colonial society. It is argued that had colonialism not intervened so directly in indigenous societies the post-colonial state would not have had to contend with ethnic politics to the same extent and greater national politicization might have been possible.

While the importance of the colonial state in mobilization of the Untouchable community is undeniable, any industrialization and urbanization would have accelerated the politicization of ethnicity.[17] The state did, however, facilitate this process by constitutional legitimization of the ethnic categories which already existed at the level of popular consciousness. Without this identification mass mobilization would not have succeeded. Ethnic elites utilized these shared values to develop a following, but did not create the culture.[18]

> The assumption that the colonial state could manipulate and invent Indian tradition at will creating a new form of caste and reconstituting the social ... is clearly inadequate and largely wrong.... Caste achieved its critical colonial position only because the British state was successful in separating caste as a social form from its dependence on precolonial political processes.[19]

There is an ambiguity here between the role of the state and the process of modernity. Caste was too intrinsic to India not to become politicized with modernity, irrespective of the state policy. However, state policy had sufficient influence to determine the measure of political power and the success the movement would have, and by extension the degree of emancipation the Untouchables could achieve. The scope for emancipation was in critical respects greater under the colonial than post-colonial state. This is a view not prevalent in the scholarly writings on the subject. There is a general acceptance of the legitimacy of the post-colonial Indian national aims and a near-universal rejection of its colonial predecessor.

The failure of the post-colonial Indian state to implement desegregation opens up the issue of alternative strategies that might be more conducive to emancipation. The relative autonomy of an autocratic colonial state from civil society no longer exists for the post-colonial state. Democracy as constitutionally circumscribed in a majority-take-all system, creates limitations on minority rights, which the state then has difficulty promoting. The democratic state by becoming beholden to indigenous elites, and most particularly rural landed elites, loses the feasibility of a desegregationist policy option. This is not to say that the colonial state ever attempted this option, but the scope for implementation has been reduced in certain respects under the post-colonial government. The influence on the state of groups opposing integration increased after independence, progressively circumscribing the possibility for radical desegregation.

Electoral politics, as prescribed by the Poona Pact, and later the Indian constitution, marginalized the Untouchables despite their significant absolute numbers. The post-colonial state like its colonial predecessor found the incorporation of Untouchables within its political agenda advantageous. Affirmative action was continued, enabling the recruitment of educated Untouchables in the state sector, where employment regulations restricted their political involvement. Untouchable politicians likewise depended on the patronage of higher-caste-dominated political parties for nomination in safe seats. The practice of job reservation once established proved attractive to other groups who were not particularly 'backward'. Dominant rural landed castes of middle rank in the traditional caste hierarchy then emulated the Untouchables in demanding reserved jobs because of alleged backwardness. The Congress party eventually acceded to this demand for 52 per cent of the Indian population and granted upper-caste poor candidates a 10 per cent job reservation.[20] Thus,

> We have the supremely paradoxical phenomenon of low-caste groups asserting their very backwardness in the caste hierarchy to claim discriminatory privileges from the state, and upper-caste groups proclaiming the sanctity of bourgeois equality and freedom (the criteria of equal opportunity mediated by skill and merit) in order to beat back the threat to their existing privileges.[21]

What began as a temporary measure for a uniquely segregated lower-caste group was eventually applied to most of the population. The state's generalization of affirmative action from a minority to a majority represents an official sanction to caste as a social category. Ironically, the contentiousness of the issue had led to the dropping of caste identification after the 1931 Census for non-Scheduled Castes and Tribes, but has now been established as the most critical social criterion.

State intervention occurs at a time of increasing debate on the efficacy of an intrusive state in social and economic affairs. With the prospect of cut-backs in the state sector being accompanied by expanded job reservation, the role of the post-colonial state in social engineering comes increasingly to the fore. As traditional upper-caste elites are forced to move to the potentially more lucrative private sector, the state becomes a repository for affirmative action and the social integration of potentially dissident groups who could destabilize the system. This does not directly affect the Untouchables, who remain segregated, nor does it improve the state's ability to implement their emancipation.

The colonial state fostered the politicization of Untouchables and the post-colonial government now manages their integration in the system so that it is not fundamentally antagonistic to dominant interests. This it does by promoting the state as an agency of protection and improvement for subordinate groups, who are thereby expected to subscribe to its legitimacy.[22] The efficacy of a state-oriented strategy of political mobilization has been challenged by grassroots NGO activists; however, their strategy has not yet been proved as decisively better for the emancipation of Untouchables.[23] The problem remains essentially in the social and cultural realm, and efforts by the colonial and post-colonial state at their emancipation have failed.

The difficulty was that to achieve Untouchable integration and empowerment constitutional protection and affirmative action needed to be accompanied by a separate electorate or proportional representation. While the concessions of the Poona Pact and the Indian constitution facilitated the politicization of an Untouchable caste identity, they were not empowering enough to enforce integration or achieve any appreciable change in the lives of most Untouchables. In present day India, a reintroduction of the colonial proposal of a separate electorate or proportional representation is too threatening to dominant interest groups to be easily placed on the political agenda.

Attention to the problem may seem unwarranted since India has taken major strides in improving the condition of Untouchables. Even when job quotas are not filled the trend has been towards increased implementation. Government policies which virtually preclude mass famine deaths ensure survival of subaltern groups in a way that never existed before.[24]

In international terms, however, India is being left behind as other nations more fully implement human rights laws. It is at a disadvantage in this respect as 'India's traditional caste system was the most closed society known' in the world.[25]

India is therefore left with the problem of how some of the most pernicious effects of untouchability can be at least ameliorated, if not entirely eradicated. The most obvious route would be to empower the Untouchables through land redistribution, which would enhance their independence. However, land reform has been considered a dead issue, given the rural vested interests involved in all the major parties in India, so any major resource redistribution is unlikely in the foreseeable future. The other route to empowerment has been through seat reservations. Without this provision very few Untouchables would be elected, given their geographic dispersion as a minority throughout the country. Whatever constitutional safeguards have been maintained have in part been due to the efforts of Scheduled Caste legislators holding reserved seats. Their contribution has, however, been weakened by dependence on higher-caste-dominated party nominations for successful election.

If one compares the Scheduled Caste movement of the colonial period with that of independent India, then the movement can be said to have suffered a relative eclipse till recently. At the leadership level there has been no national leader approaching Ambedkar's stature. The movement as a whole has been subject to the same corruption and factionalism endemic in Indian politics. Given the regional variations and status rivalries between Untouchable castes, no national leadership has ever been able to deliver the Scheduled Caste vote in a convincing manner. 'Jagjivan Ram's long unassailable position in Union politics depended upon his being seen as representing the Scheduled Castes. But he can hardly be said to have mobilized them.'[26]

Effective political mobilization for an economically and politically marginal minority group is problematic. Without an independent Scheduled Caste party with sufficient seats to hold the balance of power, their bargaining strength will be limited, and the influence, if any, is likely to be ephemeral. The electoral system itself would have to be redesigned in such a way as to give them political power proportional to their population. Constitutional remodelling could be either through the resurrection of the colonial proposal of a separate electorate for Untouchables or in proportional representation, as occurs in a number of countries. Though both models would undoubtedly enhance the power of the Scheduled Castes, they would have to overcome some inherent disadvantages and widespread public opposition.

A separate electorate is inherently divisive for the Hindu community and is likely to be resisted for the same reason Gandhi went on a 'fast unto death' to prevent its implementation. Proportional party representation without a Scheduled Caste seat reservation will allow seat allotment according to a party's percentage of the popular vote and enable Scheduled Caste parties to get representation in proportion to their vote totals. Similar advantages could accrue to all parties, but especially benefit smaller parties by increasing their influence through power-sharing coalition governments.[27] These coalitions, however, could tend to be unstable. Regional and linguistic balance could prove difficult to implement at the national level. Its greatest advantage would lie in increasing the power of Scheduled Castes without any special legislative favour being shown to them. A source of divisive caste resentment would therefore be removed. The ruling parties which regularly get elected to power with only a plurality of votes will strenuously oppose this reform. Proportional representation, like a separate electorate, despite significant merits for Untouchables, is therefore a non-starter in the foreseeable future.[28]

These obstacles to electoral change mean that solutions will have to be found within the present electoral arrangements. In a state which is both co-optive and repressive, the opportunities for major change are few. They revolve around lobbying the state for fulfilment of job quotas and better implementation of development programmes to reach Scheduled Caste beneficiaries. Publicizing atrocities against Untouchables in India and abroad can also bring better enforcement of human rights legislation. None of these amount to any sea change, but minimal Scheduled Caste resources and their own internal divisions mean that their power is limited. In any system there is arguably a tendency for those who have to get more, while those with nothing get palliatives. This system is unlikely to change in India, and the most the Scheduled Castes can expect to obtain is more effective delivery of welfare measures.

Though officially abolished by administrative fiat, untouchability persists not because of state policy, but due to a reluctance of the state to intervene in civil society. Given the cultural imperatives of village India, and the private prejudices of urban dwellers, little state action in this regard is likely. Though India is often regarded as over-governed, this does not effectively extend to intervention in Hindu religious values, of which caste is an integral part. This presents problems for India's international reputation, given the ending of segregation in the rest of the world. India can no longer defend its inaction against untouchability on the grounds that other countries have no right to interfere in its internal affairs. This policy no longer has validity in western public opinion and was never implemented in practice. Amnesty International's 1992 book detailing torture in India which made connections to the plight of Untouchables received coverage in a wide variety of quality newspapers.[29] Weiner, in making explicit the Indian neglect of the lower class/caste issues compared with other nations at equivalent stages of development, puts an academic spotlight on human rights problems.[30] These issues which traditionally have not been highlighted in foreign perceptions of India are increasingly receiving coverage. 'Tough policies of repression have given India an unwelcome, and growing, reputation for abuse of human rights.'[31] With the erosion of India's international reputation, and the linkage of foreign aid and trade preferences to human rights implementation, India is facing increasing difficulty in making a convincing case that it is fully democratic.

Thus, though a domestic constituency for the effective eradication of untouchability may be lacking, international opinion could increasingly become a significant lobby pressuring India to implement a series of human rights measures, including ending police torture, custody deaths, child labour and untouchability. However, India lacks the domestic constituency to enforce integration, and foreign pressure is unlikely to reach the point where the government will be compelled to act. Cultural values, however, are extremely flexible, and can be adjusted within limits to suit practical imperatives. Though increased urban caste integration could lead to the abolition of caste identities, this is far from certain.

The major challenge to caste relations in recent years has come not from the Scheduled Castes, but from the Backward Class movement. The proposed implementation of the Mandal Commission Report recommending extension of job reservation to Backward Classes provoked unprecedented violence from the upper castes. Unlike the Scheduled Castes, which, despite claims to the contrary, are too marginal to be a serious threat to the system of privileged access for the middle class, the Backward Classes have the population and resources to change the composition of the urban middle classes. In an economy which is becoming more oriented to the private sector, the existing upper-caste elites should be able to use their caste networks to move into the more lucrative private sector. The state sector will thus serve increasingly as an employment avenue for an urbanizing rural elite. The government will thus maintain inter-caste harmony by distributing employment benefits beyond the upper-caste minority.

The democratization of employment opportunities will be of little value to the Scheduled Castes, who are often victims of the Backward Class landowners. A case can be made that a westernized urban upper-caste elite is more likely to be sympathetic to rural desegregation and land reforms than the Backward Classes, who are often more directly involved in Scheduled Caste exploitation. Attempts to unite the Backward Classes and the Scheduled Castes are only likely to be effective in the long term if a class consciousness grows in the movement. However, as the class composition of the Backward Class movement is more heterogeneous than that of the Scheduled Castes, its multi-class character makes progressive policies more difficult to implement than would be the case with the Scheduled Caste movement. Alliances between Backward Classes, Scheduled Castes and Scheduled Tribes, while they serve to reduce the influence of traditional upper-caste elites, may not in the long term benefit the Scheduled Castes and Scheduled Tribes, who will likely continue to receive the least benefits from redistribution of job opportunities.[32] In political practice, Forward Caste–Scheduled Caste alignments against the Backward Classes have emerged, indicating the degree of realpolitik that enters the bargaining for power.[33] Rural Scheduled Caste alliances with urbanized groups may be more realistic than those with the rural elite from Backward Classes. In general though, it does not appear that the Scheduled Castes have any natural allies. Caste prejudice is so pervasive in the subcontinent that even followers of minority religions have come to develop caste-like divisions among themselves. Whatever coalitions develop with Scheduled Caste groupings may prove as fluid and subject to defection as other alliances. In this respect the Communist movement may have lost an opportunity for forming a more permanent alliance by not desegregating the states they governed. That this was never seriously attempted even on an educational level is itself indicative of the depth of caste feeling in India, and the difficulty even of leftist movements in resisting its influence.

The only pressure likely to be consistent in its advocacy of human rights implementation would therefore come from western public opinion. Unlike the Sikh movement, however, there is no diaspora ready to fund and organize the movement. Western public opinion is fluid in its causes and attachments. The resonance that the American civil rights and anti-apartheid struggle elicited in the West is unlikely to be forthcoming in the cause of Untouchables. India's role in the world is marginal, while at the same time its size and autonomy make it relatively immune to foreign pressure. In this sense the lamentable ignorance in the West about India is fortunate for India's establishment, as a well-informed foreign public would only lead to greater pressure on it for human rights implementation.

The roots of caste in civil society make state intervention for its abolition problematic. It will therefore remain embedded in Indian culture as an international embarrassment which refuses to go away. The Scheduled Caste movement is trapped in a minority position from which it can only be effective through coalitions with vacillating allies. These may range from right to left, from backward to high castes, or even with communalists of various religious persuasions. The Scheduled Caste movement has always been fragmented and unable to deliver its own community votes. With these divisions its bargaining power in such coalitions will be significantly reduced and open to numerous contenders for allegiance. Further the movement has also been divided between insiders and outsiders. In the colonial period, Ambedkar represented the outsider strategy of maintaining a separate Untouchable organization. Except for a brief change to an insider strategy as a minister, he maintained this approach all his life. However, with Ambedkar out of the cabinet, another Untouchable had to be included, and if one had not existed then Congress would have had to invent one. Jagjivan Ram represented the insider approach to Untouchable politics that utilized a presence in the ruling party to effect change within the state apparatus for Untouchable advancement. This approach was continued by Ram Vilas Paswan in subsequent non-Congress governments, though it remains to be seen if this strategy will prove any more successful.[34] Ambedkar's old Republican Party has continued the outsider strategy with very little electoral success given the nature of the constituency system in India. The most successful electoral force, the Bahujan Samaj Party (BSP), led by Kanshi Ram, has utilized a Dalit-based vote bank to ally with various other parties to ensure its own seat allotments. While this enables a sizeable number of BSP candidates to be elected, only coalitions with more powerful parties representing privileged interests makes this possible, and the compromises that this requires of the Dalits severely limits the reforms they can undertake in office. There is then the danger of disillusionment as these coalitions provide little to the lower classes, but give Dalit office-holders the same opportunities for corruption and despotism as their predecessors in office. These limitations on what Dalit leaders can do in office means that the electoral system cannot be considered the only forum for Dalit empowerment.

Religious conversion movements which have swept various castes have arguably only exacerbated the Untouchable divisions.[35] With no unified theology or politics, fragmentation rather than projection of demands has utilized much of the movement's energies. The Scheduled Caste elite have not always been effective in promoting the interests of lower-class members, preferring implementation of more elite-oriented affirmative action programmes. Much of the organization has focused on a few dominant Scheduled Castes rather than on intercaste cooperation. Any ethnic identity is by its nature exclusive; for a minority group without a geographical centre, this tendency is particularly debilitating because power is impossible without outside alliances. Caste identity makes cooperation more difficult on account of the high level of intercaste suspicion and animosity. Despite the vital need of the Scheduled Castes to form alliances with more secular groups and individuals, these relations have often been acrimonious. The history of exploitation and the individual problems of Untouchables in obtaining upward mobility leave a legacy of resentment which makes such cooperation psychologically difficult. This has often been observed among the Scheduled Caste leadership, though the reasons for these problems are not always appreciated by people of more privileged backgrounds.

The Scheduled Caste movement has had its ups and downs and, in certain respects, such as in national leadership, has declined since the death of Ambedkar. However, the movement never disappeared, and the problem of untouchability has remained on the national agenda. It remains to be seen if the problems within the Scheduled Caste community can be resolved. Without this, the movement will lack the dynamism to make its presence felt, and continue to be manipulated by dominant interest groups.

Dalit Government Policy

This pattern of dominant elite manipulation is beginning to change through growing popular consciousness and the imperatives of the electoral system. Dominant politicians are attempting to adapt themselves to popular sentiments, while new forces are coming forward to mobilize in different directions. As long as democracy is maintained traditional elites will not be able to exercise the same degree of control and face the prospect of being removed from state power. However, if democratic institutions are not maintained, there is a danger that Dalit governments will succumb to the vices of their predecessors. The imperatives of a Dalit government will mean that the old traditional elite must disappear from the state, but what direction the new order will take and how much of the old order's privileges and assets they will seize is undetermined. If democracy is to survive, some old-style accommodations will have to be made, and both sides will have to concede economic and political territory to each other. While the Forward Castes will not have the votes to maintain state control, their control over the private sector means that their displacement from the public sector will have to be gradual enough not to ruin the economy or provoke too violent a confrontation.

Attempting to analyze the policy of a non-existent government may seem like a pointless exercise.[36] Nevertheless, after a Dalit government headed by an Untouchable woman took power in Uttar Pradesh, India's politically most important state, it became probable that there would be other Dalit-controlled or Dalit-influenced governments. Without some understanding of their likely actions and compromises, a prediction of Indian politics will be incomplete. A Dalit government could lose credibility in a wave of corruption and undirected repression as have so many governments before it, but it will restructure the opportunities and dynamics of Indian democracy.

To prevent a Dalit government taking power in Uttar Pradesh the existing government disconnected the water and electricity to the home of the Untouchable woman Mayawati, who was trying to form a government. Her house was surrounded by a mob shouting obscenities at her. In a turn of events that literally defy belief, the Hindu fundamentalist BJP said that it would support her from the opposition benches. As a result, the first Dalit government took office. The new chief minister then brought charges against her predecessor for her unlawful confinement, and opened the books to show that her predecessor had been using government money to pay off his political friends and journalists (which raises the question as to why other chief ministers do not do the same on taking office). That an Untouchable government should be supported by Hindu extremists seemed an anathema to many in the Dalit movement. Muslims were arguably the most important potential allies of the Untouchables, which many of them originally were, and allowing the Hindu fundamentalists to support a Dalit government threatened the coalition the Untouchables were attempting to build. However, just the fact that for the first time in India, and in Uttar Pradesh of all places, an Untouchable was allowed to take office is a comment on how far Indian democracy has come. In fact, the Dalit government stuck to its own agenda and thereby alienated the BJP, thus bringing about its downfall. Though the party leader L.K. Advani was said to have wanted to continue support to the Dalit government, Murli Manohar Joshi and A.B. Vajpayee and the party state workers favoured its downfall. Having enabled a Dalit government to take power, they could not bring about its defeat without losing credibility with Dalit voters. They would have been better off not having supported it in the first place than withdrawing support after having put it in power, but in dealing with an Untouchable woman schoolteacher they may have overestimated the influence they could exert on the chief minister they had installed. The 1996 general and state elections repeated the earlier minority impasse while indicating the continuing support for both the Dalit and fundamentalist parties. The BJP was in a weaker position than the secular parties for, having forfeited the 12 per cent Muslim vote with an anti-Muslim campaign, it had only the Hindus to rely on, of which a considerable number were Untouchable (16 per cent of the total population). Hence, taking central power without some Untouchable support appeared difficult. But the political necessity of obtaining Untouchable support meant going against the social prejudices of its strongest supporters.

Political expediency and the desire for power has won over religious prejudices, but the downfall of the Dalit government shows that the BJP remains a base for those most opposed to the socio-economic emancipation of Untouchables. The Untouchable leadership is now placed in an awkward position. Politically, the BJP has the most to gain by eliciting Untouchable support. While the Untouchables have been able to use this to take state power, it undermines the possibility of forming a secular coalition of minority groups against the establishment parties. Ultimately, the Untouchables cannot allow their office to be used as an opportunity for Hindu fundamentalists to conduct a pogrom against Muslims. The Dalit government will have to be prepared to resign on this principle. This in itself has given it considerable manoeuvrability with the BJP, because if pushed too far by it, the Dalit government will return to the secular parties for support. Though based on the experience in Uttar Pradesh, these dynamics are likely to be in operation in future Dalit governments, as they generally form the building blocs of Indian politics.

Untouchables are in a unique position in India in being potential converts to all of the major religions. For some, such as the BJP, keeping them in the Hindu fold is particularly important, but as marginal people they have formed a basis for many Sikh, Christian, Buddhist and Muslim communities. Ambedkar felt that their position in Hinduism was untenable, and religious leaders of various communities approached him about converting the Untouchables to their religion. Ultimately, Ambedkar chose Buddhism because it was closer to his intellectual disposition and indigenous to India. Though the conversion of his followers was the largest in history, it failed to reach most of the community as he died shortly thereafter, and the Buddhist conversions did not ultimately extend much beyond his own caste. Though the Buddhist community is a rich one, it provided very little in the way of development aid and as a result, the benefits of conversion have not been realized. Maximum advantage can now be gained by Untouchables playing the various groups off against each other as potential religious and political converts, but without irrevocably converting en masse to any one camp. Restrictions on missionary activity need to be lifted to maximize development aid and encourage others to enter the competition.

Communalism is something the opposition, and in particular the BJP, is likely to throw up as a problem for a Dalit government. It is important however that the Dalits begin office with their own agenda paramount. For this there must be at least one or two items that the government must be prepared to stand or fall on. There cannot be much doubt that one of the priorities must be land reform, which for the vast majority is the only reform likely to touch their lives in a material way. Even desegregation is of secondary importance to this because with land comes relative economic independence and with that rural power. It is no coincidence that land is also the craving of the agricultural classes. Some of the best examples of land reform were undertaken by the Americans who introduced it to Japan, and indirectly to Korea and Taiwan. They offered it to the Italian Communists after the War, who rejected it for fear that it would create a yeoman class opposed to communism. The Communists have a very chequered record when it comes to land reform, and more often than not avoided it in South Asia. It has been argued that it can be an important basis for successful capitalist development. While this may be overstretching the case, it is certainly not antithetical to capitalism, and can be a bulwark against communism, at least if undertaken by non-Communists. This explains why the Americans pressed for it in Latin America, albeit unsuccessfully. That they did not have the force of an occupying power there as they had in Japan limited their influence, but the fact that it has rarely been implemented by non-Communists since the American occupation in East Asia does not make it an exclusive Communist agenda.

In India, state-level legislation will still need Presidential assent which if not immediately forthcoming should be side-stepped with grassroots land seizures, while the state government keeps the police from interfering on the landlords' behalf. This was done very effectively under Hari Krishna Konar in the Communist-dominated West Bengal United Front of the 1960s before the Communists had become too tied to landed interests to undertake serious reform. The correlation of forces has changed so much in recent years that it is doubtful the centre would want to intervene with military force, which would have to be done to stop such a movement by a popularly elected government. The fact is that every government now feels the need to court the Untouchable vote, which is the only thing of value the Untouchables have. As the vote can no longer be taken for granted, it becomes a valuable commodity, and no central government would want to unnecessarily alienate the Untouchables. Unlike provincial ethnic groups who may periodically rise up in revolt but can be militarily suppressed just as often, the Untouchables exist in every village of India. They may not take part in any movement or politics but how they really think and vote can change governments. Short of rigging elections there is no way the state can control them on election day, and in this sense they can never be suppressed even when there is no movement visible or opinion expressed. They are not likely to be in open revolt, but to alienate this electorate is to shave off up to 16 per cent of the votes, which is generally more than the votes needed to change the government at both the national and state levels. Now that it is a floating vote, and one that better communications have made more informed about national developments, politicians have to scramble ever more assiduously after it.

To facilitate better communications and consciousness among the Dalit community mass literacy is important. Though to some extent the spread of electronic communications decreases the relevance of mass literacy, it is nevertheless one of the limited number of things a Dalit government might be expected to successfully undertake. This should not be confused with the formal education system; rather, it is an adult literacy programme which has been talked about for years but never been effectively implemented. In a period of current and accumulated deficits, the funding for such a programme presents a problem; but this problem stems from within the education ministry itself. The solution to it first came to me when a high-caste political science professor at Jawaharlal Nehru University, New Delhi, complained that when he asked an Untouchable librarian for a book the man could not get it because he could not read. This was meant as a criticism of the affirmative action hiring and promotion programme, but it also reflects on the distorted nature of the Indian education system which neglects mass literacy in preference to funding university education. According to Bhupendra Kumar Joshi, Director of Lucknow's Giri Institute of Development Studies: 'Higher education has virtually collapsed in Uttar Pradesh.... There are no standards, and the state universities do not even have a regular academic session.'[37] The solution to this lies in cutting off government funding for university departments that do not perform effectively. Academics have rarely been on the side of the Dalit movement, which is hardly surprising given their caste composition, and there are insufficient Untouchable candidates to replace them, even if this were legally feasible. This could raise the objection that the government should use its influence to convert them to a new way of thinking, but this would leave the government open to charges of interference in academic affairs and censorship. It would frankly not be worth the trouble.

That it would be a futile exercise to try to change their minds was indicated by the outpouring of rage against the Mandal Commission affirmative action proposals the V.P. Singh government wished to implement. Ashis Nandy, a political philosopher, though a critic of the Mandal Commission Report proposals, wrote: 'I doubt if the Indian state can bring about the kind of social changes the report presumes ... [but] the anti-Mandal stir has revealed an aspect of the Indian elite—including many of my friends and colleagues—which I wish I had not seen.'[38] According to the *New York Times* South Asia correspondent Barbara Crossette,

> The media are dominated by upper-caste Hindus who know how small a minority they are—scarcely 10 per cent of the population. Their instinctive response was not unlike that of white South Africans who find the idea of majority rule too terrible to contemplate. The liberalism of the intellectual elite was severely tested and often found wanting.[39]

The comparison with South Africa is unfair because it puts the South African whites in the same category as the high-caste Indian elite, when in fact the Indian elite are more resistant to subaltern emancipation. It is no coincidence that apartheid has disappeared in South Africa but is rampant in India. There are profound cultural reasons why apartheid survived longer in India than South Africa. The white South African community was undermined by an assault on their western cultural values brought on by sanctions and criticism in the western world of which they were a part. This undermining of their confidence in their right to rule was particularly prominent in the English community, but came to influence the Afrikaner elite as well. By being part of the western world there were cultural ties and an identity which facilitated an opening up of the system.

The loss of faith by white South Africans in their divine right to rule has yet to have an analogous self-doubt in the Indian elite. The traditional Indian elite comes from a different cultural background than the enlightenment, and though it has adopted the technological trappings of modernity, its thinking when pushed to the wall is for lack of a better word for Brahminical. Though modern defenders of Hinduism have attempted to put a progressive interpretation to the philosophy by equating the traditional Hindu concept of duty with human rights, the concepts are very different.[40] Even the more liberal attitude towards women as compared to Untouchables in the *Laws of Manu* is hardly a basis for rights. 'In childhood a female must be subject to her father, in youth to her husband, when her lord is dead to her sons; a woman must never be independent.'[41]

Given the cultural inheritance of the dominant groups, western reason alone will thus be of little value unless backed by force, which, unlike human rights, is universally understood. The increasing democratization of Indian society is putting the traditionally dominant class on the defensive, which gradually has to accommodate itself to things it had not previously tolerated. There is therefore hope that it will continue its gradual retreat to the more dynamic private sector and allow the lower castes to take control of the state. The complaints about the deterioration in services and even criminalization of society reflect in part the failure of the state to function in their interests and protect them. This view is reflected in the academic literature as well which laments the deterioration in societal values and state governance, but fails to mention that the state never functioned for the lower classes and in fact enforced centuries of oppression on them. The democratization process in unleashing new social forces is bound to bring with it the prospect of a deterioration in the quality of life for old elites as well as offer opportunities for the creation of new ones. The insecurities suffered by the lower classes are now beginning to be felt by the middle and upper classes, which makes it a particularly acute issue in the media and academia. It is no coincidence that the democratization of South Africa had as a parallel process the development of the highest criminal homicide rate in the world. The deterioration in American law and order has likewise accompanied its period of greatest democratization. Much the same process could accompany South Asian democratization. Criminal victimization, bureaucratic indifference and exploitation by the state that the lower classes have long been subjected to could now spread to the middle and upper classes. Democratization will result in new political groups and cultures entering the ruling class. The 'crisis of the nation-state in India', when seen from a subaltern perspective, is also an opportunity for empowerment.[42] Such is the persistence of elite views that even foreign Marxists have described the situation in India as 'deteriorating' at the very time when from a subaltern perspective it is democratizing. That they do not recognize the process that is under way is indicative of the perspectives they bring to the study of India. Because it is not following the prescribed Marxist game plan does not mean it is not happening. One Marxist scholar once told me that the Marxists had made a mistake by not incorporating caste into their analysis and mobilizing caste movements accordingly. Now they find themselves marginalized from some of the most important movements sweeping India. Though the Marxists have now abandoned referring to lower-class culture as 'false consciousness', the attitude remains, and even subaltern studies are too rarefied to be able to convey lower-class views rather than intellectual views of what the lower classes might be.[43] Not having much feel for the lives of ordinary people and the way the state and its local minions treat them, many analysts have little idea that what they see as deterioration is taking place within a wider context of democratization.[44] Much of the democratization process will not be to their liking, but it is taking place with a dynamic that is moving out of their control.

Though much of the scholarship on the 'crisis of governance' reflects a genuine fear of religious fundamentalism and in that respect shares a Dalit concern as well, a good part of it suggests fear about loss of power and privilege by those of the old elite from whom the intellectual class comes. There is little in this literature which could be of any conceivable use to a Dalit movement, and reflects the musings of a class under threat of democratization. Whatever the merits of the Mandal Commission, there is no doubt that it brought out the real feelings of upper-caste Indians when they were under threat. Given their power it is perhaps fortunate that economic liberalization has opened up much more profitable outlets for their undoubted talents which will facilitate a relatively non-violent accession to state power by previously subordinate groups.

Nevertheless, the democratization process is unlikely to become institutionalized without economic stability and growth. For this to be achieved the existing elites must continue to be able to find a more profitable outlet in the private sector. It is important that the private sector remain open to them and the state not curb its initiative and investment with unnecessary restrictions. These elites, while they still have power and influence, need to find an outlet for their energies and not be reduced to unemployment through too much state intervention in the private sector hiring process. The Mandal riots against job reservations brought the prejudice and the threat this class poses out in the open temporarily, but it is the background against which any Dalit government will have to deal. Because they do not think like South African whites, one cannot expect the same acceptance of majority rule and a quiet transfer of power. The intellectual elite have not psychologically resigned themselves to their loss of power and continue to retain a divine sense of their own ruling place in society. However, like the South African whites, they will find that while their property and education give them a privileged place in society, the state, which is their ultimate guarantee of security, will no longer be theirs.

At the same time, the Dalit community is so full of rage that at the first opportunity the Dalits are liable to seek revenge for centuries of wrongs. This view might surprise many in the academic community, but as a group twice removed from this reality, first from being in the university ivory tower, and then as products (personally and/or intellectually) of this elite, they are generally unaware of grassroots feelings. In trying to bring this sense of rage to them, the case of the 'bandit queen' Phoolan Devi will have to suffice. Her killing of innocent higher-caste villagers lived out in real life the fantasy of many in the lower castes subjected to the daily humiliation of village apartheid. Of course, there are no polls to prove it, and even if they were undertaken this would not be admitted, but the subsequent dropping of the murder charges against her by the Uttar Pradesh government and her election as Member of Parliament reflects the substantial support her action received.

This has significant implications for Indian democracy, and some of the more substantive literature has recognized this dilemma. However, writers from the intellectual elite tend to see the 'crisis of governability' from the perspective of the state and those who already control it. Popular resistance then becomes something for the state to manage. The state is not something to be seized and used for popular purposes. T.V. Sathyamurthy in a review of Atul Kohli's book *Democracy and Discontent: India's Growing Crisis of Governability* sums up the history of this approach in political science.

North American students of the 'third world', following the lead given by the editors and contributors of the series on political development (published during the 1960s by Princeton University Press) and Samuel P. Huntington, the leading advocate of 'political order', have tended to devote greater attention to aspects of governance (i.e. control) and rule than aspects of the democratic rights of the mass of the people (i.e. civil society) and the accountability of the rulers to the ruled.[45]

Sathyamurthy goes on to argue that Kohli following this tradition 'starts from the premise that good governance is at the heart of the problem (or "crisis") currently faced by Indian society'.[46]

Ultimately, this approach becomes the political science of those who seek to maintain control through state improvements, but gives no advice on how state power can be utilized by subaltern groups in their own interest. For this reason the field of Indian studies has little to offer a Dalit government. However, as the Dalit leader Kanshi Ram stated, 'Those who worship dogs, cats, even stones will lose no time in worshipping social reformers like Periyar, once the Dalits come to power'.[47] Put in another context, where there is funding, academics will surely follow. In the West the dominant ideology has been under attack for some time and can now be considered to be partly on the defensive. The traditional fields have not been able to make significant breakthroughs in analyses or paradigms, and the discipline of political science to the chagrin of the traditionalists is moving into new areas of endeavour. The impact of university programmes in ethnic and feminist studies, and affirmative action recruitment is changing the composition and orientation of the discipline in ways that have yet to effectively penetrate South Asian political science, where patriotism still precludes certain perspectives. Sanctions against apartheid may have been supported, but against their own country for similar practices it is a non-issue. When, as often happens, foreign scholars are introduced to South Asia through a positive and even idealized perspective, the legacy can be equally a distortion of reality. The history of Afro-American studies has parallels in this regard. The black intellectual W.E.B. DuBois was never able to get an academic position despite a Harvard Ph.D., but this is not likely to happen today.[48] Just as the American establishment once projected its ideas as those of the nation, today elite South Asianists are attempting the same type of projection on their own country and on how it is perceived abroad. This is being done with the use of public funds, which a Dalit government should cut off. It is now clear that a Dalit government will take power before the academic community comes round to an appreciation of its views. This is perfectly understandable given its own background and interests, but it reflects a different experience from that of the West where intellectual reorientations often preceded changes in popular perceptions and electoral politics. The South Asian academic diaspora has perpetuated its own vision of South Asia abroad to the detriment of scholarship and the subaltern groups in the subcontinent. Thus, though the social science and humanities disciplines have changed in the West, in South Asia and its diaspora, traditional intellectual elites have been able to project their own perceptions much more effectively in the academic community. Only a fundamental change in the membership of this fraternity will change its orientation. Given its depth of self-interest and communal feeling, this will be a long drawn-out struggle. Though the whole discipline cannot be judged by how it appears in India, it is the Indian faculty with which a Dalit government must deal.

The transfer of employment generation to the private sector has been seen by Deepak Lal as undermining the Brahminical attitude towards business. 'The relatively shrinking rewards from public service as compared with those in the private sector are persuading many of their children to seek commercial careers. This should help to undermine the long-standing Brahminical attitudes against Banias.'[49] From a Dalit perspective, whether the Brahmins dominate or the Banias, the private sector is of relevance only in so far as it lowers Forward Caste opposition to the Dalit takeover of the state sector. To the extent that this happens, it could ease the democratizing transition from Forward Caste to Dalit state control. Lal notes that 'the very different reaction that

Prime Minister V.P. Singh's desire to implement the Mandal Commission Report on caste reservations in government jobs evoked from the universities compared with the virtual silence that greeted the Rao government's actual implementation of the report on instructions from the Supreme Court', indicates that the Forward Castes have implicitly abandoned the state as at least an employment goal.[50] Given the degree of control the state has over the private sector, which makes it such a valuable tool for Dalit empowerment and development, the actual political takeover will be seen as more of a threat to the business community than any change in state employment prospects. However, the inability of the Dalits to make a significant entry into the business community for some time to come, and their need for economic expansion should allay business concerns.

This dual state–private sector system goes to the heart of the problem facing a Dalit government. Short of some sort of Gandhian autarchy, which with market integration is no longer feasible, urban and even village economy is dependent on the industrial sector. With the virtual bankruptcy of much of the public sector enterprises, the private sector will have to be the driving force behind economic development, and this can only be maintained with private sector investment. To attract this will be, to say the least, difficult for a Dalit government. Financial constraints make it imperative to lay off large numbers of civil servants and public sector employees to get into a position where taxes will be low enough to make private investment attractive in competition with other states. However, because of the prejudices of the business classes, substantive new investment is probably unrealistic, and only a maintenance of prevailing investment levels may have to be sufficient. To avoid a flight of capital, violence against the urban upper castes will have to be prevented, and the institutions that maintain the prosperity of this class maintained however incongruous it may seem for a Dalit government. If the business class cannot maintain their lifestyle they will not invest. Reassuring the business sector will have to be an early priority, regardless of the political views the Dalits might hold. In return the Dalits will have to insist on the tacit acquiescence of big business in the reform of the countryside through land redistribution and desegregation. As their class interests are not threatened by this, this should be feasible.

The fulfilment of lower-caste aspirations need not necessarily be antithetical to free-market liberalisation, however. Many Indians believe that a non-discriminatory social order would provide a better climate for business in the long run, while a discriminatory one would always contain within it the seeds of strife and upheaval.[51]

It has been argued that the American land reforms in Japan, the KMT land reform in Taiwan and the South Korean land distribution were factors facilitating the industrialization of these countries, and it is to the benefit of big business that this be done. It is the landlords' vote bloc and their control of the villages that have prevented this, but land reforms should raise no objection from big business.

It would be unrealistic to think that land reform and desegregation can be undertaken without some violent confrontations, but without the state behind them the local elite are likely to bide their time for the most part. It would also be unrealistic not to consider the possibility of a bloodbath ensuing. This will have to be controlled since it may force the central government to intervene and dismiss the state government. For some time to come the Dalit movement will have to be content with limited land redistribution and desegregation, and may have to defer justice (revenge) to a more opportune time.

Of course, how much land reform and desegregation is possible is a critical question in itself. The composition of the local state bureaucracy makes this a serious obstacle, but dismissal and popular pressure should curb their autonomy. The central government will be more critical, and just how much room a state government will have will be determined by the centre. It is quite likely, however, that a Dalit state government will have powerful allies at the centre, and the general expectation is that future central governments will often be coalitions and minority governments. Dalit participation in the central government is likely to be more than the token presence it has been so far. It is not inconceivable that Dalit MPs in various parties, if they can achieve a certain unity, will have the balance of power at the centre and veto any attempt at President's rule over a Dalit-administered state.

In this respect a future Dalit government is less likely to have problems with the centre than within its own coalition. Whether governing on its own or as a coalition it will be dependent on non-Untouchable parties whose interests may be opposed to those of the Dalits. The most obvious candidates for this luke-warm coalition partnership are the Other Backward Classes. Though portrayed in the Mandal Commission Report as severely disadvantaged, everyone knows that in the rural areas it is often the landed elite who are among the worst exploiters of Untouch-ables.[52] The Forward Castes by contrast have often gone on to become urban middle class, and are hence less tied to the landed interests than these dubious Backward Caste allies. Andre Beteille argues against the granting of affirmative action programmes to the Backward Castes for this reason though he supports the Scheduled Caste and Scheduled Tribe reservation.[53] He has been vilified in some of the Dalit press, as this position hinders the attempt to create a coalition with the Backward Castes, but it was the position of Ambedkar as well, and for much the same rea-sons.[54] However, without supporting affirmative action for the Backward Castes, it is doubtful that an Untouchable government could maintain a coalition in power for long. The Untouchables will probably have to insist on land reform but in return give a free hand to the Backward Classes to fill their job quotas. Whe-ther the Backward Classes, given their landed bases, would even accept such a trade-off is problematic, but the Untouchables if they are to maintain support and credibility within their own con-stituency must insist upon it at an opportune time during their rule.

It is possible to have a largely unfilled 16 per cent and 8 per cent Scheduled Caste and Scheduled Tribe quota, but by adding a Backward Class quota which can be filled, either the staff has to be replaced through layoffs and hiring or the state sector greatly expanded. As the latter is not financially feasible, only the former is possible. But this will raise serious legal and political problems. Though the anti-Brahmin movement in Tamil Nadu indicates that this can be eventually accomplished, creating the state sector as the preserve of the Backward Classes and the Untouchables rele-gates them to the least dynamic sector. The Forward Castes will quickly use their connections and education to move to the more dynamic and higher-paying private sector, where they already dominate. The political compromise behind a state sector domi-nated by the Backward Classes and the Untouchables which, for budget deficit reasons will have no significant growth, and a rapidly expanding private sector, while necessary in the short term, is not going to be tolerated for long. Soon it can be expected that, as in America, the Untouchables and Backward Classes will demand quotas in the private sector and employment equity in firms that receive government contracts. This may scare away investment, and the most a Dalit government can do in the short term may be to pressure the centre to implement such policies. However, it is unlikely that once in power, the Dalits will tolerate restriction in the limited opportunities the state sector can provide and will insist on affirmative action in the private sector as well. 'The state even may be forced to apply reservation to currently exempt institutions, such as the armed forces. And equal-opportunity laws could see quotas encroach on the private sector.'[55]

Large corporations at least will eventually find they have to comply, but indiscriminate hiring of unqualified people could make business uncompetitive in the world market. The temptation of Dalit politicians once in power to do this will be enormous but must be resisted.

> Clearly, the country's new lower-caste rulers will have to tread a tightrope between pressure for more state patronage and the demands of the free market. But in a classic Catch 22, such a balancing act won't be successful without sustained economic growth—which won't come easy if the state is squeezed too hard for patronage.[56]

In these circumstances, the Dalits will have to be cautious in using their control of the state as a springboard and mechanism for diversification into the private sector and the development of an entrepreneurial class. It is doubtful, given the political imperatives involved, that they will be cautious. At a time when there is need for privatization and downsizing, the Dalits may revert to the old strategy of state expansion through deficit financing. The only way to achieve Dalit employment in the state sector and deficit reduction will be through even larger layoffs than hiring, which may become feasible in the near future if central government policy proposals are implemented. A strategy that sees Dalits taking control of a stagnant state, and the Forward Castes moving into the booming private sector will only create inequality at new levels. This is bound to anger the lower castes, who already know that now that state power is within their grasp but the powers that be have moved to downsizing the state sector and promoting liberalization. They are unlikely to see this as a world phenomenon and more likely to see it as a Forward Caste conspiracy. 'Reform could also be hampered by the anger of lower castes who feel betrayed by the reduction in state control of the economy. Indeed, some of them already see the whole reform process as a high-caste trick to deny them the fruits of advancement. 'The traditional elite can see their power being reduced as real democracy is extended,' says a lower-caste government official. 'Now that the patronage is slipping from their hands, they are all for liberalisation'.[57] However, under the circumstances the Dalit state will have to control its expenditures and substitute existing programmes and personnel rather than expand the state.

With only their predecessors as role models, the temptation to milk the private sector for jobs and campaign contributions will be irresistible, and anything as glorified as policy is likely to be lost in attempting to grab the loaves and fishes of office. Genuine Dalit business development, however, can only be achieved one step at a time, and without the control of the state, the Untouchables will be in no position to acquire the capital and skills to enter the private sector in significant numbers. Just as the Afrikaners and French Canadians used control of the state to leverage access to the private sector, so will the Dalits. Coming from a much weaker socio-economic position, and in a time of state budget austerity, it will take much longer. However, an Untouchable officer observed that among Untouchables the first generation usually becomes an office peon or clerk and the second generation an officer. It is unlikely that social mobility from the state to the private sector will be any faster, but without state support they are unlikely to be able to get there at all. While the Forward Castes will gradually have to give up their hold on the public sector and move on to the more dynamic and lucrative private sector, the Untouchables will have to follow in their footsteps a generation later. There is every indication that Indian democracy has become institutionalized enough to eventually allow these accommodations to take place, though the transitional period we are going through will be difficult and fraught with conflict. Rather than just dwelling on the disintegration and criminalization that journalists and scholars so frequently lament, it is important to recognize the popular empowerment taking place which should lead to greater democratization in India.

REFERENCES

1. Crawford Young, 'Patterns of Social Conflict: State, Class, and Ethnicity', *Daedalus*, 111, Spring 1982, p. 84.
2. Kathleen Gough, 'Harijans in Thanjavur', in Kathleen Gough and Hari P. Sharma (eds), *Imperialism and Revolution in South Asia* (New York: Monthly Review Press, 1973), p. 242.
3. Arjun Appadurai, 'Number in the Colonial Imagination', in Carol A. Breckenridge and Peter van der Veer (eds), *Orientalism and the Postcolonial Predicament: Perspectives on South Asia* (Philadelphia: University of Pennsylvania Press, 1993), pp. 331–33.
4. Mark Juergensmeyer, *Religion as Social Vision: The Movement Against Untouchability in 20th Century Punjab* (Berkeley: University of California Press, 1982).
5. Ibid., p. 277.
6. Michael Brecher, *Nehru: A Political Biography* (London: Oxford University Press, 1959), p. 189.
7. Marc Galanter, *Competing Equalities: Law and the Backward Classes in India* (Berkeley: University of California Press, 1984), p. 33.
8. Mulk Raj Anand, *Untouchable* (Harmondsworth: Penguin Books, 1986). For the Untouchable view, see B.R. Ambedkar, *What Congress and Gandhi Have Done to the Untouchables* (Bombay: Thacker & Co., 1945).
9. Juergensmeyer, *Religion as Social Vision* (n. 4 above), pp. 72–73, 243.
10. Geoffrey Hawthorn, 'Caste and Politics in India Since 1947', in Dennis B. McGilvray (ed.), *Caste Ideology and Interaction* (Cambridge: Cambridge University Press, 1982), p. 211.
11. John Broomfield, *Mostly About Bengal: Essays in Modern South Asian History* (Delhi: Manohar, 1982), p. 233.
12. Nasir Iqbal, 'More Educated are More Caste Conscious: Delhi Survey', *Dalit Voice*, Vol. 10, No. 9, 16–31 March 1991. The survey was conducted by the Delhi-based sociologist R.P. Singh.
13. World Bank, *World Development Report 1991* (Oxford: Oxford University Press, 1991), p. 242.
14. James Manor, 'How and Why Liberal and Representative Politics Emerged in India', *Political Studies*, Vol. 38, No. 1, March 1990, p. 25.
15. Sumit Sarkar, *Modern India: 1885–1947* (New York: St Martin's Press, 1989), p. xxiii.
16. Gyanendra Pandey, 'In Defence of the Fragment: Writing about Hindu–Muslim Riots in India Today', *Representations*, 37, Winter 1992, pp. 28–29, 31, 50.
17. Nicholas B. Dirks, 'Castes of Mind', *Representations*, 37, Winter 1992, p. 76.
18. Ranajit Guha, 'Dominance Without Hegemony and Its Historiography', in Ranajit Guha (ed.), *Subaltern Studies VI: Writings on South Asian History and Society* (Delhi: Oxford University Press, 1989), p. 304.

19. Dirks, 'Castes of Mind' (n. 17 above), pp. 74, 76.
20. Robert L. Hardgrave, 'After the Dynasty: Politics in India', *Current History* Vol. 91, No. 563, March 1992, p. 112.
21. Partha Chatterjee, 'Caste and Subaltern Consciousness', in Ranajit Guha (ed.), *Subaltern Studies VI* (Delhi: Oxford University Press, 1989), p. 208.
22. Pramod Parajuli, 'Power and Knowledge in Development Discourse: New Social Movements and the State in India', *International Social Science Journal*, Vol. 43, No. 127, 1991, p. 175.
23. Jana Everett, 'Incorporation versus Conflict: Lower Class Women, Collective Action, and the State in India', in Sue Ellen M. Charlton, Jana Everett and Kathleen Staudt (eds), *Women, the State, and Development* (New York: State University of New York Press, 1989).
24. Jean Dreze and Amartya Sen, *Hunger and Public Action* (Oxford: Clarendon Press, 1989), p. 8.
25. Metta Spencer, *Foundations of Modern Sociology*, (Scarborough: Prentice-Hall, 1981), p. 269.
26. Hawthorn, 'Caste and Politics in India Since 1947' (n. 10 above), p. 211.
27. Arend Lijphart, *Democracy in Plural Societies* (New Haven: Yale University Press, 1977), pp. 40–41.
28. It is perhaps significant that the idea of a Presidential system has received more attention with its possible positive prospects for more stable governance, than any new systems for increased non-elite empowerment. Jean-Alphonse Bernard, 'The Presidential Idea in the Constitutions of South Asia', *Contemporary South Asia*, Vol. 1, No. 1, 1992, p. 49.
29. Amnesty International, *India: Torture, Rape and Deaths in Custody* (New York: Amnesty International, March 1992), p. 195.
30. Myron Weiner, *The Child and the State in India* (Princeton: Princeton University Press, 1991).
31. James C. Clad, 'India: Crisis and Transition', *The Washington Quarterly*, Vol. 15, No. 1, Winter 1992, p. 94.
32. Andre Beteille, Letter to the Editor, *Dalit Voice*, Vol. 11, No. 8, 1–15 March 1992, p. 16.
33. Francine R. Frankel, 'Caste, Land and Dominance in Bihar: Breakdown of the Brahminical Social Order', in Francine R. Frankel and M.S.A. Rao (eds), *Dominance and State Power in Modern India: Decline of a Social Order* (Delhi: Oxford University Press, 1989), p. 99.
34. Sayantan Chakravarty, 'Ram Vilas Paswan: On the Gravy Train', *India Today*, 15 January 1997, pp. 18–20.
35. Jayashree B. Gokhale, 'The Evolution of a Counter-Ideology: Dalit Consciousness in Maharashtra', in Francine R. Frankel and M.S.A. Rao (eds), *Dominance and State Power in Modern India: Decline of a Social Order Vol. 2* (Delhi: Oxford University Press, 1990), p. 244.
36. John Stackhouse, 'Uttar Pradesh Main Prize as New Contest Opens Up', *The Globe and Mail*, 20 October 1995, p. A15.
37. Hamish McDonald, 'Pride and Prejudice', *Far Eastern Economic Review*, 3 November 1994, p. 29.
38. Barbara Crossette, *India: Facing the Twenty-First Century* (Bloomington: Indiana University Press, 1993), p. 28.

39. Ibid., p. 28.
40. Jack Donnelly, *Universal Human Rights in Theory and Practice* (Ithaca: Cornell University Press, 1989), pp. 55–57, 126.
41. Ibid., p. 127.
42. Sudipta Kaviraj, 'Crisis of the Nation-state in India', in John Dunn (ed.), *Contemporary Crisis of the Nation State?* (Oxford: Basil Blackwell, 1995).
43. Amal Kumar Mukhopadhyay, 'Theoretically Speaking', *The Statesman*, 15 May 1995, p. 11.
44. Olle Tornquist, *The Next Left? Democratization and Attempts to Renew the Radical Political Development Project: The Case of Kerala* (Copenhagen: Nordic Institute of Asian Studies, 1995), p. 9.
45. T.V. Sathyamurthy, Book Review, *Public Administration and Development*, Vol. 13, No. 5, 1993, pp. 524–26.
46. Ibid., p. 525.
47. *India Today*, 'Voices', 15 October 1995, p. 11.
48. Evelyn Hu-DeHart, 'The Undermining of Ethnic Studies', *The Chronicle of Higher Education*, 20 October 1995, p. B1.
49. Deepak Lal, 'India and China: Contrasts in Economic Liberalization?', *World Development*, Vol. 23, No. 9, September 1995, p. 1485.
50. Ibid., p. 1486.
51. McDonald, 'Pride and Prejudice' (n. 37 above), p. 25.
52. Hiranmay Karlekar, *In the Mirror of Mandal* (Delhi: Ajanta Books, 1992), p. 65.
53. Beteille, Letter to the Editor (n. 32 above), p. 16.
54. Thomas Sowell, 'Affirmative Action: A Worldwide Disaster', *Commentary*, Vol. 88, No. 6, December 1989, p. 37.
55. McDonald, 'Pride and Prejudice' (n. 37 above), p. 24.
56. Ibid., pp. 24–25.
57. Ibid., p. 25.

CHAPTER 11

Human Rights in South Asian Scholarship

Human rights scholarship has been dominated by theoretical debates on the topic rather than the exposure of specific abuses that could lead to criminal charges. In examining specific abuses and then drawing generalizations from them, the following two chapters attempt to expose the duplicity of scholarship in dealing with human rights abuses.

The scholarship on contemporary West Bengal is particularly interesting in this regard, for its Communist government adds an extra dimension to issues of governance and human rights in Indian studies. The performance of the Left Front government since 1977 has generated considerable praise in the academic literature, and its longevity in office would seem to confirm this analysis.

The scholarship is too large to be adequately covered in a single chapter, hence the critique is restricted primarily to western academic publications. This literature is particularly important because it has defined foreign perceptions of the West Bengal experiment, the Indian literature having limited foreign distribution. The most detailed academic analyses have been done by Atul Kohli at Princeton University and Thomas Nossiter at the London School of Economics, but their positive appraisal has been shared by such institutions as the World Bank and the Club of Rome. I have argued elsewhere that this work is inaccurate.[1] However, from the point of view of Indian studies, the most important question is how such a literature came to be accepted for such a long period in an open society with a free press and an active academic community. Are 'progressive' regimes treated differently from those with no particular reformist agenda? To what extent is the literature a creation of intellectual elite views which distort the reality on the ground?

Governance and human rights in West Bengal have been selected for analysis as the Left Front government has received particular praise for providing good and humane governance since coming to office. This is a major theme of Kohli's book *Democracy and Discontent*, which singles out West Bengal as achieving better results than the four other states he studies. This follows his earlier book *The State and Poverty in India*, which credits West Bengal with better development reform implementation than the two other states he analyses. As recently as 1996 Kohli described West Bengal as an example of 'good governance'.[2] These views are shared by Nossiter in *Marxist State Governments in India*. Together these works represent the dominant view in the literature and have received the widest circulation.

The issue of good governance and human rights in West Bengal has important political ramifications in an era of Communist discreditation and disintegration. It points a way, at least implicitly, to a radical alternative to both conventional Third World regimes supporting elite interests and unpopular repressive Communist governments. As the longest ruling democratically elected Communist government of any consequence in the world, the West Bengal Left Front is a natural pole of attraction for Third World radicals seeking a strategy for working with newly emerging democratic systems. Though the scholarship does not make this connection explicitly, a positive evaluation of the West Bengal experience relative to other states implies that it is an alternative model for development and human rights. Kohli states that 'West Bengal under the CPM (Communist Party Marxist) probably is India's best-governed state'.[3] Its positive human rights record is indicated when Kohli claims that 'the most impressive achievement of the CPM, however, has been restoration of political order— and that without repression'.[4] Nossiter gives equal credit to the Left Front, stating that 'the disappearance of communal and caste clashes; freedom from the gangsterism which has been a nightmare during Congress rule; diminished corruption in politics and government', all contributed to Left Front electoral support.[5]

My own conclusions are so fundamentally different from this as to raise questions about source selection and the sociology of knowledge in Indian studies. I argue that on both sides of this subject social position has not been transcended, and in fact the scholarship is a reflection of it. While this applies as much to myself as to other scholars, this diversity can be positive in elic-iting useful information. The problem is that diversity of scholar-ship is not adequately present and has been skewed towards the perceptions of the Indian intellectual elite.

Government performance in West Bengal is particularly ger-mane to this issue because there are certain social realities, inci-dents and statistics which have been virtually omitted from the history of the Left Front, thereby permitting a positive evaluation of its record. Why these were omitted is not always clear in each instance, but it is argued that there are cultural and political val-ues that filter information in preconceived formats. When taken into account they can reveal both scholarly preconceptions as well as something about the society being studied.

There are few political scientists today who would claim that their work is absolutely 'value free', 'scientifically objective' or 'ideologically neutral'. Yet rare—and self-destructive—is the political scientist willing to admit bias in his or her par-ticular research project or methodology. While all (or virtu-ally all) admit that some moral imperative is unavoidable in setting the research agenda, we must nevertheless invoke the rigors of the scientific method—or at least the 'coolness' of reason and logic—to justify our findings and arguments.[6]

That objectivity is seldom reached in many subjects has long been recognized as a problem in the social sciences and humani-ties. According to the then President of the American Sociological Association, Stanley Lieberson,

This difficulty in evaluating evidence is the 'double standard' that we all run into—evidence in support of an 'undesired' conclusion is subjected to much tougher standards than evidence supporting other conclusions. This is disturbing because it means there is no consensus about the grounds for deciding whether evidence strongly supports or strongly undermines a theory, or whether considerable uncertainty remains. I have no doubt that the double standard is a prob-lem in other disciplines, but it is probably an exceptionally severe problem for us because of several factors: We often deal with socially and politically sensitive topics that people have strong feelings and dispositions about; it is simply harder to develop strong evidence compared to other sciences; and we do not have even a rough set of guidelines for evaluating our evidence for a given problem.[7]

In an open society such as India, scholarship is determined less by access to information than by preconceptions formed through social background and contacts. In trying to provoke readers into rethinking their views of India my opinions may seem polemical, but in this process they will hopefully reflect on their own biases and begin to see India as it really is to a great many people in it. I will present this view using West Bengal as a case study of how a social reality has been distorted in the academic literature. That analysis of West Bengal is affected by the ideological predispositions of scholars is indicated in Tanka B. Subba's study of the Gorkhaland movement in Darjeeling, West Bengal.

Most social scientists who have attained the level of theorizing are bogged down with one or the other ideological camp. Thus they often try to see sense within the domain of their ideology and pick up only those data that fit into their preconceived notions. Those data which do not fit in or which contradict the same are in a fit of rationalization excluded or ignored.[8]

Governance

The study of human rights is particularly germane to the sociology of knowledge as all social scientists would presumably claim to be in favour of improving human rights. Empirical evidence for violations is often readily available, and any divergence from this reality in the academic literature can be easily detected. However, the determination of good governance or its comparison with other states presents serious problems of uneven reporting. Even if trends can be confirmed, it may not be justifiable to attribute them to the regime in power. According to Nossiter; 'Calcutta, under the LF [Left Front], is despite its poverty one of the safest, if not the safest, metropolis in the world.'[9] Leaving aside periods of political conflict, however, it is doubtful if Calcutta was less safe under the Congress regime or during the British rule for that matter. Public safety is not something the Left Front can credit to itself alone, even assuming it is true. Likewise the increased school enrolment under the Left Front, for which it has also been credited, if plotted on a graph back into the Congress period shows no change in the rate of increase, so presumably it would have increased at the same rate under either government.[10] As the enrolment of Scheduled Castes (Untouchables) and Scheduled Tribes has remained about the same, the gap between the lower and upper-caste/classes has increased. Thus the Left Front failed in lower-class education, which disproportionately benefits the middle and upper classes. None of this is mentioned in the academic literature praising the Left Front, though the West Bengal government's own publication 'School Education in West Bengal' admits that 'as with Primary education gross enrolment ratios of the disadvantaged sections for the age-group 11–14, women, Scheduled Castes and Scheduled Tribes have been trailing far behind the enrolment ratios of the general student'.[11]

The central government's Scheduled Castes and Scheduled Tribes Commission found that 'in Madhya Pradesh, Orissa and West Bengal, the District officers had a very vague knowledge of the Special Component Plan' for the Scheduled Castes.[12] When I pointed out to the secretary of the West Bengal government who was in charge of the programme that the state had the lowest per capita expenditure in the country, he assured me that there was no expenditure at all as the programme existed only in planning documents, which used figures from other programmes not entitled to be included. As this programme was non-existent it would presumably explain the district officers' vagueness. Amrita Basu notes that 'as the growth of the Jharkhand movement and Gurkha agitation suggest[s], minorities have become increasingly hostile to the Left Front government'.[13] However, these tribal movements appear to have been taken more seriously than the women's movement. 'When the issue was raised with CPI(M) men, they were so amused that it allayed their anxieties about being interviewed. They simply could not consider women's issues serious political issues.'[14]

These examples can serve only to hint at a larger reality that seems to have escaped much of the scholarly writing on Left

Front performance. The extent of deceit and misinformation that confronts scholars requires cross-checking and verification with the officers responsible for the programmes. Both Kohli and Nossiter have done this. I interviewed IAS secretaries of the West Bengal government who expressed surprise at the positive assessment these scholars had made of the Left Front, because they had told them what was going on but their negative information had been discounted in their publications. As these senior IAS officers had spent most of their professional lives in the field, their views cannot be easily discredited since they are more familiar with the subject and have greater access to information than visiting scholars. According to Kohli, 'senior civil servants' follow what 'almost appeared to be the bureaucratic line' in attributing problems of land reform 'to the "middle peasant" nature of the CPM's rural support'.[15] When the civil servants in charge of programmes are discounted as credible sources of information, questions on the greater reliability of other sources must be raised. Neither peasants nor party workers can be counted on to express their frank opinion publicly, and that is why personal contacts and private meetings are essential.

The way in which information is filtered or mediated between subject and scholar is critical. It is relatively straightforward at the micro level where interviewing a cross-section of villagers over an extended period can uncover inconsistencies and deception. For this reason perhaps, micro-level studies tend with some exceptions to be more critical of the Left Front than the state-level studies of Kohli and Nossiter.[16] However, micro studies cannot be generalized to the state level without a fairly large sample. The state-level statistics are too aggregated to be easily verified. Intermediaries then become essential to scholarship, and this is where class and caste are critical to the creation of knowledge. In colonial Bengal the tricaste elite made up only 6.08 per cent of the population but now occupy all but one cabinet post in the Left Front government, with a Muslim being the exception.[17] By any standard the Bengali elite are extremely narrowly caste based, but still dominate all fields of middle-class intellectual activity. This is the group through which the scholarship on Bengal is largely produced. It brought with it certain myths about its society and state which have come to be widely accepted even by visiting scholars.

Perhaps the most fallacious view is that Untouchable segregation does not exist in the state. The Vice Chairman of the West Bengal State Planning Board goes so far as to claim that 'no prejudice exists in relation to caste or creed' in West Bengal.[18] Atul Kohli argues that even as far back as the twelfth century 'the Untouchables could eat with members of cleaner castes'.[19] In travelling through rural Bengal even CPM guides admit that segregation of eating facilities is still prevalent. This is confirmed in village-level academic literature which states that this extends to government schools.[20] Considering that Untouchables comprise 22 per cent of the West Bengal population and 73 per cent of the state population is rural, the scale of the segregation and humiliation is obvious. If one drew an analogy with American studies and a scholar argued that black segregation never existed in the American South, the very least that would happen is a loss of academic credibility. Yet this sort of thing passes for scholarship of West Bengal without raising objection. This is not a tribute to the state of Indian studies. What we have here is a gross distortion of reality, though it is a common perception of the urban intelligentsia. When I express the view that from my experience living under South African apartheid was better than the situation in rural India, Indian scholars often get upset. This seems to suggest an emotional attachment to nationality which affects their academic objectivity.

This is the tip of a cultural myth about India which continues in many quarters to this day and has seriously influenced scholarship on India. The obstacles to its de-mythologization are considerable and rooted in deep-seated cultural values. This would be less of a problem for scholarship if the caste system were not closely correlated with class which excluded most lower castes/classes from educational institutions and the media. Until recently, Untouchables have been excluded from participation in modern education and their influence in the media is negligible. These hierarchical divisions result in the Indian intelligentsia not realizing just how differently Untouchables view society. For example, Untouchables of all classes tend to see the British as more just than Indians, and foreign missionaries though disliked by 'official' India are fondly remembered in Untouchable folk tradition.[21]

The way the intellectuals see society may determine how the world sees it, but this is not necessarily the reality. Bengali cultural superiority is assumed in the view that Bengali cultural and political practices are more enlightened and advanced than those in the rest of the country; a view reflected even in the non-Bengali writings of Kohli and Nossiter. While the myth of caste integration represents a qualitative improvement on traditional values, Bengali modernity is not generalized beyond a narrow intellectual elite. As long as there are no discordant notes such as I present, the myth of progressive enlightenment is reinforced by the lack of Scheduled Caste and Scheduled Tribe upward mobility and mass education which might result in attempts to contradict these views.

In fact the Bengali tricaste elite has greater dominance than the upper castes in most other states where intermediate castes with rural property have challenged upper-caste dominance through such issues as the Backward Caste job reservation movement. Amartya Sen has argued that in states such as Bihar where the high-caste elite has been partly supplanted by intermediate castes, Hindu fundamentalism is not a serious threat.[22] As positive references to Bihar are few and far between, this points to a need to re-examine the relative position of Indian states in social change. The Bengali elite has been able to project itself as representative of the whole society, and its political and intellectual discourses have hardly been challenged. The leftist orientation gives this discourse added credibility by downplaying the significance of traditional identities and assuming a concerted effort to achieve lower-class emancipation. The masses, however, are portrayed as the intellectual elite see them, not as they really are.[23] The ignorance of the desegregation issue is indicative of just how out of touch this intellectual elite is with rural society. This is perhaps not surprising, given the urban intelligentsia's long separation from rural life and property.

The human rights record of the Left Front government, which both Kohli and Nossiter praise for the relative absence of political and communal violence, is difficult to assess in relative terms. Comparing the Congress and Left Front period is problematic given the changes in politics over time, and comparison with other states with different traditions is equally difficult. Since much of the political violence was caused by the Communists and the government's repression of them, their entry into government naturally brought an end to a lot of this violence. Crediting the Communists for not rioting against themselves would be distorting the political picture. Kohli points to a decrease in the number of riots per million population under the Left Front. Whether this was due to better repression or to co-option is difficult to determine, since historically much of the violence was politically inspired by Left Front parties.[24]

There are limitations on what any state government can do to control crime or mass violence. There are, however, issues over which the government could have exercised its influence to implement human rights and remove corruption. When the Left Front first came to power, police torturers were reputedly apprehensive of facing criminal charges because the Left Front had evidence against them. However, their services were retained by the new government, and their practices continued. I was offered an interview with a well-known police torturer which I declined. When I tried to obtain the publications of Maoist insurgents, a CPM friend warned me that I could be tortured by the police and being a scholar would not save me. He had used contacts in his party to keep Maoist friends out of jail because even though the Maoists and CPM were killing each other then, when the revolution came they would be on the same side. As the *New York Times* South Asia correspondent observed, jailed Maoists whose good behaviour was 'guaranteed by some relative or friend of established status…could go free…. But if there were no "respectable" persons to guarantee their good behaviour, they could just stay in jail, whatever they promised. In many cases, therefore, the real crime was not revolutionary violence but lack of connections.'[25] When I enquired of my host in Calcutta about possible police interference in my research on Indian communism, he assured me that because of his position in government, the police would approach him first and he would ask them to leave me alone as I had only an academic interest in the subject. Though there has been a circulation of political elites since the Left Front came to power, the system of influence peddling remains unchanged under the Communists. This is only a glimpse of how power is exercised in the state, but it indicates that good governance and human rights are more illusive than the academic literature indicates. Estimates suggest at least 6,000 political murders since the Communists took power.[26] Reports by groups such as Amnesty International have by their own acknowledgement revealed only part of the picture. 'Jyoti Basu, Chief Minister of West Bengal where Amnesty International has recorded 43 deaths allegedly following torture since 1985, proclaimed in October 1987: "Deaths in police custody are unthinkable in any civilised society. It is illegal and absolutely sickening. Nothing could be worse."'[27] By 1995 there had been 198 deaths in police custody since the Communists came to power, though no policeman was ever punished. Even when there were witnesses, such as among the 68 rapes in custody, only two policemen were charged. That West Bengal had more deaths in custody than any other state was attributed by the Home Secretary to possibly better record keeping.[28] Which state keeps the most accurate statistics on torture deaths is debatable; but what is more significant is that nothing has been done about it since the Communists came to power. As avowed Stalinists, they are aware of the importance of having the coercive apparatus of the state on their side, and investigating the police would cause their alienation from the party in power and hinder the ability of the state to intimidate people by the threat of torturing them to death with impunity. This is not to say that torture is random or arbitrary. The society is in fact informally divided into the torturable and the untorturable, depending on the connections of those involved. Though people may not see themselves in these terms, the police are perfectly well aware of whom they can brutalize. Though changes of government may make some slight change in who is untorturable, the categories remain.

The fact is that there is such a backlog of criminal cases(8,00,000 in West Bengal, 2,30,000 in the Calcutta High Court alone) that justice cannot be done. Perhaps as a result mobs lynched 77 people between January and September 1995 (including a 12-year-old for allegedly stealing a bicycle). An *India Today* correspondent speculated that the CPM control of the police and its replacement of traditional community-based arbitration had resulted in people outside the party nexus finding the system unresponsive.[29] Such violations of human rights are perpetrated by the low-level police or uncontrollable mobs. The chief minister's alleged involvement in political killings, however, though known to government officials, goes unreported. When the veteran CPM leader and former Chief Minister of Tripura criticized Jyoti Basu for widely reported influence peddling on behalf of his son's business interests in a case reminiscent of the 'young tigers' (children of Chinese Communist leaders using their family connections in business dealings), he was expelled from the party. When the Left Front lost control after the Calcutta municipal elections, it formed a coalition with a well-known organized crime figure, who had been elected as an independent, to stay in power.[30] While these sordid details may have little place in scholarship, when scholars proclaim good governance the underside of the West Bengal 'miracle' needs to be examined.

The decrease in corruption under the Communists has often been referred to in the academic literature without corroborative evidence. Nossiter's comment that 'for an anti-Communist newspaper, a little corruption goes a long way' may be valid.[31] The difficulty is in quantifying the amount. Press reports of hundreds of crores misappropriated by the CPM in Bengal are under investigation, but there is visible evidence that the CPM owns some of the best office buildings in district towns. These assets appear to have been acquired through the provision of state services in return for party donations. When I enquired of a Bengali professor with contacts at the highest level of the state CPM how a neighbourhood property occupied by squatters could be cleared for development, he said that a donation to the party would be required to obtain the use of the police for the eviction. I asked if receiving bribes for police eviction of slum dwellers on behalf of capitalist real estate developers was an appropriate role for a Communist party, he replied that I could hire Congress gangsters instead. In essence, being in the opposition meant resorting to organized crime to raise funds, while holding state power enabled the use of police.

If threats of torture and requests for bribes seem a poor way of influencing scholars, it must be recognized that most visitors would never be confronted with either possibility. One's position in society and the direction of research can determine the view of society. Some knowledge is encouraged, some ignored or never brought to light.

An accurate interstate comparison of good governance is probably impossible. Though Kohli and Nossiter make favourable evaluations of West Bengal, these are without corroborative empirical data. It is not that the rest of India is any better than West Bengal, or that there are not states with greater repression and corruption, but what the favourable ranking scholars have put forward is unverifiable. States with active insurgencies are likely to have the worst human rights abuses, and some others have long histories of communal and caste violence. While hundreds of Scheduled Castes and Scheduled Tribes have been killed by the Left Front government, this is not because they were poor minorities, though this facilitated the repression, but because they defied the government. This is different from some other states where violence is more likely to be between communal groups, with the state having to maintain civic harmony. That West Bengal repression is state directed makes the government more responsible for excesses. International opinion has increasingly placed a restricted interpretation on the rights of states to repress minorities, though interference in internal affairs has been deemed inappropriate by the Indian government.

Massacres in Indian History

In West Bengal I came across an alleged massacre which was widely known but omitted from academic literature because no one was interested in writing about it. Hence, I found myself being a chronicler of 'forgotten' history. The difficulty in getting it accepted by scholarly referees raises questions of academic objectivity and the political bias in Indian studies.

When the Left Front first came to power it had to reckon with the expectations of its supporters that their campaign promises would be kept. One of the biggest problems of West Bengal was the influx of millions of East Bengal refugees. The poorest Untouchable refugees who were dependent on government assistance were forced by the Congress government to settle at Dandakaranya in central India. In opposition, the Communists demanded that these refugees be settled in the uninhabited Sundarbans Ganges delta of West Bengal. When the Communists took power in West Bengal their refugee supporters took them at their word and sold their belongings in Dandakaranya to return to West Bengal. About 30,000 Untouchable refugees managed to reach the delta forest area, and settled at Marichjhapi. By their own efforts they established a viable fishing industry, salt pans, health centres and schools.[32]

The state government was not disposed to countenance such settlement, stating that the refugees were 'in unauthorised occupation of Marichjhapi which is a part of the Sundarbans Government Reserve Forest violating thereby the Forest Acts'.[33] It is debatable whether the CPM placed primacy on ecology or merely feared that this might be a precedent for an unmanageable refugee influx with loss of political support. When persuasion failed to make the refugees abandon their settlement, the West Bengal government started on 26 January 1979 an economic blockade of the settlement with 30 police launches. The community was teargassed, huts razed and fisheries and tubewells destroyed in an attempt to deprive them of food and water. The Calcutta High Court ordered a lifting of the blockade, but this was ignored. Though some died of starvation and disease, the refugees would not give up. When these police actions failed to persuade the Untouchable refugees to leave, the state government ordered the forcible evacuation of the refugees, which took place from 14 to 16 May 1979. Muslim gangs were hired to assist the police, as it was thought that they would be less sympathetic to refugees from Muslim-ruled East Pakistan (now Bangladesh).[34] Several hundred men, women and children were said to have been killed in the operation and their bodies dumped in the river. Photographs were published in the *Ananda Bazaar Patrika* and opposition members in the state assembly staged a walk-out in protest.[35] However, no criminal charges were brought against any of those involved nor was any investigation undertaken. The then Prime Minister, Morarji Desai, wishing to maintain the support of the Communists for his government, decided not to pursue the matter.[36] The central government's Scheduled Castes and Scheduled Tribes Commission said in its annual report that there were no atrocities against Untouchables in West Bengal, even though its Marichjhapi file contains newspaper clippings, petitions, and a list with the names and ages of 236 men, women and children killed by police at Marichjhapi *prior* to the massacre.[37] The refugees themselves complained to visiting members of parliament that 1,000 had died of disease and starvation during the occupation and blockade.[38] 'Out of the 14,388 families who deserted, 10,260 families returned to their previous places...and the remaining 4,128 families perished in transit, died of starvation, exhaustion, and many were killed in Kashipur, Kumirmari, and Marichjhapi by police firings.'[39]

Within the CPM—which had taken the decision—there was some dissatisfaction with the way the party leadership had handled the situation. Many CPM cadre felt that the leadership had dealt with the problem in a 'bureaucratic way' when it could have used the issue to develop a mass movement on behalf of the refugees. The Communists had large refugee organizations which could have mobilized the refugees and brought them to West Bengal. Instead of utilizing the situation to rehabilitate the refugees and in the process develop a solid Communist base among them, only force was resorted to by the CPM. Those in the CPM who were unhappy with the policy could do nothing; no one on the CPM State Committee opposed the State Secretary Promode Das Gupta on this issue. However, not all parties and ministers in the Left Front coalition cabinet favoured the eviction, preferring to support the refugees instead. The Revolutionary Socialist Party, which had a political base in the Sundarbans and was in the Left Front government, opposed the decision, as did other Left Front supporters.

> Even if it is admitted that the refugees should not have left Dandakaranya in so sudden a manner after selling out everything they had, the Left Front Government should have shown some consideration for those whose total participation in the Left's struggle against the Establishment and whose kith and kin in West Bengal voting concertedly for the Left Front enabled it to hit the Writers' Buildings [take state power].[40]

In a final twist to the episode, the CPM settled its own supporters in Marichjhapi, occupying and utilizing the facilities left behind by the evicted refugees.[41] The need for environmental preservation and compliance with the Forest Act were forgotten. A professor of Community Medicine from the All India Institute of Medical Sciences, who visited the refugees in Dandakaranya shortly after their return, told me that those who came back were now dispossessed, having sold their land and belongings to make the trip to West Bengal, while those who had remained behind were better off. A pall of gloom hung over the refugee colonies. Though IAS secretaries of the West Bengal government who worked on a daily basis with the Left Front ministers revealed to me the divisions in the cabinet over the eviction, and informed me about the hiring of Muslims, killing, raping, and resettlement by CPM supporters, they did not have the names of the gangsters and policemen who actually perpetrated this. The failure of the government to investigate what happened means that this was never recorded. Had the Left Front government felt it was being unfairly maligned by these reports it could have ordered an independent inquiry to exonerate itself. The accuracy of the allegations and the involvement through acts of commission and omission of the chief minister and Prime Minister Desai among others make such an investigation unlikely. A journalist of the Bengali daily *Jugantar* noted:

> The refugees of Dandakaranya are...mainly cultivators, fishermen, day-labourers, artisans, the exploited mass of the society. I am sorry to mention that they have no relation with the elite of society. If it is a matter of anybody of the family of a Zamindar, doctor, lawyer or engineer, the stir is felt from Calcutta to Delhi, but in this classified and exploited society, we do not feel anything for the landless poor cultivators and fishermen. So long as the state machinery will remain in the hands of the upper class elite, the poor, the helpless, the beggar, the refugees will continue to be victimised.[42]

If the massacre is recorded in history at all it is because I am writing about it now. This is an unfortunate statement of fact since some scholars, including Nossiter, were informed of it, yet none considered it fit to mention.

The closest to an academic reference of the massacre is in a summary of the West Bengal human rights record by Sajal Basu.[43]

> Both the CPI(M) led left parties and Congress (I) prefer to continue in violence-prone activities, causing casualties and eviction of cadres from localities. As a ruling party, CPI(M) has forcefully evicted middle peasants belonging to non-CPI(M) groups. Police torture on CPI(M-L) [Communist Party

of India Marxist-Leninist] and SUC [Socialist Unity Centre] cadres, violent eviction of Marichjhapi refugees, incidents at Panshila symbolise CPI(M)'s violent orientation. The Congress (I) too has its inner troubles being expressed in street fights, its affiliated mastans are again active in violent activities.

Kohli states that the CPM restored order in the state 'without repression', yet he refers to Sajal Basu's two books on violence in West Bengal and acknowledges the author's assistance in collecting primary data on his behalf.[44] Though Kohli refers to Sajal Basu as an observer for Amnesty International, Amnesty makes no mention of the massacre, and my mailing of information to the organization went unacknowledged. As Kohli was aware of the literature on West Bengal violence, his conclusions raise questions of research perspective. The problem is not the availability of data, which both Nossiter and Kohli were in fact exposed to, but what is selected for inclusion in their academic publications.

The number of the Marichjhapi massacre victims may have exceeded that of the Jallianwalla Bagh massacre and the massacre of 80 Communists in West Bengal in 1958, but the refugees had no influential backers to publicize their cause in movies and history books. Jallianwalla Bagh was investigated by the Hunter Commission, but Marichjhapi was soon forgotten, except by the Untouchable refugees themselves. The 'crime was white-washed and most culprits went not only unpunished, but remained in service and...in some cases were even rewarded'.[45] Though M.K. Gandhi refers here to Jallianwalla Bagh it could just as easily apply to CPM and Congress massacres. While the massacre of nationalists and Communists elicits the reaction of powerful constituencies with an intellectual community to publicize their cause, in this case the refugees had nothing. After the massacre of Communists by the Congress government Jyoti Basu stated in the assembly that there was nothing but dead bodies between him and the government benches. This incident has been commemorated ever since on 'Martyr's Day'. The Communists' own massacre created a much more muted reaction and was soon forgotten. In the treatment of refugees, when Congress faced a similar situation it cut off aid, but did not resort to blockade, eviction and police firing, unlike the Left Front. In this respect the Left

Front was more repressive. Whether this reflected an ideological difference between self-avowed Gandhianism and Stalinism is difficult to determine.

> In 1961 when Dr. Roy [West Bengal Congress Chief Minister] ordered the despatch of the camp refugees to Dandakaranya and when 10,000 of them refused to move he did not use force to transport them there although he suspended the payment of cash and dry doles and withdrew the amenities enjoyed by the camp refugees. He did not also force them out of the camps. The refugees continued to live at the ex-camp sites and to fend for themselves without any government help and finally got themselves integrated into the economy of the region. But the Marxist Government had no compunction in driving out precisely those refugees who, according to their own statistical evaluation of the amount of surplus land available in West Bengal, could have been absorbed in West Bengal.[46]

The Congress failed where the CPM succeeded because it was not prepared to be as ruthless as the Stalinists and kill men, women and children. Neither the Congress nor the CPM were good practitioners of their respective idols' philosophy and practice; but ideology even in the context of Indian politics can make some difference. By not mentioning the massacre no unfavourable comparisons between the Congress and CPM refugee policies need be made, and the reputation of a non-repressive Left Front government can be maintained. The Marichjhapi massacre cannot be compared to human rights violations in Cambodia or the Soviet Union—though many in the CPM see Stalin's regime as a model to be emulated. The charges of genocide have no substance. It was simply that the CPM at a particular point decided that it was politically more expedient to evict the refugees, and accurately made the calculation that there would be no repercussions. Had there been a more influential human rights lobby this might not have been a realistic policy option. Even after the massacre the failure to force an investigation is indicative of the weakness of human rights interests.

In over a decade of attempts to get details of the Marichjhapi massacre published, the resistance of members in the academic community to its publication has revealed the prevalent views on the subject of human rights in South Asia. The editor of one major journal of Asian studies wrote me 'that after all this time...we have yet to obtain one solid outside referee report on your manuscript. We have solicited several referees and some have even accepted the task, only to have the ms [manuscript] returned to us in a few weeks with a terse statement that they felt unable to provide the promised report'. To the editor's credit, he went to an unusual effort to obtain favourable reviews, but in so doing revealed the degree of resistance in the profession to the exposure of human rights abuses, and the tolerance in the academic community towards its continuance. No one, however, could refute any of the evidence of the massacre, or even attempted to do so, though that presumably would be the only morally justifiable grounds for refusing publication about the massacre.

'Progressive' Regime History

There is a long history of western radical scholarship failing to understand the inner workings of progressive regimes and ignoring their human rights abuses. Perhaps this stems from the optimism of politically committed social scientists. The people living in these societies soon understood the nature of their regimes, but the scholars realized it long after it should have been obvious.

Nossiter states that the Communist movement 'has sustained its values far more successfully than any other movement or party in independent India'.[47] By contrast, I could not find them adhering to any values. What values a self-avowed Stalinist party should be expected to follow is a matter of debate.[48] If the Stalinists are taken at their word then they should be pursuing the interests of the poor, but this is the very group they have repressed the most. While the democratic rights of the already powerful middle and upper classes are maintained and they are solicited with pay increments and investment opportunities, the poor, who have the least power, are manipulated and controlled. This is understandable since lower class dissent threatens the CPM's ideology, membership and electoral base. According to Nossiter: 'If, and I believe it, Rajiv Gandhi, did say at his first meeting with Jyoti Basu after becoming prime minister that the chief minister was more fit for the role, the comment was not only a gracious courtesy but a proper tribute to Basu's standing.'[49] No mention is made of the chief minister's role in the Marichjhapi massacre or his being responsible for other human rights abuses. If a scholar gave similar praise to the Chinese premier there would be enough people familiar with the Tiananmen Square massacre (which the CPM supported) to make an independent judgement. In the case of West Bengal the human rights situation is obscured by the foreign academic literature which makes a critical assessment such as this difficult. Though the display of Stalin's rather than Gorbachev's portrait at the 1989 CPM Congress was reported in the Indian press and subsequently mentioned in two American publications, the CPM's Stalinism is not mentioned in either Nossiter's or Kohli's books. As I have seen Stalin's portrait in CPM offices, calendars, and on pen holders, this was not an isolated incident. The CPM's theory is in something of an ideological time warp, set in the era when Stalin was alive and the present Indian Communist leaders were being politicized. The failure to mention CPM Stalinism makes the theories of Kohli and Nossiter on its social-democratic-type reformism seem more plausible. This is not to say that institutionalization in the democratic system is not taking place, but omitting to mention CPM Stalinism and human rights abuses creates a deceptive impression of what is going on.

None of the secretaries of the West Bengal government (top ministry bureaucrats) I interviewed could credit the Left Front government with any successful programmes even though many were themselves leftist. The number two CPM minister in the Left Front government, Benoy Chowdhury, stated: 'The Government is corrupt. After 18 years in power, we have fallen prey to corruption....I may be called mad for saying so, but this is the bitter truth.' To this Chief Minister Jyoti Basu responded: 'If he thinks the Government is corrupt, why is he continuing to be in the Government?'[50] The CPM cadre was likewise disillusioned. According to a Burdwan CPM District Committee internal 1985 report, which was withdrawn from inner party circulation by the party leadership,

> The Left Front government has not been able to meet the aspirations of the people....People feel that even the limited

powers at the disposal of the Left Front government has not been properly used....There is considerable slackness and corrupt practices are followed in the implementation of these social programs by the government....The youth are no longer carried away by the Communist movement at the international and national level. The call to Communism has considerably waned among the youth....The Communist Party is no longer seen as a totally different party from other political parties....All the aberrations of petty bourgeois class have pervaded our party today.[51]

My analysis of the West Bengal case literature is not only a critique of the state of Indian studies but, because West Bengal has a Communist government, it is also a critique of Third World radical studies in general. Few today have any illusions about Communist regimes or regimes of the Third World liberation movements.[52] Yet, whether there is any learning process in operation is debatable. The illusions surrounding the West Bengal experiment are particularly surprising since it is an open society and has adequate English language primary and secondary literature which is accessible to foreigners. It is implicit in the nature of the subject that no specialized training is required to understand what is going on. Yet, to the extent that West Bengal is studied in the West at all, it is through the writings of Kohli and Nossiter. Some of the best literature is being published in India, but as it is not easily available abroad, course offerings depend largely on the publications of such scholars as Kohli and Nossiter.

These publications follow a standard academic format. Though colleagues are aware of the ideology of social science authors, this bias is carefully avoided in the writing. Minor reservations and criticisms are included, so to the unsuspecting reader the work appears academically balanced and objective. However, it really consists of value judgements and political stands backed by little empirical evidence or by evidence uncritically taken from data that have already been distorted by the government in its own favour. What is unknown to the non-specialist is the mass of countervailing information the authors were exposed to but chose to ignore. There is a critically determinant political bias underlying this which is never revealed. What is required is an understanding of how cognitive dissonance is resolved among social scientists who claim some degree of objectivity but publish highly skewed findings. Part of the reason may be cultural, but in the West Bengal case the political value judgements appear to be primary. The length of exposure to the state government may also be an important factor. Bengali Marxist scholars are usually more critical than the foreign admirers of the West Bengal experiment, perhaps because foreigners do not have to stay in the country long enough to experience Communist governance in all its aspects.

The growing number of radical Third World regimes that have come to be discredited on account of their political conduct and economic performance raises issues of how social scientists have perceived them. Minority views that do not tally with prevailing ideas can be ignored if they lack influential support. Ethnic minorities with a middle and upper class have an advantage in obtaining world attention over those that are almost exclusively lower class. Those that develop their ideas to fit western lobbies would presumably have an edge. Certainly, some nations such as Nicaragua, Mozambique, Tanzania and Guinea Bissau obtained disproportionate western aid by appealing to political constituencies. Development efforts largely failed, but the way western and Third World groups feed on each other's interests to gain attention and patronage raises questions about how movements are packaged in the West. Are they really what they are proclaimed to be in the foreign literature, and do their leaders really believe it themselves, or is there a mutual delusion about movements among both the westernized indigenous leaders and their foreign supporters?[53]

In West Bengal it was clear to policy implementers within a couple of years of taking power that the experiment was failing, yet foreign observers continue to publish optimistic appraisals years after these failures. Once a political position has been published there is an incentive to stick to it, as a reappraisal threatens credibility. As regime failures accumulate the discrepancy makes a loss of credibility inevitable but to stick to the position further endangers credibility. A switch in position at the earliest opportunity then becomes imperative. The time-lag between when a regime gets discredited at home and becomes so abroad is bound to vary with the circumstances; however, the greater the political commitment and academic investment in the regime, the longer this is likely to be. This change in attitude often appears only gradually in print, with the previously neglected countervailing evidence starting to be accepted by mainstream academics, and qualified reappraisals turning to increasingly frank admissions. The switch often follows the irrefutable revelation of human rights violations (as in Cambodia) and poor economic performance, or most likely both.

The West Bengal Left Front is different in the sense that it can survive with its present plurality of votes for a long time, and the limited nature of its power—confined to one state—precludes expectations of revolutionary changes.[54] The narrowness of its policy options created an ambiguity about what it could be expected to implement, which facilitated multiple interpretations of its achievements. As I had sources involved in key Left Front programmes, the failures were immediately apparent to me. Even so, these problems were no secret. This suggests that a reappraisal of how scholars view radical regimes is in order. When and from where does the first critical academic writing emerge? When does the regime lose domestic credibility, and how long does it take for foreign scholarship to accept this? Has the time-lag been reduced over the years as scholars became better informed from historical experiences, improved communications, and a proliferation of academic publications? In the radical regime life cycle, West Bengal is at the stage where its programmes have been largely discredited domestically but continue to receive endorsement internationally. How long it will take the international scholarship to catch up with domestic West Bengal realities is difficult to predict but it will eventually happen.

As one Bengali Marxist scholar put it, there is a sense of deja vu in West Bengal. It is like the 1950s when the Congress government was discredited. Now it is the Communists who have been discredited. The difference is that in the 1950s there was a Communist party waiting in the opposition to take over the government, now there are no credible alternatives, so the Communists hang on to power but do nothing constructive. Since his comments, the BJP has emerged as an alternative which threatens the future of secular democratic India. Had the Congress and Communists been more efficient and honest in government this challenge might have been diminished.

It has been claimed that the chief minister by his conciliatory strategy has achieved a necessary accommodation with the establishment and the central government, thereby legitimizing the Communist party and facilitating the institutionalization of Indian democracy. While accurate as far as it goes, the negative side of this strategy is that it offers nothing of substance to the underprivileged and exploited. Had something more substantive been offered the communal and caste forces might not have made the inroads they did among the lower classes. By not even implementing a human rights policy it alienated a lot of people who might have formed part of its natural constituency. If this is to be undertaken, past offences have to be investigated and charges laid. Had West Bengal been Serbia, the chief minister and others would have been charged by the UN War Crimes Tribunal for 'crimes against humanity'. Unfortunately, South Asia is not Europe, so until an effective international regime is in place that investigates and charges politicians responsible for major human rights abuses, no justice will come to the state. Jyoti Basu described in an interview with the *Asian Age* how his attempt to become prime minister in May 1996 was thwarted in a 'historic blunder' by the CPM Central Committee, which voted 35 to 20 against the move.[55] The Central Committee undoubtedly knows more about his record than most observers, and had clearly placed some limits on the accommodations and political opportunism it would tolerate. Had he become prime minister, media scrutiny would likely have revealed more than the CPM would have wished about the chief minister's period in office.

The acquiescence of the academic community in covering up human rights abuses is particularly disturbing because it shows how unreliable the scholarship is. West Bengal is in a sense doubly obscured, because the leftist intellectuals, who might have articulated an alternative view to nationalist scholarship in other states, are themselves in part committed to the West Bengal Communist regime. There are sharp differences of opinion among Indian scholars on Left Front performance, which may appear to make foreign scholars more objective; however, both groups operate in much the same intellectual mould. The problem is that these views are limited by cultural values and political biases that leave out much that is relevant about the state and society in West Bengal. Scholars, by failing to mention segregation, CPM Stalinism, torture and mass murder, while at the same time accepting inaccurate and misleading Communist government statistics, can portray

West Bengal as a socialist transition model. For a society that is relatively open to investigation, formulating such an analysis must require a highly selective data analysis. How this has been done would be a worthwhile subject for study, but scholars are often more reticent about examining their own ideology and work methods than those of their subjects. The Left Front experiment has been used to show that a state can be effective in poverty alleviation and popular empowerment. Though governments can arguably achieve this, the West Bengal case is an example of how this went wrong. That it continues to be portrayed in the academic literature as successful is indicative of just how wrong scholarship can be.

REFERENCES

1. Ross Mallick, *Development Policy of a Communist Government: West Bengal Since 1977* (Cambridge: Cambridge University Press, 1993).
   Ross Mallick, *Indian Communism: Opposition, Collaboration, and Institutionalization* (Delhi: Oxford University Press, 1993).
2. Atul Kohli, 'Can the Periphery Control the Center? Indian Politics at the Crossroads', *The Washington Quarterly*, Vol. 19, No. 4, Autumn 1996, p. 121.
3. Atul Kohli, *Democracy and Discontent* (Cambridge: Cambridge University Press, 1990), p. 268.
4. Ibid., p. 294.
5. T.J. Nossiter, *Marxist State Governments in India* (London: Pinter Publishers, 1988), p. 195.
6. William F.S. Miles, 'Motives, Morality and Methodology in Third World Research', *PS: Political Science and Politics*, Vol. 22, No. 4, December 1989, p. 853.
7. Stanley Lieberson, 'Einstein, Renoir, and Greeley: Some Thoughts About Evidence in Sociology—1991 Presidential Address', *American Sociological Review*, Vol. 57, No. 1, February 1992, pp. 1–2.
8. Tanka B. Subba, *Ethnicity, State and Development: A Case Study of the Gorkhaland Movement in Darjeeling* (Delhi: Vikas Publishing House, 1992), p. 102.
9. Nossiter, *Marxist State Governments in India* (n. 5 above), p. 181.
10. Mallick, *Development Policy of a Communist Government* (n. 1 above).
11. Government of West Bengal, Department of Information and Cultural Affairs, *School Education in West Bengal 1984*, (Calcutta: Director of Information, 1984), p. 25.
12. Government of India, *Report of the Commission for Scheduled Castes and Scheduled Tribes: Fifth Report April 1982–March 1983*, Delhi: Government of India Press, p. 3.

13. Amrita Basu, 'Democratic Centralism in the Home and the World: Bengali Women and the Communist Movement', in Sonia Kruks, Rayna Rapp and Marilyn B. Young (eds), *Promissory Notes: Women in the Transition to Socialism* (New York: Monthly Review Press, 1989), p. 229.

14. Ibid., p. 226.

15. Atul Kohli, *The State and Poverty in India* (Cambridge: Cambridge University Press, 1987), p. 127.

16. Micro-level studies that are critical of Left Front implementation include Kirsten Westergaard, *People's Participation, Local Government and Rural Development: The Case of West Bengal*, Centre for Development Research Report No. 8, Copenhagen, March 1986; Neil Webster, *Panchayati Raj and the Decentralisation of Development Planning in West Bengal*, Centre for Development Research Project Paper 90.7, Copenhagen, December 1990; Suraj Bandyopadhyay and Donald von Eschen, 'The Impact of Politics on Rural Production and Distribution', Paper for Association for Asian Studies, Annual Meeting, 26 March 1988, San Francisco; John Echeverri-Gent, 'Politics Takes Command: Implementation of the National Rural Employment Program in West Bengal', unpublished manuscript, June 1991. For a positive micro-level study of the Left Front performance, see G.K. Lieten, 'Panchayat Leaders in a West Bengal District', *Economic and Political Weekly*, Vol. XXIII, No. 40, 1 October 1988, pp. 2069–73.

17. Atul Kohli, 'From Elite Activism to Democratic Consolidation: The Rise of Reform Communism in West Bengal', in Françine R. Frankel and M.S.A. Rao (eds), *Dominance and State Power in Modern India Vol. II* (Delhi: Oxford University Press, 1990), pp. 374, 390.

18. Arun Ghosh, *West Bengal Landscapes*. (Calcutta: K.P. Bagchi & Co., 1989), p. 208.

19. Kohli, 'From Elite Activism to Democratic Consolidation' (n. 17 above), p. 395.

20. Marvin Davis, *Rank and Rivalry: The Politics of Inequality in Rural West Bengal*. (Cambridge: Cambridge University Press, 1983), p. 76; Linda C. Mayoux, 'Income Generation for Women in India: Problems and Prospects', *Development Policy Review*, Vol. 7, No. 1, March 1989, p. 23; Ronald P. Rohner and Manjusri Chaki-Sircar, *Women and Children in a Bengali Village*. (Hanover: University Press of New England, 1988), pp. 40–41.

21. Kathleen Gough, 'Harijans in Thanjavur', in Kathleen Gough and Hari P. Sharma (eds), *Imperialism and Revolution in South Asia* (New York: Monthly Review Press, 1973), p. 242.

22. Amartya Sen, 'The Threats to Secular India', *The New York Review of Books*, 8 April 1993, p. 32.

23. Himani Bannerji, 'Language and Liberation: A Study of Political Theatre in West Bengal', *Ariel*, Vol. 15, No. 4, 1984, pp. 131–44; Partha Chatterjee, 'Caste and Subaltern Consciousness', In Ranajit Guha (ed.), *Subaltern Studies VI* (Delhi: Oxford University Press, 1989), p. 169.

24. Kohli, *Democracy and Discontent* (n. 3 above), p. 275.

25. Joseph Lelyveld, *Calcutta* (Hong Kong: The Perennial Press, 1975), p. 31.

26. N.K. Singh and Farzand Ahmed, 'Crime and Politics: The Nexus', *India Today*, 31 August 1995, p. 31.

27. Amnesty International, *India: Torture, Rape and Deaths in Custody* (New York: Amnesty International, March 1992), p. 2.
28. Ruben Banerjee, 'West Bengal: Damning the Police', *India Today*, 30 November 1995, p. 56.
29. Ibid., 'West Bengal: Law Unto Themselves: A Failing System Leads to a Rise in Mob-led Vigilante Justice', *India Today*, 15 September, 1995, p. 137.
30. N.K. Singh and Farzand Ahmed, 'Crime and Politics: The Nexus', *India Today*, 31 August 1995, p. 28.
31. 'Coming Clean', *India Today*, 12 January 1998, p. 9; Nossiter, *Marxist State Governments* (n. 5 above), p. 181.
32. Prasannbhai Mehta MP, Laxmi Narayan Pandey MP, and Mangaldev Visharat MP, 'Report on Marichjhapi Affairs' (members of parliament nominated by Prime Minister Desai to visit and investigate Marichjhapi prior to the eviction), 18 April 1979, Mimeo; Ranjit Kumar Sikdar, 'Marichjhapi Massacre', *The Oppressed Indian*, July 1982, p. 21.
33. Letter from Deputy Secretary, Refugee Relief and Rehabilitation Department, Government of West Bengal, to Zonal Director, Ministry of Home Affairs, Government of India, Office of the Zonal Director, Backward Classes and Ex-officio Deputy Commissioner for Scheduled Castes and Scheduled Tribes, Eastern Zone, Subject: 'Problems of Refugees from Dandkaranya to West Bengal', No. 3223–Rehab/DNK–6/79.
34. Interview with a secretary (IAS) of the West Bengal Government.
35. Interviews with IAS and WBCS officers.
36. Interviews with ICS officers.
37. Letter from All-India Scheduled Castes/Tribes and Backward Classes Employees Co-ordination Council to Bhola Paswan Shastri MP, Chairman of the Commission for Scheduled Castes and Scheduled Tribes, Subject: 'Genocide Committed on the Scheduled Caste Refugees of Marichjhapi Island'.
38. Sikdar, 'Marichjhapi Massacre' (n. 32 above), p. 23.
39. Atharobaki Biswas, 'Why Dandakaranya a Failure, Why Mass Exodus, Where Solution?' *The Oppressed Indian*, July 1982, p. 19.
40. Prafulla K. Chakrabarti, *The Marginal Men: The Refugees and the Left Political Syndrome in West Bengal*, (Kalyani, West Bengal: Lumiere Books, 1990), p. 434.
41. Interview with a secretary (IAS) of the West Bengal Government.
42. Sikdar, 'Marichjhaphi Massacre' (n. 32 above), p. 23, quoting *Jugantar*, 29 May 1979.
43. Sajal Basu, *The Politics of Violence: A Case Study of West Bengal* (Calcutta: Minerva Publications, 1982), p. 168.
44. Kohli, 'From Elite Activism to Democratic Consolidation' (n. 17 above), pp. 374, 414.
45. M.K. Gandhi, *Collected Works*, Vol. 23, p. 116 cited in Ranajit Guha, 'Dominance Without Hegemony and its Historiography', in Ranajit Guha (ed.), *Subaltern Studies VI* (Delhi: Oxford University Press, 1989), p. 279.
46. Chakrabarti, *The Marginal Men* (n. 40 above), p. 434.
47. T.J. Nossiter quoted in Mark Tully, *No Full Stops in India* (London: Viking, 1991), p. 209.
48. Mark Tully, *No Full Stops in India* (n. 47 above), p. 181.

49. Nossiter, *Marxist State Governments* (n. 5 above), p. 139.
50. R. Banerjee, 'Benoy Chowdhury: Blowing the Whistle', *India Today*, 15 January 1996, p. 17.
51. Communist Party of India-Marxist, Burdwan District Committee, *Shamiksha Astham Lok Sabha Nirbachan* ('Analysis of Eighth Lok Sabha Elections') 28 February 1985, p. 26–27, 31–32. Burdwan is arguably the strongest Communist district base in the state. Communist programmes should therefore work better there than in other districts. According to Neil Webster: 'Politically Burdwan District has been a stronghold for the communist movement from its earliest days and continues to be so for the C.P.I.(M). The All India Kisan Sabha [the communist-led peasant movement] was established in [Burdwan]...in 1933 and a significant number of communist and kisan leaders have subsequently emerged from the district, including Harekrishna Konar and Benoy Chowdhury, past and present Land Ministers in the State government.' Neil Webster, *Panchayati Raj and the Decentralization of Development Planning in West Bengal*, Centre for Development Research, Project Paper 90.7, Copenhagen, December 1990, p. 48.
52. Linda M. Heywood, 'UNITA and Ethnic Nationalism in Angola', *The Journal of Modern African Studies*, Vol. 27, No. 1, March 1989, p. 48.
53. Brian H. Smith, *More Than Altruism: The Politics of Private Foreign Aid* (Princeton: Princeton University Press, 1990).
54. The 12 per cent vote for the BJP in 1991 indicates that differences with other states may have been somewhat exaggerated. With 46 per cent of the popular vote the Left Front is in office due to the divisions in the opposition. A less discredited Congress would likely lead to a Communist defeat. Left Front rule is to a great extent a result of fractious conflicts in the Congress opposition, which traditionally got around 40 per cent of the vote.
55. Subrata Nagchoudhury, 'Jyoti Basu: Off to New Pastures', *India Today*, 11 January 1997.

CHAPTER 12

Imagining South Asia

Not long ago someone outspokenly remarked: 'There hasn't been an honest book written on Indian politics.' This may have been intended to be arresting and wild, but it was not silly. It did not mean that the authors had been lying, only that the whole truth had not yet come out.[1]

More than two decades later, this statement is still relevant, although hardly confined to India.[2] Morris-Jones goes on to state that

every state's political life has an 'inside story' and every 'honest' book on politics has to try to bring it out. But is there some special difficulty in being 'honest' about Indian politics? Is its inside story very concealed and very different from outside appearances?[3]

An indication of the continued illusions of the South Asian political science community was Atul Kohli's statement to *Time* magazine in reaction to the Hawala scandal: 'Corruption in India doesn't surprise me. What does surprise me is how widespread and how high up it goes.'[4] That it was only one person's diary shows what a small piece of the action the scandal really reveals.

It will be argued that not only has the 'whole truth' not come out in the academic literature, but that there are deep-seated cultural and ideological reasons why honesty about Indian politics has generally not been forthcoming. There are obvious reasons for the failure of social scientists to adequately understand South Asia. Not the least of these has been the scale and diversity of the subcontinent, which often makes empirical verification impossible, and any generalizations fraught with exceptions. Scholarly perceptions of India have a long history, and much of the literature, as with any subject, has failed to stand the test of time. However, one of the advantages of South Asian studies has been its scholarly accessibility in both the colonial and post-colonial periods. Nevertheless, the literature is often grossly inaccurate and misleading. These misrepresentations result from the theoretical and ideological bias of social scientists and the often inadequately diversified informant base on which they rely. Ronald Inden in a take-off of Edward Said's work on Western attitudes to the Islamic world has indicated how, in contrast to Islam, Christian scholars have in part come to portray positives images of Hinduism. Unlike Islam, which is a bitter rival of its Christian 'cousin', Hinduism is different without the inherent challenge to the West that Islam represents, a challenge Samuel Huntington at least sees as the fundamental conflict of the current era.[5] According to Inden the dominant western view, whether of Mill or Marx, sees India as inherently inferior. But there is also the perception of a 'romantic India' by a 'loyal opposition' of scholars initiated by Sir William Jones and the Asiatic Society, but continued to the present day by Sanskritists and their contemporary social science counterparts who see in Indian spiritualism an answer to the difficulties of the West. As the assumptions of western superiority become 'politically incorrect' to publish, the positive attributes of Indian culture become 'hegemonic' in contemporary literature. This is aided by the Indian elite's wish to promote positive images of its culture and nation.

> The romantics take those very features of Indian civilization which the utilitarian-minded criticize and see as worthless and find them worthy of study and perhaps even of praise. The very ascetic practices, philosophies, cosmologies, customs, visual art forms, and myths which the utilitarian or materialist finds wasteful, deluded, or even repulsive, the romantic idealist takes up with great fascination.[6]

Inden sees this division between rationalists and cultural relativists as continuing to play itself out in contemporary academic discourse.

> The holders of the dominant view, best exemplified in the past in imperial administrative discourse (and today probably by that of 'development economics'), would place a

traditional, superstition-ridden India in a position of perpet-
ual tutelage to a modern, rational West. The adherents of the
romantic view, best exemplified academically in the discourses of Christian liberalism and analytic psychology, concede this realm of the public and the impersonal to the
positivist. Taking their succour not from governments and
big business, but from a plethora of religious foundations
and self-help institutes, and from allies in the 'consciousness
industry', not to mention the important industry of tourism,
the romantics insist that India embodies a private realm of
the imagination and the religious which modern, western
man lacks but needs.[7]

In practice the boundaries between the two are much blurred.
Christian theology generally imposed western hegemony, and
though not mentioned, the Indian diaspora and its endowments
are having an increasing impact, both positive and negative, on
the western impressions of India. Though different, India is not a
threat to the West, so an indulgent attitude to it is acceptable, and
its values even promoted in off-mainstream circles. Far from
remaining confined to the 'romantics' and cultural relativists, this
positive imagery has also come to pervade more mainstream circles, as exemplified in social science research. What was historically seen as hegemonic and derogatory towards Indian culture
has been replaced by cultural relativism in recent times. The loss
of imperial scholarship has been replaced by a timidity in criticizing other societies that results in distortions of Third World
cultures through lack of critical analysis. Far from representing
western values and institutions, social science has become an
apologist for elite Indian values and institutions with the resultant
erosion of scholarship that arises from this culturally biased positive perception of India.

That these distortions have not totally escaped the attention of
the South Asian studies social science fraternity is indicated by
Brass's critique of how American scholars have become

agents of the government of India rather than the CIA....
Scholars of India in general do research that supports the
image that the government of India wishes to present to the
world, whether of its ancient culture or of its present goals

and aspirations. And we are prevented from doing the research we want to do which the government of India feels will not serve its purposes. The only word for this is pre-censorship. Some of us manage to escape it one way or another, but we as a scholarly community, including our fellowship-granting agencies, have become implicated in this process. We interpret and publicise the information to fellowship applicants that the government of India is un-likely to approve certain topics, and most of us discourage our students from proposing such topics. We allow our projects to be vetted by government bureaucrats, not just for legitimate security concern, but on broadly political and personal grounds as well.[8]

These grounds are determined by 'the appreciation of upper class and upper caste Indians for certain headings and categories of scholarship ... [which] feeds into a nearly two-centuries long political drive by upper caste elites to establish a "national culture" for India based on their own values and interpretation of Indian history'.[9] 'We [scholars] have not as a group lobbied, agitated, or signed statements of protest against the policies of the government of India, despite the fact that its human rights record has been severely criticised by all the leading, impartial international human rights monitoring agencies.'[10] Sunil Dasgupta is even more explicit in naming the institutions responsible for this deception. After frankly stating that 'like all other things Indian, Indian studies is not even at the periphery of American research agendas', he observes that most of this scholarship does not even deal with contemporary social science. The American Institute of Indian Studies (AIIS) commemorative volume had only seven of 30 chapters on contemporary social science. 'The Government of India, and the Indian elite, has for long pursued a policy of discouraging inconvenient research projects such as the continuing existence of "untouchables".' This is also attributed to the Hindu project of the 'NRI activism' which has 'the acquiescence of American scholars'. 'The AIIS, the biggest financier of South Asian studies set-up with crores of PL-480 rupees, has an unstated policy of funding non-controversial projects. This not only encourages research on arcane, Orientalist subjects, but also ensures that access—and this translates basically into visas—

continues to be available for these "softer" projects.' With the rupee funds of the AIIS finally running out there is a danger that in searching for new funding 'the discipline could instead move away, towards a narrower niche, catering for rich, nostalgic Hindus in the West. And then, contemporary India can be truly written off academic agendas'. Stephen Cohen, a professor at the University of Illinois, is quoted as saying,

> Of course, the Government of India will try and keep us out—it is a bureaucracy and bureaucracies do this all over the world—but what upsets me most is being sold down the drain by my own colleagues just for the sake of their own visas. We should have taken a stand on this long ago.[11]

Indians' misrepresentations of their country to westerners has a long history, but the antecedents of the protests against this deception went further back than I had expected. The All-Bengal Namasudra Association protested to the Simon Commission in 1929:

> It has been seen in more than one case that British members of the Indian Civil Service, on account of their living in this country for a long time, and by coming into contact with only a section of the people, are mentally captured by the ideas of those few people who are in the position of social aristocrats.[12]

This historical deception of the British ICS officers continues today with academics, tourists and businessmen, who often lack the interest, time, or opportunity to meet more diversified contacts in non-elite groups.

Indian studies has been divided into foreign and domestic scholarship since the first European contact. Western perceptions of the Middle East have been critiqued by Edward Said as reflecting a pejorative view of Christendom's arch Islamic rivals, but in the case of India, Ronald Inden argues that western perceptions have been more positive.[13] 'The British Orientalists largely ignored the living Hindus and the concrete Hindu practices which surrounded them', preferring to deal with an idealized classical age.[14] 'The "good" Orient was invariably a classical period somewhere in a long-gone India, whereas the "bad" Orient lingered in present-day Asia.'[15] Here the West looks for things lacking in its own society, and sure enough manages to find them. This of course distorts Indian realities, but because it is a positive distortion there is all too ready a confirmation among Indian elites trying to find foreign affirmation for their own culture. In both the Western and Asian interpretations negative realities get downplayed in favour of positive affirmation. For instance, during the Emergency, the government-owned radio would quote every positive comment on the Emergency it could find among foreign observers. More generally, such affirmation points to a lack of western interest in being too hard or critical of India, as reflected in the difficulty of getting human rights abuses recorded in the literature. This also applies to the academic community which all too often adopts the views of the local elites about their society. There is now a body of scholarship which argues that much of the way India is viewed is a result of the distorted perceptions of foreigners, which have come to be accepted not only in the West, but by Indians themselves.[16] This has been criticized as conceding too much influence to the scholarly community, and this is well taken, but aside from the folk traditions of villagers, there is really no other interpretation of India.[17]

There is however a more neglected issue of how the local elites have interpreted Indian traditions to foreigners. Did the Brahmin translators of Hindu codes do an accurate job, or was this merely their view of reality passed off as Indian tradition? In fact, how the foreign scholar views India is largely determined by local elites, and this trend could increase with the burgeoning of domestic scholarship. Marxist interpretations in subaltern studies can read their own values into the lower classes and dismiss the rest as 'false consciousness'.[18]

The foreign versus Indian elite view is illustrated by E.M. Forster's preface to Mulk Raj Anand's novel *Untouchable* which makes a profoundly incorrect assessment of the relative merits of Europeans and Indians writing on India.

> No European, however sympathetic, could have created the character of Bakha, because he would not have known enough about his troubles. And no Untouchable could have written the book, because he would have been involved in

indignation and self-pity. Mr. Anand stands in the ideal position.[19]

European values should enable a greater objectivity and appreciation of reality, but all too often foreign scholars defer, as Forster does here, to the assumed greater knowledge of local intellectual elites. A European might have been better placed to study the subject given less prior knowledge, than a high-caste Indian steeped in his own identity. In his novel Mulk Raj Anand presents an upper-caste Gandhian view of the Untouchable, which is at variance with reality, but which comes to be accepted by readers as authentic.

> *Untouchable* represents the untouchables as they appear to the gaze of an upper class, upper-caste kshatriya Hindu, albeit a Marxist. This caste and class distance between writer and the people he represents results in the erasure in the novel of the voice of the untouchable community as a dissonant discourse in the Indian social fabric. This absence is then substituted by the voices of the nationalist bourgeoisie 'speaking for' the untouchables.[20]

The problems in representing the subalterns are thus common to the humanities and social sciences. Even scholars who consider themselves sympathetic to these people have difficulty authenticating representative opinions from groups they do not belong to. Some Dalit writing is discounted because it does not fit into the paradigms of the dominant academic discourse. While the language of these writings may not be suitable for establishing better public relations with potentially sympathetic audiences in the dominant society, they may have resonance within their own community. These writings then become the raw material for academics in the dominant society to analyze and translate into their paradigms. This can easily result in a loss of authenticity. Publication of this material requires fitting it within conventional approaches acceptable in mainstream outlets. Because India continues to be one of the most inegalitarian and hierarchical societies in the world, there is a lot of room for misrepresentation of uncomfortable realities by nationalist and

Marxist intellectuals claiming to represent the people. Foreigners are in a better position to see through these cultural values. Their views, however, tend to be influenced by the Indian intellectual elites who unconsciously distort the realities they often do not understand themselves. An Indian anthropologist who published her Indian fieldwork memoirs noted that all the American readers of the manuscript stated that they 'didn't know Indians could feel so outside of their own country'.[21] Untouchables have no illusions that the Indian intellectual elites understand their views, but Untouchables are not in the circles visiting scholars normally frequent. Rather foreign and local scholars transmit and reinforce each others' view so that hardly a discordant note need sound, and Untouchable realities are erased. These misconceptions in an increasingly politicized and polarized society can make mutual understanding more difficult given the suspicions that have arisen. A high-caste anthropologist who undertook a study of Untouchable Chamars was told: 'The longer the inquiry the more sinister could be your motive.... In these times why would somebody (especially an Indian) like to know the Chamar in depth? Nobody enquires these days simply for the sake of knowledge. It could be another Brahminical trap.'[22]

Academic researchers are under no obligation to participate in human rights activities, but the absence of any mention of abuses in their writings makes for poor social science research. Most academics do not do original research on human rights, but it is nevertheless incumbent on them to be objective enough not to prevent others from publishing on the subject. This is particularly the case at the empirical level, which exposes specific abuses. It is well known that even a single negative reader evaluation of a book can often block publication, hence the minority view becomes extremely difficult to publish in the more competitive academic presses. As these presses take manuscripts to the stage of evaluation only in exceptional cases, influence and contacts become particularly important in getting even this evaluation done. The academic community in the West has gone to considerable lengths and faced a lot of opposition to achieve affirmative action in faculty hiring, but, ironically, this may have contributed to the views of the Indian elite being entrenched in the profession. The problems of subaltern representation are therefore more acute in India than in other parts of the world where the intelligentsia is more diversified.

One of the few Indian contributions to social science discourse has been that of 'subaltern studies', which is now being replicated in Latin America.[23] Coming from what is arguably the most inegalitarian and socially exclusive country in the world, it is understandable that subaltern scholars should be disproportionately made up of Bengali Brahmins and others of the national and provincial tricaste elite. As West Bengal is more educationally backward than most of the rest of India, and has been officially classified as such, it is perhaps inevitable that subaltern views should be represented by its provincial elites. However, despite claiming to represent subalterns, their views conform to an elite discourse which has little or nothing to do with the way subalterns perceive their world. As intellectuals applying their paradigms to the poor, they need to exercise a great deal of caution in the process to avoid imposing elite political and cultural agendas on them, supposedly in their interest, but also to further their own career objectives. In fact, if there is a theme that unifies the field it is its irrelevance to any conceivable struggle the subalterns might undertake. It is not that subaltern scholars are unaware of the problem; indeed, their theory has taken some of them at least to this conclusion, but they have yet to apply this theory to an actual analysis relevant to a contemporary struggle. For instance, as all informed people in West Bengal were aware of the Marichjhapi massacre, as far as I could tell, it could not have escaped the notice of scholars. Although they cannot be expected to analyze every human rights abuse, there is a significant silence here. Despite their theory taking them to a recognition of the importance of presenting the subalterns without the teleological assumptions of a world capitalist system and class, they are inescapably products of their own class and culture.[24] To really apply their subaltern theory they would have to go outside their caste and culture and not only accept subaltern views on the topics they have chosen, but allow subalterns to choose their subjects of research as well. They would not only have to allow news of the Marichjhapi massacre to be published, they would have to write about it too.

To achieve a more authentic subaltern literature learned articles would then appear with such titles as 'How the London Missionary

Society liberated the Untouchables from the Eternal Damnation of Hinduism'. They must not only let the Untouchables choose their topics, but they must be allowed to express their rage in the writings as well. Considering that there are 16 million Untouchable Christians, their silence in the subaltern literature is significant.[25] Such suggestions may be provocative but they make the point that scholars are really writing about their own values while claiming to represent the poor, so these pretensions need to be exposed.

The fact that colonialism was emancipatory for Untouchables is not reflected in the subaltern literature because it is an affront to the ideology of its authors. While colonialism was genocidal for many Amerindians, the differential ways in which it was received by subaltern groups needs to be analyzed even if it conflicts with the beliefs of upper-caste nationalist authors. Until they break their silence on the issue they have no right to claim to be projecting or representing subaltern views. The reason for the silence of subaltern voices in subaltern studies of course has nothing to do with the inability of the subalterns to speak (if anything they talk too much for the amount that is written), but everything to do with the agendas of the dominant society of which the intellectuals are a part. O'Hanlon and Washbrook are right in pointing out this limitation.

> Ethnographic texts are subject to external as well as to internal relations of production, which include a professional academic apparatus of seminars, lectures and conferences, funding bodies, research councils and committees of appointment. It would be very difficult to deny that this intellectual and institutional apparatus helps set to a considerable extent the agendas and framing questions which ethnographers take with them into the field and that it also exerts a large control in shaping professional standards, styles of writing, and access to publication; in awarding recognition and conferring academic authority; and in approving and financing further research. Local writer-collaborators may indeed have long-lasting and intimate connections with individual ethnographers. It is much less clear what access and influence they, let alone wider and less privileged indigenous audiences, are able to command in these complex external contexts of a text's production.[26]

In my field research in Dandakaranya among the Untouchables whose community members attempted to settle in Marichjhapi, I was told about a missionary who had helped emancipate their caste. Finding it extraordinary that a foreign missionary from a century ago should be remembered by peasants living in mud and thatch huts, I looked up the subaltern literature on the subject. The Brahmin historian Sekhar Bandyopadhyay[27] has undertaken an extensive study of this caste's history. The missionary effort was mentioned in the text, but what was extraordinary was that there was no indication of how the Untouchables as either leaders or followers felt. Though it was clear from the bibliography that the author had collected a considerable number of Untouchable publications of the period, they were rarely quoted or analyzed and the humiliations of untouchability completely sanitized, with the lack of response of the elite caste response to emancipation mentioned but not elaborated. In trying to 'read against the grain'[28] of this subaltern literature it was impossible to understand the views of the Untouchables as I had heard them speak. Even a partial account of the movement is an important contribution, but it is crucial to historical understanding that the subaltern voice not be sanitized in subaltern literature. That this voice is not being presented indicates how much scholars are a product of their nation, class and caste.

As the gap between the Bengali Brahmin and the Untouchable is arguably among the widest between people of the same ethnic group, it is understandable that subaltern scholars have difficulty in bridging it. It is nevertheless important that the alienation of Untouchables be reflected in the literature. The extent of the social distance was indicated to me when a professor related to his experience of taking one of the leading scholars of subaltern studies to the Alipore court where the subaltern scholar was fighting to have his tenant evicted. The professor had achieved almost unprecedented success in getting his own tenant evicted and was hence being requested for hands-on advice. However, in court the subaltern scholar did not behave in a way that would expedite the case. The professor had to tell him that he should not have said that he could not wait because he had a conference to attend in Australia when the clerks and office peons he was talking to did not have enough to eat. He would have to make small talk with them and offer them tea and sit in court repeatedly to ensure that they moved his files. This illustrates the class gap between fellow caste men. In the case of the rural Untouchables, this is even greater, which may explain though not justify the lack of the subaltern in subaltern studies. A Bengali North American professor recounted how at a Calcutta bank he was asked what country he came from. When he asked how they could tell he was a foreigner, they said he had shut the taxi door when he got out. Coming from a culture like this it is not realistic to expect the tricaste elites to access and accurately represent subaltern views. While the logic of their various positions has led them to understand the theoretical necessity of doing so, they have yet to implement it. 'Unless and until such theory joins hands with a language that respects them [subalterns] as possible subjects and speaks in their voices' it will fail.[29]

Finding intellectually appropriate education for and about the subalterns is fraught with difficulties. Those most familiar or most a part of them may not be the most perceptive, or detached enough to make a useful contribution in some types of forum.[30] The parochialism of ethnic movements may make their perspectives of limited academic use. Nevertheless, when accounts of human rights abuse cannot find a place in academic discourse, something about the nature of society is missing that is relevant as at least raw material for more erudite scholarly analysis.

Though Indian subalterns are too marginalized to be effectively heard in scholarship, others such as Amerindians have recently been able to impose their own agenda on academics. Scholars now have to sign legally binding contracts specifying the work the community wants them to do in order to obtain access to it. When the Smithsonian Institution's Museum of the American Indian was handed over to a Native Indian Board, access to its vast collection became difficult for scholars. Federal law now requires museums to return Indian artifacts to the tribes even when this will result in their ceremonial destruction. However, with control moving from scholars to the subalterns other problems arise. By controlling access they can now control criticism, with the result that the scholarship on contemporary Indians has weakened. The lack of contemporary critical literature has meant that Native people have greater scope for projecting their beliefs, but the lack of criticism does not necessarily foster their empowerment. The role of the leadership in moving subaltern consciousness in critical and scientific directions rather than the celebratory directions it might naturally take should not be underestimated. This paramount role is something that subaltern studies have hardly touched on. However the lack of it in the movement is only likely to become visible once the subalterns take state power.

As it becomes increasingly probable that the subalterns will take power through the democratic process, it is unlikely to be a coincidence that scholars of subalterns are leaving the field. In a truculent critique of the subaltern scholars entitled 'Beyond Bhadralok and Bankim Studies', Ramachandra Guha points out that in the first two volumes all 12 chapters were about subalterns but in the two latest volumes only two of the 11 were.[31] Subaltern studies have thus become bhadralok studies, in other words, studies of their own provincial caste/class elite. Having come to the theoretical conclusion that subalterns must be studied in their own terms, they abandon or avoid the field research this would entail and take recourse to the relatively comfortable library research that elite bhadralok studies require. Guha undertakes a personal rendition of the career paths of individual scholars to prove his point, and makes the most charitable interpretation possible that middle age is making rural studies increasingly difficult for these scholars. Less charitably, this could be interpreted as a cause of the failure of Marxism as a field, which should serve to spur the Marxist scholars to look again at subalterns to see how they misinterpreted them. However, rather than study their own mistakes, the field has been abandoned in favour of studies of what they know best, namely, themselves, the bhadralok. For studying their own relatives and ancestors no ideological dissonance or new understanding is required. With an increasingly hostile subaltern population, retreat to the ancestral archives is wholly appropriate. By studying their bhadralok ancestors who made this subaltern hostility inevitable, we may get some insights into how the limitations of their ideologies caused them to lose power.

While tenured academics are in a position to defend their own writing, and have the connections and outlets to do so, the fundamental question must be of who will present the position of human rights victims if the majority of South Asian scholars will not do so, and oppose the publication of the minority that does attempt to expose what is happening in the subcontinent. This is not to say that a determined effort might not result in eventual publication, but for the more prestigious and widely read journals, where only a fraction of articles are accepted, a minority view is unlikely to get past reviewers, even though reviewers make claims to objectivity. However, with journals at least a reader evaluation is generally undertaken, while book manuscripts usually receive only a few minutes of attention and are not read.[32] According to a survey by the Association of American University Presses, 68.6 per cent of books published by university presses are subsidized by outside sources.[33] The only substantive difference from the vanity presses is in the peer review process, though even this is subject to insider bias. The subvention/bribe is beyond the means of many western individual scholars, let alone subalterns from South Asia. With unintroduced manuscripts having a 0.38 and 0.57 per cent publication rate according to two surveys, 'to get a book published, recommendation through an informal circle or network is close to being an absolute necessity'.[34] Untouchables who have approached me about getting their manuscripts published in the West have been disappointed. There were no scholars I knew who had both sympathy and influence. Those who had written on Untouchable issues were not in gatekeeping positions with publishers. Editors who work for publishers change positions frequently, so prior publication does not ensure continuing access. Most foreign scholars came to South Asian subjects enamoured with the field and I knew of none who came looking to expose human rights abuses. Even if fieldwork created a more realistic assessment of the situation, the tendency was not to expose abuses in their field. Though details of the Marichjhapi massacre were published in the more obscure Indian media, and the alternative press exists in both India and the West, their marginal impact implies that mainstream publication is essential for justice to be obtained from authorities. While it is clear that some scholars in the South Asian academic community are prepared to tolerate the exposure of human rights violations, that these appear, from the evidence in the Marichjhapi massacre, to be a minority is an indictment of the academic profession. As people responsible for disseminating the views of the world to students who will become opinion makers, their lack of interest in human rights is disturbing. A course content evaluation of South Asian studies would presumably reflect their lack of concern for human rights. One Harvard professor who noted that the human conditions in India were atrocious found that colleagues in the field had in effect become desensitized to it, concentrating on their particular academic interests instead. Ignoring human rights violations in both publications and lectures, however, leads to a distorted view of the subcontinent.

Anonymous reviewers of academic journals could easily approve articles without fear of reprisal. There is however a group consensus in any profession that mitigates against self-criticism. One university administrator who read this chapter commented that academic egos were fragile enough, and I would never get a university job if I published such things. In this sense independent scholars are free from reprisal and the necessity to conform in a way that university academics are not. That South Asian studies have chosen for so long to avoid paramount human rights questions is indicative both of the mindset in the profession, and the pressures that can be brought to bear on dissenters.

However, academics are usually dependent on informants at various levels, who can either obstruct or facilitate their research. The Dalits have therefore to decide what course to take with them. Attempts to 'pollute' them through offers of food, as happened to Khare,[35] are not likely to expose the prejudices of modern academics, who can in any case 'purify' themselves afterwards. What they need to do instead is insist on seeing their CVs and publications with a request that they point out what has been written about Dalits. While this may not be possible with doctoral students, more senior scholars should have a paper trail that exposes their beliefs. This has been effectively done with Congressional appointment hearings in the United States. If, as is likely, there is not much written of a sympathetic nature, it is a fair bet that future writing will be in a similar vein. Verbal claims of friendship and sympathy should not generally be taken too seriously. Despite what one might think, more in-depth studies aimed specifically at Untouchables are more likely to be sympathetic or become so than those on a larger issue. Though academics might appear rich, their funding is unlikely to permit more than the hiring of an assistant or two. Generally, they have neither the resources to uplift a whole community nor links with the development agencies or government to get them to do this. In fact, development agencies tend not to hold academics in high regard, so unless scholars have personal links their connection with practitioners tend to be tenuous. Except for a few favours to individuals, they are unlikely to bring any direct benefits to the community, and if there is any positive effect at all it will be through their writings. It is therefore incumbent on a community to have these publications surveyed. Beating up academics and journalists as has happened in the past is not good public relations and therefore should be avoided. As the Marichjhapi incident illustrates, the academic community is generally either indifferent or hostile to Untouchable emancipation. The submission of the article put the anonymous referees in the position of being participants in either a cover-up or an exposure of the massacres. Though cover-ups are usually associated with the police, bureaucrats and politicians, in this case they came to apply to scholars as well. That the scholars either refused to take a position or were hostile reveals that when they cannot be held accountable they act in ways detrimental to Untouchables. Only the editors and referees know their identity, but the anonymous sampling is an illustration of attitudes prevalent in the South Asian academic community.

Writing about the massacre, because of its high-level political involvement, was likely to give offence to a number of groups, including Indian nationalists, Marxists, and Caste Hindus, not to mention those with particular party affiliations or friends of the accused. However, even when I excluded criticisms of the academic coverage and stuck to the massacre, the reaction of the referees and editors was still negative, indicating a lack of interest in human rights abuses as a topic for scholarship. By sticking to the facts of the massacre one can argue that the exposure of human rights abuses is not suitable for academic journals, but if one situates it in the academic literature by showing how academics have covered up the incident, thereby making the submission relevant to an academic publication, it offends academic sensibilities. Either way the submission will likely be rejected, so it is impossible to win. After some years I gave up expecting a positive result and submitted in the hope of getting some insight into the mindset of the academic community. Unfortunately, terse rejections without any evaluation was the norm, making any in-depth analysis impossible.

As I became aware of this hostility from submitting variations of these chapters over the years, I had the opportunity to include mention of it in other publications. I had come upon the idea from an interview with a Czech filmmaker who explained how under the Communist regime he submitted safe scripts for the requisite censorship, and at the last moment filmed it differently after which it was too expensive to have the scenes reshot. I did this alteration after the drafts had been passed by the referee/censors at the final copy-editing and proofing stages, but changing a sentence or two hardly does justice to the subject. Ultimately I found the best strategy was to write the South Asian material in a chapter or two of a book on a wider subject, thereby avoiding having to go through the South Asian community during the review process. Fields such as indigenous studies or environmental studies tend to be more receptive to critical analysis than South Asian studies. This will in time no doubt change but it is likely to be government rather than academically driven, with Dalit-demanded government funding being used to promote the field, rather than academics fostering it. The massacre was peripheral to my research and I included it more out of a moral obligation to my informants than any professional utility. It was something to be placed on record and forgotten. However, in attempting publication I came to realize just how strong the resistance was to human rights exposure in the South Asian academic community; and the more opposition I met, the more I was determined to pursue the matter. This was an education for me that I would not have obtained had I not been presented with information on the massacre and felt obliged to put it on record. In this respect Untouchables are unfortunate in being too 'backward' a community to be able to challenge academic perceptions effectively.

In the West faculty who have been accused on often flimsy and trivial grounds (at least compared to India) of racism or sexism have been forced to undergo sensitivity training. In one case, court-ordered sensitivity training was given by blacks to members of the white racist Ku Klux Klan.[36] It is doubtful if forced re-education has the desired effect; it may indeed accentuate initial prejudices, but it does serve to preclude the expression of prejudices. A stronger case can perhaps be made for removing this censorship and allowing the prejudices to come out and be challenged. The difficulty is that this can only work well if there

are people to challenge these ideas on a somewhat equal foot-
ing. This does not exist in South Asian academia, as the difficulty
in getting the massacre exposed illustrates. The very fact of being
able to complain implies the privilege of being enrolled in a
western university to begin with. The Indians who are enrolled
are either from the Indian elite or the children of immigrants who
were themselves generally privileged enough to afford to emi-
grate. The skewing of the diaspora towards certain ethnic groups
and castes means that only certain South Asian issues find a following on western campuses. That the diaspora idealizes their
origins means that their endowments are aimed at a positive projection of whatever they are interested in. It does not stretch the
imagination to presume that if an Untouchable were ever hired
by a western university a presentation of the reality of the community would be offensive to the diaspora which increasingly
funds South Asian university research. What is wanted are 'feel
good' images, and the scholarship contributes to this by presenting sanitized versions of the brutal realities of South Asia. In the
interests of being erudite and theoretical, scholarship leaves out
daily realities in favour of abstractions, which have only a notional bearing on these realities.

The creation of positive images of other cultures in the name of
multiculturalism follows the same course as those it challenges
for projecting the virtues of western civilization.

> It makes sense to demand as a matter of right that we ap-
> proach the study of certain cultures with a presumption of
> their value.... But it can't make sense to demand as a matter
> of right that we come up with a final concluding judgment
> that their value is great, or equal to others.[37]

It would be difficult to argue that Hindu civilization has a concept
of human rights equal to that of the West, though the argument
itself implies a belief in the superiority of the Western view.
When Indians discuss human rights they do so on western terms.
The promoters of Hindu culture are therefore perfectly justified
in not dealing with human rights because it is an alien concept.
For the scholarly community to ignore human rights is to imply their
acceptance of the Hindu terms of reference. This approach is
consistent with cultural relativism in not making value judgements

of other cultures. However, today even the anthropologists who traditionally 'respect every culture-pattern but their own' have recognized that there may be internal cultural criticisms and some values such as opposition to human sacrifice which should be adhered to.[38] Gayatri Chakravorty Spivak's comment about white men saving Indian women from sati (burning widows on their husbands' funeral pyres) raises the point of how far the debate has shifted to western terms of reference. That the reintroduction of sati is not a major issue in India represents a triumph of western values. Once the abolition of sati is justified, it becomes difficult to argue that other western values cannot be imposed as well. And once this is conceded, it may also be accepted that far from the British imposing too much on South Asia, they left the traditional structure too much to its own devices. Their western civilizing mission did not go far enough, or perhaps the natives were just too resistant to enable it to succeed.

Whatever the fault, human rights becomes a major problem in South Asia once the western agenda is accepted. There is no doubt that western values have made inroads into Hindu society over the years. As Andre Beteille observed about caste: 'How does one account for the continued existence of a social arrangement which everyone is eager to attack and no one is prepared to defend?'[39] Though he gives the politicization of caste as an explanation, a more fundamental reason also exists. For lack of a better term it must be called hypocrisy: public utterance versus private thought. None of the editors or referees was prepared to put in writing a defence of the massacre or even state that it should not be recorded, but they nevertheless made sure that it was not published. The CPM at least is more forthright in this respect. The CPM Speaker of the West Bengal Assembly and World President of the United Nations Association in supporting the Tiananmen Square massacre said they were prepared to do the same thing in Calcutta. Such frankness, however, is rare in the academic community. The public and academic debate has often shifted to western values even while the thoughts and actions remain quintessentially Indian. Prime ministers Indira Gandhi and Rao may have appeared westernized in their education and public discourse but followed astrologers and swamis for their political and private direction. In fact, seemingly westernized Indians frequently have only a veneer of westernization. Public discourse is often on a western terrain and even more so in the press and academia, but the thinking and operations behind it are within an Indian mode which includes concerns about caste.

Though variously described as rational versus irrational or non-rational, or modern versus feudal, the unconscious mixture of the modern and traditional makes for the coexistence of constitutional prohibitions on segregation and its unhampered continuance. This is why India can never really be understood by reading academic literature. Contemporary politics and society fits into too many fields to be adequately conveyed. Integrating the psychological, cultural and political views of politicians almost defies non-fiction writing. Non-Indians are extremely reluctant to criticize Indian culture for fear of ethnocentrism, while caste Indians are too steeped in its virtues to truly free themselves of it. The personification of this was Gandhi, who recognized what a challenge untouchability presented to his modernizing Hindu values, yet could not distance himself sufficiently from his culture to allow the emancipation of Untouchables. A comparison with Thomas Jefferson on the question of slavery would make for an interesting study. The best critique of India could perhaps come from an Untouchable who is both within the culture and a victim of it. However, Untouchables do not have the outlets to do this, so the so-called myths of India continue to be perpetuated.

Given the scale of the prejudice and the lack of an Untouchable lobby, sensitivity training for South Asianists will not be forthcoming in western universities, even though it is being increasingly used by women and minorities on individual 'deviants'. This new 'inquisition' which has come to be feared at some universities, represents a challenge from hitherto marginalized groups. But as these groups are not 'truly disadvantaged' in global terms, it raises questions as to the types of complaints that can obtain a hearing. It comes from groups who are privileged enough to be in a position to complain, and this process leaves out a great many people not in a position to challenge the way they are portrayed by academics. Caste Hindus could legitimately claim that sensitivity training is a suppression of their religious beliefs and an imposition of western values, and therefore violates their constitutional rights to freedom of religion and expression. To concede this, however, would mean that regulations can be applied only on a non-religious basis. In India, the idea of sensitivity training would seem almost ludicrous and Untouch-ables providing it in court-ordered courses to Brahmins and violators of human rights would similarly seem absurd. The Com-monwealth Secretariat which undertook human rights training courses for civil servants of Commonwealth countries, found, according to the programme head, that Indians were the most obstructive and detrimental in mobilizing other Third World countries against such sensitivity training. It will be some time before the democratization process in India can weed out these policies. It would be a mistake to think that the academic com-munity in India and abroad can escape the consequences of this process. Already Brahmins have been virtually excluded from many jobs in Tamil Nadu, and this exclusion is spreading else-where. Though the first Untouchable graduated from university only in this century, there is a growing number of Untouchables able to evaluate the academic contribution to their emancipation, and find it wanting. At one Learneds Conference a political scien-tist observed that in the Third World it was now difficult to do research without local academic collaborators even though they were not much good. The problem of access will grow as people become aware of how they are portrayed in the literature. Even if the latest theories give them a greater role in their own history, scholars will be judged, whether fairly or not, on the academic legacy. This is more likely to lead to blanket prohibitions than selective evaluations, which is unfortunate for there are individu-als who have attempted to bring issues such as Untouchable and tribal emancipation to the world community. With democratiza-tion, these people are likely to find more favour than those who were deafening in their silence. By then most of the academics will have retired, but the consequences for better or for worse will be passed on to their students, who are likely to find access restricted at the national, state and local levels. This has already happened in the Native American communities where social sci-entists can obtain access only through committing themselves to undertaking research in accordance with an aboriginal agenda. They have to state half-truths in court as expert witnesses and avoid uncomplimentary assessments that would result in loss of community access, with the result that scholarship has been badly affected. Others, preferring not to deal directly with Natives, have resorted to library work on ethnohistory.

One overseas Untouchable observed that the only university lectures he had given were those organized by himself, as the South Asian studies programme never invited him to speak despite his knowing the professors for years. The faculty was perfectly aware of the existence of untouchability but chose to omit it from the curriculum, perhaps because of the possible negative consequences from the east Indian diaspora and Indian government. These consequences are probably exaggerated, and may reflect more on the personal prejudices and beliefs of the professors themselves, but in either case the silence on the issue speaks volumes about the profession. What is needed is to provide incentives for them to deal with untouchability, but this would require a lot of money for endowments and research funding, which is not available. Only negative sanctions are therefore available to subordinate groups, but lack of suitable information has prevented their being used effectively. Fortunately, with the Internet this problem is being resolved and plans are under way to take the Internet to the district level. When this is achieved it will be possible for villagers to access information about visiting scholars quickly and at an affordable cost from people who know about them. With this information they will be in a position to corroborate or contradict the claims scholars may make about their views and intentions. If they have nothing in their course curriculum about untouchability it will become known to the local Dalits who can then decide what they want to do with this information. At lectures they can boycott or question scholars about their positions. Though foreign scholars may be employed by influential institutions and funding agencies, these institutions can be intimidating for individual scholars. Universities now have ethics committees which scrutinize the research proposals concerning human issues. As one sociology professor observed: 'Those familiar with fieldwork conditions in Latin America, Africa, or Asia know how exceptional is Mexico's unfettered freedom to do research. Indeed, I encountered more difficulties doing research on my own campus (especially from the petty bureaucracy of the Human Subjects Review Committee) than I have in Mexico.'[40] With e-mail addresses, these committees can be supplied with current information on their scholar's activities through the assistance of local and foreign NGOs even before the scholar has returned home. In some universities it is now the practice for professors to leave their office doors open when meeting students out of fear of being subjected to harassment charges. The possibilities the Internet provides will no doubt result in false or trivial complaints, but it is the only avenue subordinate groups will have of obtaining redress since their own national institutions do not work for them. The faculty will generally say whatever seems appropriate to obtain community access, but by using the Internet the claims can be verified by others in the scholars' home countries who keep track of scholarly paper trails, and can supply these to the local villagers. Before the Internet, it was in the interest of scholars to remain in the good books of foreign governments and intellectual elites for visas and affiliations, and therefore curb their criticisms. Now for the first time subordinate peoples will be in a position to also act as gatekeepers on the basis of substantive information.

The role of scholars is marginal to most subaltern activities and likely to be insignificant to villagers. Development agencies by contrast have considerable patronage to dispense and are therefore much more important institutions. These agencies have little to do with scholars except in so far as they are hired as consultants. Since there is relatively little research on agency activities that is not dependent on them, their findings tend to be compromised. Likewise, internal reviews are even less likely to reveal defects in programme implementation since these are often meant for fund-raising activities. Aid is dispensed through local patronage networks usually formed of local elites whose relatives or ancestors are or were generally the local exploiters of subordinate peoples. Subordinate groups may do better work but lack the connections with development agencies to access funding agencies directly. Once patronage connections are established, the foreign aid agencies have no incentive to look further afield for new groups outside the existing networks. Long established organizations are perceived to be less likely to be fraudulent, and able to undertake the book keeping and escorted tours for visitors aid donors require. Foreign aid agencies therefore have a bureaucratic interest in sticking to known people and organizations and not disturbing the relationship. There are few truly independent evaluations, as most that do take place are for publicity or for preventing fraud. National and local elites control the patronage at the village level. They pay lip service to the line the aid agency is currently promoting, since people who do not do so will lose the funding. Aid agencies have adopted human rights as a current interest but according to one South Asian human rights activist, these agencies rarely push the issue. Like their policies of transparency, human rights policies are usually observed in the breach, with a rhetorical adherence for the purposes of public relations back home. I know of no foreign aid agency which goes even so far as to follow the Indian government's job reservation quotas for tribals or Untouchables. There is a high degree of hypocrisy in criticizing the Indian government when they do even less about employment equity within their own organizations than the government they criticize. Unlike the Indian government which, for all its faults, is still subject to an electorate that includes a lot of poor people, foreign aid agencies are subject to no one except perhaps their donors, who have a hazy notion of what their money is being used for, thanks to the agency publicity material and the self-interested evaluations provided by the consultancy industry. Nor are the largest southern NGOs substantially different.

The biggest and best known Southern NGOs—Sarvodaya in Sri Lanka; BRAC (the Bangladesh Rural Advancement Committee), Proshika and Grameen Bank in Bangladesh; the Aga Khan Rural Support Programmes (AKRSP) in India and Pakistan—none are membership organizations in the Korten sense; none have more than traces of what could be described as democratic management; and few would survive in recognizable form if they were forced to become financially self-reliant in a short space of time.[41]

Until now development agencies have been able to control access to information about their programmes for purposes of bureaucratic self-preservation and fund raising. New subordinate groups are rarely included except when recommended by local dominant groups, with the result that some of the worst tendencies can get exacerbated and genuine grassroots organizations ignored or co-opted. The last thing aid agencies want are independent evaluations of their work, for this threatens their reputation with funders. Development agencies are particularly sensitive to complaints that go to the foundations and donors who pay their salaries and keep them employed. With the Internet it will be possible for subordinate groups to report on nepotism and local patronage from anywhere in the world to the people supplying the funding. Though agencies keep the identities of individual donors confidential, the larger donors are generally known. In the case where an agency is a government institution, complaints to Congressmen, members of parliament and ministers are most likely to obtain results. It has never ceased to amaze me how intimidated bureaucrats with secure jobs can be by complaints from MPs and ministers. However, access to government is also the most difficult.

The difference between policy and implementation can only be exposed if local non-beneficiaries can participate in the evaluation process. When scholars undertake independent research on development projects their work tends not to be widely read even by the organizations which fund them. The gap between scholars and development administrators was revealed by the case of the vice president of a multibillion dollar government international development agency who had never heard of the academic journal *World Development* despite a lifetime in the field. Development policy represents a rhetorical device for the donor public but rarely gets applied that way on the ground. Organizations that represent minority groups or marginalized groups are particularly handicapped because, despite all the rhetorical claims of development agencies about human rights, they are unwilling to offend host governments and local elites. In one case the South Asian Partnership, which is a consortium of Canadian Aid organizations working in South Asia, agreed to organize a press conference for a visiting Dalit activist only to admit just before the meeting that they had done nothing about it. Whether from deliberate sabotage or cold feet, the reaction is typical of development agencies which feel the need to justify their existence by proclaiming adherence to human rights issues, while doing nothing about it in practice. This is the general pattern in fact.

Overseas the actual projects supported by indigenous non-profits in Third World countries are far less threatening to the established order than their image or the rhetoric of North Atlantic donor PVOs/NGOs would indicate. They too represent diverse interests, normally including quite politically and economically conservative grassroots groups that they aid.... Hence, the international nonprofit sector does not present serious threat to nation-state stability at present, but actually enhances it. In so doing, however, it is acting in pursuit of agendas that extend well beyond charity and altruism, at times with the appearance (albeit not in actuality) of being a serious foe of nation state interests.[42]

With the Internet it will be possible to expose fraudulent activities to donors and for the first time in history make agencies responsive to people outside the patronage network and to those who donate money but do not have an accurate idea of what is happening to it. The development of such networks to curb the power of scholars and aid agencies to misrepresent the peoples in whose name they claim to be working will not be welcomed despite some rhetorical adherence to transparency.

In the present circumstances, where the perpetrators of prejudice cannot be effectively challenged, the responsibility for coming to terms with their own situation must fall on the victims. A professor told me of an Untouchable faculty member at his former institution who arrived humble and diffident, but over the years became increasingly difficult, and obstructive to the working environment at the university. In a similar case in British India, the Bengal Governor Lord Brabourne in his confidential report to the Viceroy Lord Linlithgow stated that the first Untouchable Minister was 'quite able but he, unfortunately, suffers from a severe inferiority complex which results in frequent outbursts of offensiveness towards members of the Services and people whom he fears are laughing at him behind his back'.[43] A professor who has studied the neo-Buddhist movement in India observed that Dr Ambedkar had similar difficulties. Such problems under conditions of discrimination will perhaps inevitably lead to some overreaction, and the imagining of prejudices which are not always there. Bell Hooks argues that for Afro-Americans 'politicised mental care is the next revolutionary frontier' and psychoanalysis offers hope if suitably adapted to redemption from history.[44] Whether or not it can make a difference, it is impractical in the poverty of Indian conditions, and reflects a western middle-class solution which is beyond the means of even the Untouchable elites who have too many family obligations to be able to afford to indulge in it. It therefore appears that once the Untouchables take power, the higher castes, for the sins of their ancestors, will have to put up with them.

An observer of the Soviet experience noted the effect of 'group think' on Sovietology where predominant paradigms got accepted and only a few voices of dissent were heard, which in a very few cases got it right and predicted the collapse of the Soviet bloc. In an open society such as India, access to information is not the primary problem; the problem lies in the selection of what is appropriate for research and publication. This reflects the values of intellectual elites in both South Asia and the West. The intellectual elites may represent an example of the 'Stockholm syndrome', named after an incident in Sweden where the victim identified with the captor. A more pertinent case might be of the *New York Times* correspondents who adopted the positions of the respective sides they were covering in the Spanish Civil War. Scholars like everyone else get socialized in the society they live in, and since visiting scholars tend to move in the more intellectual elite circles, they may have a tendency to adopt the positions of the host elite. As this indigenous elite is arguably the most narrowly based in the world, yet large in number (India has 190 universities, 7,000 colleges, and 1,700 research institutes[45]), there is plenty of scope and material for the transmission of Indian elite views to western scholars. Marshall Sahlins, in his controversy with the Sri Lankan Gananath Obeyesekere, states that South Asians 'are historically more closely related to native Western anthropologists than they are to Hawaiians'.[46] It can also be added that Western scholars have more in common with their counterparts in South Asia than with the lower classes in each other's country. The old colonial concept of 'going Native' is now replaced by the question of which Natives do you go with. Whether it is the Brahmin or the tribal makes a big difference in outlook, and the hegemonic culture of the dominant society will always have an advantage in cultural transmission for western scholars, save those actively pursuing subaltern research. By contrast, there are hardly any Untouchable Ph.Ds. One book published in the 1980s refers to the discriminatory practices by colleagues against the only Untouchable Ph.D. in a south Indian state.[47] According to the *New York Times* South Asia correspondent: 'A dominant regional power, in this case India, with a polished diplomatic corps and dedicated supporters abroad, can manipulate international opinion to the disadvantage of weaker parties. The result often frames the rest of the world's views of the disputes.'[48]

This negative influence on South Asian human rights issues was probably compounded by the American university affirmative action programmes meant for black faculty hiring. Since the number of qualified blacks was insufficient, Indians came to take some of these positions. Thus an American intellectual elite intent on diversifying its membership to include marginalized blacks, ended up hiring an even more narrowly based elite from India. An intellectual elite generally opposed to affirmative action in India thus took advantage of it in America. This hiring substitution was unknown to me until a Brahmin professor at the City University of New York (CUNY) explained what had happened in the immigration wave of the 1960s and 1970s. This Indian intellectual diaspora has perpetuated elite cultural myths about India abroad and hindered a more balanced and negative view of the country. In the case of endowed chairs funded by the Sikh community, they have even attempted to regulate uncritical study of their own religion. On account of the lack of Untouchable social scientists in western universities the alternative view has been represented by white American academics, who with few exceptions soon move on to other fields given the limited interest in the subject. When I suggested to a Dean at Harvard the possibility of launching an academic journal on Untouchables, who comprise nearly 3 per cent of the human race, he rightly pointed out that there was neither the funding for the project nor sufficient specialists in the field to write for such a journal. By contrast, Jews and American blacks, though far fewer in number but with much greater resources, were able to develop their ethnic studies into a legitimate and recognized academic field.

One reader objected that India now has human rights organizations and therefore a local interest exists. However, one wonders whether it is a coincidence that these organizations should arise just when there is funding for them from the West. As one former Pakistani government official observed, the explosion in the number of NGOs there is more likely to reflect outside interest from the donor community than any equivalent groundswell in civil society. It is only rational for organizations in the Third World to tailor their agenda to obtain foreign funding.[49] When I first worked in India and moved in Indian government circles I had the impression that things were domestically driven. But when I subsequently returned as a consultant to the Canadian foreign ministry I was able to use a different network to access the NGO community. In one case I visited a human rights organization without an appointment in case their phone was tapped, as they claimed it was. They also knew that their mail was opened, as they received mail on Sunday and once their mail was switched with Oxfam's. They wanted to launch a joint protest to the Indian government but Oxfam declined to be drawn into the issue. However, they did maintain contacts and had support from foreign embassies and so an Indian intelligence interest was understandable. Even the human rights organizations admitted that compared to India's neighbours this monitoring function was more sophisticated and less obtrusive. Though there are undoubtedly many genuine promoters of human rights in South Asia, I have serious doubts that they would have the clout and wherewithal to make such an impact if it were not on the western agenda.

It has been frequently pointed out that the West also has its violations of human rights, but the failures of one system do not justify those of the other. There is no doubt that there is a fair degree of hypocrisy in western allegations of human rights abuses. This was illustrated when the Canadian prime minister and most of the provincial premiers went to India and Pakistan to promote Canadian business interests, while playing to the gallery back home by denouncing human rights abuses in South Asia. They did not take any steps to do anything that would interfere with their business interests, however. A former colleague at the Canadian foreign ministry who helped organize the South Asia trip told a group of friends how he had arranged with the local hotel staff to have the 13-year-old Canadian child labour activist Craig Kielburger trapped in an elevator to prevent him meeting Prime Minister Chrétien. This attempt at Indo-Canadian cooperation failed when the media took up the issue and Chrétien had to meet Mr Kielburger in New Delhi. They had barely got back home when they went to court to prevent their own Royal Commission on AIDS from assigning individual, Red Cross, or government responsibility for infecting patients with AIDS through failure to test or get rid of infected blood supplies, as was occurring at the time in other western countries. By taking the Royal Commission they had appointed to court and dragging on the case till the AIDS victims had died, the Red Cross, all but one provincial government, and the Federal government hoped to avoid legal consequences for their actions.[50] This was followed not long after by the government taking the unprecedented step of closing down the inquiry they had appointed to look into the torture and murder of civilians by Canadian UN peacekeeping troops in Somalia. As the inquiry was reaching the stage where a cover-up by the current government might be revealed in the run-up to a general election, the negative comments by the media and opposition parties were presumably a small price to pay to prevent embarrassing revelations. However, with the wide publicity these cases generated, the individuals and governments would be discredited regardless of the outcome, and politicians, bureaucrats and the governments in general held in the almost universal disrepute that has come to be felt by civil society around the world. Politicians and bureaucrats behave in much the same way the world over if given the opportunity to abuse their power, and having seen something of how they operate in South Asia and the West I am not so sure that such a great difference exists between administrations as northerners like to think. IAS officers who have to put down police mutinies and communal riots have duties that would be beyond the capabilities of many of their western counterparts. Having indicated by this that I do not hold a brief for the Canadian government, it must also be said that institutional and civil constraints on the abuse of power in advanced democracies are qualitatively different from those in South Asia. This does not mean that civil liberties do not have to be continuously fought for in the West, but the institutions of the state tend to operate more independently of the particular interests of powerful individuals. That Indian institutions are beginning to show some of this independence in the courts through bringing cases against leading politicians is indicative that this democratization process is occurring in South Asia as well. The anti-corruption drives of Italy and Korea are an indication that India may become a participant in this global movement.[51] If it does not then the movement will have to rely on external pressures, which means getting South Asian human rights issues on the western agenda.

Getting on the western agenda is no mean feat. When I visited the London headquarters of Amnesty International as a representative of the Native Council of Canada to enquire about their aboriginal rights activities I was told that increasing the aboriginal profile required emulating the homosexual's strategy. The homosexuals had over many years targeted Amnesty and become actively involved as members in order to push the gay rights agenda higher up on the organization's priorities. The difficulty with this strategy is that while there are many gays in London and other western capitals, aboriginals in such places are few and far between. When it comes to Untouchables, their lack of education and money, and virtual absence from the Indian diaspora makes such a strategy impossible. At the United Nations in Geneva, the Human Rights Centre admitted to me that they were flooded every year by thousands of complaints and were unable to handle the load. Perhaps this was the reason my three letters and reports on Marichjhapi to Human Rights Watch received only a form-letter response with no indication of the material having been read. With the human rights organizations overwhelmed with complaints, it is perfectly understandable why nothing much gets done about individual massacres that have no lobby backing the protest. This gap in the dissemination of information on human rights abuses can be filled by scholarly publications.

Even if a South Asian cause were to get on the western agenda, staying on it presents practically insurmountable obstacles, for western interests are changeable and follow trends that have little to do with South Asian needs. South Asian constituencies have to package their causes according to the current western ideas and influential lobby groups. The most prominent of these are the environmental and feminist movements in the West, the Marxist movement having at least temporarily lost its salience there. Unique South Asian causes such as untouchability that do not relate to contemporary western experiences do not have a ready-made western constituency that can be mobilized. Even groups such as the Sikhs and Tamils for all their funding and contacts have had to rely on their own diaspora and have never made significant inroads into the western NGO movement. The most recent success story in terms of Third World causes making First World connections has been of aboriginal peoples tying their human rights with the environmental movement. However, the western movement quickly picked up and subsequently dropped various indigenous leaders and organizations which did not perform to its expectations. Indigenous

power exists only so long as Indians' political identities resonate with Western ideas and symbols; transnational symbolic politics accommodates indigenous definitions of identity and goals only to the extent that they coincide with global concerns and trends of the moment.... In capitalizing on symbolic values bestowed from the outside, native Amazonian activists may, ironically, have substituted one form of political dependency for another.[52]

The lack of sustainable western interest in many South Asian human rights causes means that much of the agenda will be dependent on domestic constituencies even when jump-started by foreign agencies. This relative autonomy from foreign movements may give the domestic sources of human rights activism greater resilience and longevity than more externally dependent peoples and causes. The more domestically driven the agenda, the less anti-national these issues are likely to be perceived. The weaker the domestic constituency, the more imperative it is to obtain foreign backing.

REFERENCES

1. W.H. Morris-Jones, 'India's Political Idioms', in C.H. Philips (ed.), *Politics and Society in India* (London: George Allen & Unwin Ltd, 1963), p. 133.
2. Marguerite S. Robinson, *Local Politics: The Law of the Fishes* (Delhi: Oxford University Press, 1988), p. 150.
3. Morris-Jones 'India's Political Idioms' (n. 1 above), p. 133.
4. James Walsh, 'India: Special Report', *Time*, 25 March 1996, p. 38.
5. Samuel P. Huntington, 'The Clash of Civilizations?', *Foreign Affairs*, Vol. 72, No. 3, Summer 1993, pp. 22–49.
6. Ronald Inden, 'Orientalist Constructions of India', *Modern Asian Studies*, Vol. 20, No. 3, 1986, p. 430.
7. Ibid., p. 442.
8. Paul R. Brass, 'American Political Science and South Asian Studies: Virtue Unrewarded', *Economic and Political Weekly*, Vol. XXX, No. 36, 9 September 1995, p. 2261.
9. Ibid., p. 2260.

10. Ibid., p. 2261.
11. Sunil Dasgupta, 'Hung-up on the Past: Research on India is Dominated by History', *India Today*, North American Edition, 15 December 1996, p. 48f.
12. *Simon Commission Report on India (Indian Statutory Commission)* Volume XVII Selections from Memoranda and Oral Evidence by Non-Officials (Part II) (reprinted by Swati Publications, Delhi, 1988), pp. 92–93, quoted in A.K. Biswas, 'The Namasudras of Bengal: Profile of a Persecuted People', Paper presented at the 19th Indian Social Sciences Congress, Allahabad, 11–14 March 1996, p. 14.
13. Edward Said, *Orientalism* (New York: Vintage, 1992); Ramachandra Guha, 'Radical American Environmentalism and Wilderness Preservation: A Third World Critique', *Environmental Ethics*, Vol. 11, No. 1, Spring 1989, p. 77, citing Ronald Inden, 'Orientalist Constructions of India' (n. 6 above), p. 442.
14. Andrea Grace Diem and James R. Lewis, 'Imagining India: The Influence of Hinduism on the New Age Movement', in James R. Lewis and J. Gordon Melton (eds), *Perspectives on the New Age* (Albany: State University of New York Press, 1992), p. 52.
15. Edward W. Said, *Orientalism* (n. 13 above), p. 99.
16. Ronald Inden, *Imagining India* (Oxford: Basil Blackwell, 1990). Edward W. Said, *Orientalism* (n. 15 above).
17. Declan Quigley, Review of *Imagining India* by Ronald Inden, in *Modern Asian Studies*, Vol. 20, No. 2, 1991, p. 406.
18. Partha Chatterjee, *Nationalist Thought and the Colonial World: A Derivative Discourse*, (London: Zed Books, 1986), p. 100; Sumit Sarkar, *Modern India, 1885–1947* (New York: St Martin's Press, 1989), p. xxiii.
19. Mulk Raj Anand, *Untouchable*, with a Preface by E.M. Forster (London: Penguin Books, 1940), p. vii.
20. Arun P. Mukherjee, 'The Exclusions of Postcolonial Theory and Mulk Raj Anand's *Untouchable*: A Case Study', *Ariel*, Vol. 22, No. 3, July 1991, p. 36.
21. Nita Kumar, *Friends, Brothers, Informants: Fieldwork Memoirs of Banaras* (Berkeley: University of California Press, 1992), p. 5.
22. R.S. Khare, *The Untouchable as Himself: Ideology, Identity, and Pragmatism Among the Lucknow Chamars* (Cambridge: Cambridge University Press, 1984), p. 13.
23. Florencia E. Mallon, 'The Promise and Dilemma of Subaltern Studies: Perspectives from Latin American History', *American Historical Review*, Vol. 99, No. 5, December 1994, p. 1491.
24. Gyan Prakash, 'Can the "Subaltern" Ride? A Reply to O'Hanlon and Washbrook', *Comparative Studies in Society and History*, Vol. 34, No. 1, January 1992, p. 182.
25. A.M.M. Vetticad, 'Mother Teresa: Cause with a Difference', *India Today*, 15 December 1995, p. 17.
26. Rosalind O'Hanlon and David Washbrook, 'After Orientalism: Culture, Criticism, and Politics in the Third World', *Comparative Studies in Society and History*, Vol. 34, No. 1, January 1992, p. 163.
27. Shekhar Bandopadhyay, *Caste, Politics and the Raj* (New Delhi: K.P. Bagchi & Co. 1990) and 'From Alienation to Integration: Changes in the Politics of

Caste in Bengal, 1937–47', *The Economic and Social History Review*, Vol. 31, No. 3, 1994.
28. Florencia E. Mallon, 'The Promise and Dilemma of Subaltern Studies: Perspectives from Latin American History', *American Historical Review*, Vol. 99, No. 5, December 1994, p. 1506.
29. Larry M. Preston, 'Theorizing Difference: Voices from the Margins', *American Political Science Review*, Vol. 89, No. 4, December 1995, p. 946.
30. Susan Moller Okin, 'Gender Inequality and Cultural Differences', *Political Theory*, Vol. 22, No. 1, February 1994, p. 19.
31. Ramachandra Guha, 'Discussion: Beyond Bhadralok and Bankim Studies', *Economic and Political Weekly*, Vol. XXXI, No. 8, 24 February 1996, p. 496.
32. Walter W. Powell, *Getting into Print: The Decision-Making Process in Scholarly Publishing* (Chicago: The University of Chicago Press, 1985), p. 227.
33. Ibid., p. 230.
34. Ibid., pp. 169, 171–72.
35. R.S. Khare, *The Untouchable as Himself: Ideology, Identity and Pragmatism Among the Lucknow Chamars* (Cambridge: Cambridge University Press, 1984).
36. Dinesh D'Souza, *The End of Racism* (New York: The Free Press, 1995), p. 393.
37. Charles Taylor, *Multiculturalism* (Princeton: Princeton University Press, 1994), pp. 68–69.
38. Wilcomb E. Washburn, 'Cultural Relativism, Human Rights, and the AAA [American Anthropological Association]', *American Anthropologist*, Vol. 89, No. 4, December 1987, p. 939.
39. Andre Beteille, 'The Reproduction of Inequality: Occupation, Caste and Family', *Contributions to Indian Sociology*, Vol. 25, No. 1, 1991, p. 23.
40. Pierre L. van Den Berghe, *The Quest for the Other: Ethnic Tourism in San Cristobal, Mexico* (Seattle: University of Washington Press, 1994), p. 24.
41. Ian Smillie, *The Alms Bazaar: Altruism under Fire—Non-Profit Organizations and International Development*, (Ottawa: International Development Research Centre, 1995), pp. 32–33.
42. Brian H. Smith, *More than Altruism: The Politics of Private Foreign Aid* (Princeton: Princeton University Press, 1990), p. 23.
43. Lord Brabourne, Governor's Half Yearly Report on Ministers to Viceroy Lord Linlithgow, 20 June 1939, London, India Office Library, p. 125.
44. Bell Hooks quoted in Sian Griffiths, 'A Class Sister Act', *The Times Higher Education Supplement*, 13 October 1995, p. 20.
45. Paul Kennedy, *Preparing for the Twenty-First Century* (New York: Harper Collins Publishers Ltd, 1993), p. 179.
46. Marshall Sahlins, 'How "Natives" Think', *Times Literary Supplement*, 2 June 1995, p. 12.
47. Partap Chand Aggarwal, *Halfway to Equality* (Delhi: Manohar, 1983), p. 147.
48. Barbara Crossette, 'Hatreds, Human Rights, and the News: What We Ignore', *SAIS Review*, Vol. 13, No. 1, Winter–Spring 1993, p. 5.
49. C.A. Meyer, 'Opportunism and NGOs: Entrepreneurship and Green North-South Transfers', *World Development*, Vol. 23, No. 8, August 1995, pp. 1277–90.

50. David Spurgeon, 'Legal Action "May End Search for Truth" in Canada's HIV Inquiry', *Nature*, Vol. 379, No. 6565 8 February 1996, p. 479.
51. John F. Burns, 'High-Level Graft Case Rocks India's Political Establishment', *The New York Times*, 22 January 1996, p. A5.
52. Beth A. Conklin and Laura R. Graham, 'The Shifting Middle Ground: Amazonian Indians and Eco-Politics', *American Anthropologist*, Vol. 97, No. 4, December 1995, p. 705.

CHAPTER 13

The New World Order

The extinction of the Soviet Union put South Asia in a difficult position, requiring a reappraisal of the region's place in the world. The promotion of non-alignment in a world which is no longer bipolar has ceased to be a policy option. South Asia will have to determine its role in an era in which the Third World has increasingly limited power and policy options. Finding a niche in this 'new world order' points to the limitations of a nation-state in a world which may dictate terms to South Asia or simply ignore it.

The Colonial Legacy and Politicized Ethnicity

The political scientist and former Indian Planning Commission member Rajni Kothari states that 'large sections of the administration are being forced to act as middlemen of corruption and criminal actions of ministers and their relatives and henchmen'.[1] The situation in neighbouring nations is if anything even worse.

The fact of the matter is that concepts of merit, equality and justice were alien values which never really extended beyond the western-influenced elite. What remains of these values in the institutions of the post-colonial state are colonial legacies and western values coexisting uneasily with local cultures. The post-independent Indian state was already basically in place by the mid-1930s. The affirmative action programmes were colonial impositions as were the administrative services that the Congress party chose to continue. The post-colonial elites maintained these institutions and accommodated opposition groups or repressed them if they turned violent. It is this accommodation process rather than the colonial institutions of governance left by the imperial powers that has made India almost unique in the Third World. Other countries such as Sri Lanka maintained the democratic colonial institutions but failed to accommodate minorities, making their democracy only a nominal one. This accommodation process is part of the Nehru and Congress legacy, but it occurred in a milieu conducive to it. The country was too ethnically diverse and the elite too diffused for any one group to dominate. As long as the Hindu majority did not coalesce in following a religious party the basis for ethnic dominance was not there.

When the colonial powers left, their institutions were gradually eroded by corruption, inefficiency and the politicized ethnicity of dominant groups. Western influence has continued, but more in the areas of technology and entertainment. The superficial has been adopted and the more developmental values conveniently ignored. This is likely to be accelerated by the spread of satellite television. The values of the colonial era have disappeared and been replaced by mores not conducive to rapid development. The cultural values that enabled the phenomenal growth of East Asia are not sufficiently prevalent in South Asia to be determinants in societal development.

A central feature of Indian civilization [is its] extraordinary capacity to bend without breaking, to accommodate themselves to change without discontinuity or collapse. They have more than held their own in the encounter with market forces over recent decades and have managed to produce curious hybrids of traditional social structures and capitalism.[2]

In retrospect, it is clear that the post-colonial state is actually the colonial state with new rulers. The foundations were laid in the Government of India Act of 1935 and with modifications continue to the present day.[3] The new rulers were in many ways more circumscribed in their ability to radically restructure and reform society than their colonial predecessors. While the British had to accommodate local elites to sustain their rule, they were more prepared to undertake fundamental restructuring of traditional society than the Congress system which succeeded it. For instance, they did more for the radical political mobilization of Untouchables than the Congress ever did. Alien conquering rulers are often in a better position to restructure subject societies than indigenous rulers with only local sources of political support, which was the fundamental dilemma of the Congress system. While the socialist idealists might prefer a secular democratic society, this did not prove to be a workable combination.[4] Democracy enabled and promoted political mobilization but in a skewed direction under the auspices of dominant rural elites that came to have a veto power over legislation detrimental to their interests; hence, the continuance of caste apartheid and other traditional customs. Secularism had no basis beyond the elite, and ethnicity soon proved a political basis for mobilization. The system's deliverance lay in the fact that ethnicity was divided by language, caste and religion, so no group could achieve hegemony and most accepted a modus operandi that enabled them to achieve limited powers and privileges for their own constituencies.[5] Only the rise of the BJP has threatened this accommodative politics, though whether its base can be expanded sufficiently to take power, and whether it will restructure the system if it takes office, remains to be seen. The rise of the BJP does not necessarily imply a holocaust for Muslims, but an erosion of rights and further discrimination seems inevitable. India will then become a country for the new religious majority in a way it was not before. Muslims will then be second-class citizens like minorities in neighbouring states. However, should the BJP's dominance be achieved splits will soon appear, making for renewed coalitions and accommodations with minorities. For the sake of electoral necessity even the BJP proved willing to solicit Dalit support, and the Hindu fundamentalists no longer appear with the unity they once claimed.

In some ways the recent growth of ethnicity is a throwback to the colonial era, when politics was consciously divided on religious and ethnic lines, with only the Congress attempting to claim a national universal following. The use of ethnicity for maintaining power was widespread in the British empire, but was repressed by post-colonial states as subversive to the nation-building process.

India has avoided the repression of non-violent uses of ethnicity, which would in any case have been difficult given the country's diversity. There has, however, been an attempt in nationalist historiography to present ethnic manifestations as a product of colonial manipulation, with the implication that ethnicity is somehow less legitimate as a result. By contrast the nation-state, which uses its educational system and media to promote national unity, is considered totally legitimate. This view has come about from reading present perspectives into the past. Historians look back to the period when modern politicized ethnicity first manifested itself under colonial rule, and in reading the reactions of colonial rulers who first recorded the phenomena attribute sinister motives to them, when they were merely reacting to events and possibly assisting them in directions politically favourable to the colonial state.

This view is most clearly illustrated in the scholarly argument that Hinduism, as commonly conceived, is a European creation, adopted and politicized by Indian elites among a population which never really considered themselves as belonging to a larger tradition. 'In many respects the intellectual activities of the orientalist have even produced in India the very Orient which it produced in its discourse.'[6] This assigns a degree of importance to the intelligentsia out of proportion to the reality on the ground. The orientalists studied castes and religions with the same motives as they catalogued plants and animals, and while this intellectual curiosity may have led colonial administrators and westernized Indians to see the country in a certain way, it was largely irrelevant to how the vast majority of the people saw themselves. To regard ethnicity, and particularly religion, as a colonial construct is to gloss over a folk tradition that would inevitably adapt to wider fields of communication and economic interaction in the face of colonial integration in the global market. 'The enlargement of the potentially effective scales of social relationships' set the stage for the politicization of ethnicity brought on by the nationalist movement and the colonial state's counter mobilization.[7] The effect of seeing ethnicity as a colonial construct is to negate the real divisions in Indian society which existed for centuries and rationalized considerable exploitation and oppression. The British Raj came and went but hardly made an impact on the local traditions of village life. To attribute to colonial rule the politicization of ethnicity is to ignore its inevitability in a plural society mobilizing itself. Colonialism could not have worked with material that was not already there, and if it worked at all it was because indigenous interests wished it so.

The problem was not excessive colonial manipulation, but that colonial rulers did not manipulate and restructure society sufficiently to lay the groundwork for making India an industrialized dynamic force in the modern world. The British were too few and the Indians too numerous for colonial rule to be maintained without accommodations to local customs and interest groups. This accommodation to Indian values was inevitable given the size of the country, but it meant that traditional values survived intact into the post-independence period. Thus, 'many would maintain, for example, that the principle of hierarchy is layered deeply in the Indian tradition in a manner that the rule of impersonal law is not'.[8] The transplanted institutions of modern society established by the British never really operated at the lower levels as the colonial rulers intended, corruption and nepotism being commonplace even then.[9] What the departure of the British and the rise of new types of post-colonial politicians permitted was the entry, into previously corruption-free upper-level institutions, of politicians operating almost entirely within Indian cultural norms. The institutions essential to a modern society had ceased to operate on western premises and adapted to Indian values which were not conducive to efficiency or productivity.

> The crisis in contemporary Indian society ... [is] a consequence of our collective difficulty in working with institutions of Western derivation which have been implanted in India during and after the colonial period: legislatures, courts, universities, banks and so forth. Our difficulty arises perhaps in a lack of fit between the principles which have gone into the designing of these institutions, over many long centuries in Europe, and those which inform institutions to which we in India have traditionally been heir: family, caste, village, pilgrimage centre, little kingdom, and so forth.[10]

Development scholars and organizations such as UNESCO promote the concept of combining indigenous culture with development, but in most of the Third World the two do not go easily together, and if they fit at all it is not a development oriented to long-term growth. Those non-western societies that had indigenous cultures adaptable or conducive to development have already taken off, as in East Asia, while the rest are unlikely to find a good fit between their own culture and the imperatives of development. India did not make this transition under British rule and western influence, and is unlikely to do so now.

The failure of the Congress to restructure traditional India is attributable to the policy of Nehru. It is said that the Untouchable leader Dr Ambedkar, when he was law minister, urged Nehru to implement land reform before the propertied interests consolidated their hold over the state, but this was never seriously implemented. Nehru's failure to act decisively in favour of the poor was a reflection of the vacillation in his socialism. Given the traditions of rural India, distribution and development were inevitably skewed towards those who already had property. Only decisive action early in the Congress regime could have prevented it. Ironically, the development of the 'democratic' system soon foreclosed the opportunity for an authoritarian state intervention in favour of land reform or any other restructuring of rural society. Democracy and the universal franchise gave the landed elites the power to control the government through their feudal-like social and economic influence over the rural poor. Once consolidated, these landed vote blocs determined state policy in their own favour, as seen in the continuing reduction in land tax and the growth of farm subsidies. Their influence became so pervasive that even when the Communists took state power they failed to implement land reform and promoted landed interests instead.[11] From right to left, the whole political spectrum had become part of traditional India, and in the rural areas parties ceased to be social modernizers.

The Contemporary Impasse

If one views India's position in the region and the world in terms of the old concept of 'comparative advantage', India will be relegated to the position of a supplier of cheap labour, both skilled and unskilled. However, even this dubious distinction is under serious threat with the integration of Mexico into the North American economy and the former Soviet bloc into the EEC. India is geographically more isolated from the northern industrial states which have closer sources of cheap labour, while the oil economies of the Middle East have proved unreliable employers of labour and show no signs of an industrial revolution either. India's economy will therefore have to remain primarily domestically driven, but open to competitive export opportunities.

The traditional autarchic policies of the post-colonial era have seen the creation of a new middle class and a significant degree of industrialization. This absolute growth has not, however, kept up with the rest of the world as India's relative position has fallen behind many other countries. According to *The Economist,*

> In 1950 India accounted for 2% of world exports and 6% of Third World exports; by 1980 the respective figures were 0.4% and 1.4%. In 1955, just before India began its industry-based growth strategy, it was the world's tenth biggest industrial power; less than 20 years later it ranked 20th. The world's other poor behemoth, China, could claim average annual growth in real GNP per person of 5.2% during the years 1965–87. India's score over the same period was 1.8%.[12]

On the social front India is still tied to 'feudal' cultural values and isolated from world currents which have moved on to other beliefs. Indian social institutions have proved both remarkably durable and flexible in the face of the challenges of modernity. The advent of modern consumerism has not prevented the continued traditional practices of pogroms against Muslims and Untouchables. The world has largely ignored such human rights abuses, but this cannot be taken for granted in the future. Already there are calls for sanctions against South Asia by the year 2000 if desegregation is not implemented. The Asia NGO regional meeting of the United Nations World Conference on Human Rights passed a resolution stating: 'We call on the UN to take appropriate steps to eradicate the practice of untouchability which is a crime against humanity, and discrimination on the basis of caste, religion and other factors by the year 2000, failing which sanctions will be imposed.'[13]

The recently increased attention of groups such as Amnesty International and the World Council of Churches to South Asian human rights abuses indicates a new interest in the region. The former head of the Commonwealth Secretariat, Human Rights Unit observed that the Indian government was a major obstacle to human rights training of civil servants by the Commonwealth

Secretariat, even though no investigation or criticism of member countries was allowed. He observed that flexibility did not work with the Indian government as it gave them room for evasion. Only concerted international pressure for human rights implementation might lead to government concessions as happened when Amnesty International was allowed to visit India. This pressure led to the setting up of an Indian human rights commission, along the lines of commissions set up for minorities and Scheduled Castes and Scheduled Tribes. There is a sensitivity among the political elite towards international and domestic criticism of human rights abuses which might be utilized to create a better monitoring system and enforcement of human rights legislation.

India has proved unwilling to implement human rights conventions and may now face increased international pressure to do so. In an article in *The Washington Quarterly*, James C. Clad notes that 'Washington is not without leverage' in India.

> The United States remains India's largest external market and its largest source of foreign investment. On human rights, the careful documentation found in successive reports by such groups as Asia Watch or Amnesty International is slowly widening a constituency of concern in the United States and, more generally, throughout the West. Because India's influence in Washington is weak, these issues must necessarily cloud the attitude of the U.S. Congress.[14]

Though the underlying motive in tying foreign aid to human rights implementation might be to justify budget cut-backs in periods of austerity, this linkage is a recent phenomenon which shows every sign of becoming more and more dominant in western foreign policy. It is questionable, however, just how high a priority western donors will be prepared to place on human rights. The United States threatened trade sanctions if India did not extend pharmaceutical patent protection from six to 14 years.[15] For a country where a third of the population suffers from malnutrition to attempt to extort higher drug profits is an unconscionable violation of human rights. It would not be unduly cynical to predict that human rights will continue to be a lower priority than national interest in western foreign policy. If human rights can be put on the agenda some significant improvements may be possible. However, trade sanctions are more likely to be imposed for the most questionable of priorities, and there is no evidence this will be changed by the new world order.

As long as India remains one of the few democracies in the Third World, the human rights critique can be countered by the dismal records of its neighbours, but as democracy spreads in the Third World this response will lose much of its validity. The Indian domestic constituency for ending the abuse of human rights is too weak to be effective; hence international sanctions will be the only way to enforce adherence to human rights conventions. The forces behind these abuses, rooted as they often are in the rural landed elite, are too politically influential to be easily controlled. This could result in an increasingly poor international reputation for India. Although the issue of human rights has never been the top priority in the West, with the collapse of Communism India will no longer be able to play one side off against the other; there is now only one side, which India will have to come to terms with, namely, the northern international community. India's most vulnerable point is its human rights record. Though it is largely ignored by scholars and not given high priority by development agencies, both groups will be vulnerable to pressure for accountability from subordinate groups and donors.

The North has all the bargaining chips, and with the poor financial management of recent Indian governments, India is particularly vulnerable to foreign influence. This influence will be primarily economic; an attempt to break down Indian trade barriers without necessarily lowering the barriers to imports from India. The recent financial difficulties reflect a northern assault on Indian nationalism. India has had to face its diminished importance in the world, and dispense with any illusion it might have had in the Nehru era that it had a role as a world player. 'As distressing as the notion may be, Delhi does not count as a major player in international trade or politics.'[16] Even in its regional capacity India has been unable to translate its economic and military 'preeminence into predominance' due to the resistance of smaller neighbouring states.[17]

The domestic obstacles to India's putting its own house in order are considerable. Aside from the influence of the heavily subsidized surplus-producing farmers, lethargic government employees are a considerable political force, soaking up resources without any commensurate productivity. Pranab Bardhan's apt description of them as 'salaried parasites' points to a major problem of all intrusive state bureaucracies which have a vested interest in self-perpetuation.[18] Pressure from the IMF and World Bank may not be enough to alter this situation significantly, but they do give the much-needed direction which would be politically difficult to follow in a non-crisis situation. Opposition parties usually take advantage of such threats to a valued public sector constituency and denounce the influence of the 'foreign hand'. In this case the influence is there, but the policy option of following old courses is no longer tenable.

Putting together a constituency for structural reform will not be easy, but India has a number of assets which most other Third World nations lack. 'China's economic base is far stronger than India's but its institutional framework is weaker. India has regular elections, at least a lukewarm adherence to the rule of law and a real stock market. China has none of these things.'[19] The top-heavy Indian educational system has produced an educated class which could provide skills for a much larger industrial base as well as emigration. There is an entrepreneurial class, which though not in the same league as the Chinese, is nevertheless diversified. However, India is constrained by cultural defects in both mass and elite culture. In Guyana I met a leading local East Indian businessman who had been approached by an Indian trade representative about buying Indian products from his country of origin rather than from China. He responded that his experience of Indian businesses was of being cheated with substandard goods unreliably delivered, while the Chinese could be depended on to honour their agreements, so he travelled every year to China to buy their products. With this conduct, Indian business will fail to compete internationally, and the gap with China will grow not only on the economic front but militarily as well.

If India is to be internationally competitive and respected in human rights practices it must cut back on unproductive expenditures, including huge military acquisitions, and implement the much-needed social reforms. This involves providing basic needs to the poorer third of the population so that South Asia would no longer have half of the world's absolute poor. Desegregation of Untouchables and the cessation of police torture and state-sanctioned atrocities against minorities must be implemented. A country where ministers can get away with mass murder is not a full-fledged democracy. The legal and educational system is long overdue for reform. At present it does not appear likely that India will be willing to implement many of these reforms as the lobbies against change are too influential. In that event India will become even more of an international backwater than it is already. South Asia will remain more advanced than much of Africa but will fall increasingly behind an industrializing East Asia which once had a similar level of development. With an economy the size of Los Angeles and a population which is 1/7th of the world total, the constraints on India are considerable. However, if the problems are to be resolved, India and the subcontinent must rise above the more parochial aspects of ethnicity, and incorporate new values into their culture instead of reverting to old ones. In this regard the subcontinent has not been well served by its intellectuals, who have been blinded by their own ethnicity and nationalism. The failure to promote the human rights of their own minorities is a reflection on their culture which they must come to terms with. Though much of the doomsaying comes from an elite fearful of losing their privileges in the face of genuine democratization, the greatest danger is that this group and many others will revert to political religiosity and bring about a breakdown in the democratic institutions of the subcontinent. This counter-revolution will come from threatened elites rather than the poor, whose role in Indian politics has been marginal. The failure of secularism to deliver good governance, however, makes it imperative that minorities be incorporated into the system to present an effective vote bloc against fundamentalism. If this holds true for India, the fate of its smaller neighbours is even more precarious. Lacking institutionalized democracy their prospects seem even less certain, and the possibilities for reversion to military rule more likely.

REFERENCES

1. Rajni Kothari, *State Against Democracy* (New York: New Horizons Press, 1989), p. 297.
2. James Manor, 'How and Why Liberal and Representative Politics Emerged in India', *Political Studies*, Vol. 38, No. 1, 1991, p. 25.

3. Ibid., p. 33.
4. Ainslie T. Embree, *Utopias in Conflict: Religion and Nationalism in Modern India* (Berkeley: University of California, 1990), p. 87.
5. Subrata Kumar Mitra, 'Crisis and Resilience in Indian Democracy', *International Social Science Journal*, Vol. 43, No. 129, 1991, p. 567.
6. Ronald Inden, *Imagining India* (Oxford: Basil Blackwell, 1990), p. 38.
7. Satish Saberwal, *India: The Roots of Crisis* (Delhi: Oxford University Press, 1986), p. 3.
8. Ibid., p. 5.
9. David Arnold, 'Bureaucratic Recruitment and Subordination in Colonial India: The Madras Constabulary, 1859–1947', in Ranajit Guha (ed.), *Subaltern Studies IV* (Delhi: Oxford University Press, 1985), p. 53.
10. Saberwal, *India: The Roots of Crisis* (n. 7 above), p. 2.
11. Ross Mallick, *Development Policy of a Communist Government: West Bengal Since 1977* (Cambridge: Cambridge University Press, 1993) and *Indian Communism: Opposition, Collaboration, and Institutionalization* (Delhi: Oxford University Press, 1993).
12. *The Economist*, 23 June 1990, p. 27.
13. Regional Meeting for Asia, World Conference on Human Rights, United Nations General Assembly, Bangkok, 29 March–2 April 1993, A/Conf. 157/ASRM/4, 30 March 1993, p. 17.
14. James C. Clad, 'India: Crisis and Transition', *The Washington Quarterly*, Vol. 15, No. 1, Winter 1992, p. 100.
15. Brahma Chellaney, 'Drama in Delhi', *World Monitor*, Vol. 4, December 1991, p. 44.
16. Clad, *India: Crisis* (n. 14 above), p. 103.
17. Mohammed Ayoob, 'The Primacy of the Political: South Asian Regional Cooperation (SARC) in Comparative Perspective', *Asian Survey*, Vol. 25, No. 4, April 1985, p. 455.
18. Pranab Bardhan, 'Dominant Proprietary Classes and India's Democracy', in Atul Kohli (ed.), *India's Democracy* (Princeton: Princeton University Press, 1990), p. 218.
19. Jim Rohwer, 'The East is Ready', in *The World in 1992* (Toronto: Globe and Mail and *The Economist*, January 1992), p. 77.

Bibliography

Aggarwal, Partap Chand, *Halfway to Equality*, Delhi: Manohar, 1983.

Agrarian Research and Training Institute (ARTI), *Anuradhapura Dry Zone Agricultural Project: A Socio-Economic Study of the Project Beneficiaries*, Occasional Publication No. 40, Colombo, August 1991.

Ahsan, Syed Aziz-al, 'Islamization of the State in a Dualistic Culture: The Case of Bangladesh', Ph.D. thesis, McGill University, Montreal, October 1990.

Akram-Lodhi, A. Haroon, 'Book Review', *Journal of Peasant Studies*, Vol. 22, No. 2, January 1995.

Alam, Almas, *South Asia Newsweek*, CFMT Television, Ottawa, 25 September and 9 October 1994.

Alam, Javeed, 'Political Articulation of Mass Consciousness in Present-day India', in Zoya Hasan, S.N. Jha and Rasheeduddin Khan (eds), *The State, Political Processes, and Identity: Reflections on Modern India*, New Delhi: Sage Publications, 1989.

Ali, S. Mahmud, *The Fearful State: Power, People and Internal War in South Asia*, London: Zed Books, 1993.

All India National Central Assembly, 'A First Call to Convene an All India National Central Assembly of all the Ethnic Indigenous and Tribal Groups', Draft, 30 November 1992.

All India Scheduled Castes/Tribes and Backward Classes Employees Co-ordination Council, Letter to Bhola Paswan Shastri MP, Chairman of the Commission for Scheduled Castes and Scheduled Tribes, Subject: Genocide Committed on the Scheduled Caste Refugees of Marichjhapi Island.

Ambedkar, Babasaheb, *Writings and Speeches*, Vol. 2, ed. Vasant Moon, Bombay: Education Department, Government of Maharashtra, 1982.

———, *What Congress and Gandhi Have Done to the Untouchables*, Bombay: Thacker & Co., 1945.

Amnesty International, *India: Torture, Rape and Deaths in Custody*, New York: Amnesty International, March 1992.

———, *Appeal: 1992 India Campaign*, 'Mass Rape of Tribal Women in Ujan Maidan Village, West Tripura'.

Anam, Mahmudul and **Rahman, Syed Sajjadur**, 'Economic Integration in South Asia: An Exploratory Analysis in Trade, Investment and Finance', *Journal of Developing Societies*, Vol. 7, No. 1, January–April 1991.

Anand, Mulk Raj, *Untouchable*, with a Preface by E.M. Forster, London: Penguin Books, 1940.

Anderson, Robert S. and **Walter Huber**, *The Hour of the Fox: Tropical Forests, the World Bank, and Indigenous People in Central India*, Seattle: University of Washington Press, 1988.

Appadurai, Arjun, 'Number in the Colonial Imagination', in Carol A. Brecken-ridge and Peter van der Veer (eds), *Orientalism and the Postcolonial Predica-ment: Perspectives on South Asia*, Philadelphia: University of Pennsylvania Press, 1993.

Arnold, David, 'Bureaucratic Recruitment and Subordination in Colonial India: The Madras Constabulary, 1859–1947', in Ranajit Guha (ed.), *Subaltern Studies IV*, Delhi: Oxford University Press, 1985.

Awasthi, Dilip, 'Mathura: Back From the Brink', *India Today*, 15 September 1995.

Axline, W. Andrew, 'Underdevelopment, Dependence, and Integration: The Politics of Regionalism in the Third World', *International Organizations*, Vol. 31, Nos. 1–2, 1977.

———, 'Regional Co-operation and National Security: External Forces in Carib-bean Integration', *Journal of Common Market Studies* Vol. 27, No. 1, Septem-ber 1988.

———, 'The Comparative Analysis of Regional Cooperation Among Developing Countries', Paper presented at the Fifteenth World Congress of the Interna-tional Political Science Association, 21–25 July 1991, Buenos Aires.

Ayoob, Mohammed, 'The Primacy of the Political: South Asian Regional Coop-eration (SARC) in Comparative Perspective', *Asian Survey*, Vol. 25, No. 4, April 1985.

———, 'India in South Asia: The Quest for Regional Predominance', *World Pol-icy Journal*, Vol. 7, No. 1.

Bajpai, Kanti Prasad, 'The Origins of Association in South Asia: SAARC 1979–1989', unpublished Ph.D. dissertation, University of Illinois at Urbana-Cham-paign, Urbana, Illinois 1990.

Balassa, Bela and **Ardy Stoutjesdijk**, 'Economic Integration Among Develop-ing Countries', *Journal of Common Market Studies*, Vol. 14, No. 1. September 1975.

Bandyopadhyaya, Nripen, 'Evaluation of Land Reform Measures in West Ben-gal', Mimeo, Calcutta: Centre for Studies in Social Sciences, 1983.

Bandyopadhyay, Sekhar, 'Social Protest or Politics of Backwardness?', in Basudeb Chattopadhyay, Hari S. Vasudevan and Rajat Kanta Ray (eds), *Dissent and Consensus: Protest in Pre-Industrial Societies*, Delhi: K.P. Bagchi & Co., 1989.

———, *Caste, Politics and the Raj*, Delhi: K.P. Bagchi & Co., 1990.

———, 'A Peasant Caste in Protest: The Namasudras of Eastern Bengal 1872–1945', in Suranjan Das and Sekhar Bandopadhyay (eds), *Caste and Com-munal Politics in South Asia*, Calcutta: K.P. Bagchi & Co., 1993.

Bandyopadhyay, Suraj and **Donald von Eschen**, 'The Impact of Politics on Rural Production and Distribution: A Comparative Study of Rural Policies and Their Implementation Under Congress and Left Front Governments in West Bengal', Paper delivered at the annual meeting of the Association of Asian Studies, San Francisco, 26 March 1988.

Banerjee, Ruben, 'West Bengal: Law Unto Themselves: A Failing System Leads to a Rise in Mob-Led Vigilante Justice', *India Today*, 15 September 1995.

———, 'West Bengal: Damning the Police', *India Today*, 30 November 1995.

———, 'Benoy Chowdhury: Blowing the Whistle', *India Today*, 15 January 1996.

Bannerji, Himani, 'Language and Liberation: A Study of Political Theatre in West Bengal', *Ariel*, Vol. 15, No. 4, 1984.

Bara, Dominic and **Boniface Minz**, *Towards Building a Self-Reliant Tribal Community: Vikas Maitri Approach to Development*, Vikas Maitri: Ranchi, 1981.

Bardhan, Pranab, *The Political Economy of Development in India*, Oxford: Basil Blackwell, 1984.

———, 'Dominant Proprietary Classes and India's Democracy', in Atul Kohli (ed.), *India's Democracy*, Princeton: Princeton University Press, 1990.

Barlas, Asthma, *Democracy, Nationalism and Communalism: The Colonial Legacy in South Asia*, Boulder: Westview Press, 1995.

Basu, Amrita, 'Democratic Centralism in the Home and the World: Bengali Women and the Communist Movement', in Sonia Kruks, Rayna Rapp and Marilyn B. Young (eds), *Promissory Notes: Women in the Transition to Socialism*, New York: Monthly Review Press, 1989.

Basu, Jyoti, 'Tin Bachar Bamfront Sarkar Parichalanar Aviggyata Samparke Kichhu Baktyavba' ('Something to Say Regarding the Experience of Running the Left Front Government for the Last Three Years'), *Deshhitaishee* Annual Puja Issue, 1980.

Basu, Kalipada, *West Bengal Economy: Past, Present, and Future*, Calcutta: Firma KLM, 1989.

Basu, Sajal, *The Politics of Violence: A Case Study of West Bengal*, Calcutta: Minerva Publications, 1982.

———, *Jharkhand Movement: Ethnicity and Cultural Silence*, Shimla: Indian Institute of Advanced Study, 1994.

Baviskar, Amita, 'Development, Nature and Resistance: The Case of Bhilala Tribals in the Narmada Valley', Ph.D. thesis, Cornell University, Ithaca, 1992.

Behura, N.K., 'Santal Sub-Nationalism and New Identity: The Orissa Situation' in Buddhadeb Chaudhuri (ed.), *Ethnopolitics and Identity Crisis*, Delhi, M.C. Mittal, 1992.

Berghe, Pierre L. van Den, *The Quest for the Other: Ethnic Tourism in San Cristobal, Mexico*, Seattle: University of Washington Press, 1994.

Bergmann, Theodor, *Agrarian Reform in India*, Delhi: Agricole Publishing Academy, 1984.

Bernard, Jean-Alphonse, 'The Presidential Idea in the Constitutions of South Asia', *Contemporary South Asia*, Vol. 1, No. 1, 1992.

Berwick, Dennison, 'Sacred and Profane', *The Sunday Times Magazine*, 1 July 1990.

Beteille, Andre, 'The Reproduction of Inequality: Occupation, Caste and Family', *Contributions to Indian Sociology*, Vol. 25, No. 1, 1991.

———, Letter to Editor, *Dalit Voice*, 1–15 March, Vol. 11, No. 8, 1992.

Bhalla, Surjit S. and **Paul Glewwe**, 'Growth and Equity in Developing Countries: A Reinterpretation of the Sri Lankan Experience', *The World Bank Economic Review*, Vol. 1, No. 1, September 1986.

Bhanage, N.P., *Tribal Commissions and Committees in India*, Bombay: Himalaya Publishing House, 1993.

Bhattacharyya, Dwaipayan, 'Agrarian Reforms and Politics of the Left in West Bengal', Ph.D. dissertation, University of Cambridge, Cambridge, March 1993.

Biswas, Atharobaki, 'Why Dandakaranya a Failure, Why Mass Exodus, Where Solution?' *The Oppressed Indian*, July 1982.

Blair, Harry, 'Civil Society, Democratic Development and International Donors: A Case Study from Bangladesh', Paper presented at the annual meeting of the American Political Science Association, New York City, 1–4 September 1994.

Bose, Arun, *India's Social Crisis*, Delhi: Oxford University Press, 1989.

Boyce, James K., 'Agricultural Growth in Bangladesh and West Bengal', Ph.D. dissertation, Oxford University, Oxford, 1984.

Brabourne, Lord, 'Governor's Half Yearly Report on Ministers to Viceroy Lord Linlithgow', 20 June 1939, London: India Office Library.

Brass, Paul R., 'Elite Groups, Symbol Manipulation and Ethnic Identity Among the Muslims of South Asia', in David Taylor and Malcolm Yapp (eds), *Political Identity in South Asia*, London: Curzon Press Ltd, 1979.

———, *The New Cambridge History of India IV: I—The Politics of India Since Independence*, Cambridge: Cambridge University Press, 1990.

———, *Ethnicity and Nationalism: Theory and Comparison*, New Delhi: Sage Publications, 1991.

———, 'American Political Science and South Asian Studies: Virtues Unrewarded', *Economic and Political Weekly*, Vol. XXX, No. 36, 9 September 1995.

Brecher, Michael, *Nehru: A Political Biography*, London: Oxford University Press, 1959.

———, 'India and Canada: Origin and Assessment of the Shastri Institute', in Arthur G. Rubinoff (ed.), *Canada and South Asia: Political and Strategic Relations*, Toronto: University of Toronto, 1992.

Broomfield, J.H., *Elite Conflict in a Plural Society: Twentieth-Century Bengal*, Berkeley, CA: University of California Press, 1968.

———, *Mostly About Bengal: Essays in Modern South Asian History*, Delhi: Manohar, 1982.

Bruton, Henry J., *The Political Economy of Poverty, Equity, and Growth: Sri Lanka and Malaysia*, Oxford: Published by Oxford University Press for the World Bank, 1992.

Burchell, Graham, Colin Gordon and **Peter Miller** (eds), *The Foucault Effect: Studies in Governmentality*, Chicago, The University of Chicago Press, 1991.

Burger, Julian, *Report from the Frontier: The State of the World's Indigenous Peoples*, London: Zed Books, 1987.

Burki, Shahid Javed, 'Pakistan's Economy in the Year 2000: Two Possible Scenarios', in J. Henry Korson (ed.), *Contemporary Problems of Pakistan*, Boulder: Westview Press, 1993.

Burns, John F., 'High-Level Graft Case Rocks India's Political Establishment', *The New York Times*, 22 January, 1996.

Buzan, Barry, 'A Framework for Regional Security Analysis', in Barry Buzan and Gowher Rizvi (eds), *South Asian Insecurity and the Great Powers*, London: Macmillan, 1986.

Canadian Commission for UNESCO, *Final Report*, International Workshop on the Cultural Dimension of Development, Ottawa, 14–15 March 1991, January 1992.

Chakrabarti, Prafulla K., *The Marginal Men: The Refugees and the Left Political Syndrome in West Bengal*, Kalyani: Lumiere Books, 1990.

Chakravarty, Sayantan, 'Ram Vilas Paswan: On the Gravy Train', *India Today*, 15 January, 1997.

Chatterjee, Meera, *ICDS Service Delivery Among Tribal Populations in Bihar and Madhya Pradesh*, New Delhi, World Bank, October 1992.

Chatterjee, Nilanjana, 'Midnight's Unwanted Children: East Bengali Refugees and the Politics of Rehabilitation', unpublished Ph.D. thesis, Brown University, Providence, May 1992.

Chatterjee, Partha, 'Caste and Subaltern Consciousness', in Ranajit Guha (ed.), *Subaltern Studies VI*, Delhi: Oxford University Press, 1989.

———, *Nationalist Thought and the Colonial World: A Derivative Discourse*, London: Zed Books, 1986.

Chatterji, Joya, *Bengal Divided: Hindu Communalism and Partition, 1932–1947*, Cambridge: Cambridge University Press, 1994.

Chaudhuri, Buddhadeb, 'Ethnic Conflict in the Chittagong Hill Tracts of Bangladesh', in S.W.R. de A. Samarasinghe and Reed Coughlan (eds), *Economic Dimensions of Ethnic Conflict: International Perspectives*, London: Pinter Publishers, 1991.

Chaudhuri, Nirad C., *Thy Hand, Great Anarch! India 1921–1952*, Reading, Massachusetts: Addison-Wesley, 1989.

Chellaney, Brahma, 'Drama in Delhi', *World Monitor*, 4 December 1991.

Chittagong Hill Tracts Jumma Refugees Welfare Association, 'Report on the Visit of Jumma Refugee Team to Chittagong Hill Tracts', Takumbari Relief Camp, PO Dumburnagar (Jatanbari) South Tripura, India, 19–23 September 1993.

Chopra, Pran, 'SAARC and ASEAN: Comparative Analysis of Structures and Aims', in Bhabani Sen Gupta (ed.), *SAARC–ASEAN: Prospects and Problems of Inter-regional Cooperation*, Delhi: South Asian Publishers, 1988.

Chowdhury, Akram H., in David P. Forsythe (ed.), *Human Rights and Development*, New York: St Martin's Press, 1989.

Clad, James C., 'India: Crisis and Transition', *The Washington Quarterly*, Vol. 15, No. 1, Winter 1992.

Claude, Inis L., Jr., *Swords into Plowshares: The Problems and Progress of International Organization*, New York: Random House, 5th edition, 1971.

Communist Party of India-Marxist, *Reports and Resolution on Organization*, adopted by the Salkia Plenum, 27–31 December 1978, Delhi: Communist Party of India-Marxist, 1979.

———, Burdwan District Committee, *Shamiksha Astham Lok Sabha Nirbachan*, (Analysis of Eighth Lok Sabha Elections), Burdwan: CPM District Committee, 28 February 1985.

———, West Bengal State Conference, *Rajnaitik-Sangathanik Report*, 27 December 1981–1 January 1982, Calcutta: West Bengal State Committee, Communist Party of India-Marxist, March 1982.

Conklin, Beth A. and **Laura R. Graham**, 'The Shifting Middle Ground: Amazonian Indians and Eco-Politics', *American Anthropologist*, Vol. 47, No. 4, December 1995.

Corbridge, Stuart, 'Ousting Singbronga: The Struggle for India's Jharkhand', in Peter Robb (ed.), *Dalit Movements and the Meaning of Labour in India*, Delhi: Oxford University Press, 1993.

Cose, Ellis, *The Rage of a Privileged Class*, New York: Harper Collins, 1995.

Crossette, Barbara, *India: Facing the Twenty-First Century*, Bloomington: Indiana University Press, 1993.

———, 'Hatreds, Human Rights, and the News: What We Ignore', *SAIS Review*, Vol. 13, No. 1, Winter–Spring 1993.

Dasgupta, Biplab, 'Some Aspects of Land Reform in West Bengal', *Land Reform: Land Settlement and Cooperatives*, No. 1/2, 1982.

Dasgupta, Sunil, 'Hung-up on the Past: Research on India is Dominated by History', *India Today*, North American Edition, 15 December, 1996.

Das Gupta, Jyotirindra, 'Ethnicity, Democracy, and Development in India: Assam in a General Perspective', in Atul Kohli (ed.), *India's Democracy*, Princeton: Princeton University Press, 1988.

Davis, Marvin, *Rank and Rivalry: The Politics of Inequality in Rural West Bengal*, Cambridge: Cambridge University Press, 1983.

de Kadt, Emanuel, 'Some Basic Questions on Human Rights and Development', *World Development*, Vol. 8, No. 2, February 1980.

Delhi Domestic Service, Foreign Broadcast Information Service, South Asia, NES-91-067, 8 April 1991, 6 April 1991.

Devalle, Susana B.C., *Discourses of Ethnicity*, New Delhi: Sage Publications, 1992.

Dewan, Aditya Kumar, 'Class and Ethnicity in the Hills of Bangladesh', unpublished Ph.D. thesis, McGill University, Montreal, October 1990.

———, 'International Development and Indigenous Peoples in the Chittagong Hill Tracts in Bangladesh', Paper presented at the Annual Meeting of the Canadian Association for the Study of International Development, Learned Societies Conference held at the University of Quebec, Montreal, 4–6 June 1995.

Dewan, Ramendu Shekhar, 'A Report on the Fifth Round of the Dialogue Held Between the Bangladesh Government Commission and the Jana Samhati Samiti' on 18 September 1993, at Khagrachari Circuit House.

Diem, Andrea Grace and **James R. Lewis**, 'Imagining India: The Influence of Hinduism on the New Age Movement', in James R. Lewis and J. Gordon Melton (eds), *Perspectives on the New Age*, Albany: State University of New York Press, 1992.

Dirks, Nicholas B., 'Castes of Mind', *Representations* 37, Winter 1992.

Dogra, Bharat, 'Mandal Commission: Will Tribal Interests Suffer?' *Economic and Political Weekly*, Vol. XXV, No. 39, 29 September 1990.

Donnelly, Jack, 'Human Rights and Development', *World Politics*, Vol. 36, No. 4, January 1984.

———, *Universal Human Rights in Theory and Practice*, Ithaca: Cornell University Press, 1989.

Dreze, Jean and **Amartya Sen**, *Hunger and Public Action*, Oxford: Clarendon Press, 1989.

D'Souza, Dinesh, *The End of Racism*, New York: The Free Press, 1995.

Dunham, David, 'Politics and Land Settlement Schemes: The Case of Sri Lanka', *Development and Change*, Vol. 13, No. 1, January 1982, pp. 43–61.

Echeverri-Gent, John, 'Politics Takes Command: Implementation of the National Rural Employment Program in West Bengal', unpublished manuscript, June 1991.

Echeverri-Gent, John, 'Public Participation and Poverty Alleviation: The Experience of Reform Communists in India's West Bengal', *World Development*, Vol. 20, No. 10, October 1992.

Economic and Political Weekly, 'Commentary: Sardar Sarovar Project: Review of Resettlement and Rehabilitation in Maharashtra', 21 August 1993.

Embree, Ainslie T., *Utopias in Conflict: Religion and Nationalism in Modern India*, Berkeley: University of California Press, 1990.

Etienne, Gilbert, *India's Changing Rural Scene: 1963–1979*, Delhi: Oxford University Press, 1982.

Everett, Jana, 'Incorporation versus Conflict: Lower Class Women, Collective Action, and the State in India', in Sue Ellen M. Charlton, Jana Everett and Kathleen Staudt (eds), *Women, the State, and Development*, New York: State University of New York Press, 1989.

Fernandes, Walter, 'Meetings of Non-tribal Observers During the General Assembly', Council of Indigenous and Tribal Peoples, 15–20 November 1993, New Delhi, unpublished typescript.

Fernandes, Walter, J.C. Das and **Sam Rao**, 'Displacement and Rehabilitation: An Estimate of Extent and Prospects', in Walter Fernandes and Enakshi Ganguly Thukral (eds), *Development, Displacement and Rehabilitation* Delhi: Indian Social Institute, 1989.

Fernandes, Walter and **S. Anthony Raj**, *Development, Displacement and Rehabilitation in the Tribal Areas of Orissa*, Delhi: Indian Social Institute, 1992.

Franda, Marcus, *India's Rural Development*, Bloomington: Indiana University Press, 1979.

Frankel, Francine R., 'Caste, Land and Dominance in Bihar: Breakdown of the Brahminical Social Order', in Francine R. Frankel and M.S.A. Rao (eds), *Dominance and State Power in Modern India: Decline of a Social Order*, Delhi: Oxford University Press, 1989.

Freeman, Derek, 'Fooled in Paradise', *The Times Higher Education Supplement*, 27 December, 1996.

Freeman, James M., *Untouchable: An Indian Life History*, Stanford: Stanford University Press, 1979.

Furer-Haimendorf, Christoph von, *Tribes of India: The Struggle for Survival*, Berkeley: University of California Press, 1982.

Galanter, Marc, *Competing Equalities: Law and the Backward Classes in India*, Berkeley: University of California Press, 1984.

——, 'Pursuing Equality: An Assessment of India's Policy of Compensatory Discrimination for Disadvantaged Groups' in Dilip K. Basu and Richard Sisson (eds), *Social and Economic Development in India*, New Delhi: Sage Publications, 1986.

——, Lecture at Ambedkar Centenary Celebration, 14 April 1991, New York: Columbia University.

Gandhi, M.K., *Collected Works*, Vol. 23, p. 116 cited in Ranajit Guha, 'Dominance Without Hegemony and its Historiography', in Ranajit Guha (ed.), *Subaltern Studies VI*, Delhi: Oxford University Press, 1989.

Ganguly Thukral, Enakshi (ed.), *Big Dams, Displaced People*, New Delhi: Sage Publications, 1992.

Gankovsky, Yuri V., 'The Social Structure of Society in the People's Republic of Bangladesh', *Asian Survey*, Vol. 14, No. 3, March 1974.

Gavaskar, Mahesh, 'Bahujans as Vanguards: BSP and BMS in Maharashtra Politics', *Economic and Political Weekly*, Vol. XXIX, Nos. 16–17, 16–23 April 1994.

Gazdar, Haris, 'Rural Poverty, Public Policy and Social Change: Some Findings from Surveys of Six Villages', WIDER Working Paper, WP 98, May 1992.

George, Paul, 'Indian Naval Expansion', Working Paper No. 32, Ottawa: Canadian Institute for International Peace and Security, February 1991.

Ghose, Ajit Kumar, 'Agrarian Reform in West Bengal', World Employment Program Research Working Paper, Geneva: International Labour Organization, May 1980.

Ghosh, Anjali, *Peaceful Transition in Power: A Study of Marxist Political Strategies in West Bengal 1967–1977*, Calcutta: Firma KLM, 1981.

Ghosh, Arun, *West Bengal Landscapes*, Calcutta: K.P. Bagchi & Co., 1989.

Ghosh, Arunabha, 'Probing the Jharkhand Question', *Economic and Political Weekly*, Vol. XXVI, No. 18, 4 May 1991.

Ghosh, Partha S., 'Bangladesh at the Crossroads: Religion and Politics', *Asian Survey*, Vol. 33, No. 7, July 1993.

Ghosh, S.K., 'Land and Agricultural Development', in Manjula Bose (ed.), *Land Reforms in Eastern India*, Calcutta: Jadavpur University, 1981.

Gillies, David, *Between Principle and Practice: Human Rights in North-South Relations*, Montreal, McGill-Queen's University Press, 1996.

———, 'Canadian Aid, Human Rights, and Conflict in Sri Lanka', in Robert Miller (ed.), *Aid as Peacemaker: Canadian Development Assistance and Third World Conflict*, Ottawa: Carleton University Press, 1992.

Gokhale, Jayashree B., 'The Evolution of a Counter-Ideology: Dalit Consciousness in Maharashtra', in Francine R. Frankel and M.S.A. Rao (eds), *Dominance and State Power in Modern India: Decline of a Social Order Vol. 2*, Delhi: Oxford University Press, 1990.

Gonsalves, Eric, 'An Agenda for the Next Decade', *South Asia Journal*, Vol. 1, No. 1, July–September 1987.

Gough, Kathleen, 'Harijans in Thanjavur', in Kathleen Gough and Hari P. Sharma (eds), *Imperialism and Revolution in South Asia*, New York: Monthly Review Press, 1973.

Government of India, *Report of the Committee on Panchayati Raj Institutions*, Delhi: Government of India, Ministry of Agriculture and Irrigation, Department of Rural Development, 1978.

———, *Report of the Commission for Scheduled Castes and Scheduled Tribes: Second Report, April 1979–March 1980*, Delhi: Government of India Press, 1981.

———, *Report of the Commission for Scheduled Castes and Scheduled Tribes: Fifth Report, April 1982–March 1983*, Delhi: Government of India Press, 1984.

———, *Report of the Commission for Scheduled Castes and Scheduled Tribes: Eighth Report, April 1985–March 1986*, Delhi: Government of India Press, 1988.

———, *Report of the Commissioner for Scheduled Castes and Scheduled Tribes: Twentyseventh Report, 1979–1981, Part I*, Delhi: Government of India Press, 1982.

Government of India, *Report of the Commissioner for Scheduled Castes and Scheduled Tribes: Twentyeighth Report, 1986–1987,* Delhi: Government of India Press, 1988.

———, *Report of the Commissioner for Scheduled Castes and Scheduled Tribes: Twentyninth Report, 1987–1989,* Faridabad: Government of India Press, 1990.

———, Ministry of Home Affairs, *Selected Statistics on Scheduled Castes,* Occasional Papers on Development of Scheduled Castes (2), Delhi: Government of India Press, 1984.

———, *National Sample Survey,* West Bengal No. 215, 26th Round, July 1971–September 1972, Delhi: Ministry of Planning, 1972.

———, *Sarvekshana,* Delhi: National Sample Survey Organization, 1979.

———, Planning Commission, 'Report of the Working Group on the Development of Scheduled Castes During the Seventh Five Year Plan 1985–90', Mimeo, Delhi, 1985.

———, Programme Evaluation Organization, Planning Commission, *Evaluation of Food for Work Programme: Final Report,* Delhi: Government of India Press, 1981.

———, Registrar General and Census Commissioner, *Census of India, 1981, Provisional Population Totals: Workers and Non-Workers,* Series–1, Paper 3, Delhi: Government of India Press, 1982.

———, Registrar General and Census Commissioner, 'Primary Census Abstract for Scheduled Castes and Scheduled Tribes', Paper 1 of 1993, Census of India 1991, Registrar General and Census Commissioner, India, Delhi: Government of India Press, 1993.

———, Ministry of Welfare, *Report of the Working Group on Development and Welfare of Scheduled Tribes During Eighth Five-Year Plan 1990–95,* Delhi: Ministry of Welfare, Government of India, 1989.

Government of West Bengal, 'Adarsh Gramin Abash' ('Ideal Village Habitation'), leaflet.

———, Board of Revenue and Directorate of Agriculture, *Agricultural Census 1976–77,* Calcutta: Board of Revenue and Directorate of Agriculture, 1979.

———, Board of Revenue, *Dynamics of the Rural Situation in West Bengal,* Calcutta: West Bengal Government Press, 1979.

———, *Economic Review 1980–81,* Alipore: West Bengal Government Press, 1981.

———, *Economic Review: Statistical Appendix,* Calcutta: West Bengal Government Press, Annual.

———, Department of Information and Cultural Affairs, *School Education in West Bengal 1984,* Calcutta: Director of Information, 1984.

———, Department of Information and Cultural Affairs, *12 Years of Left Front Government,* Calcutta: Director of Information, June 1989.

———, Department of Labour, *Labour in West Bengal,* Calcutta: Department of Labour, Annual.

———, Legislative Department, *The West Bengal Panchayat Act, 1973* as modified up to November 1980, Alipore: West Bengal Government Press, 1980.

———, Land Reforms Office, *Bargadars in West Bengal and an Assessment of Their Position in the Field,* Mimeo, Calcutta: West Bengal Land Reforms Office, August 1985.

Government of West Bengal, Department of Panchayats and Community Development, *The Working of Panchayat System in West Bengal, A Review of Main Events and Activities*, Calcutta: Department of Panchayats and Community Development, March 1980.

————, Directorate of Panchayats, *Panchayats in West Bengal*, Calcutta: Directorate of Panchayats, 1981.

————, Department of Panchayats and Community Development, *Panchayats in West Bengal From 1978–79 to 1980–81: A Review*, Calcutta: Department of Panchayats and Community Development, January 1982.

————, Deputy Secretary, Refugee Relief and Rehabilitation Department, Letter to Zonal Director, Ministry of Home Affairs, Government of India, Office of the Zonal Director, Backward Classes and Ex-officio Deputy Commissioner for Scheduled Castes and Scheduled Tribes, Eastern Zone, Subject: 'Problems of Refugees from Dandakaranya to West Bengal', No. 3223-Rehab/DNK-6/79.

Griffiths, Sian, 'A Class Sister Act', *The Times Higher Education Supplement*, 13 October, 1995.

Guha, Ramachandra, 'Radical American Environmentalism and Wilderness Preservation: A Third World Critique', *Environmental Ethics*, Vol. 11, No. 1, Spring 1989.

————, 'Discussion: Beyond Bhadralok and Bankim Studies', *Economic and Political Weekly*, Vol. XXXI, No. 8, 24 February, 1996.

Guha, Ranajit, 'The Prose of Counter-Insurgency', in Ranajit Guha and Gayatri Chakravorty Spivak (eds), *Selected Subaltern Studies*, New York: Oxford University Press, 1988.

————, 'Dominance Without Hegemony and Its Historiography', in Ranajit Guha (ed.), *Subaltern Studies VI: Writings on South Asian History and Society*, Delhi: Oxford University Press, 1989.

Gupta, Ranjit Kumar, *Agrarian West Bengal: Three Field Studies*, Calcutta: Institute of Social Research and Applied Anthropology, August 1977.

Haas, Ernst B., 'The Uniting of Europe and the Uniting of Latin America', *Journal of Common Market Studies*, Vol. 5, No. 4, June 1967, pp. 315–43.

Hardgrave, Robert L., 'After the Dynasty: Politics in India', *Current History*, Vol. 91, No. 563, March 1992.

Harper, Edward B., 'Comparative Analysis of Caste: The United States and India', in Milton Singer and Bernard S. Cohn (eds), *Structure and Change in Indian Society*, Chicago: Wenner-Gren Foundation for Anthropological Research, Inc., 1968.

Harris, John, 'What is Happening in Rural West Bengal? Agrarian Reform, Growth and Distribution', *Economic and Political Weekly*, Vol. XXVIII, No. 24, 12 June, 1993.

Hawthorn, Geoffrey, 'Caste and Politics in India Since 1947', in Dennis B. McGilvray (ed.), *Caste Ideology and Interaction*, Cambridge: Cambridge University Press, 1982.

————, '"Waiting for a Text?": Comparing Third World Politics', in James Manor (ed.), *Rethinking Third World Politics*, Harlow, Essex: Longmans, 1991.

Heywood, Linda M., 'UNITA and Ethnic Nationalism in Angola', *The Journal of Modern African Studies*, Vol. 27, No. 1, 1989.

Horowitz, Donald L., *Ethnic Groups in Conflict*, Berkeley: University of California Press, 1985.

Hu-DeHart, Evelyn, 'The Undermining of Ethnic Studies', *The Chronicle of Higher Education*, 15 October, 1995.

Huntington, Samuel P., 'The Goals of Development', in Myron Weiner and Samuel P. Huntington (eds), *Understanding Political Development*, Boston: Little, Brown & Co., 1987.

———, 'The Clash of Civilizations', *Foreign Affairs*, Vol. 72, No. 3, Summer 1993.

Hussain, Akmal, *Strategic Issues in Pakistan's Economic Policy*, Lahore: Progressive Publishers, 1988.

———, 'The Crisis of State Power in Pakistan: Militarization and Dependence' in Ponna Wignaraja and Akmal Hussain (eds), *The Challenge in South Asia: Development, Democracy and Regional Cooperation*, New Delhi: Sage Publications, 1989.

Ilaiah, Kancha, 'BSP and Caste as Ideology', *Economic and Political Weekly*, Vol. 29, No. 12, 19 March 1994, pp. 668–69.

Inden, Ronald, 'Orientalist Constructions of India', *Modern Asian Studies*, Vol. 20, No. 3, 1986.

———, *Imagining India*, Oxford: Basil Blackwell, 1990.

Institute for Financial Management and Research, *An Economic Assessment of Poverty Eradication and Rural Unemployment Alleviation Programmes and their Prospects*, Part III, Madras: Institute for Financial Management and Research, April 1984.

Interviews with IAS Officers and WBCS Officers.

Interview, IAS Secretary of the West Bengal Government.

Interviews with ICS Officers.

Interview, West Bengal Land Reforms Commissioner.

International Labour Organization, *Report of the Committee of Experts on the Application of Conventions and Recommendations: General Report and Observations Concerning Particular Countries*, 80th Session, Report III (Part 4A) Geneva, 1993.

Iqbal, Nasir, 'More Educated are More Caste Conscious: Delhi Survey', *Dalit Voice*, Vol. 10, No. 9, 16–31 March 1991.

Isaacs, Harold R., *India's Ex-Untouchables*, New York: Harper and Row, 1965.

Jalal, Ayesha, *The State of Martial Rule: The Origins of Pakistan's Political Economy of Defence*, Cambridge: Cambridge University Press, 1990.

———, *Democracy and Authoritarianism in South Asia*, Cambridge: Cambridge University Press, 1995.

Jayewardene, Ruwani Anush, 'The Impact of Malaria on New Setters in the Mahaweli Development Project, Sri Lanka', unpublished Ph.D. dissertation, University of Connecticut, Connecticut, 1988.

Jha, A.K., 'Jharkhand Politics of Bihar: Paradigm of Non-Performance', in S. Narayan (ed.), *Jharkhand Movement: Origin and Evolution*, Delhi: Inter-India Publications, 1992.

Jones, Steve, 'Tribal Underdevelopment in India', *Development and Change*, Vol. 9, No. 1, 1978.

Jose, A.V., 'Agricultural Wages in India', *Economic and Political Weekly*, Vol. XXIII, No. 26, 25 June 1988.

Juergensmeyer, Mark, *Religion as Social Vision: The Movement Against Untouchability in 20th Century Punjab*, Berkeley: University of California Press, 1982.

S.K., 'Diminishing Returns from Blaming Centre', *Economic and Political Weekly*, Vol. XX, No. 15, 13 April 1985.

Kabir, Muhammad Ghulam, *Minority Politics in Bangladesh*, Delhi: Vikas Publishing House, 1980.

Kamble, J.R., *Rise and Awakening of Depressed Classes in India*, Delhi: National, 1979.

Karlekar, Hiranmay, *In the Mirror of Mandal*, Delhi: Ajanta Books, 1992.

Kaviraj, Sudipta, 'On State, Society and Discourse in India', in James Manor (ed.), *Rethinking Third World Politics*, Harlow, Essex: Longmans, 1991.

———, 'Crisis of the Nation-state in India', in John Dunn (ed.), *Contemporary Crisis of the Nation State?* Oxford: Basil Blackwell, 1995.

Kennedy, Charles H., 'Policies of Redistributional Preference in Pakistan', in Neil Nevitte and Charles H. Kennedy (eds), *Ethnic Preference and Public Policy in Developing States*, Boulder, Colorado: Lynne Rienner Publishers, 1986.

Kennedy, Paul, *Preparing for the Twenty-First Century*, New York: Harper Collins, 1993.

Keshari, B.P., 'Development of Political Organizations in Chotanagpur', in S. Bosu Mullick (ed.), *Cultural Chotanagpur: Unity in Diversity*, Delhi: Uppal Publishing House, 1991.

Khare, R.S., *The Untouchable as Himself: Ideology, Identity, and Pragmatism Among the Lucknow Chamars*, Cambridge: Cambridge University Press, 1984.

Kohli, Atul, 'Parliamentary Communism and Agrarian Reform', *Asian Survey*, Vol. 33, No. 7, July 1983.

———, *The State and Poverty in India: The Politics of Reform*, Cambridge: Cambridge University Press, 1987.

———, 'From Elite Activism to Democratic Consolidation: The Rise of Reform Communism in West Bengal', in Francine R. Frankel and M.S.A. Rao (eds), *Dominance and State Power in Modern India Vol. II*, Delhi: Oxford University Press, 1990.

———, *Democracy and Discontent*, Cambridge: Cambridge University Press, 1990.

———, 'Can the Periphery Control the Center? Indian Politics at the Crossroads', *The Washington Quarterly*, Vol. 19, No. 4, Autumn 1996.

Korten, David C., 'Community Organization and Rural Development: A Learning Process Approach', *Public Administration Review*, Vol. 40, No. 5, September/October 1980.

Kothari, Rajni, *State Against Democracy*, New York: New Horizons Press, 1989.

Kumar, Nita, *Friends, Brothers, Informants: Fieldwork Memoirs of Banaras*, Berkeley: University of California Press, 1992.

Kumar, Prem, 'CIDA and Canada's Visible Minorities', *Policy Options*, Vol. 10, No. 7, September 1989.

Kumar, Shanti P., 'The Mahaweli Scheme and Rural Women in Sri Lanka' in Noeleen Heyzer (ed.), *Women Farmers and Rural Change in Asia: Towards Equal Access and Participation*, Kuala Lumpur: Asia and Pacific Development Centre, 1987.

Kumar, T.M. Vinod and **Jatin De**, *Basic Needs and the Provision of Government Services: An Areas Study of Ranaghat Block in West Bengal*, Geneva: International Labour Organization, World Employment Program Working Paper, February 1980.

Lal, Deepak, 'India and China: Contrasts in Economic Liberalization?' *World Development*, Vol. 23, No. 9, September 1995.

Lee, Shin-Wha, 'Environmental Change, Refugees, and Conflict in the Third World: A Framework for Inquiry Applied to Case Studies of Sudan and Bangladesh', Ph.D. thesis, University of Maryland, College Park, 1994.

Lelyveld, Joseph, *Calcutta*, Hong Kong: The Perennial Press, 1975.

Levy, Brian, 'Foreign Aid in the Making of Economic Policy in Sri Lanka, 1977–1983', *Policy Sciences*, Vol. 22, Nos. 3–4, 1989.

Lewis, Martin W., *Green Delusions*, Durham: Duke University Press, 1992.

Lieberson, Stanley, 'Einstein, Renoir, and Greeley: Some Thoughts About Evidence in Sociology–1991 Presidential Address', *American Sociological Review*, Vol. 57, No. 1, February 1992.

Lieten, G.K., 'Panchayat Leaders in a West Bengal District', *Economic and Political Weekly*, Vol. XXIII, No. 40, 1 October 1988.

———, 'Caste, Gender and Class in Panchayats: Case of Barddhaman, West Bengal', *Economic and Political Weekly*, Vol. XXVII, No. 29, 18 July 1992.

———, *Continuity and Change in Rural West Bengal*, New Delhi: Sage Publications, 1992.

———, 'Land Reforms at Centre Stage: The Evidence on West Bengal', *Development and Change*, Vol. 27, No. 1, January 1996.

———, *Development, Devolution and Democracy: Village Discourse in West Bengal*, New Delhi: Sage Publications, 1996.

Lijphart, Arend, *Democracy in Plural Societies*, New Haven: Yale University Press, 1977.

Lin, Sharat G. and **Madan C. Paul**, 'Bangladesh Migrants in Delhi: Social Insecurity, State Power, and Captive Vote Banks', *Bulletin of Concerned Asian Scholars*, Vol. 27, No. 1, 1995.

Lomnitz, Larissa Adler and **Marisol Perez-Lizaur**, *A Mexican Elite Family: 1820–1980*, Princeton: Princeton University Press, 1987.

Looney, Robert E., 'Pakistani Defence Expenditures and the Macroeconomy: Alternative Strategies to the Year 2000', *Contemporary South Asia*, Vol. 4, No. 3, 1995.

Lynch, Owen, *The Politics of Untouchability*, New York: Columbia University Press, 1969.

Maitra, Tares, *Expansion of Employment Through Local Resource Mobilisation: A Study of a Cluster of Villages in West Bengal*, Bangkok: Asian Employment Program, International Labour Organization, 1982.

Mallick, Ross, 'Limits to Radical Intervention: Agricultural Taxation in West Bengal', *Development and Change*, Vol. 21, No. 1, January 1990.

———, *Development Policy of a Communist Government: West Bengal Since 1977*, Cambridge: Cambridge University Press, 1993.

———, *Indian Communism: Opposition, Collaboration, and Institutionalization*, Delhi: Oxford University Press, 1993.

Mallon, Florencia E., 'The Promise and Dilemma of Subaltern Studies: Perspectives from Latin American History', *American Historical Review*, Vol. 99, No. 5, December 1994.

Manogaran, Chelvadurai, *Ethnic Conflict and Reconciliation in Sri Lanka*, Honolulu: University of Hawaii Press, 1987.

Manor, James, 'Tried, Then Abandoned: Economic Liberalisation in India', *IDS Bulletin*, Vol. 18, No. 4, 1987.

———, 'How and Why Liberal and Representative Politics Emerged in India', *Political Studies*, Vol. 38, No. 1, 1990.

Matthews, Bruce, 'Sinhala Cultural and Buddhist Patriotic Organizations in Contemporary Sri Lanka', *Pacific Affairs*, Vol. 61, No. 4, Winter 1988–89.

Maybury-Lewis, David, 'A Special Sort of Pleading: Anthropology at the Service of Ethnic Groups', in John H. Bodley (ed.), *Tribal Peoples and Development Issues: A Global Overview*, Mountain View, California: Mayfield Publishing Company, 1988.

Mayoux, Linda C., 'Income Generation for Women in India: Problems and Prospects', *Development Policy Review*, Vol. 7, No. 1, March 1989.

McDonald, Hamish, 'Pride and Prejudice', *Far Eastern Economic Review*, 3 November, 1994.

Mehta MP, Prasannbhai, Pandey MP, Laxmi Narayan and **Visharat MP, Mangaldev**. 'Report on Marichjhapi Affairs', Mimeo, 18 April 1979.

Mencher, Joan P., 'On Being an Untouchable in India: A Materialist Perspective', in *Beyond the Myths of Culture*, New York: Academic Press, Inc. 1980.

Meyer, C.A., 'Opportunism and NGOs: Entrepreneurship and Green North-South Transfers', *World Development*, Vol. 23, No. 8, August 1995.

Michels, Robert, *Political Parties*, New York: Collier Books, 1962.

Mikesell, Raymond F. and **Lawrence F. Williams**, *International Banks and the Environment*, San Francisco: Sierra Club Books, 1992.

Miles, William F.S., 'Motives, Morality and Methodology in Third World Research', *PS: Political Science and Politics*, Vol. 22, No. 4, 1989.

Minz, Boniface, 'The Jharkhand Movement', in Walter Fernandes (ed.), *National Development and Tribal Deprivation*, Delhi: Indian Social Institute, 1992.

Minz, Nirmal, 'Identity of Tribals in India' in Walter Fernandes (ed.), *The Indigenous Question: In Search for an Identity*, Delhi: Indian Social Institute, 1993.

Mitra, Subrata Kumar, 'Crisis and Resilience in Indian Democracy', *International Social Science Journal*, Vol. 43, No. 129, 1991.

———, 'Book Review', *The Journal of Commonwealth & Comparative Politics*, Vol. 33, No. 2, July 1995.

Mitter, Swasti, *Peasant Movements in West Bengal*, Cambridge: Department of Land Economy, 1977.

Monshipouri, Mahmood and **Amjad Samuel**, 'Development and Democracy in Pakistan', *Asian Survey*, Vol. 35, No. 11, November, 1995.

Moore, Barrington, *Injustice: The Social Base of Obedience and Revolt*, New York: M.E. Sharpe Inc. 1978.

Moore, Mick, 'The Ideological History of the Sri Lankan Peasantry', *Modern Asian Studies*, Vol. 23, Part. 1, February 1989.

Morris-Jones, W.H., 'India's Political Idioms', in C.H. Philips (ed.), *Politics and Society in India*, by London: George Allen & Unwin Ltd, 1963.

Mukherjee, Arun P., 'The Exclusions of Postcolonial Theory and Mulk Raj Anand's *Untouchable*: A Case Study', *Ariel*, Vol. 22, No. 3, 1991.

Mukherji, B.C., 'The Impact of Panchayats on Socio-Economic Development of Rural Bengal', in *Panchayats in West Bengal from 1978–79 to 1980–81: A Review*, Calcutta: Department of Panchayats and Community Development, Government of West Bengal, January 1982.

Mukhopadhyay, Amal Kumar, 'Theoretically Speaking', *The Statesman*, 15 May, 1995.

Mukhopadhyay, Rajatasubhra, 'Resource Distribution and,Power Structure: A Case Study of a West Bengal Village', *Eastern Anthropologist*, Vol. 35, No. 1, January–March 1982.

Mullick, S. Bosu, 'Jharkhand Movement Through Time', *Religion and Society*, Vol. 38, September–December 1991.

Muni, S.D., 'South Asian Regional Cooperation: Evolution and Prospects', *IDSA Journal*, Vol. 19, No. 1, July–September 1986.

Mytelka, Lynn Krieger, 'The Salience of Gains in Third World Integrative Systems', *World Politics*, Vol. 25, No. 2, January 1973.

———, 'Fiscal Politics and Regional Redistribution: Bargaining Strategies in Asymmetrical Integrative Systems', *Journal of Conflict Resolution*, Vol. 19, No. 1, March 1975, pp. 138–60.

Nagchoudhury, Subrata, 'Jyoti Basu: Off to New Pastures', *India Today*, 11 January 1997.

Nagchoudhury, Subrata and **Arnab Neil Sengupta**, 'West Bengal: Projecting a Cleaner Face', *India Today*, 31 March 1996.

Namboodiripad, E.M.S., *A Brief Critical Note on the Programme Drafts*, Delhi: Communist Party of India, 1964.

Newman, Saul, 'Does Modernization Breed Ethnic Political Conflict?', *World Politics*, Vol. 43, No. 3, April 1991.

Newsmith, Cathy, 'Gender, Trees, and Fuel: Social Forestry in West Bengal, India', *Human Organization*, Vol. 50, No. 4, Winter 1991.

Nietschmann, Bernard, 'Third World Colonial Expansion: Indonesia, Disguised Invasion of Indigenous Nations', in John H. Bodley (ed.), *Tribal Peoples and Development Issues: A Global Overview*, Mountain View, California: Mayfield Publishing Company, 1998.

Nossiter, T.J., *Marxist State Governments in India*, London: Pinter Publishers, 1988.

Nye, J.S., 'Patterns and Catalysts in Regional Integration', *International Organization*, Vol. 19, No. 4, Autumn 1965, pp. 870–84.

Nye, Joseph, *Bound to Lead: The Changing Nature of American Power*, New York: Basic Books, 1991.

O'Hanlon Rosalind and **David Washbrook**, 'After Orientalism: Culture, Criticism and Politics in the Third World', *Comparative Studies in Society and History*, Vol. 34, No. 1, January 1992.

Okin, Susan Moller, 'Gender, Inequality and Cultural Differences', *Political Theory*, Vol. 22, No. 1, February 1994.

O'Neill, Juliet, 'Bidding for Foreign-Aid Contracts to Become Fairer, Quicker Process', *Ottawa Citizen*, 11 December, 1996.

Page, David, *Prelude to Partition: The Indian Muslims and the Imperial System of Control: 1920–1932*, Delhi: Oxford University Press, 1982.

Pandey, Gyanendra, 'In Defence of the Fragment: Writing about Hindu–Muslim Riots in India Today', *Representations*, 37, Winter 1992.

Parajuli, Pramod, 'Power and Knowledge in Development Discourse: New Social Movements and the State in India', *International Social Science Journal*, Vol. 43, No. 127, 1991.

Peebles, Patrick, 'Colonization and Ethnic Conflict in the Dry Zone of Sri Lanka', *Journal of Asian Studies*, Vol. 49, No. 1, February 1990, pp. 30–55.

Phadnis, Urmila, *Ethnicity and Nation-building in South Asia*, New Delhi: Sage Publications, 1989.

Poole, Richard, *The Inca Smiled: The Growing Pains of an Aid Worker in Ecuador*, Oxford: One World, 1993.

Powell, Walter W., *Getting into Print: The Decision-Making Process in Scholarly Publishing*. Chicago: The University of Chicago Press, 1985.

Prakash, Gyan, 'Can the "Subaltern" Ride? A Reply to O'Hanlon and Washbrook', *Comparative Studies in Society and History*, Vol. 34, No. 1, January 1992.

Preston, Larry M., 'Theorizing Difference: Voices from the Margins', *American Political Science Review*, Vol. 89, No. 4, December 1995.

Quigley, Declan, Review of *Imagining India*, by Ronald Inden, in *Modern Asian Studies*, Vol. 20, No. 2, 1991.

Querishi, Saleem M.M., 'Regionalism, Ethnic Conflict and Islam in Pakistan: Impact on Foreign Policy', in Hafeez Malik (ed.), *Dilemmas of National Security and Cooperation in India and Pakistan*, London: St Martin's Press, 1993.

Rachowiecki, Rob, *Ecuador & the Galapagos Islands—A Travel Survival Kit*, Hawthorn, Vic, Australia: Lonely Planet Publications, 1992.

Raizada, Ajit, *Tribal Development in Madhya Pradesh: A Planning Perspective*, Delhi: Inter-India Publications, 1984.

Raj, A.L., 'Ideology and Hegemony in Jharkhand Movement', *Economic and Political Weekly*, Vol. XXVII, No. 5, 1 February 1992.

Ram, Nandu, *The Mobile Scheduled Castes*, Delhi: Hindustan Publishing Co., 1988.

Ray, Rabindra, *The Naxalites and their Ideology*, Delhi: Oxford University Press, 1988.

Riaz, Ali, 'Taslima Nasrin: Breaking the Structured Silence', *Bulletin of Concerned Asian Scholars*, Vol. 27, No. 1, 1995.

Richardson, John M., Jr. and **S.W.R. de A. Samarasinghe**, 'Measuring the Economic Dimensions of Ethnic Conflict' in S.W.R. de A. Samarasinghe and Reed Coughlan (eds), *The Economic Dimensions of Ethnic Conflict*, London: Pinter Publishers, 1991.

Rizvi, Gowher, 'The Role of the Smaller States in the South Asian Complex', in Barry Buzan and Gowher Rizvi (eds), *South Asian Insecurity and the Great Powers*, London: Macmillan, 1986.

Robinson, Marguerite S., *Local Politics: The Law of the Fishes*, Delhi: Oxford University Press, 1988.

Rohner, Ronald P. and **Manjusri Chaki-Sircar**, *Women and Children in a Bengali Village*, Hanover, NH: University Press of New England, 1988.

Rohwer, Jim, 'The East is Ready', in *The World in 1992*, Toronto: Globe and Mail and *The Economist*, January 1992.

Roland, Alan, *In Search of Self in India and Japan*, Princeton: Princeton University Press, 1988.

Roy, Ramashray and **V.B. Singh**, *Between Two Worlds: A Study of Harijan Elites*, Delhi: Discovery Publishing House, 1987.

Roy Burman, B.K., 'Indigenous People and Their Quest for Justice', in Buddhadeb Chaudhuri (ed), *Ethnopolitics and Identity Crisis*, Delhi: Inter-India Publications, 1992.

————, Letter to Professor Kisku, the then General Secretary ICITP, 21 January 1993.

Roy Burman, J.J., 'Shifting Cultivation: A Need for Reappraisal', in *Report of National Seminar on Contemporary Tribal Economy in India*, Delhi: Jigyanau Tribal Research Centre, 1989.

Roy Choudhury, P., 'Land Reforms: Promises and Fulfilment', *Economic and Political Weekly*, Vol. XV, No. 52, 27 December 1980.

Rudolph, Lloyd I. and **Susanne Hoeber Rudolph**, *The Modernity of Tradition*, Chicago: University of Chicago Press, 1967.

————, *In Pursuit of Lakshmi: The Political Economy of the Indian State*, Chicago: The University of Chicago Press, 1987.

Rutherford, Sir Thomas, 'The Governor's Half-Yearly Report on Ministers to the Viceroy, Lord Linlithgow', 16 September 1943. London: India Office Library.

Rutland, Peter, 'Sovietology: Notes for a Post-Mortem', *National Interest*, No. 31, Spring 1993.

Saberwal, Satish, *India: The Roots of Crisis*, Delhi: Oxford University Press, 1986.

Sachchidananda, *The Harijan Elite*, Delhi: Thompson Press, 1977.

————, 'Patterns of Political-Economic Change Among Tribals in Middle India', in Francine R. Frankel and M.S.A. Rao (eds), *Dominance and State Power in Modern India*, Vol. II, Delhi: Oxford University Press, 1990.

Sahlins, Marshall, *How 'Natives' Think: About Captain Cook, For Example*, Chicago: The Chicago University Press, 1995.

Said, Edward W., *Orientalism*, New York: Vintage, 1992.

Samad, Yunas, 'The Military and Democracy in Pakistan', *Contemporary South Asia*, Vol. 3, No. 3, 1994.

Sanwal, Mukul, 'The Implementation of Decentralization: A Case Study of District Planning in Agra District, Uttar Pradesh, India', *Public Administration and Development*, Vol. 7, No. 4, 1987.

Sarkar, Sumit, *Modern India: 1885–1947*, New York: St Martin's Press, 1989.

Sathyamurthy, T.V., 'Book Review', *Public Administration and Development*, Vol. 13, No. 5, 1993.

Schneider, Bertrand, *The Barefoot Revolution: A Report to the Club of Rome*, London: Intermediate Technology Publications, 1988.

Sen, Amartya, 'The Threats to Secular India', *The New York Review of Books*, 8 April 1993.

Sen, Sumanta, 'Grassroots Power', *India Today*, 15 June 1983.

Sen Gupta, Bhabani, *CPI-M: Promises, Prospects, Problems*, Delhi, Young Asia Publications, 1979.

———, 'Time to Take Stock', *India Today*, 31 December 1982.

Shah, Ghanshyam, *Social Movements in India: A Review of the Literature*, New Delhi: Sage Publications, 1990.

Shah, Mehtab Ali, 'The Kashmir Problem: A View from Four Provinces of Pakistan', *Contemporary South Asia*, Vol. 4, No. 1, March 1995.

Shahataj, 'Dalits: Indigenous Peoples of India' in *Proceedings of the First Asian Indigenous Women's Conference Sharing Commonalities and Diversities: Forging Unity Towards Indigenous Women's Empowerment*, Teachers' Camp, Cordillera Region, Philippines, 24–30 January 1993.

Sharma, Miriam, *The Politics of Inequality: Competition and Control in an Indian Village*, Honolulu: University of Hawaii Press, 1978.

Shastri Indo-Canadian Institute, *Programme Guide 1995–1996*, New Delhi, 1995.

Shivian, M., K.B. Srivastava and **A.C. Jena**, *Panchayati Raj Election in West Bengal, 1978: A Study in Institution Building for Rural Development*, Hyderabad: National Institute of Rural Development, 1980.

Shoesmith, Brian, 'The Evolution of Political Consciousness', BA Honours dissertation, University of Western Australia, 1976.

Siebert, John, *Ottawa Citizen*, 25 April 1991, p. 13.

Sikdar, Ranjit Kumar, 'Marichjhapi Massacre', *The Oppressed Indian*, July 1982.

Singh, Anita Inder, *The Origins of the Partition of India: 1936–1947*, Delhi: Oxford University Press, 1987.

Singh, N.K. and **Farzand Ahmed**, 'Crime and Politics: The Nexus', *India Today*, 31 August, 1995.

Sinha, Arun, *Against the Few: Struggles of India's Rural Poor*, London: Zed Books, 1991.

Simon, Lord, Chairman, *Report of the Indian Statutory Commission*, Vol. XVII, Selections from Memoranda and Oral Evidence, 21 January 1929, reprinted by Delhi: Swati Publications, 1988.

Sinha, Surajit, 'Tribal Solidarity Movements in India: A Review', in K. Suresh Singh (ed.), *Tribal Situation in India*, Shimla: Indian Institute of Advanced Study, 1972.

Sisson, Richard and **Leo E. Rose**, *War and Secession: Pakistan, India and the Creation of Bangladesh*, Berkeley: University of California Press, 1990.

Slater, Richard and **John Watson**, 'Democratic Decentralization or Local Government Reform in Karnataka', *Public Administration and Development*, Vol. 9, No. 2, April–May 1989.

Sloan, John W., 'The Strategy of Developmental Regionalism: Benefits, Distribution, Obstacles, and Capabilities', *Journal of Common Market Studies*, Vol. 10, No. 2, December 1971.

Smillie, Ian, *The Alms Bazar: Altruism under Fire—Non-Profit Organizations and International Development*, Ottawa: International Development Research Centre, 1995.

Smith, Brian H., *More than Altruism: The Politics of Private Foreign Aid*, Princeton: Princeton University Press, 1990.

Sood, Krishnalekha, *Trade and Economic Development: India, Pakistan and Bangladesh*, New Delhi: Sage Publications, 1989.

Sorbo, Gunnar M., **Grete Brochmann, Reidar Dale, Mick Moore** and **Erik Whist**, *Sri Lanka: Country Study and Norwegian Aid Review*, Bergen: Centre for Development Studies, University of Bergen, April 1987.

South Asian Human Rights Documentation Centre, 'No Secure Refuge', Delhi: South Asian Human Rights Documentation Centre, February 1994.

————, 'The Jumma Refugees: Post-Script as Prologue', Delhi: South Asian Human Rights Documentation Centre, June 1994.

South Asia Newsweek, CFMT Television, Ottawa, 11 September 1994.

Sowell, Thomas, 'Affirmative Action: A Worldwide Disaster', *Commentary*, Vol. 88, No. 6, December 1989.

Spencer, Metta, *Foundations of Modern Sociology*, Scarborough: Prentice-Hall Canada Inc., 1981.

Spurgeon, David, 'Legal Action "May End Search for Truth" in Canada's HIV Inquiry', *Nature*, Vol. 379, No. 6565, 8 February, 1996.

Sri Lankan Canada Development Fund: Annual Report (Colombo, Sri Lanka: 1996).

Stackhouse, John, 'Uttar Pradesh Main Prize as New Contest Opens Up', *The Globe and Mail*, 20 October 1995.

————, 'Labourers Fight for Rights in West Bengal', *The Globe and Mail*, 30 December 1996.

Starn, Orin, 'Missing the Revolution: Anthropologists and the War in Peru', in George E. Marcus (ed.), *Rereading Cultural Anthropology*, Durham: Duke University Press, 1992.

Stein, Janice Gross, 'Detection and Defection: Security "Regimes" and the Management of International Conflict', *International Journal*, Vol. XL, No. 4, Autumn 1985.

Stevens, Jacqueline, 'Beyond Tocqueville, Please!', *American Political Science Review*, Vol. 89, No. 4, December 1995.

Subba, Tanka B., *Ethnicity, State and Development: A Case Study of the Gorkhaland Movement in Darjeeling*, Delhi: Vikas Publishing House, 1992.

Subrahmanyam, K., *India's Security: The North and North-East Dimension*, London: The Centre for Security and Conflict Studies, Conflict Studies 215, October 1988.

Sundaram, K. and **Suresh D. Tendulkar**, *Integrated Rural Development Programme in India*, Kuala Lumpur: The Asian and Pacific Development Centre, May 1984.

Sundarayya, P., *An Explanatory Note on the Central Committee Resolution on Certain Agrarian Issues*, Calcutta: Communist Party-Marxist, 1973.

Survival International, 'Violation of Human Rights and Fundamental Freedoms in the Chittagong Hill Tracts', Commission on Human Rights: Sub-Commission on the Prevention of Discrimination and Protection of Minorities, 45th Session, August 2–27, Agenda Item 6.

Tambiah, Stanley Jeyaraja, *Buddhism Betrayed? Religion, Politics, and Violence in Sri Lanka*, Chicago: The University of Chicago Press, 1992.

Taylor, Charles, *Multiculturalism*, Princeton: Princeton University Press, 1994.

Tendler, Judith, *Inside Foreign Aid*, Baltimore: The Johns Hopkins University Press, 1975.

Tennekoon, N. Serena, 'Rituals of Development: The Accelerated Mahaweli Development Program of Sri Lanka', *American Ethnologist*, Vol. 15, No. 2, 1988.

The Economist, 23 June 1990.

————, 15 June 1996.

————, 21 December 1996.

————, 8 February 1997, 'Last Chance in Pakistan'.

The Editors, 'Withdraw from Sardar Sarovar, Now', *The Ecologist*, Vol. 22, No. 5, September–October 1992.

Tilak, Jandhyala B.G., 'How Free is "Free" Primary Education in India?' *Economic and Political Weekly*, Vol. XXXI, No. 5, 3 February, 1996.

Timm, Father R.W., *The Adivasis of Bangladesh*, London: Minority Rights Group International Report, December 1991, 92/1.

Tornquist, Olle, *The Next Left? Democratization and Attempts to Renew the Radical Political Development Project: The Case of Kerala*, Copenhagen: Nordic Institute of Asian Studies, 1995.

Tow, William T., *Subregional Security Cooperation in the Third World*, Boulder, Colorado: Lynne Rienner Publishers, 1990.

Tully, Mark, *No Full Stops in India*, London: Viking, 1991.

United Nations Development Programme, *Human Development Report*, New York: Oxford University Press, various years.

United Nations General Assembly, Regional Meeting for Asia, World Conference on Human Rights, Bangkok, 29 March–2 April 1993, A/Conf. 157/ASRM/4, 30 March 1993.

United Nations Working Group on Indigenous Peoples, 8th Session, 31 July 1990, Agenda Item 5, p. 4.

Uphoff, Norman, *Learning from Gal Oya*, Ithaca: Cornell University Press, 1992.

Vanaik, Achin, 'A Liberal–Pluralist Paradigm', *Economic and Political Weekly*, Vol. XXVII, No. 3, 18 January 1992.

Verba, Sidney, *Elites and the Idea of Equality*, Cambridge: Harvard University Press, 1987.

Vetticad, A.M.M., 'Mother Teresa: Cause with a Difference', *India Today*, 15 December, 1995.

Wali, M.M.K., *Tribal People of India*, Geneva: International Labour Organization, 1993.

Walker, Dennis, 'Matua Untouchable Writers: Religious Protest and Indianist Accommodation', unpublished article, 1993.

Walsh, James, 'India: Special Report', *Time*, 25 March 1996.

Washbrook, D.A., 'Caste, Class and Dominance in Modern Tamil Nadu', in Francine R. Frankel and M.S.A. Rao (eds), *Dominance and State Power in Modern India: The Decline of a Social Order: Vol. 1*, Delhi: Oxford University Press, 1989.

Washburn, Wilcomb E., 'Cultural Relativism, Human Rights, and the AAA [American Anthropological Association]', *American Anthropologist*, Vol. 89, No. 4, December 1987.

Watson, C.W., 'Autobiography, Anthropology and the Experience of Indonesia', in Judith Okely and Hellen Callaway (eds), *Anthropology and Autobiography*, London: Routledge, 1992.

Webster, Neil, *Panchayati Raj and the Decentralization of Development Planning in West Bengal,* Copenhagen: Centre for Development Research, Project Paper 90.7, December 1990.

————, 'Panchayati Raj in West Bengal: Popular Participation for the People or the Party?' *Development and Change,* Vol. 23, No. 4, 1992.

Weinbaum, Marvin G., 'The Impact and Legacy of the Afghan Refugees in Pakistan', in J. Henry Korson (ed.), *Contemporary Problems of Pakistan,* Boulder: Westview Press, 1993.

Weiner, Myron, *Sons of the Soil: Migration and Ethnic Conflict in India,* Delhi: Oxford University Press, 1988.

————, *The Child and the State in India,* Princeton: Princeton University Press, 1991.

Weisgrau, Maxine Kay, 'The Social and Political Relations of Development: NGOs and Adivasi Bhils in Rural Rajasthan', Ph.D. thesis, Columbia University, New York, 1993.

Westergaard, Kirsten, 'People's Participation, Local Government and Rural Development: The Case of West Bengal', Copenhagen: Centre for Development Research, Report No. 8, March 1986.

Whaites, Alan, 'The State and Civil Society in Pakistan', *Contemporary South Asia,* Vol. 4, No. 3.

Wilder, Andrew R., 'Changing Patterns of Punjab Politics in Pakistan: National Assembly Election Results, 1988 and 1993', *Asian Survey,* Vol. 35, No. 4, April 1995.

Wilson, A. Jeyaratnam, *The Break-up of Sri Lanka,* London: C. Hurst & Co., 1988.

Wood, John R., 'Sardar Sarovar Under Siege: The World Bank and India's Narmada River Dam Projects', Paper presented at Learneds Conference, Canadian Asian Studies Association, Carleton University, Ottawa, 10 June 1993.

World Bank, *India: Poverty, Employment, and Social Services,* Washington, DC: World Bank, 1989.

————, *World Development Report 1990,* New York: Oxford University Press, 1990.

————, *World Development Report 1991,* New York: Oxford University Press, 1991.

————, *World Development Report 1995,* New York: Oxford University Press, 1995.

Wright, Theodore P., Jr., 'Centre–Periphery Relations and Ethnic Conflict in Pakistan: Sindhis, Muhajirs, and Punjabis', *Comparative Politics,* Vol. 23, No. 3, April 1991.

————, 'Can There be a Melting Pot in Pakistan? Interprovincial Marriage and National Integration', *Contemporary South Asia,* Vol. 3, No. 2, 1994.

Yapp, Malcolm, 'Language, Religion and Political Identity: A General Framework', in David Taylor and Malcolm Yapp (eds), *Political Identity in South Asia,* London: Curzon Press, 1979.

Young, Crawford, 'Patterns of Social Conflict: State, Class, and Ethnicity', *Daedalus,* Vol. 111, No. 2, Spring 1982.

Zhisui, Li, *The Private Life of Chairman Mao: The Memoirs of Mao's Personal Physician,* New York: Random House, 1994.

Index

About the Author

Ross Mallick is an independent development consultant based in Canada. He has previously been Research Director at the Native Council of Canada; a Research Fellow at the Canadian Institute for International Peace and Security; and a Consultant to the Department of Foreign Affairs and International Trade, Government of Canada and to the Canadian International Development Agency. Besides contributing research articles to various well known journals, Dr Mallick has previously published *Development Policy of a Communist Government: West Bengal since 1977* (1993) and *Indian Communism: Opposition, Collaboration and Institutionalization* (1994).